Home
Sweet
Home
Okinawa
(main island)

Last year, I returned home to Okinawa seven times! Every visit was for a different reason, and I'm sure I'll be going back there a lot this year too!! I've got plans…yep. Heh heh heh… (My current weight is… 68 kg!! That's more like it!!)

–Mitsutoshi Shimabukuro, 2013

Mitsutoshi Shimabukuro made his debut in **Weekly Shonen Jump** in 1996. He is best known for **Seikimatsu Leader Den Takeshi!** for which he won the 46th Shogakukan Manga Award for children's manga in 2001. His current series, **Toriko**, began serialization in Japan in 2008.

TORIKO VOL. 23
SHONEN JUMP Manga Edition

STORY AND ART BY **MITSUTOSHI SHIMABUKURO**

Translation/Christine Dashiell
Weekly Shonen Jump Lettering/Erika Terriquez
Graphic Novel Touch-Up Art & Lettering/Elena Diaz
Design/Matt Hinrichs
Editor/Hope Donovan

Printed in Canada

Published by VIZ Media, LLC
P.O. Box 77010
San Francisco, CA 94107

10 9 8 7 6 5 4 3 2 1
First printing, August 2014

www.viz.com

www.shonenjump.com

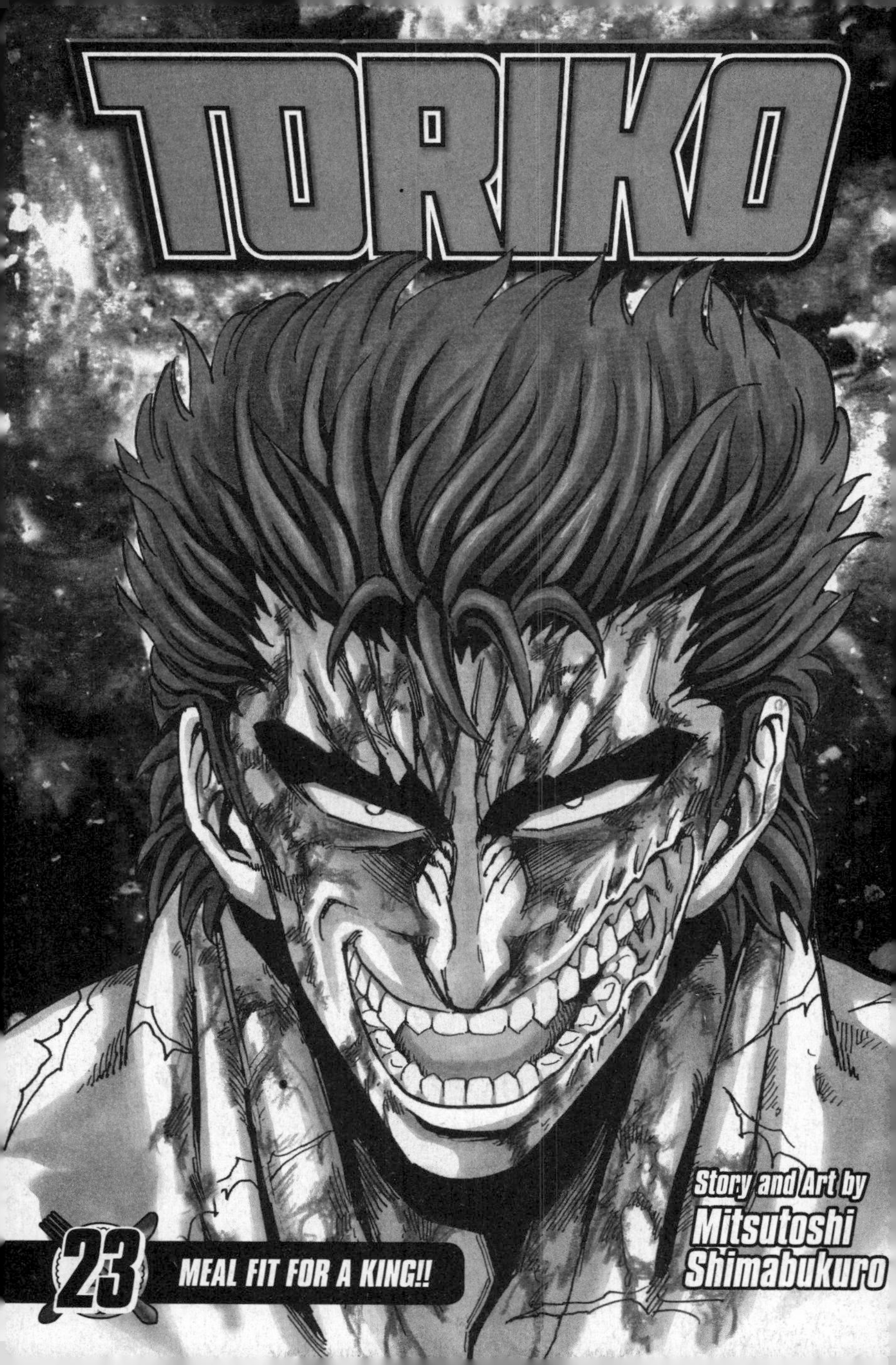
TORIKO
23
MEAL FIT FOR A KING!!
Story and Art by
Mitsutoshi Shimabukuro

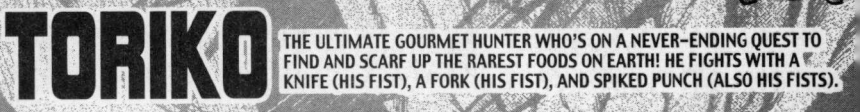

TORIKO

THE ULTIMATE GOURMET HUNTER WHO'S ON A NEVER-ENDING QUEST TO FIND AND SCARF UP THE RAREST FOODS ON EARTH! HE FIGHTS WITH A KNIFE (HIS FIST), A FORK (HIS FIST), AND SPIKED PUNCH (ALSO HIS FISTS).

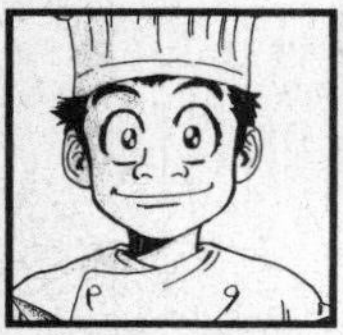

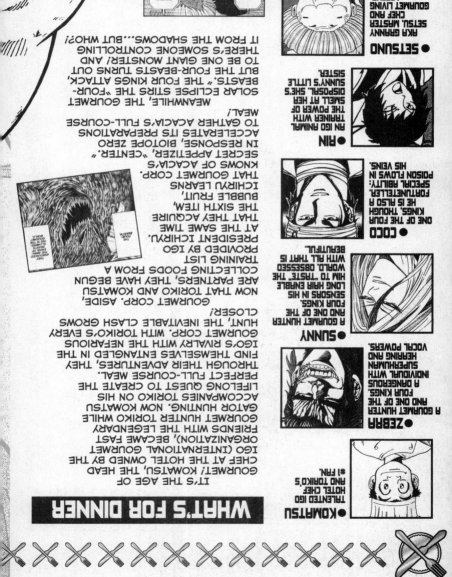

● **KOMATSU**

TALENTED IGO HOTEL CHEF AND TORIKO'S #1 FAN.

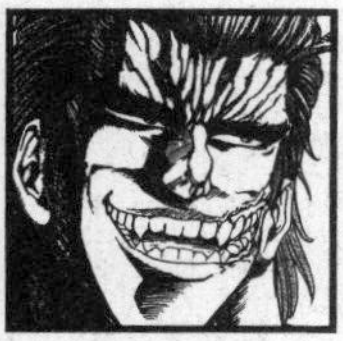

● **ZEBRA**

A GOURMET HUNTER AND ONE OF THE FOUR KINGS. A DANGEROUS INDIVIDUAL WITH SUPERHUMAN HEARING AND VOCAL POWERS.

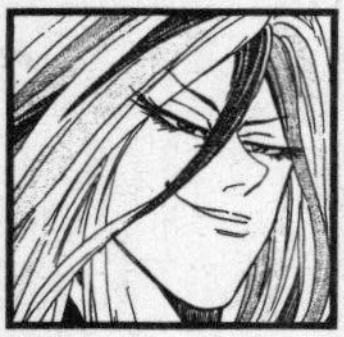

● **SUNNY**

A GOURMET HUNTER AND ONE OF THE FOUR KINGS. SENSORS IN HIS LONG HAIR ENABLE HIM TO "TASTE" THE WORLD. OBSESSED WITH ALL THAT IS BEAUTIFUL.

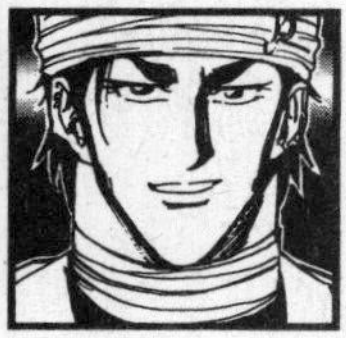

● **COCO**

ONE OF THE FOUR KINGS, THOUGH HE IS ALSO A FORTUNETELLER. SPECIAL ABILITY: POISON FLOWS IN HIS VEINS.

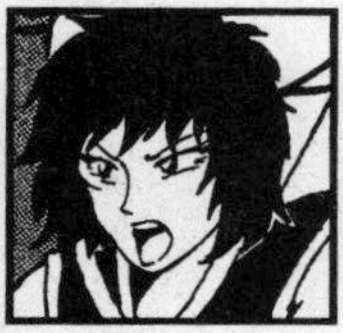

● **RIN**

AN IGO ANIMAL TRAINER WITH THE POWER OF SMELL AT HER DISPOSAL. SHE'S SUNNY'S LITTLE SISTER.

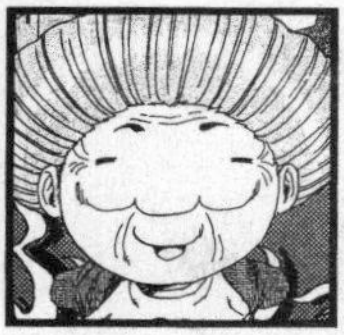

● **SETSUNO**

AKA GRANNY SETSU. MASTER CHEF AND GOURMET LIVING LEGEND.

WHAT'S FOR DINNER

IT'S THE AGE OF GOURMET! KOMATSU, THE HEAD CHEF AT THE HOTEL OWNED BY THE IGO (INTERNATIONAL GOURMET ORGANIZATION), BECAME FAST FRIENDS WITH THE LEGENDARY GOURMET HUNTER TORIKO WHILE GATOR HUNTING. NOW KOMATSU ACCOMPANIES TORIKO ON HIS LIFELONG QUEST TO CREATE THE PERFECT FULL-COURSE MEAL. THROUGH THEIR ADVENTURES, THEY FIND THEMSELVES ENTANGLED IN THE IGO'S RIVALRY WITH THE NEFARIOUS GOURMET CORP. WITH TORIKO'S EVERY HUNT, THE INEVITABLE CLASH GROWS CLOSER!

GOURMET CORP. ASIDE, NOW THAT TORIKO AND KOMATSU ARE PARTNERS, THEY HAVE BEGUN COLLECTING FOODS FROM A TRAINING LIST PROVIDED BY IGO PRESIDENT ICHIRYU. AT THE SAME TIME THAT THEY ACQUIRE THE SIXTH ITEM, BUBBLE FRUIT, ICHIRYU LEARNS THAT GOURMET CORP. KNOWS OF ACACIA'S SECRET APPETIZER, "CENTER." IN RESPONSE, BIOTOPE ZERO ACCELERATES ITS PREPARATIONS TO GATHER ACACIA'S FULL-COURSE MEAL!

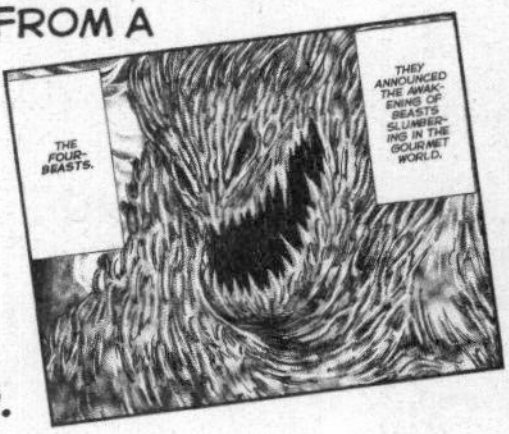
THEY ANNOUNCED THE AWAKENING OF BEASTS SLUMBERING IN THE GOURMET WORLD.
THE FOUR-BEASTS.

MEANWHILE, THE GOURMET SOLAR ECLIPSE STIRS THE "FOUR-BEASTS." THE FOUR KINGS ATTACK, BUT THE FOUR-BEASTS TURNS OUT TO BE ONE GIANT MONSTER! AND THERE'S SOMEONE CONTROLLING IT FROM THE SHADOWS...BUT WHO?!

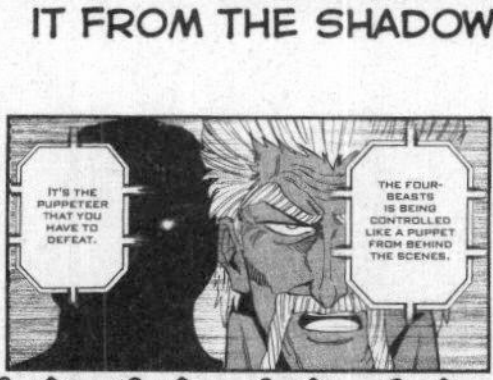
THE FOUR-BEASTS IS BEING CONTROLLED LIKE A PUPPET FROM BEHIND THE SCENES.
IT'S THE PUPPETEER THAT YOU HAVE TO DEFEAT.

Contents

Gourmet 199: Four Battles Settled!! 7

Gourmet 200: The Four-Beasts' True Form!! 26

Gourmet 201: Chaos in the Human World!! 47

Gourmet 202: Green Rain!! 67

Gourmet 203: Antidote Meal!! 87

Gourmet 204: A New Way to Cook!! 107

Gourmet 205: Curiosity About the Taste!! 126

Gourmet 206: Appetite!! 149

Gourmet 207: Meal Fit for a King!! 169

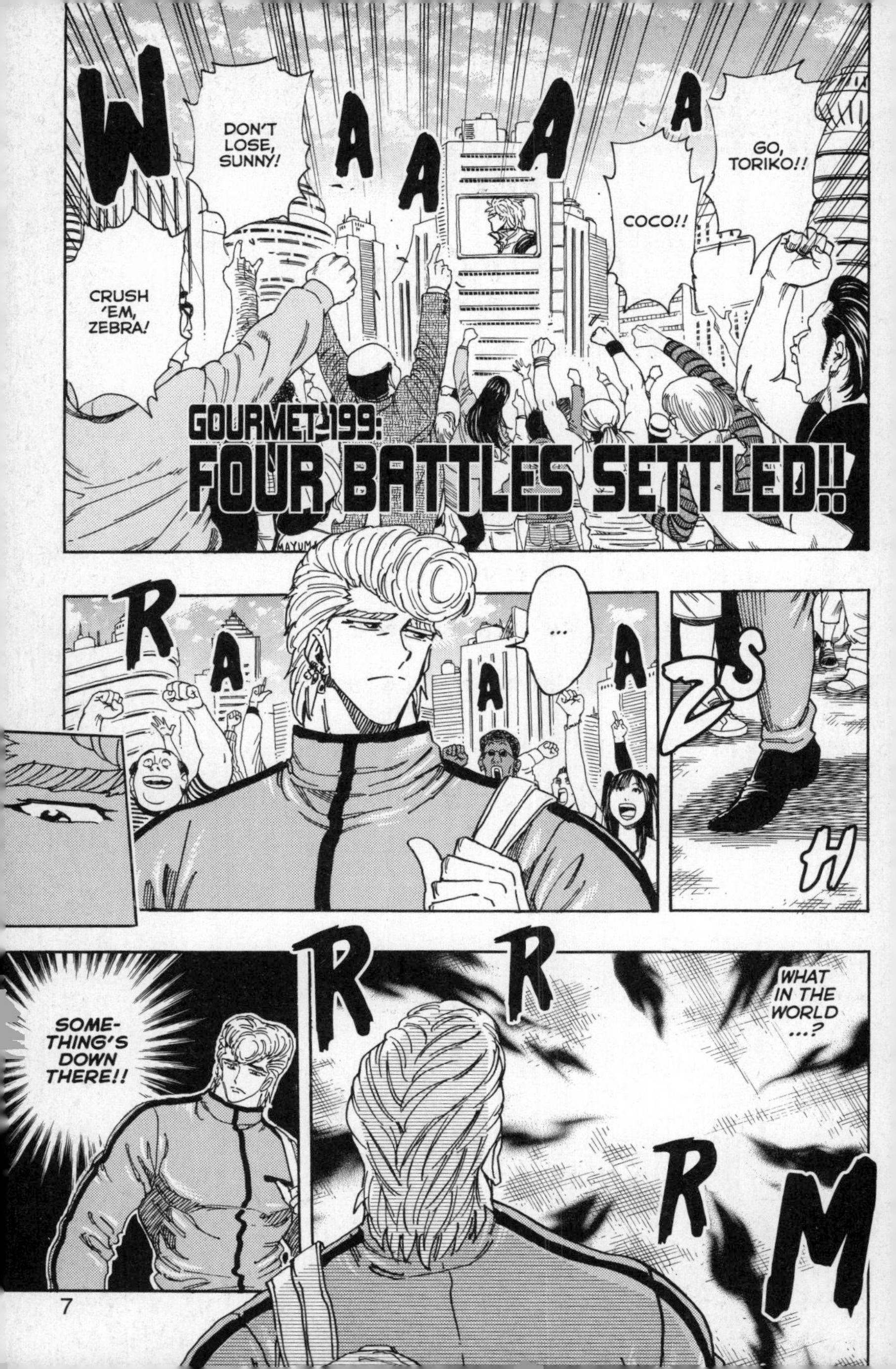
GO, TORIKO!!
COCO!!
DON'T LOSE, SUNNY!
CRUSH 'EM, ZEBRA!
WAAAAA
GOURMET 199:
FOUR BATTLES SETTLED!!
SZZZH
RAAA
...
WHAT IN THE WORLD ...?
RRRRM
SOME-THING'S DOWN THERE!!

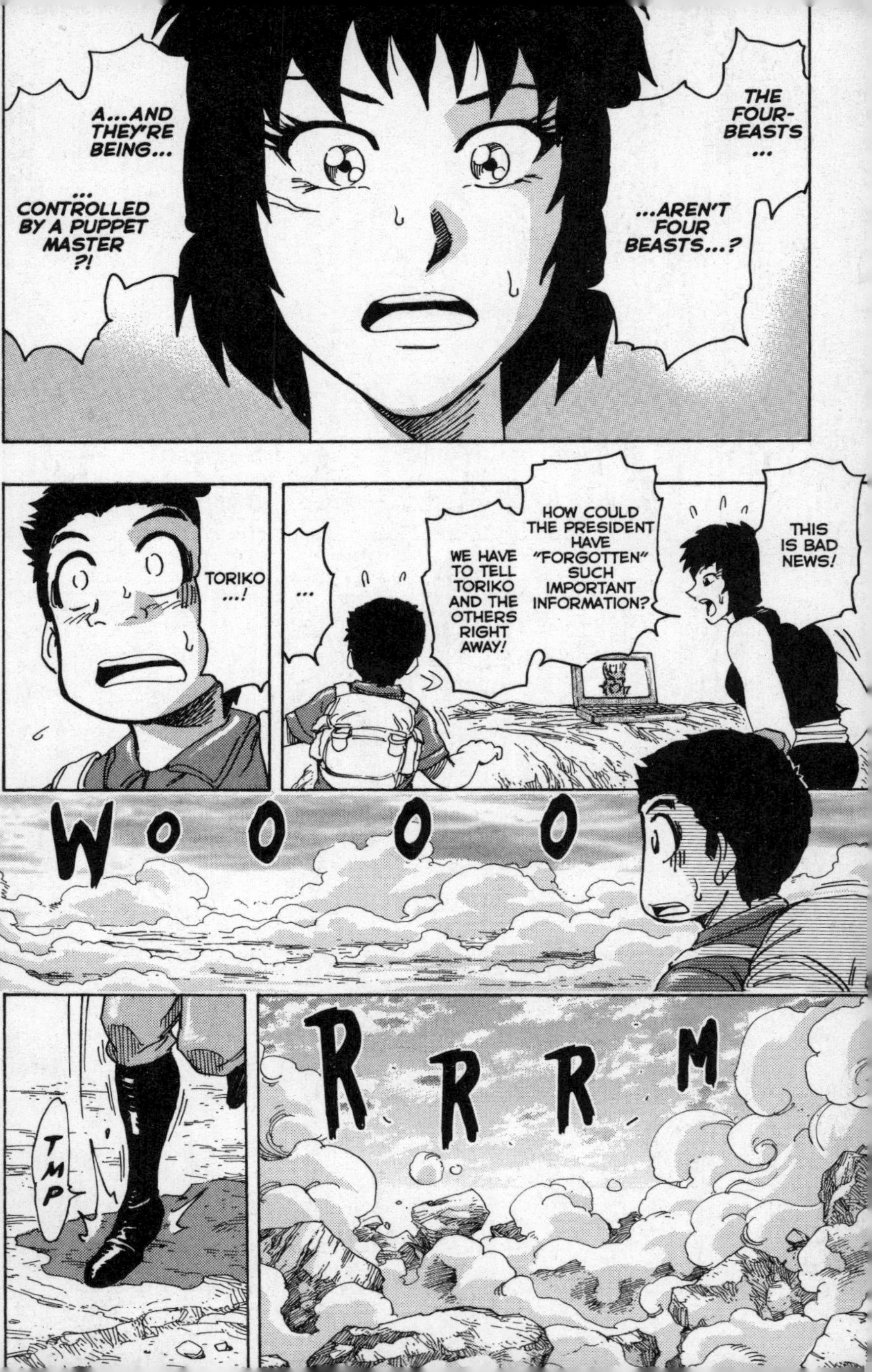
THE FOUR-BEASTS...
...AREN'T FOUR BEASTS...?
A...AND THEY'RE BEING...
...CONTROLLED BY A PUPPET MASTER?!
THIS IS BAD NEWS!
HOW COULD THE PRESIDENT HAVE "FORGOTTEN" SUCH IMPORTANT INFORMATION?
WE HAVE TO TELL TORIKO AND THE OTHERS RIGHT AWAY!
...
TORIKO...!
WOOO
RRRM
TMP

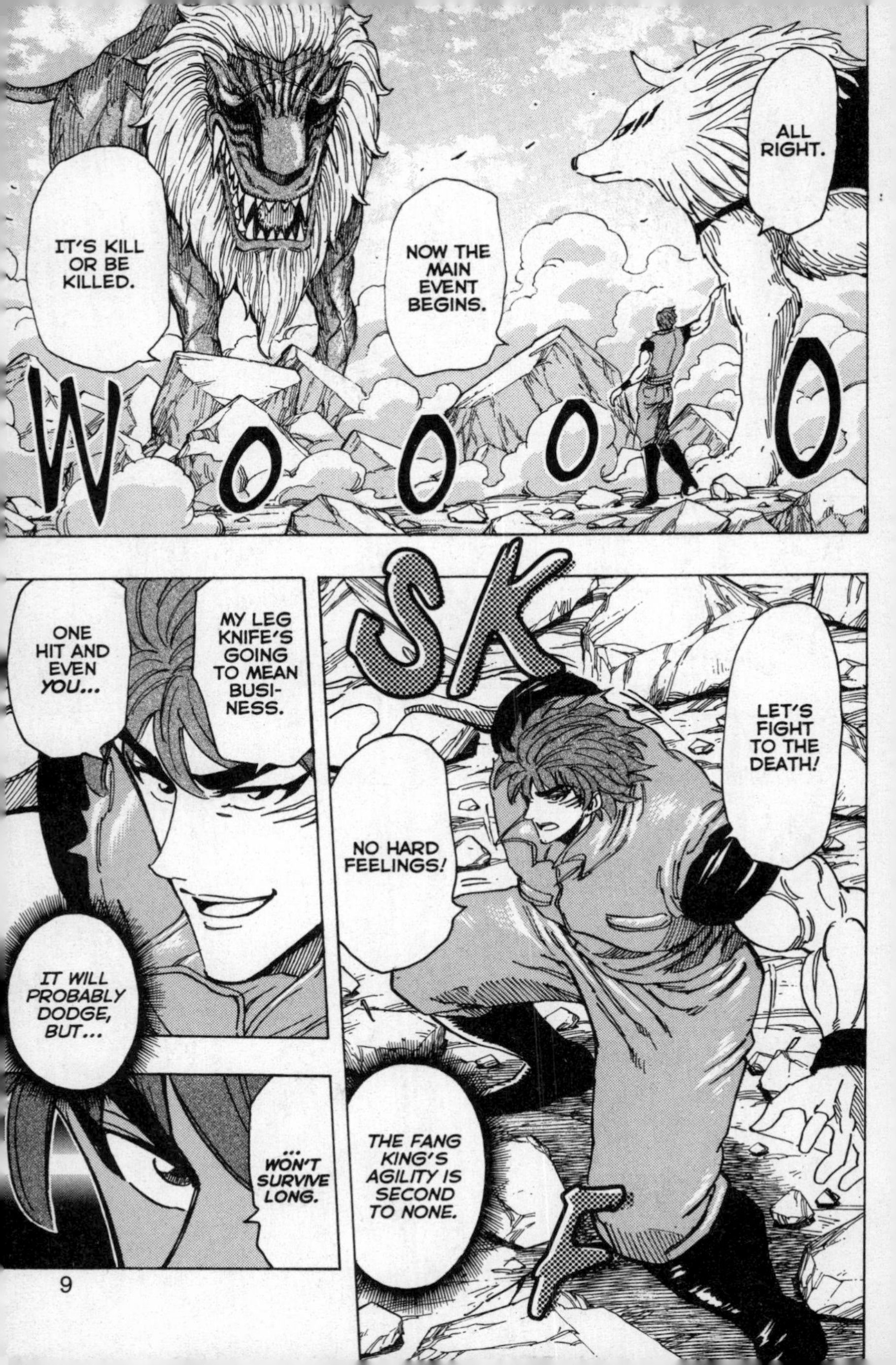
ALL RIGHT.
NOW THE MAIN EVENT BEGINS.
IT'S KILL OR BE KILLED.
WOOOOO
SK
LET'S FIGHT TO THE DEATH!
NO HARD FEELINGS!
THE FANG KING'S AGILITY IS SECOND TO NONE.
MY LEG KNIFE'S GOING TO MEAN BUSI-NESS.
ONE HIT AND EVEN YOU...
IT WILL PROBABLY DODGE, BUT...
...WON'T SURVIVE LONG.

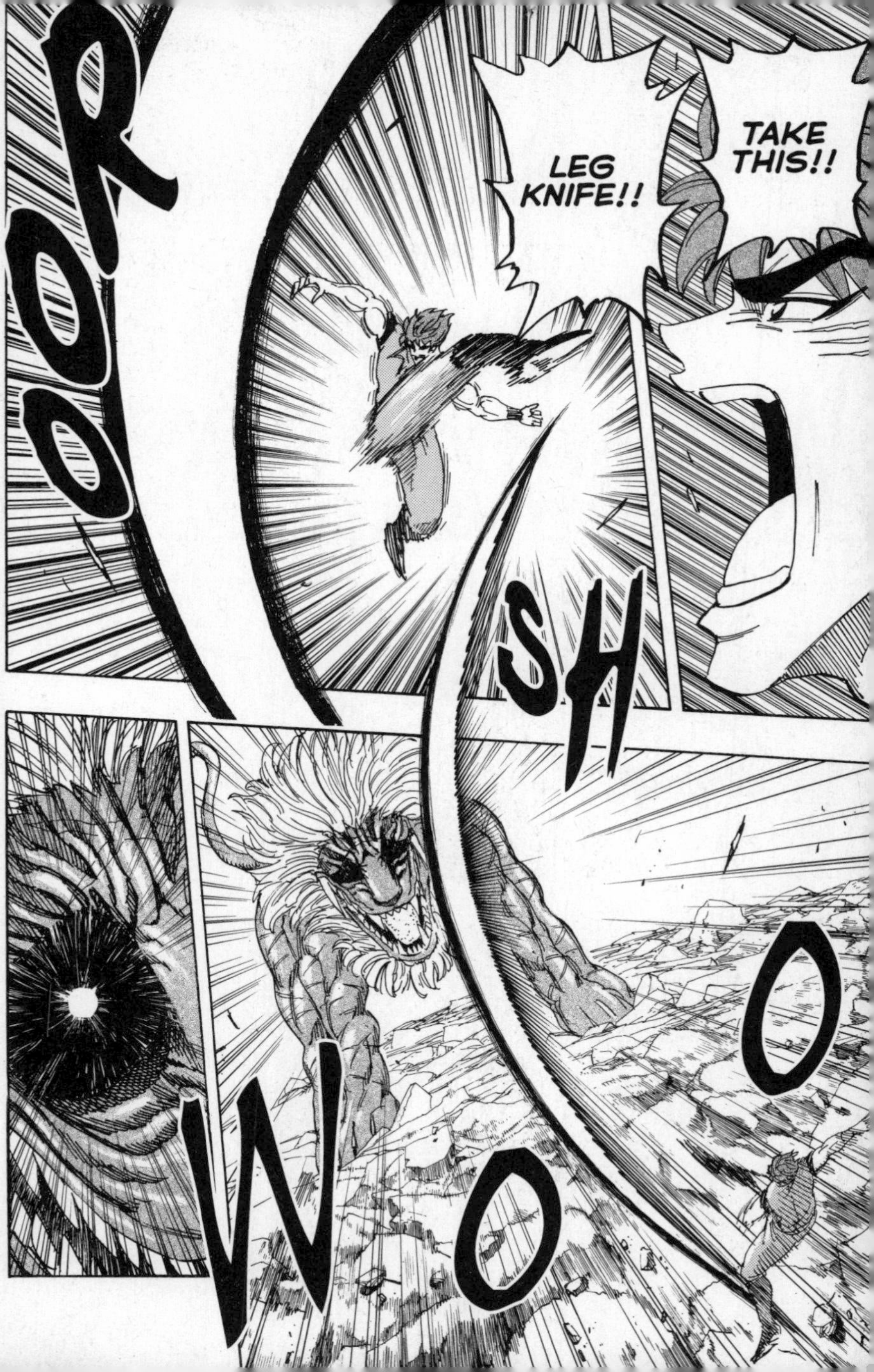
TAKE THIS!!
LEG KNIFE!!
ROOOO
SH
WOOO

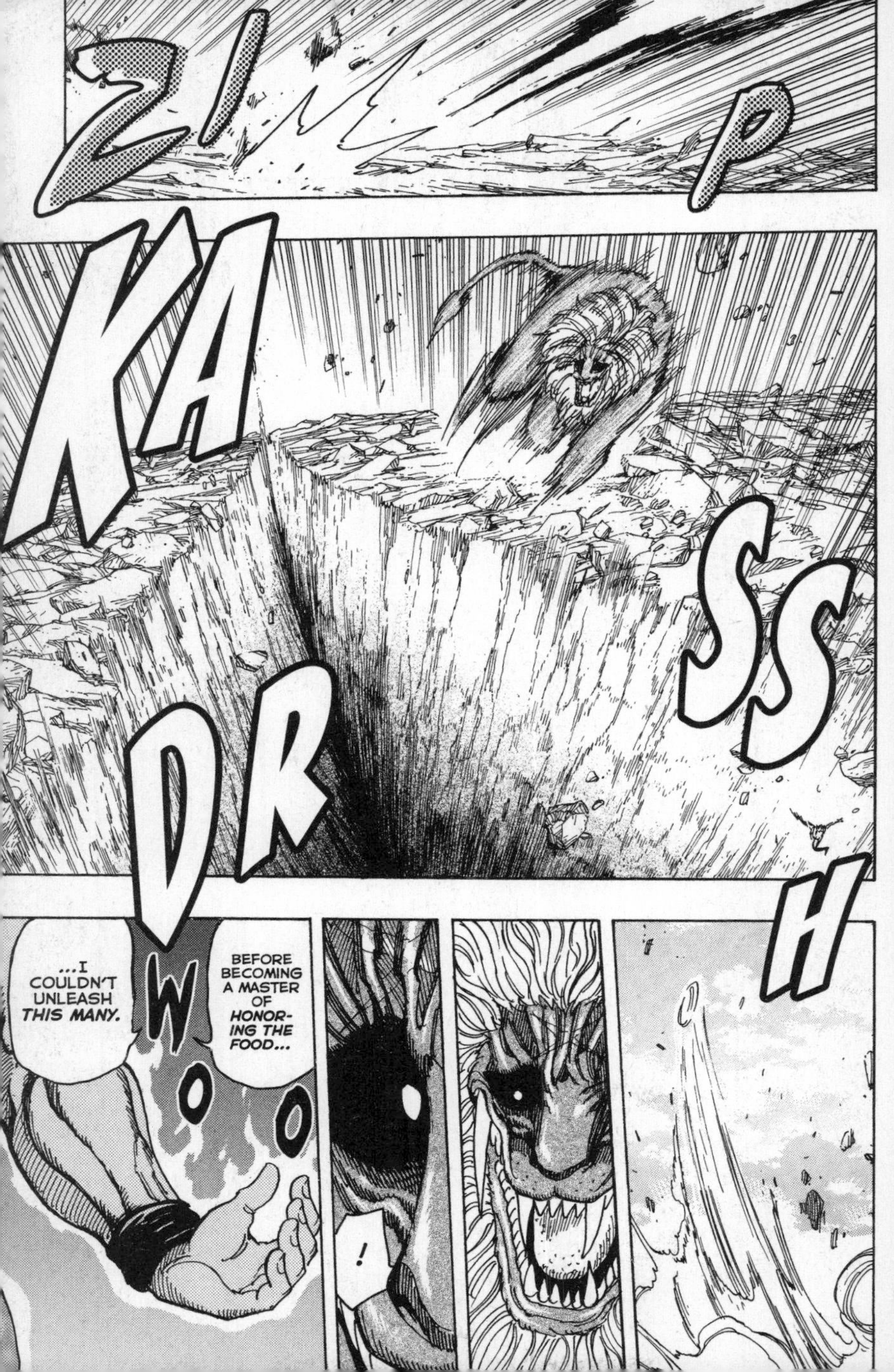
ZIP
KA
DR
SS
H
!
BEFORE BECOMING A MASTER OF *HONORING THE FOOD*...
...I COULDN'T UNLEASH *THIS MANY.*
WOOO

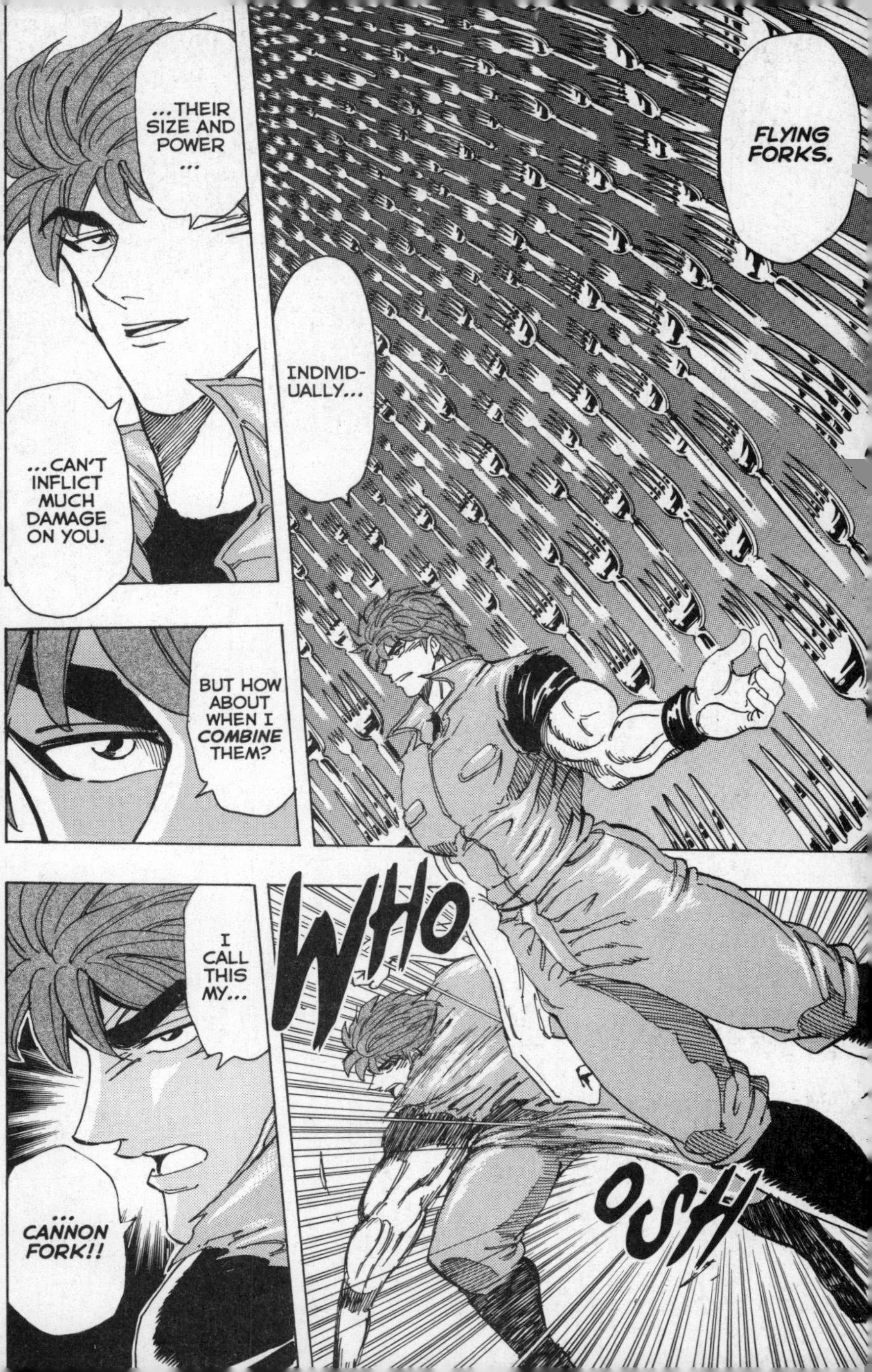
FLYING FORKS.
INDIVID-UALLY...
...THEIR SIZE AND POWER...
...CAN'T INFLICT MUCH DAMAGE ON YOU.
BUT HOW ABOUT WHEN I *COMBINE* THEM?
WHO
OSH
I CALL THIS MY...
...CANNON FORK!!

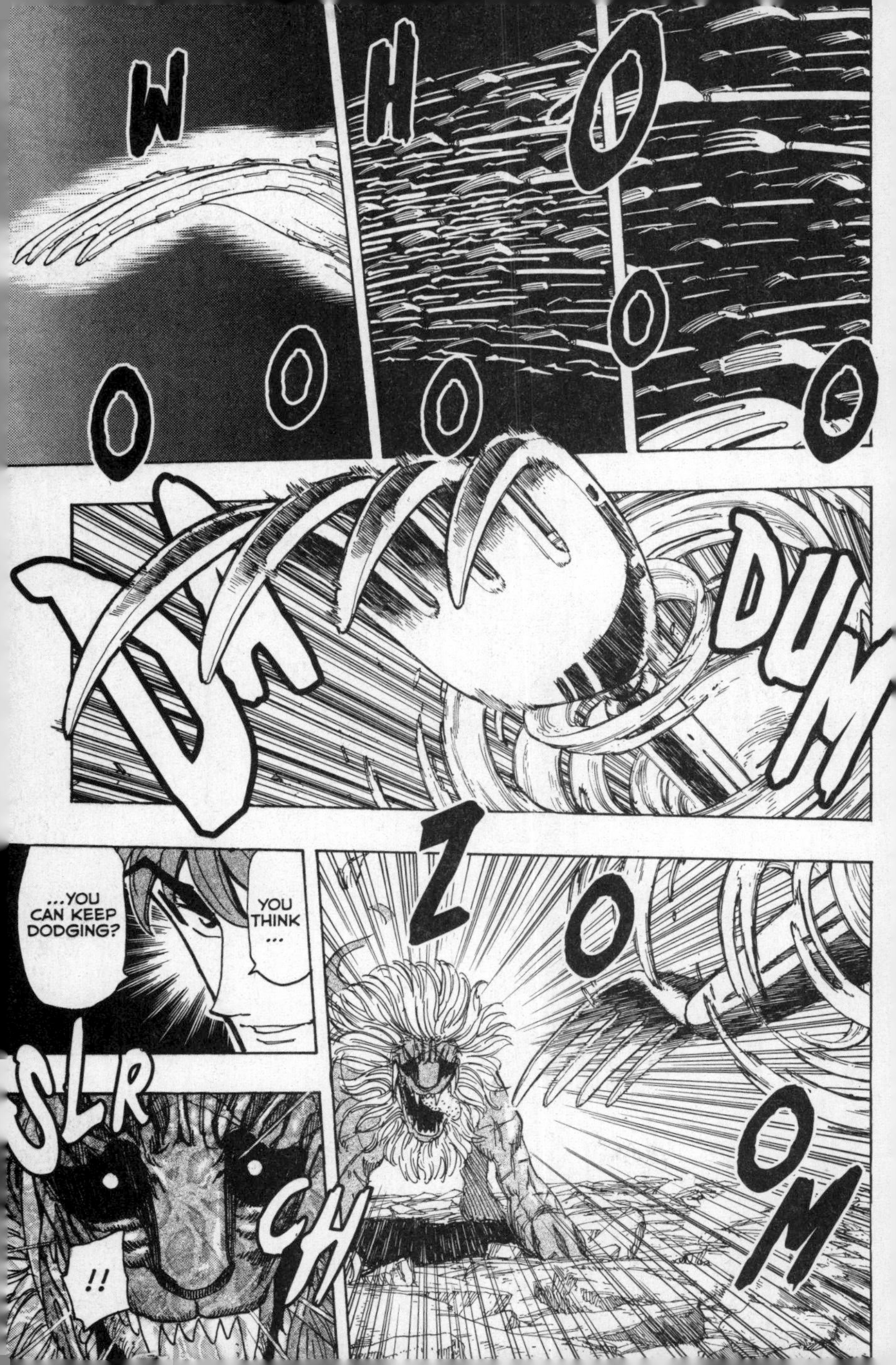
WHOOOOOOO
DUM
ZOOOM
YOU THINK ...
...YOU CAN KEEP DODGING?
SLRCH
!!

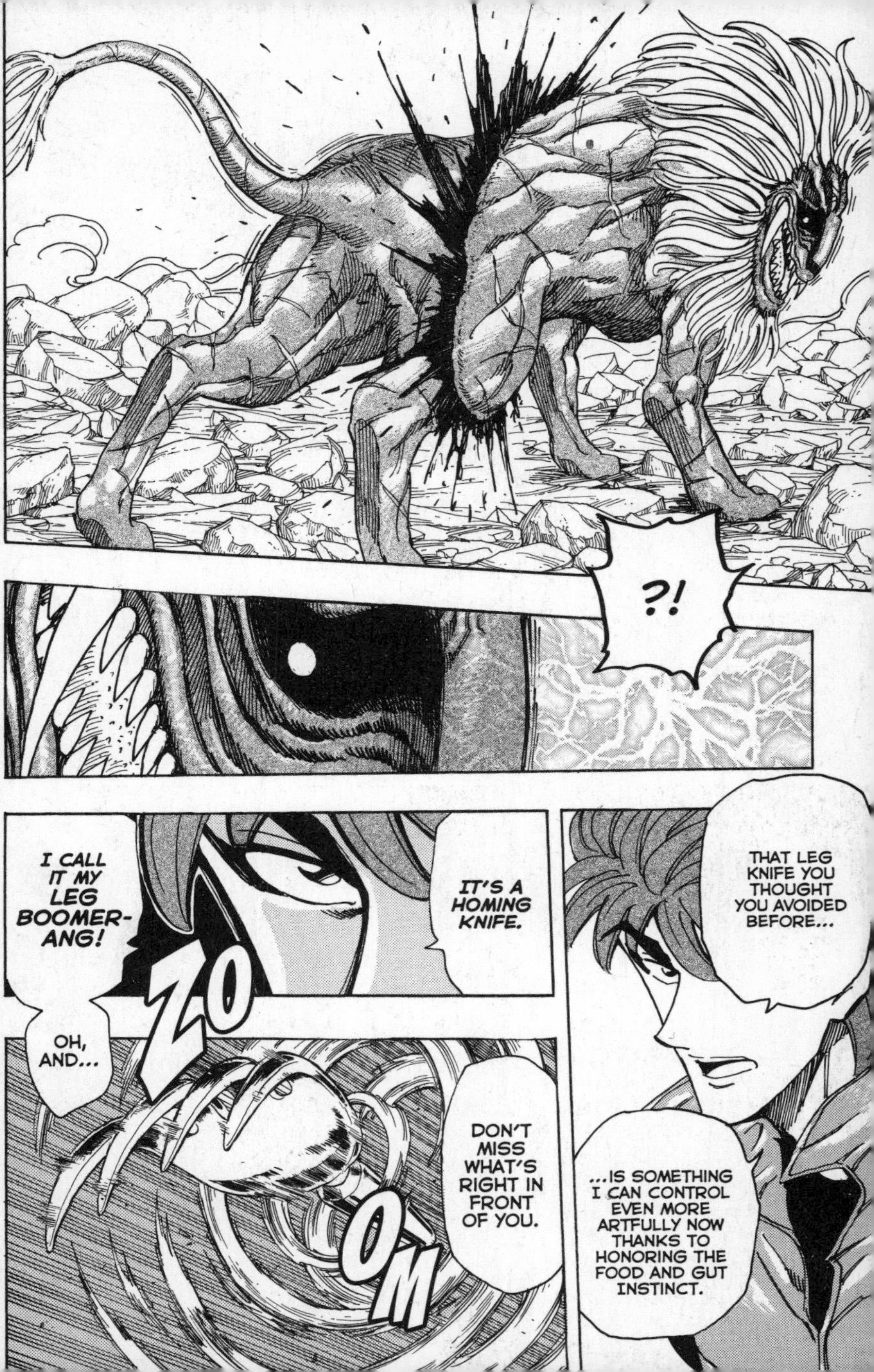
?!
THAT LEG KNIFE YOU THOUGHT YOU AVOIDED BEFORE...
...IS SOMETHING I CAN CONTROL EVEN MORE ARTFULLY NOW THANKS TO HONORING THE FOOD AND GUT INSTINCT.
IT'S A HOMING KNIFE.
I CALL IT MY LEG BOOMER-ANG!
OH, AND...
DON'T MISS WHAT'S RIGHT IN FRONT OF YOU.
ZOOM

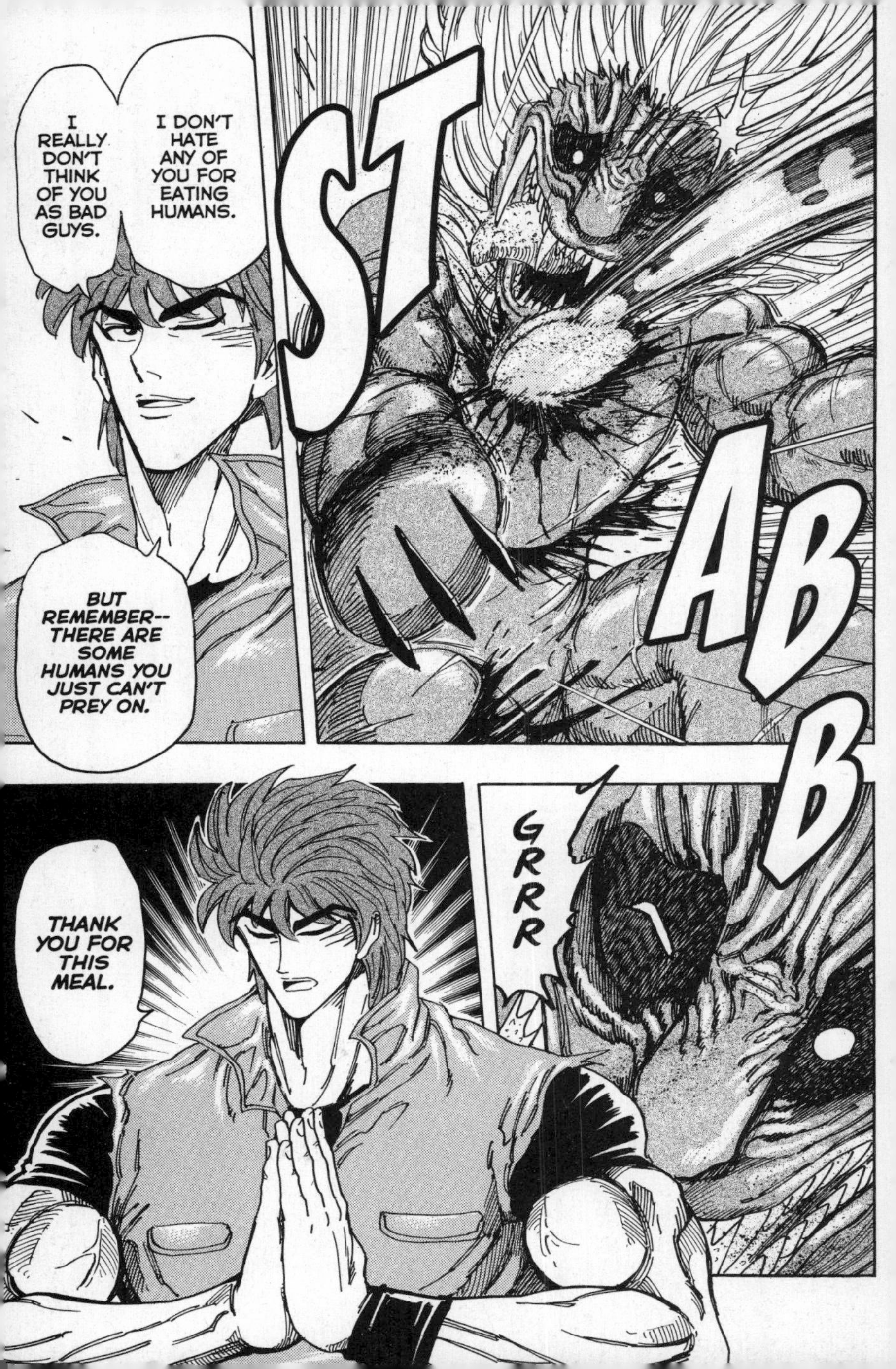
STABB
I DON'T HATE ANY OF YOU FOR EATING HUMANS.
I REALLY DON'T THINK OF YOU AS BAD GUYS.
BUT REMEMBER-- THERE ARE SOME HUMANS YOU JUST CAN'T PREY ON.
GRRR
THANK YOU FOR THIS MEAL.

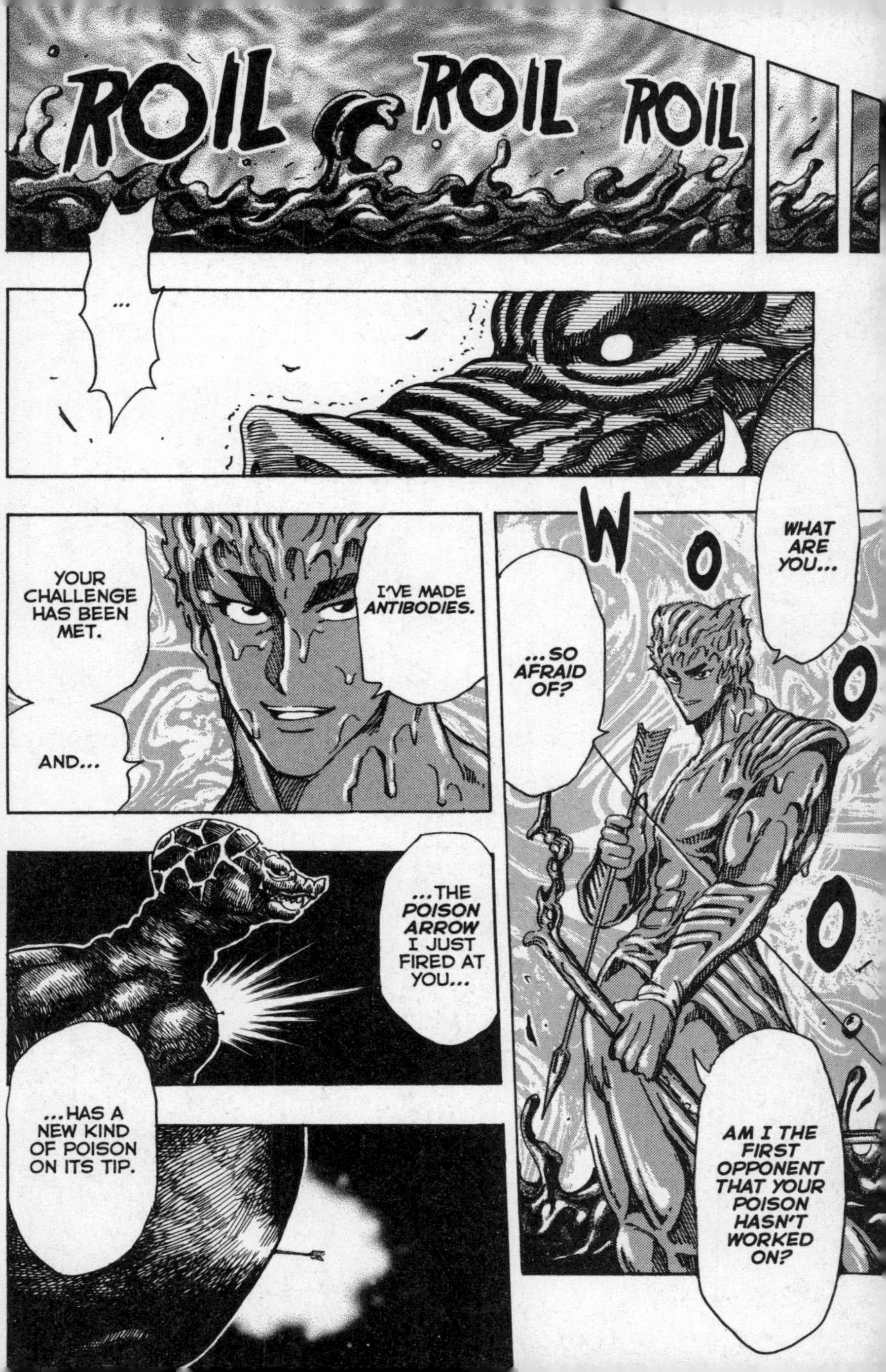
ROIL ROIL ROIL
...
WHAT ARE YOU...
WOOO
...SO AFRAID OF?
AM I THE FIRST OPPONENT THAT YOUR POISON HASN'T WORKED ON?
YOUR CHALLENGE HAS BEEN MET.
I'VE MADE ANTIBODIES.
AND...
...THE POISON ARROW I JUST FIRED AT YOU...
...HAS A NEW KIND OF POISON ON ITS TIP.

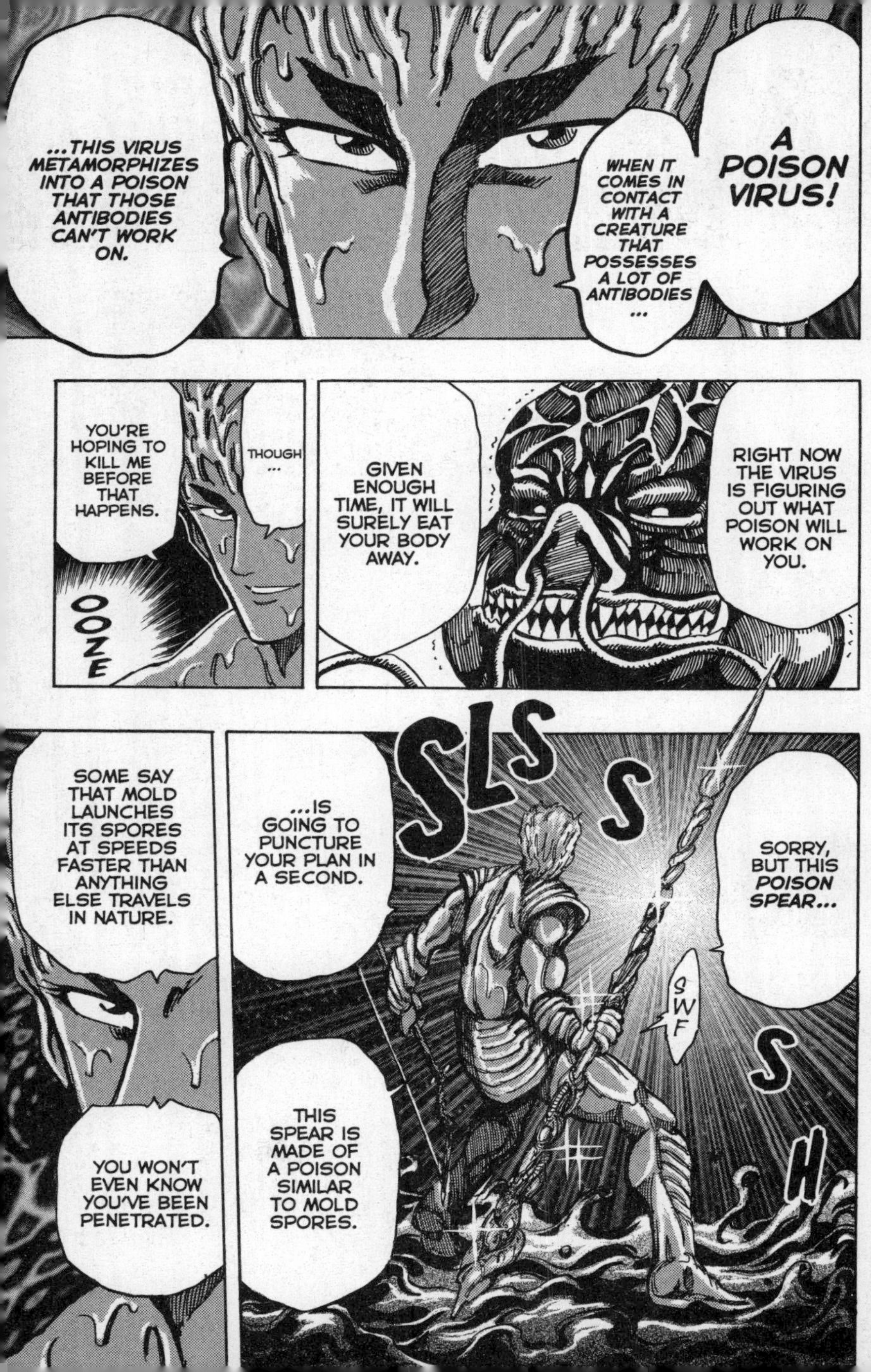
A POISON VIRUS!
WHEN IT COMES IN CONTACT WITH A CREATURE THAT POSSESSES A LOT OF ANTIBODIES ...
...THIS VIRUS METAMORPHIZES INTO A POISON THAT THOSE ANTIBODIES CAN'T WORK ON.
RIGHT NOW THE VIRUS IS FIGURING OUT WHAT POISON WILL WORK ON YOU.
GIVEN ENOUGH TIME, IT WILL SURELY EAT YOUR BODY AWAY.
THOUGH ...
YOU'RE HOPING TO KILL ME BEFORE THAT HAPPENS.
OOZE
SORRY, BUT THIS POISON SPEAR...
SWF
SLS
S
S
H
...IS GOING TO PUNCTURE YOUR PLAN IN A SECOND.
THIS SPEAR IS MADE OF A POISON SIMILAR TO MOLD SPORES.
SOME SAY THAT MOLD LAUNCHES ITS SPORES AT SPEEDS FASTER THAN ANYTHING ELSE TRAVELS IN NATURE.
YOU WON'T EVEN KNOW YOU'VE BEEN PENETRATED.

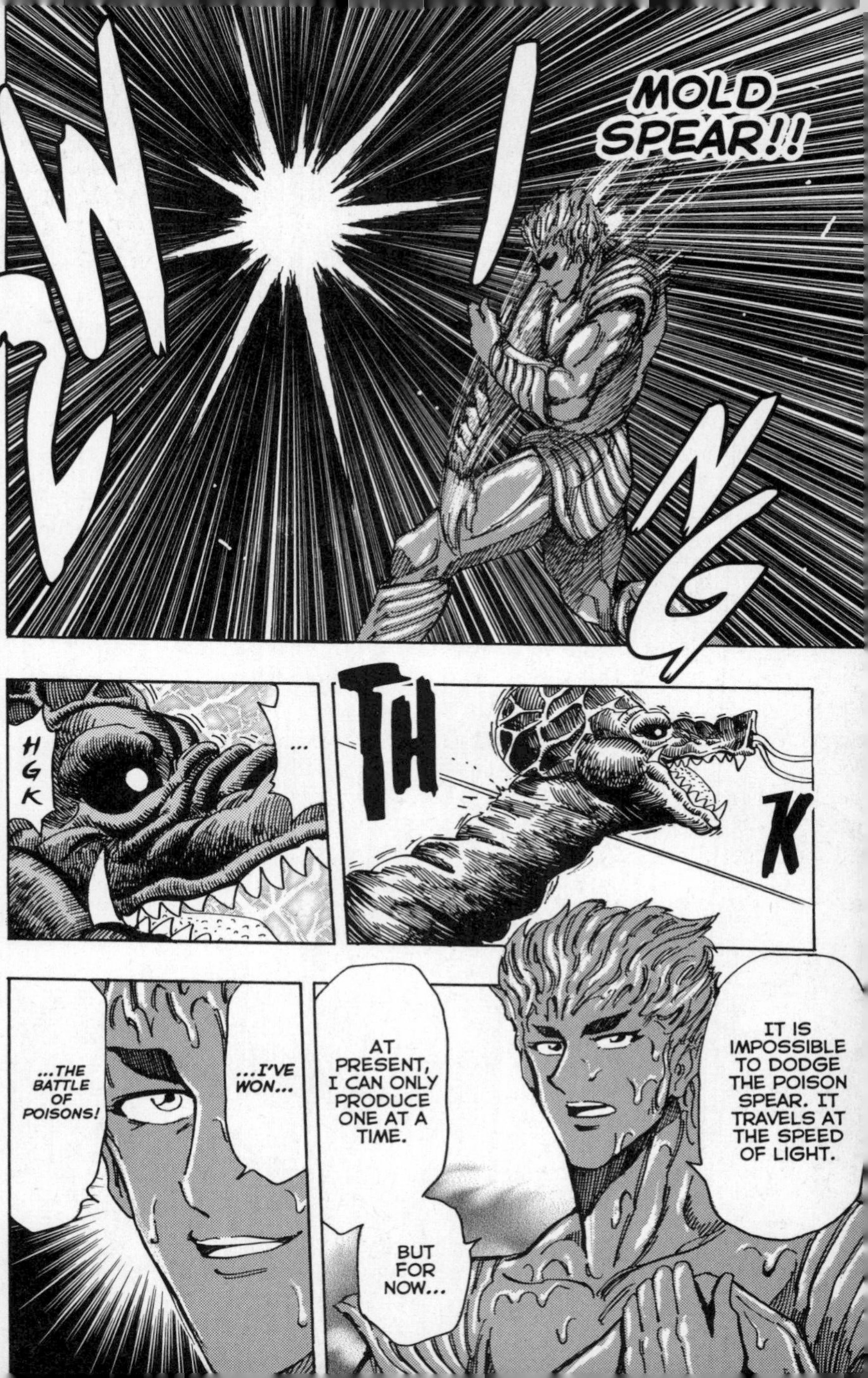
MOLD SPEAR!!
SWING
TH
K
...
HGK
IT IS IMPOSSIBLE TO DODGE THE POISON SPEAR. IT TRAVELS AT THE SPEED OF LIGHT.
AT PRESENT, I CAN ONLY PRODUCE ONE AT A TIME.
BUT FOR NOW...
...I'VE WON...
...THE BATTLE OF POISONS!

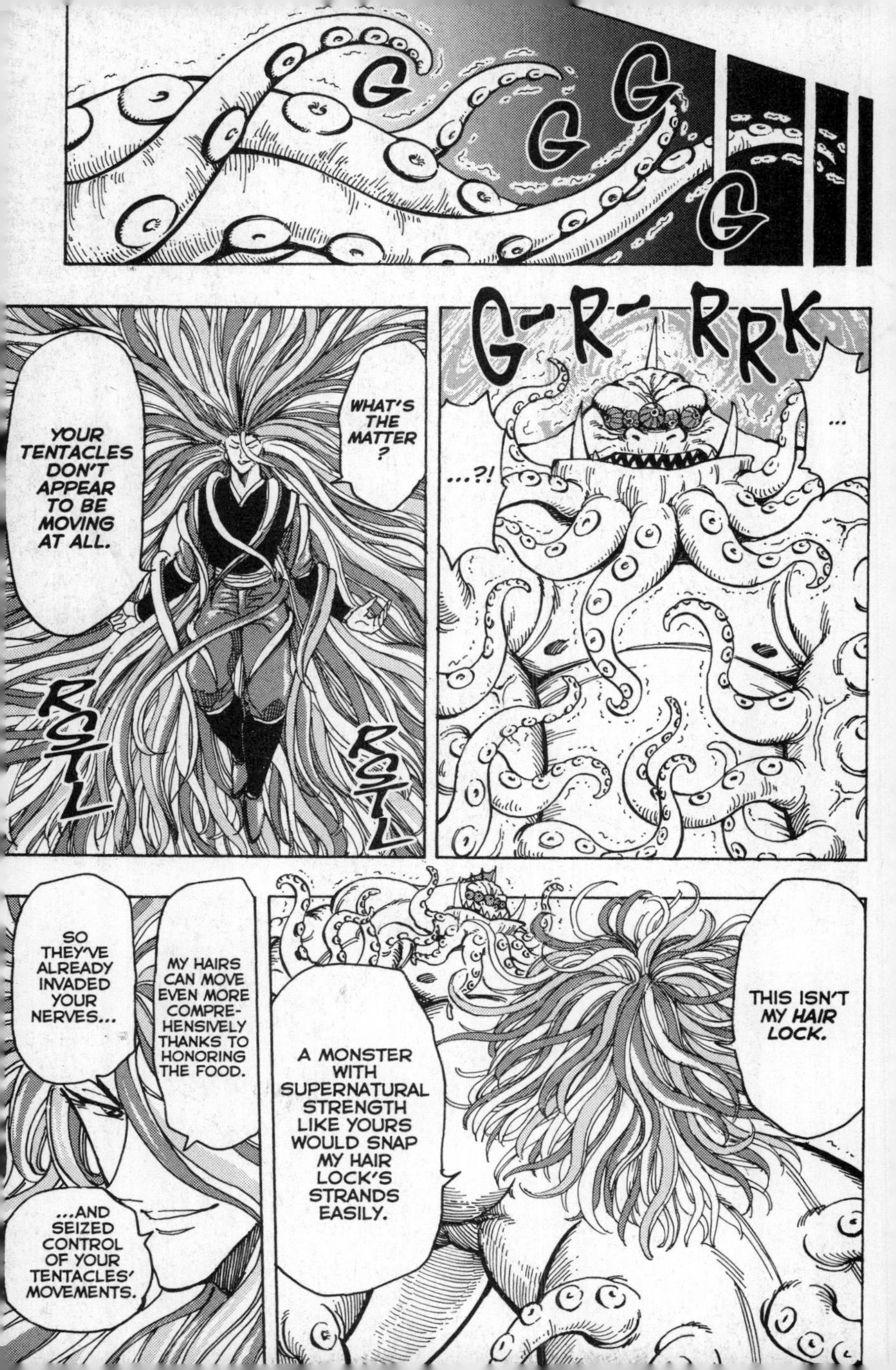
G G G G
G-R- RRK
...
...?!
YOUR TENTACLES DON'T APPEAR TO BE MOVING AT ALL.
WHAT'S THE MATTER?
RSTL
RSTL
THIS ISN'T MY HAIR LOCK.
A MONSTER WITH SUPERNATURAL STRENGTH LIKE YOURS WOULD SNAP MY HAIR LOCK'S STRANDS EASILY.
MY HAIRS CAN MOVE EVEN MORE COMPREHENSIVELY THANKS TO HONORING THE FOOD.
SO THEY'VE ALREADY INVADED YOUR NERVES...
...AND SEIZED CONTROL OF YOUR TENTACLES' MOVEMENTS.

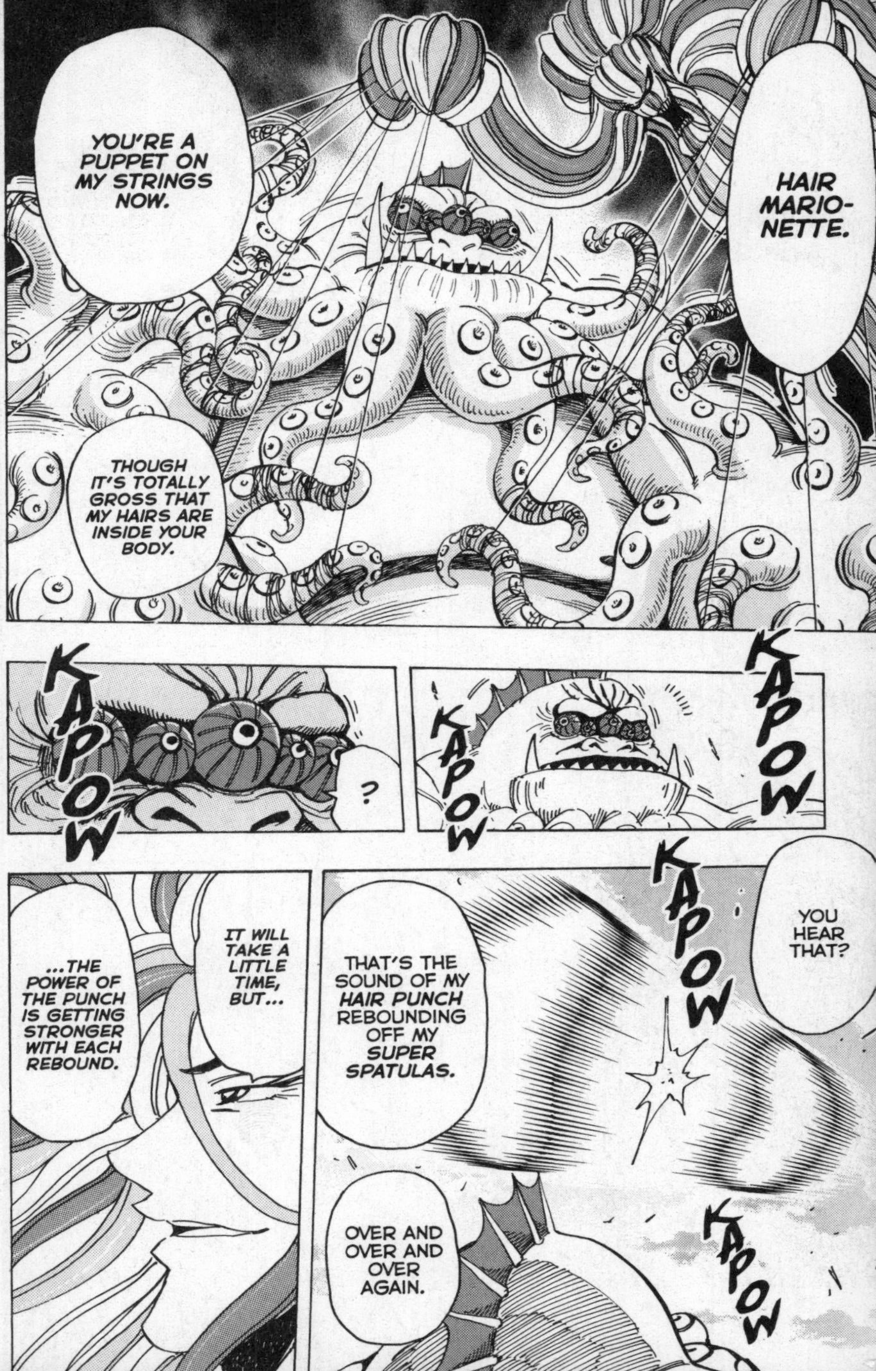
HAIR MARIONETTE.
YOU'RE A PUPPET ON MY STRINGS NOW.
THOUGH IT'S TOTALLY GROSS THAT MY HAIRS ARE INSIDE YOUR BODY.
KAPOW
KAPOW
?
KAPOW
YOU HEAR THAT?
KAPOW
THAT'S THE SOUND OF MY HAIR PUNCH REBOUNDING OFF MY SUPER SPATULAS.
OVER AND OVER AND OVER AGAIN.
KAPOW
IT WILL TAKE A LITTLE TIME, BUT...
...THE POWER OF THE PUNCH IS GETTING STRONGER WITH EACH REBOUND.

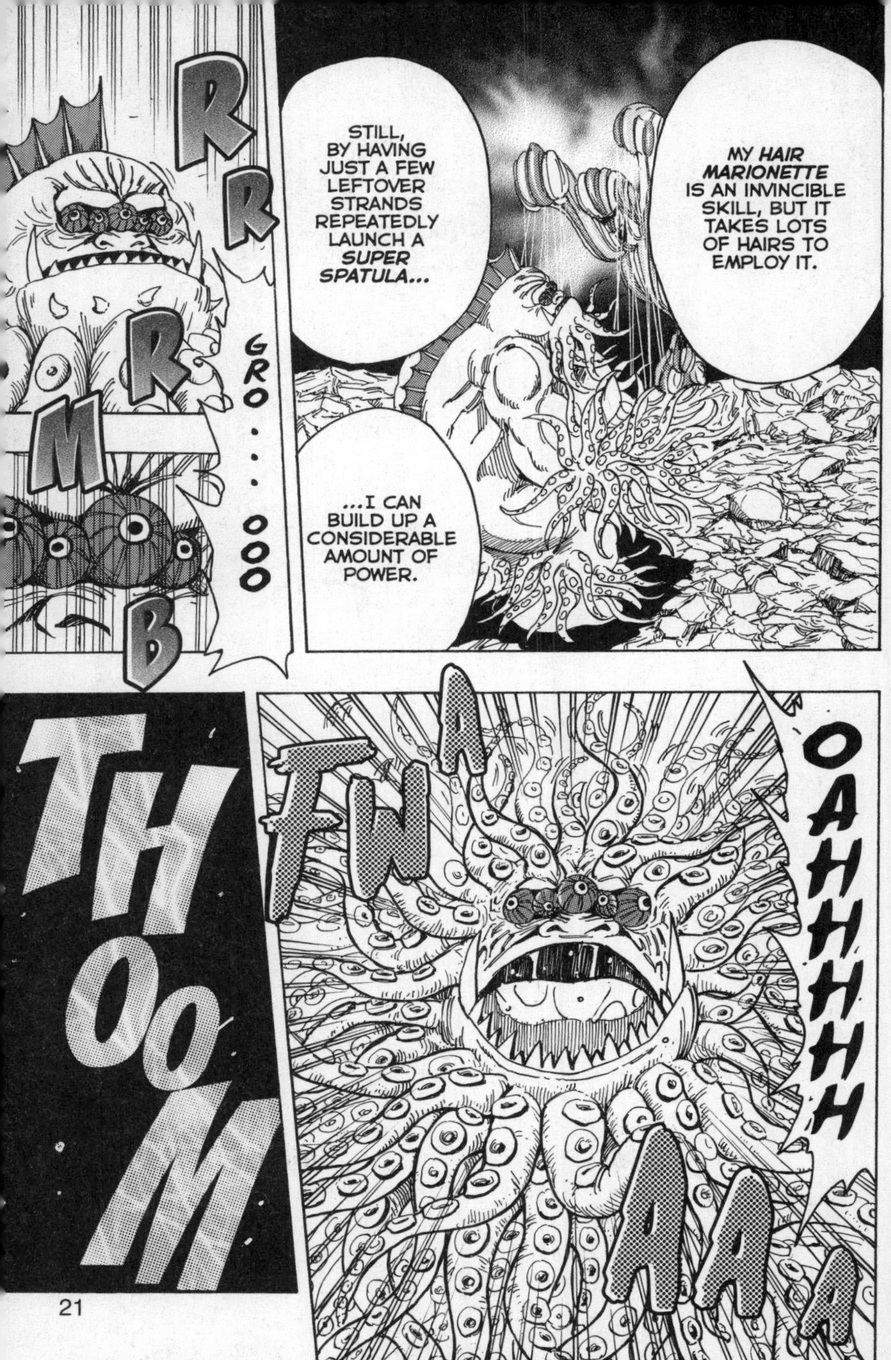
MY *HAIR MARIONETTE* IS AN INVINCIBLE SKILL, BUT IT TAKES LOTS OF HAIRS TO EMPLOY IT.
STILL, BY HAVING JUST A FEW LEFTOVER STRANDS REPEATEDLY LAUNCH A *SUPER SPATULA*...
...I CAN BUILD UP A CONSIDERABLE AMOUNT OF POWER.
GRO... OOO
RRRMB
OAHHHHHH
FWA
AAA
THOOM

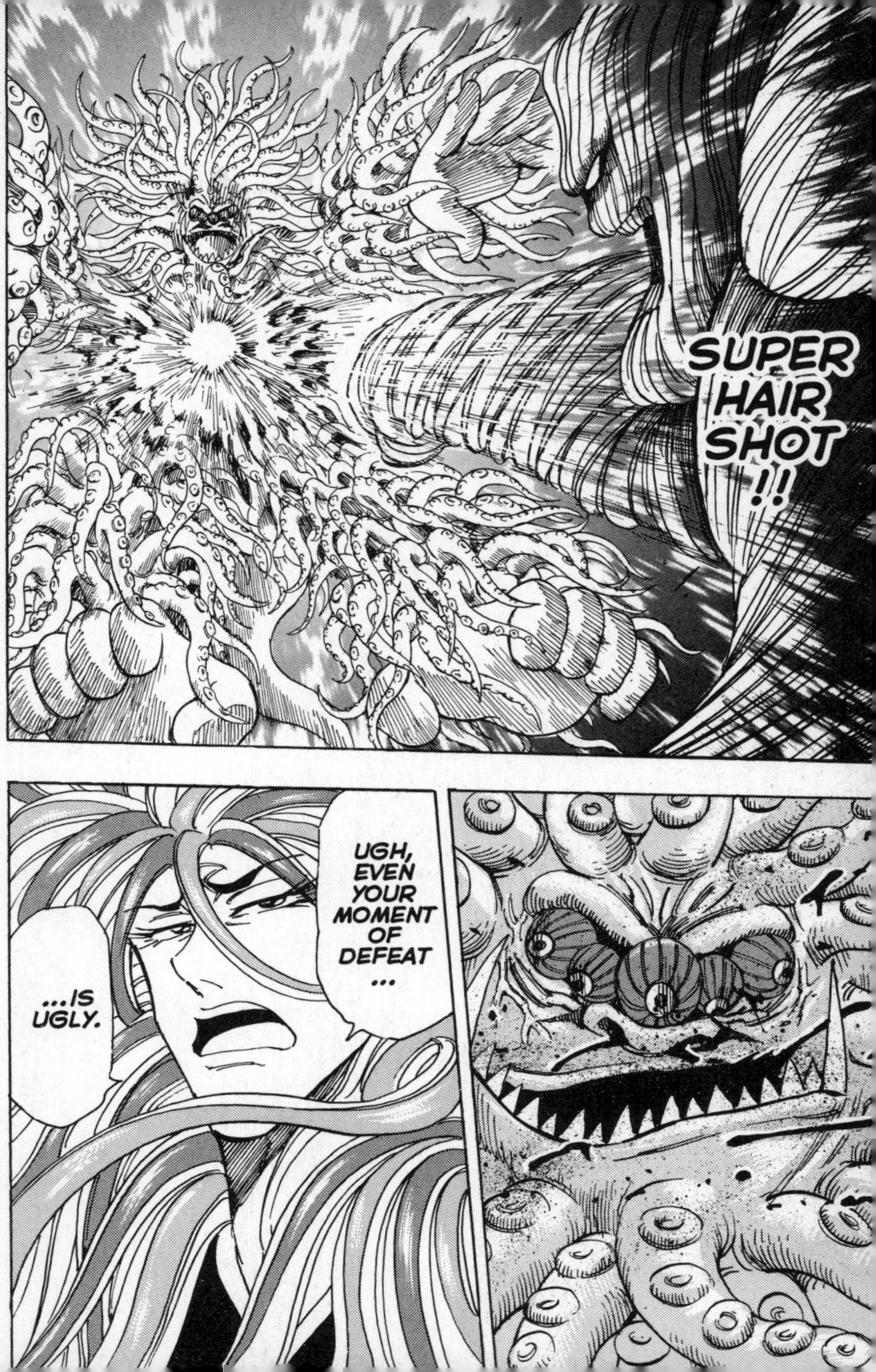
SUPER HAIR SHOT !!
UGH, EVEN YOUR MOMENT OF DEFEAT ...
...IS UGLY.

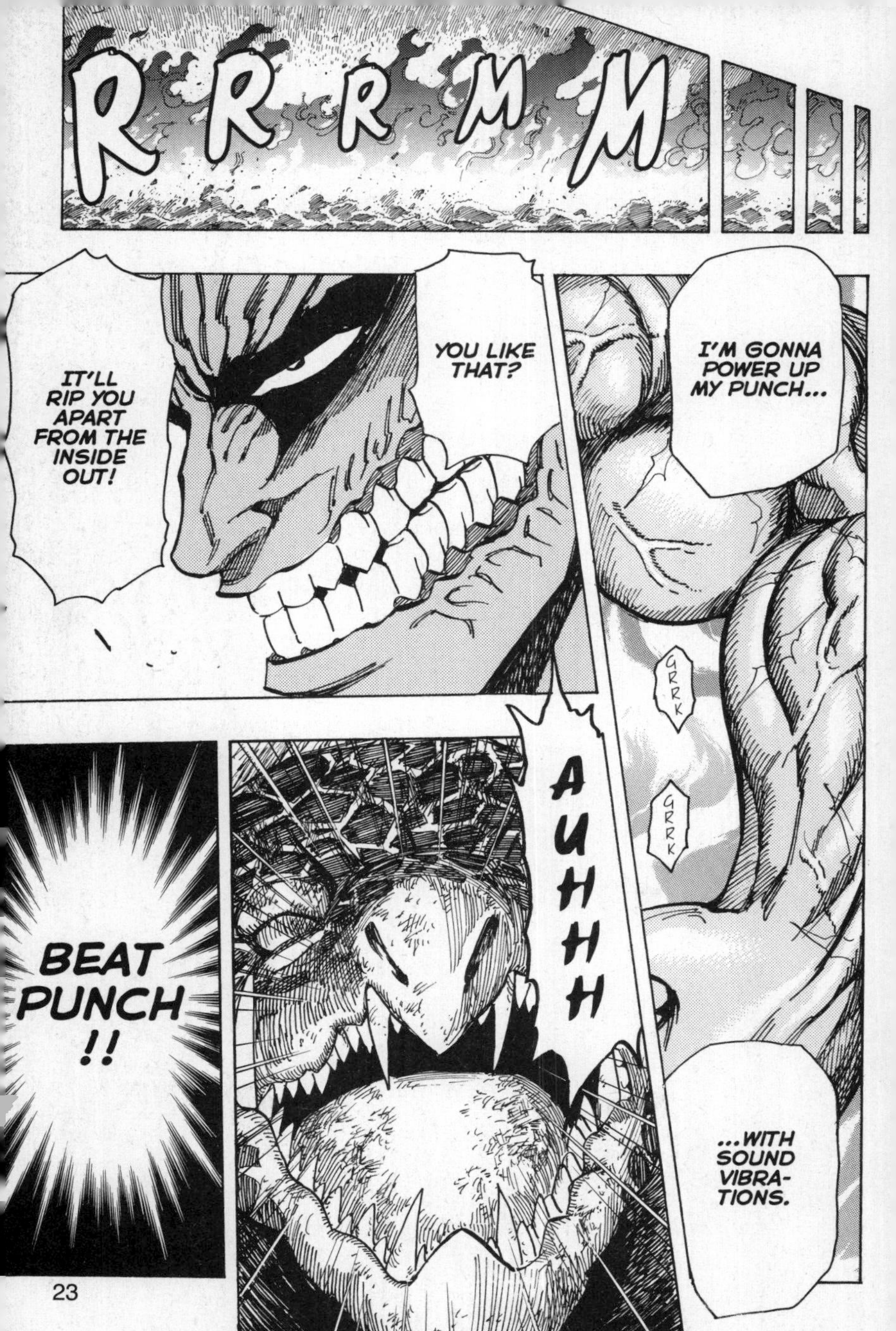
RRRMM
I'M GONNA POWER UP MY PUNCH...
YOU LIKE THAT?
IT'LL RIP YOU APART FROM THE INSIDE OUT!
GRRK
GRRK
...WITH SOUND VIBRATIONS.
AUHHH
BEAT PUNCH !!

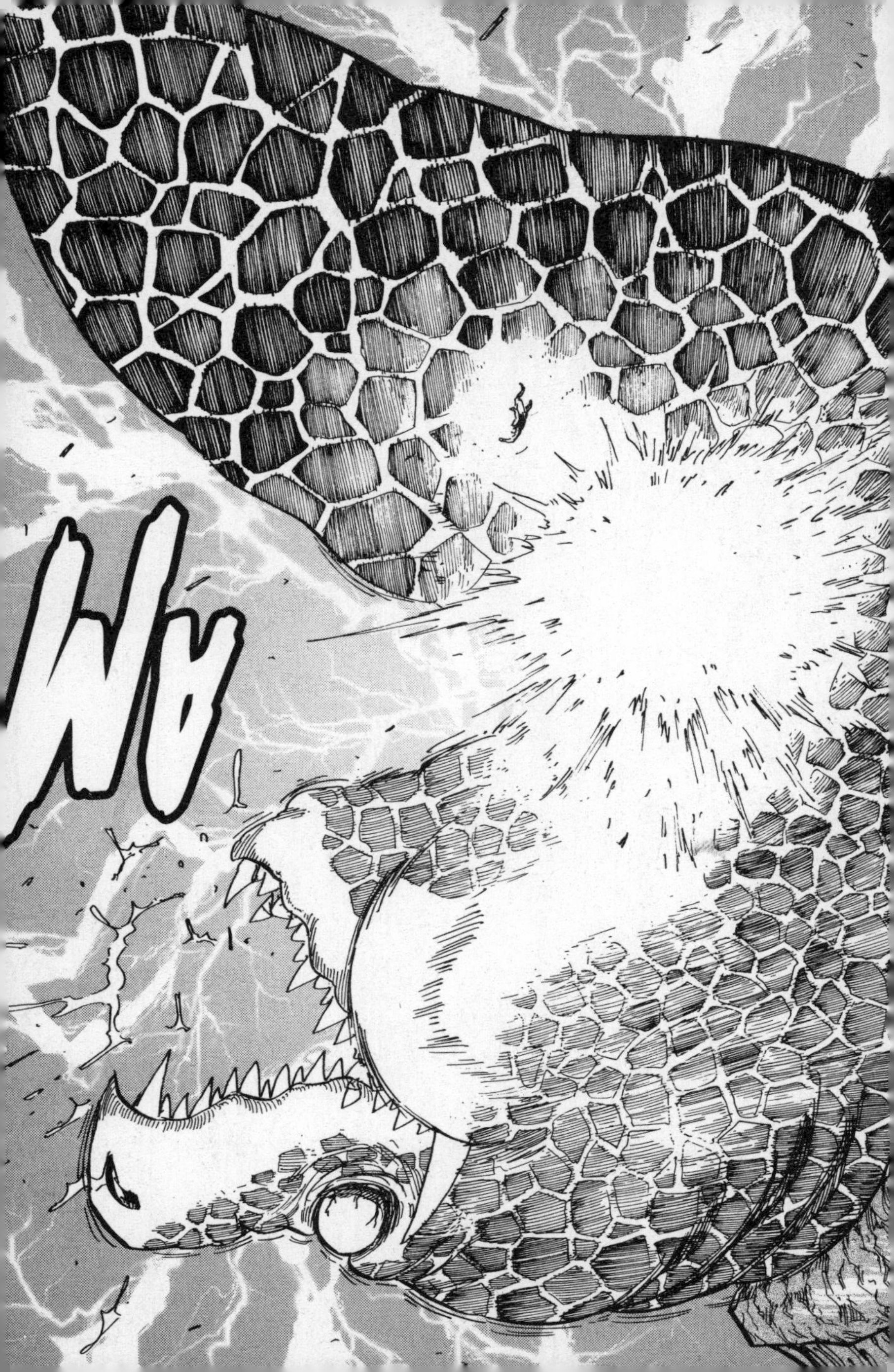
Wo

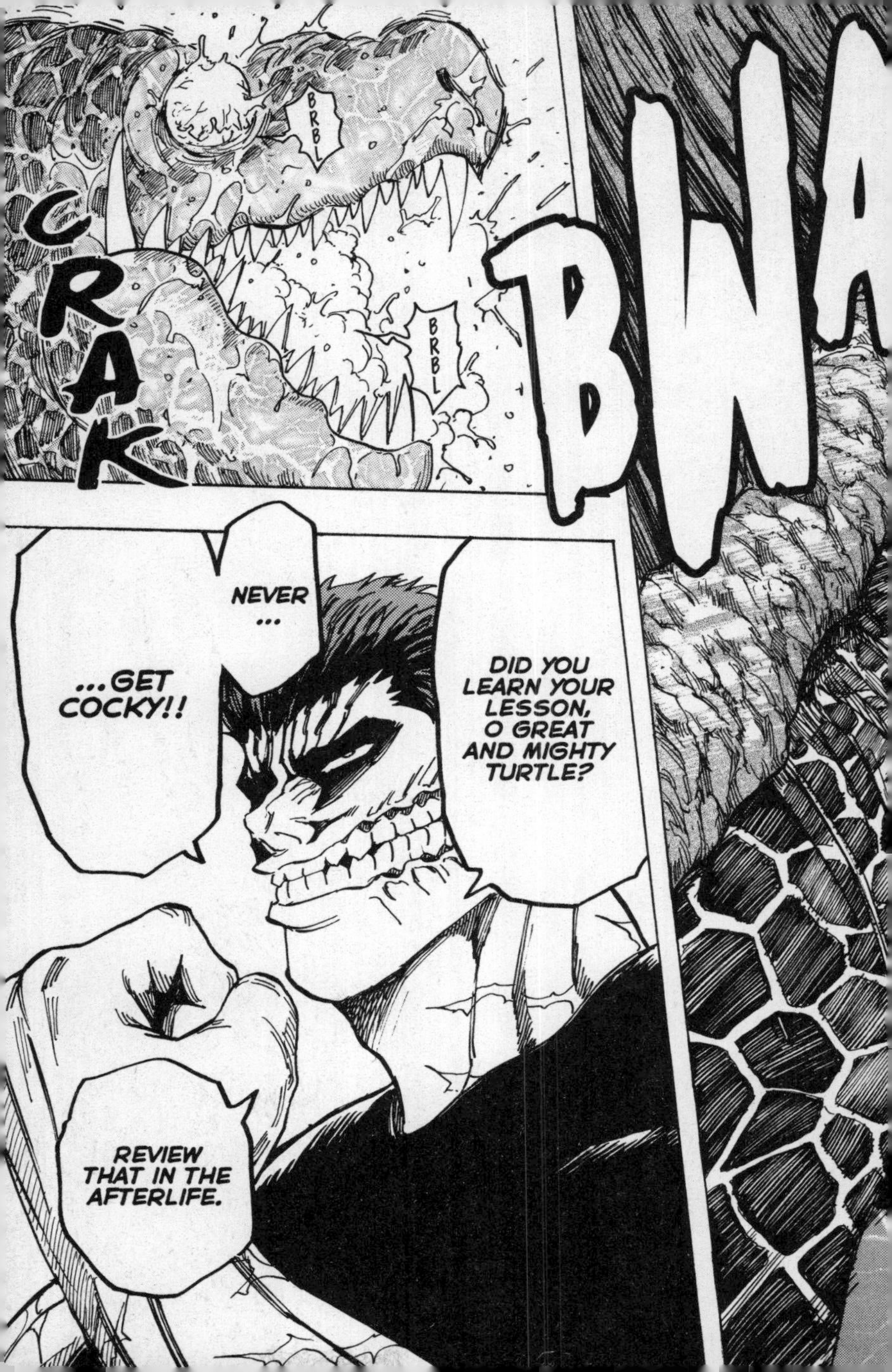
BWA
BRBL
BRBL
CRAK
DID YOU LEARN YOUR LESSON, O GREAT AND MIGHTY TURTLE?
NEVER...
...GET COCKY!!
REVIEW THAT IN THE AFTERLIFE.

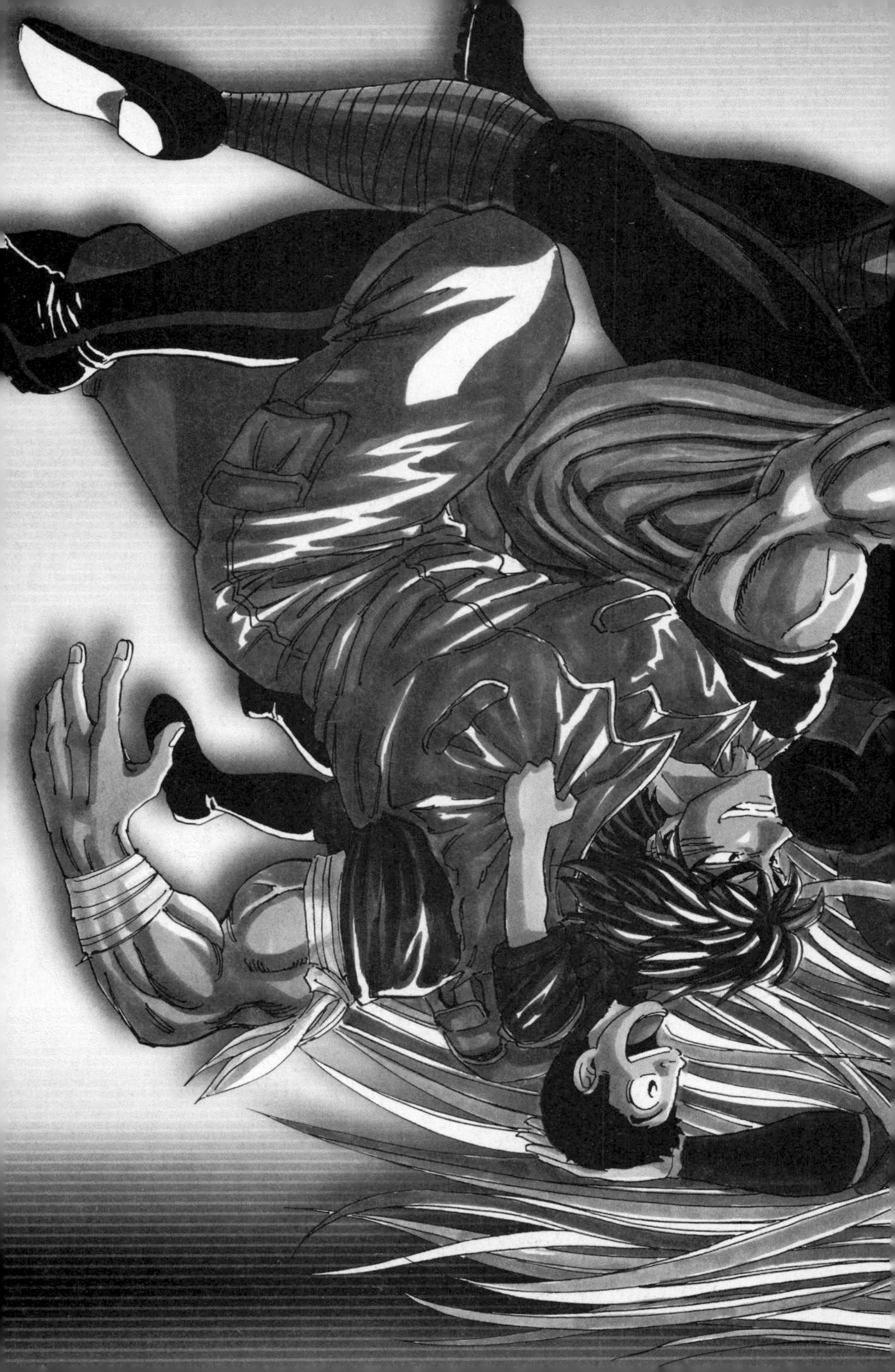

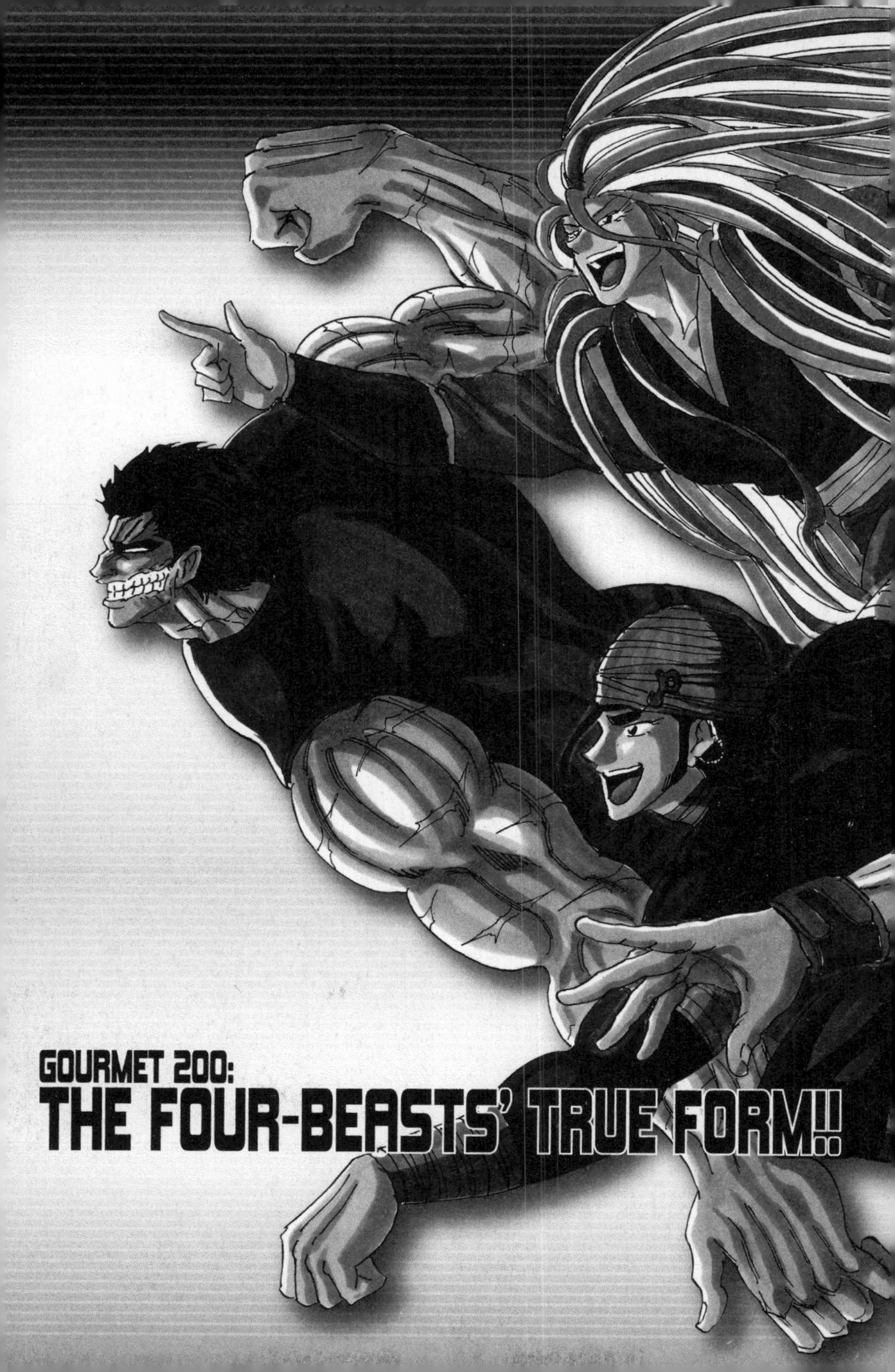
GOURMET 200:
THE FOUR-BEASTS' TRUE FORM!!

TORIKO

GOURMET CHECKLIST

Vol. 235

GOURMET COIN
(CASINO CURRENCY)

CAPTURE LEVEL: ---
HABITAT: GOURMET CASINO
SIZE: LARGER=HIGHER VALUE
HEIGHT: ---
WEIGHT: HEAVIER=HIGHER VALUE
PRICE: 1,000 YEN—100,000,000
YEN PER COIN

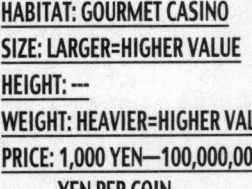

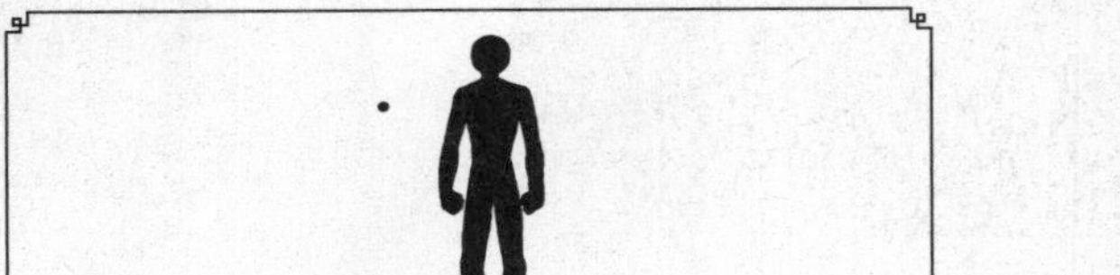

SCALE

A COIN USED AT GOURMET CASINO. IT'S MEANT TO BE USED FOR BETTING ON GAMES, BUT IT CAN BE EATEN AS WELL. THE HIGHER THE COIN'S VALUE, THE BETTER ITS TASTE. GOURMET COINS CAN BE SO ADDICTIVE, IN FACT, THAT PLENTY OF GLUTTONOUS GAMBLERS WILL GORGE ON COINS INSTEAD OF GAMBLING WITH THEM, AND END UP RUINING THEMSELVES.

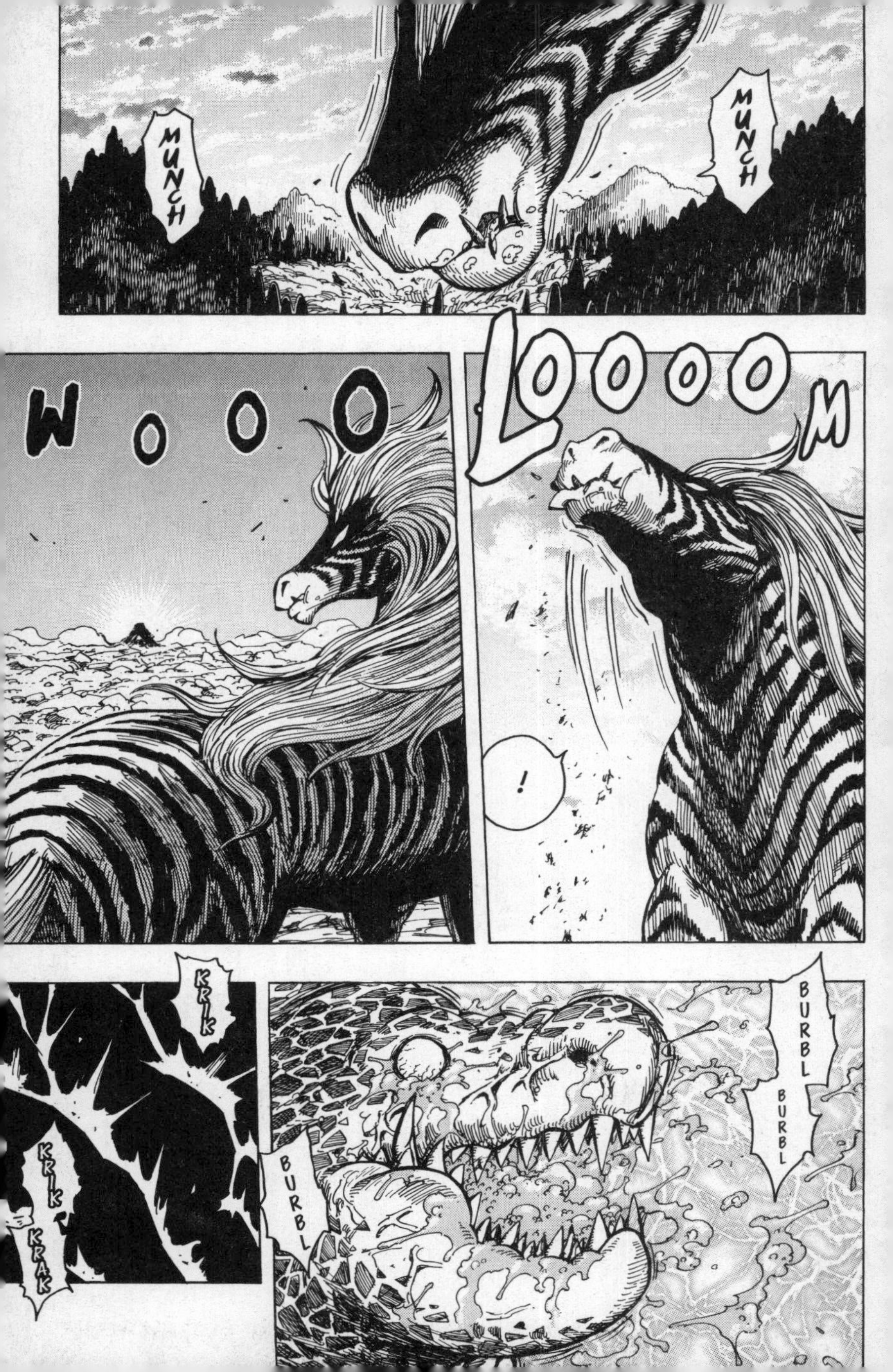
MUNCH
MUNCH
LOOOOM
!
WOOO
BURBL
BURBL
BURBL
KRIK
KRIK KRAK

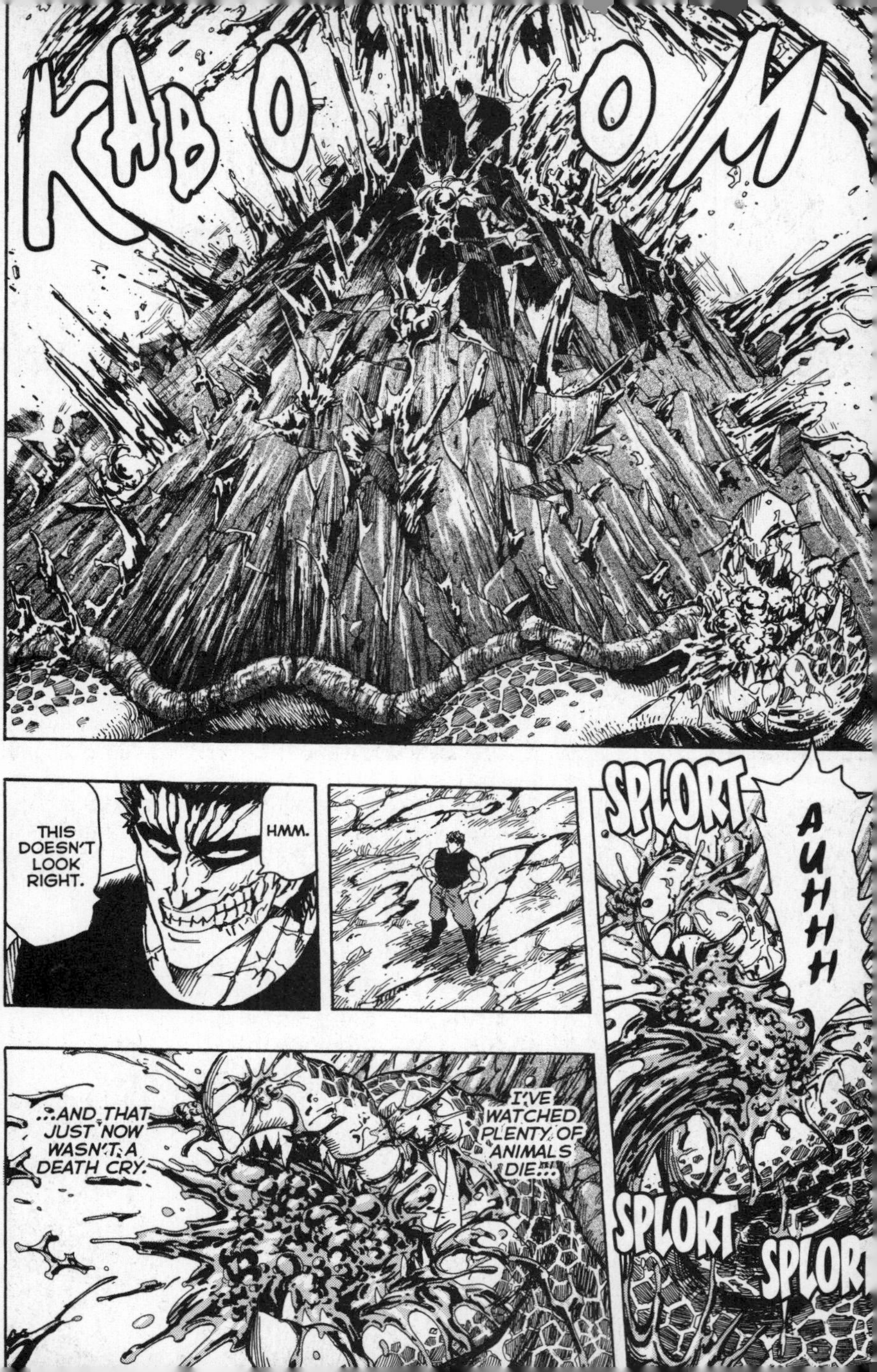
KABOOM
SPLORT
AUHHH
SPLORT
SPLOR
HMM.
THIS DOESN'T LOOK RIGHT.
I'VE WATCHED PLENTY OF ANIMALS DIE...
...AND THAT JUST NOW WASN'T A DEATH CRY.

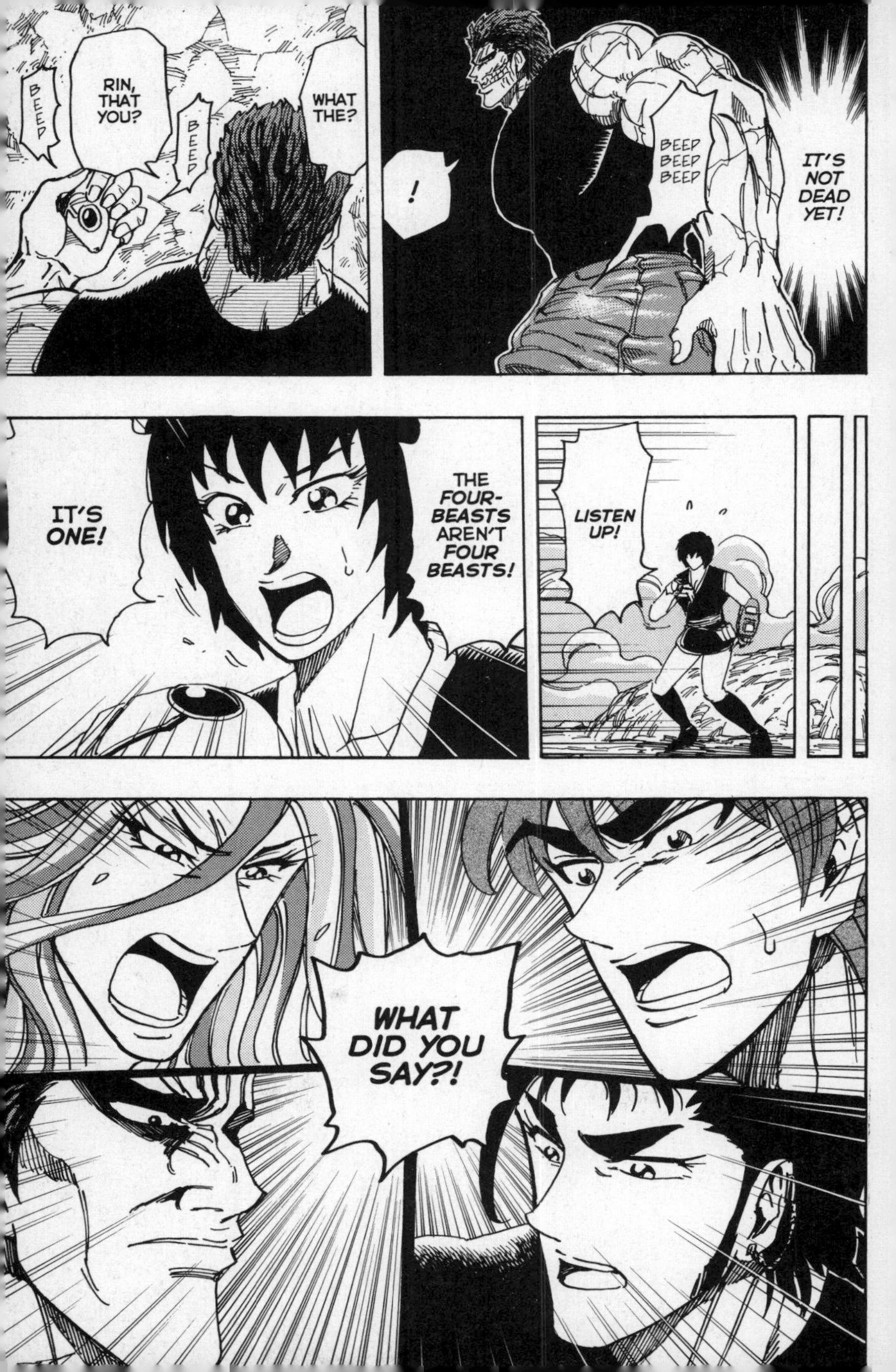
IT'S NOT DEAD YET!
BEEP BEEP BEEP
!
WHAT THE?
BEEP
RIN, THAT YOU?
BEEP
LISTEN UP!
THE FOUR-BEASTS AREN'T FOUR BEASTS!
IT'S ONE!
WHAT DID YOU SAY?!

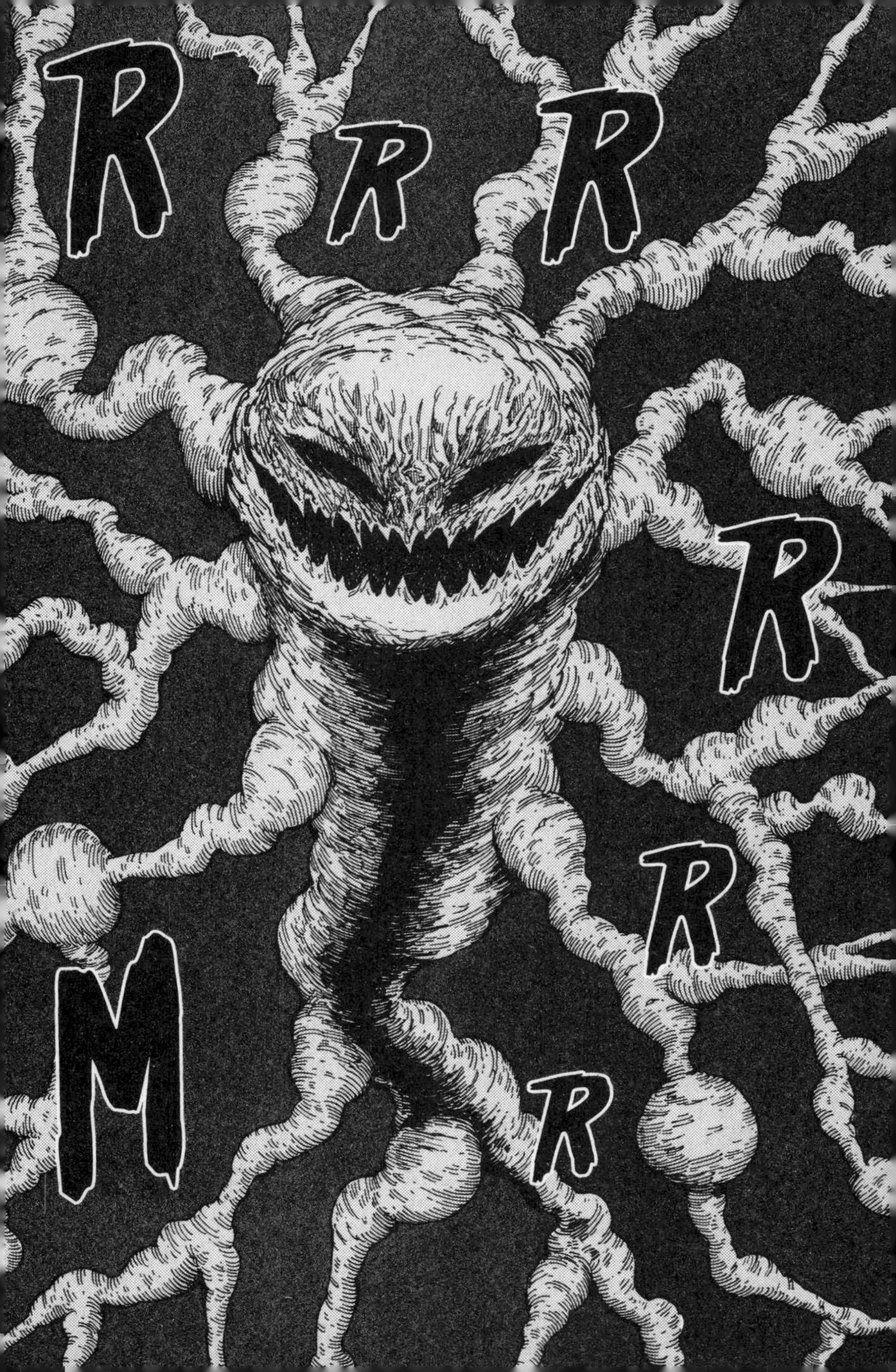
RRRRRRM

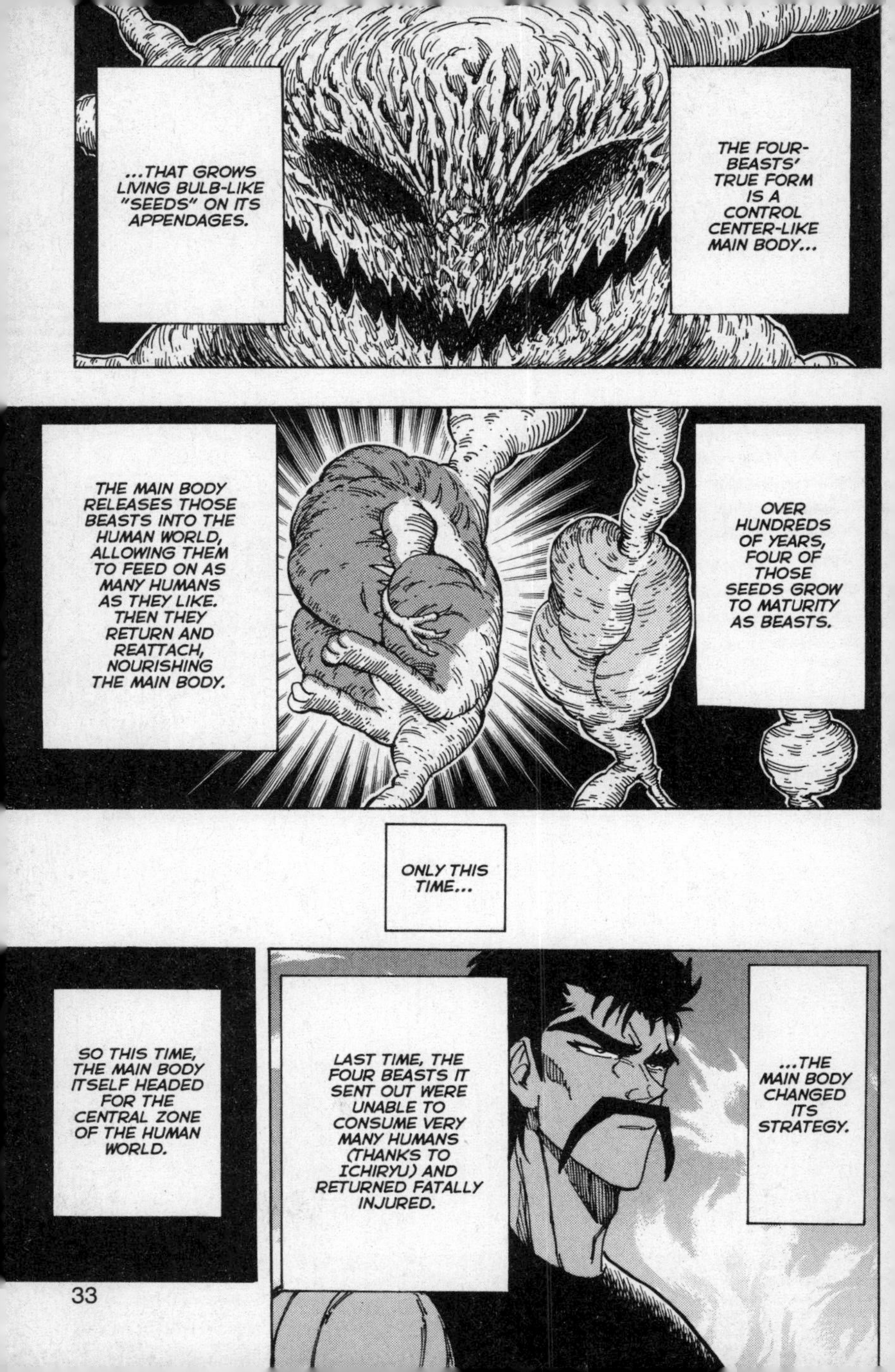
THE FOUR-BEASTS' TRUE FORM IS A CONTROL CENTER-LIKE MAIN BODY...
...THAT GROWS LIVING BULB-LIKE "SEEDS" ON ITS APPENDAGES.
OVER HUNDREDS OF YEARS, FOUR OF THOSE SEEDS GROW TO MATURITY AS BEASTS.
THE MAIN BODY RELEASES THOSE BEASTS INTO THE HUMAN WORLD, ALLOWING THEM TO FEED ON AS MANY HUMANS AS THEY LIKE. THEN THEY RETURN AND REATTACH, NOURISHING THE MAIN BODY.
ONLY THIS TIME...
...THE MAIN BODY CHANGED ITS STRATEGY.
LAST TIME, THE FOUR BEASTS IT SENT OUT WERE UNABLE TO CONSUME VERY MANY HUMANS (THANKS TO ICHIRYU) AND RETURNED FATALLY INJURED.
SO THIS TIME, THE MAIN BODY ITSELF HEADED FOR THE CENTRAL ZONE OF THE HUMAN WORLD.

FROM THE GOURMET WORLD IT UNLEASHED ITS LIMBS, THE FOUR BEASTS...
...AND DROVE ITS HUMAN PREY TO GATHER LIKE CATTLE IN THE CENTRAL ZONE OF THE HUMAN WORLD.
ALL IN ORDER ...

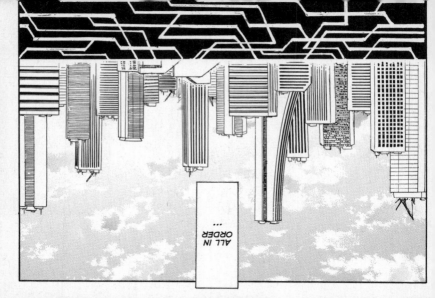

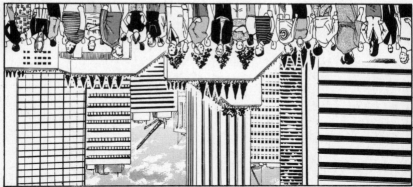

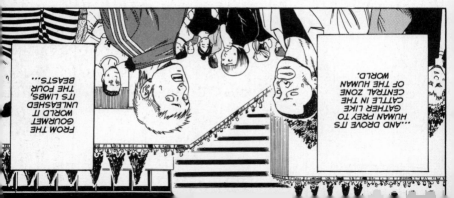

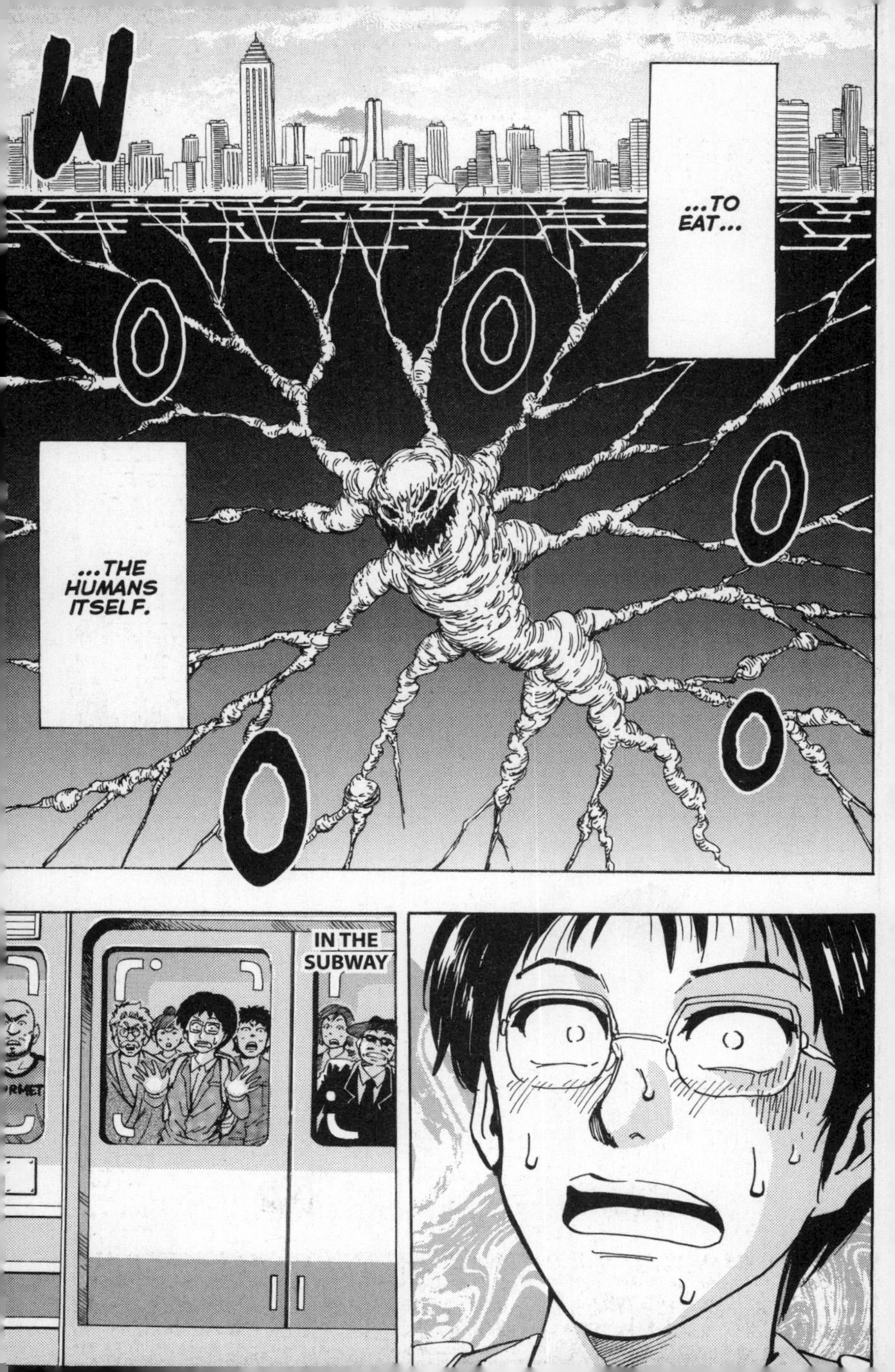
...TO EAT...
...THE HUMANS ITSELF.
W
IN THE SUBWAY

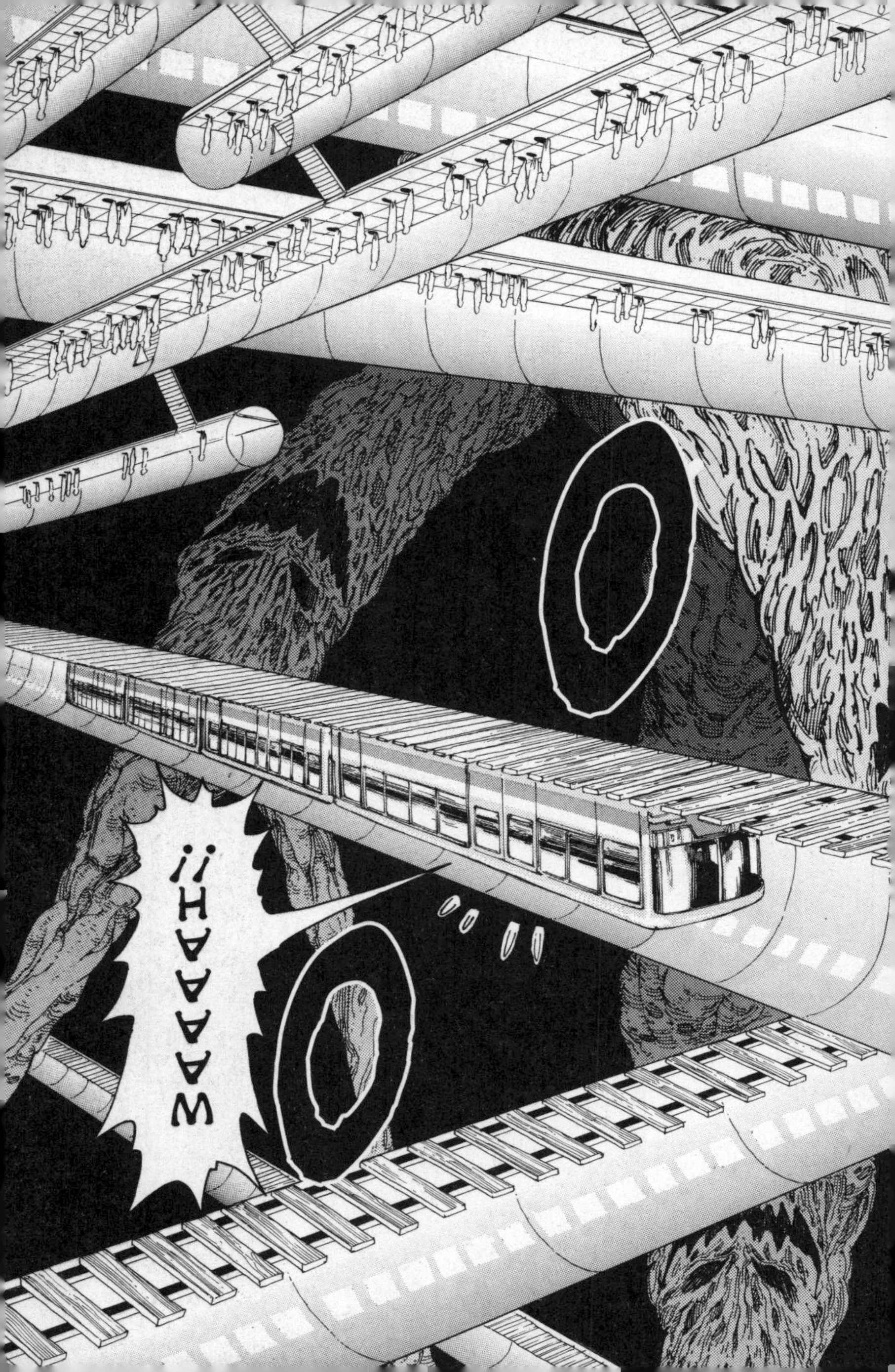
WAAAAH!!

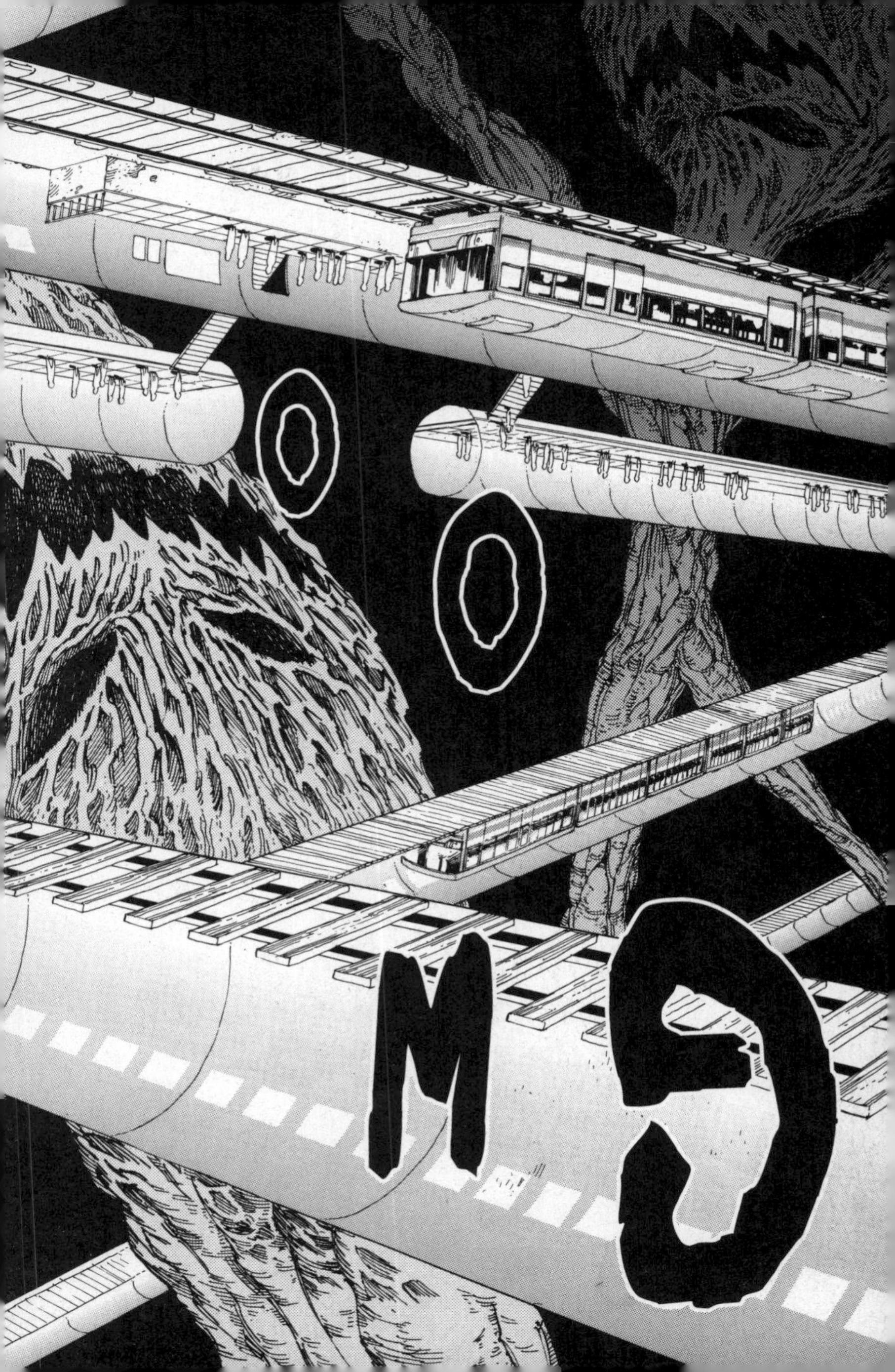

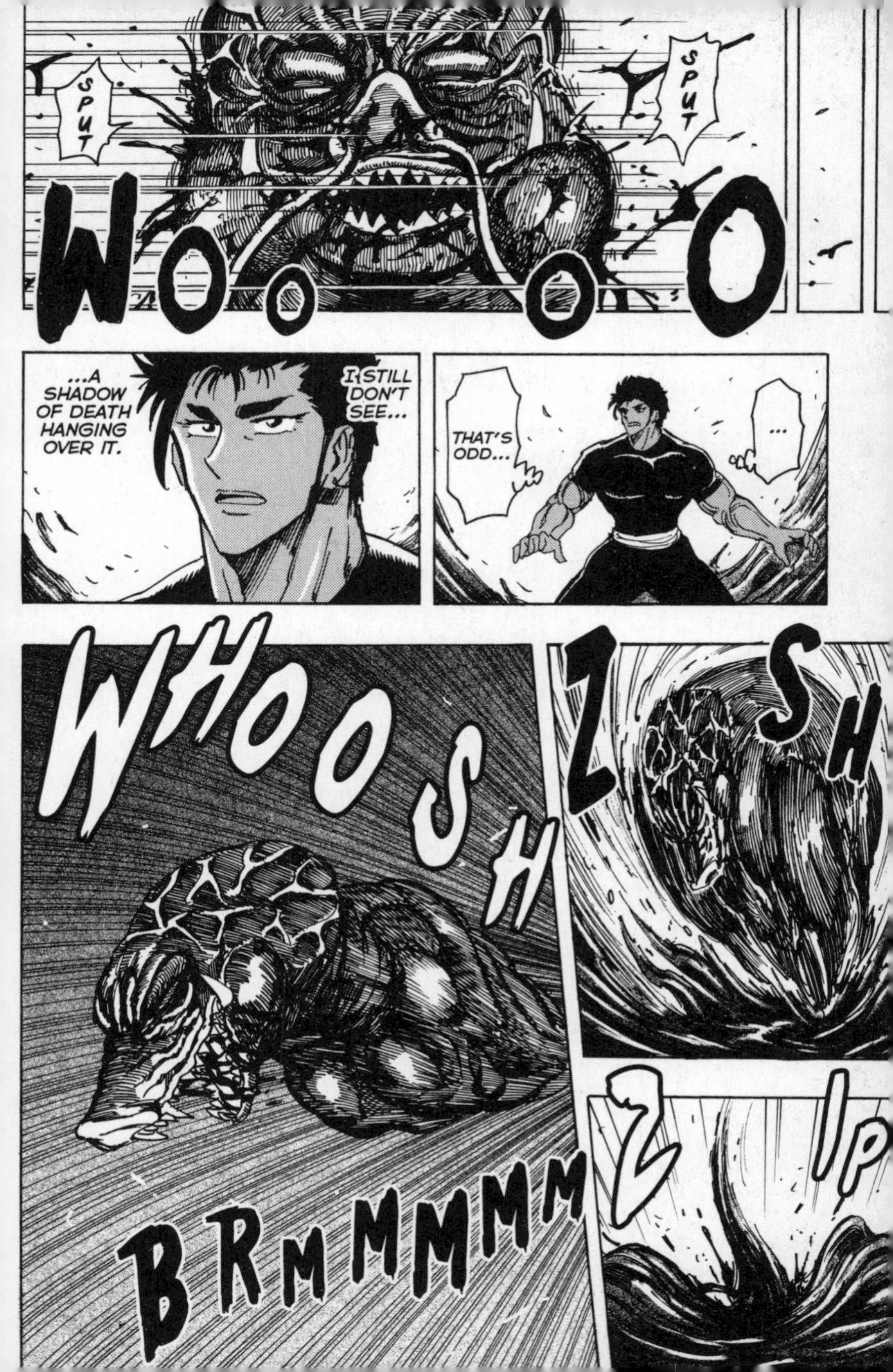
SPUT
SPUT
WOOOOO
THAT'S ODD...
...
I STILL DON'T SEE...
...A SHADOW OF DEATH HANGING OVER IT.
ZSH
WHOOSH
ZZIP
BRMMMMMM

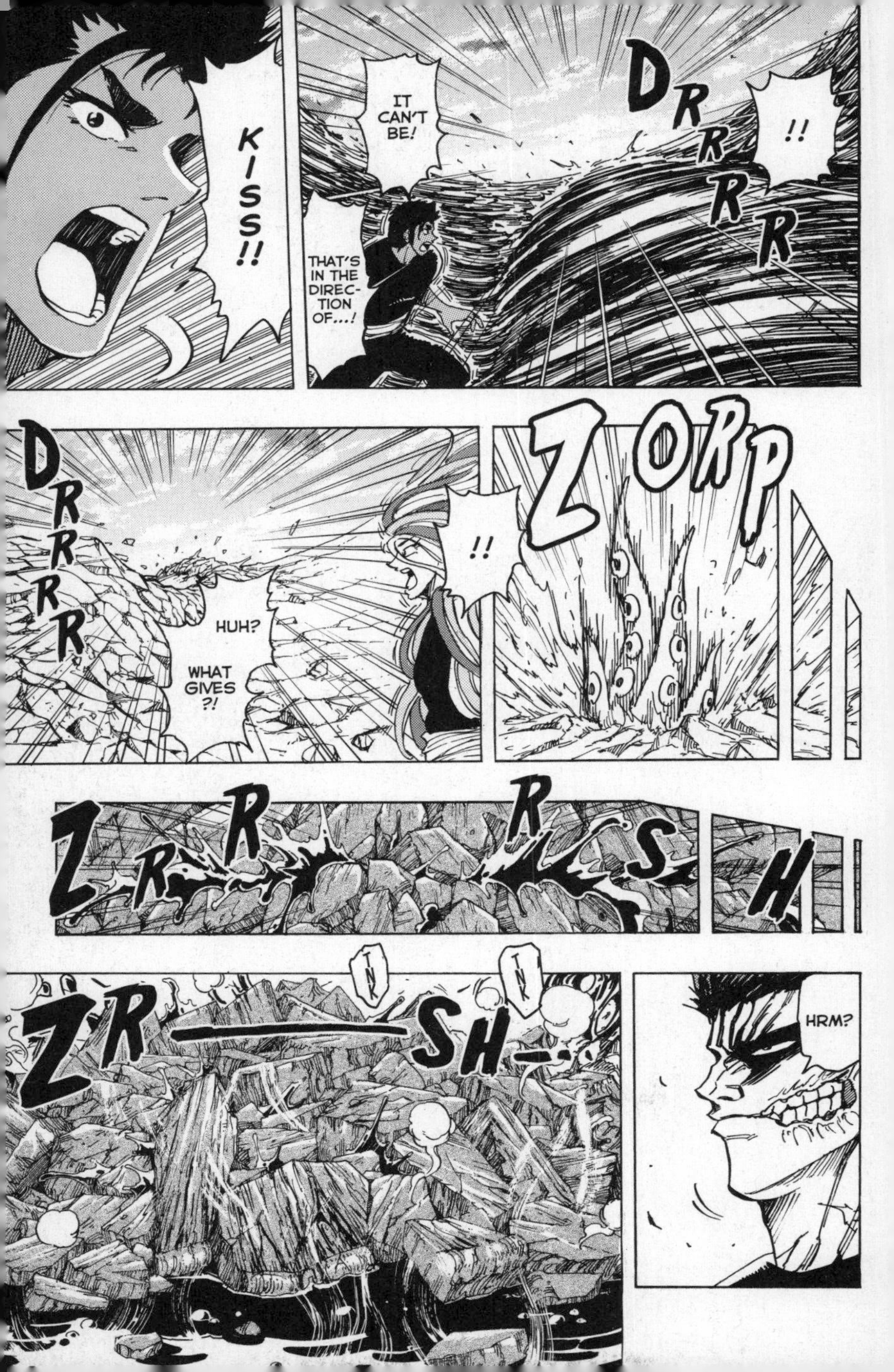
!!
DRRRR
IT CAN'T BE!
THAT'S IN THE DIREC-TION OF...!
KISS!!
ZORP
!!
HUH?
WHAT GIVES ?!
DRRRR
ZRRRSH
HRM?
TNK
TNK
ZR——SH—

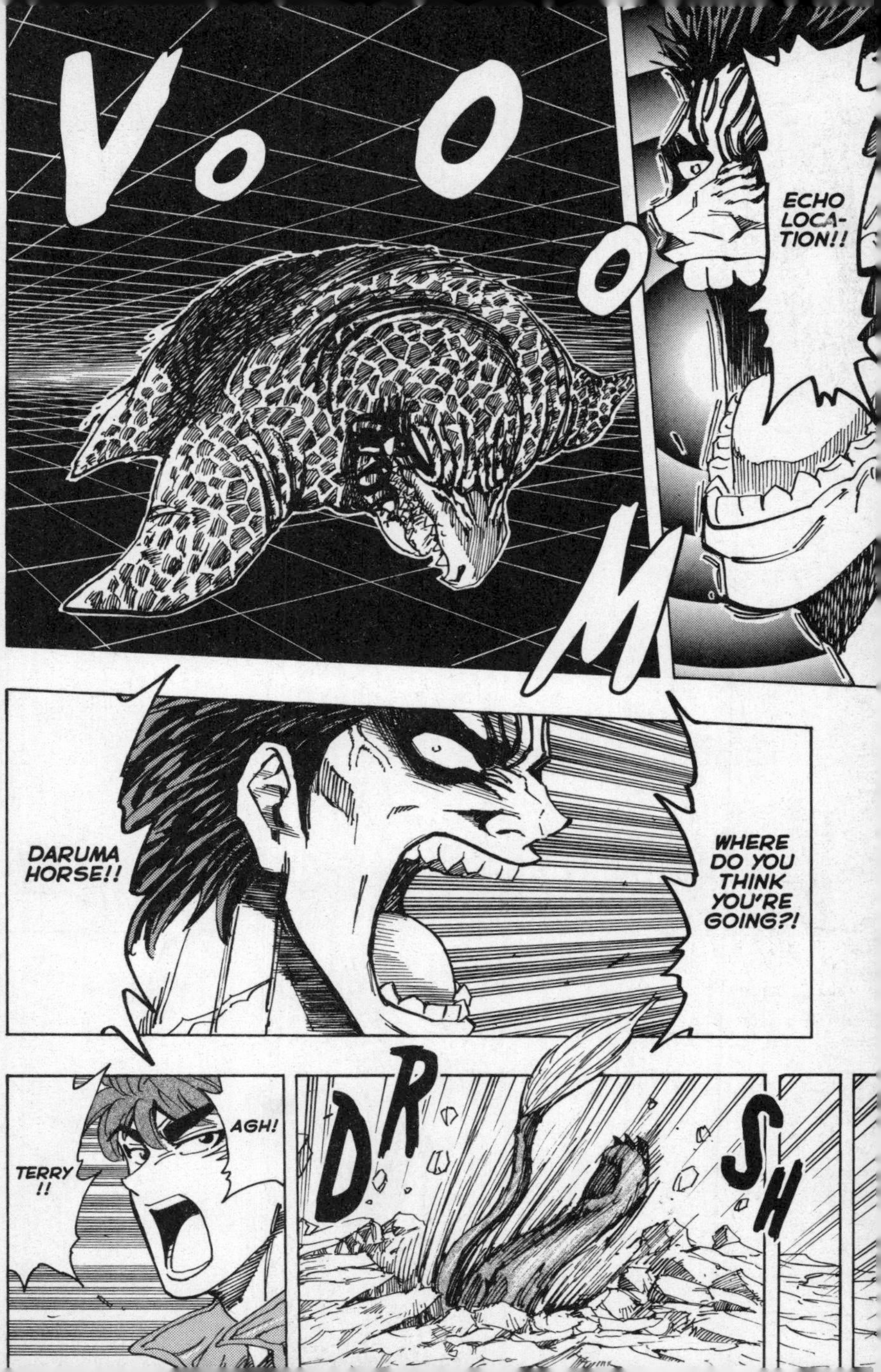
ECHO LOCA-TION!!
VOOOM
WHERE DO YOU THINK YOU'RE GOING?!
DARUMA HORSE!!
DRSH
AGH!
TERRY !!

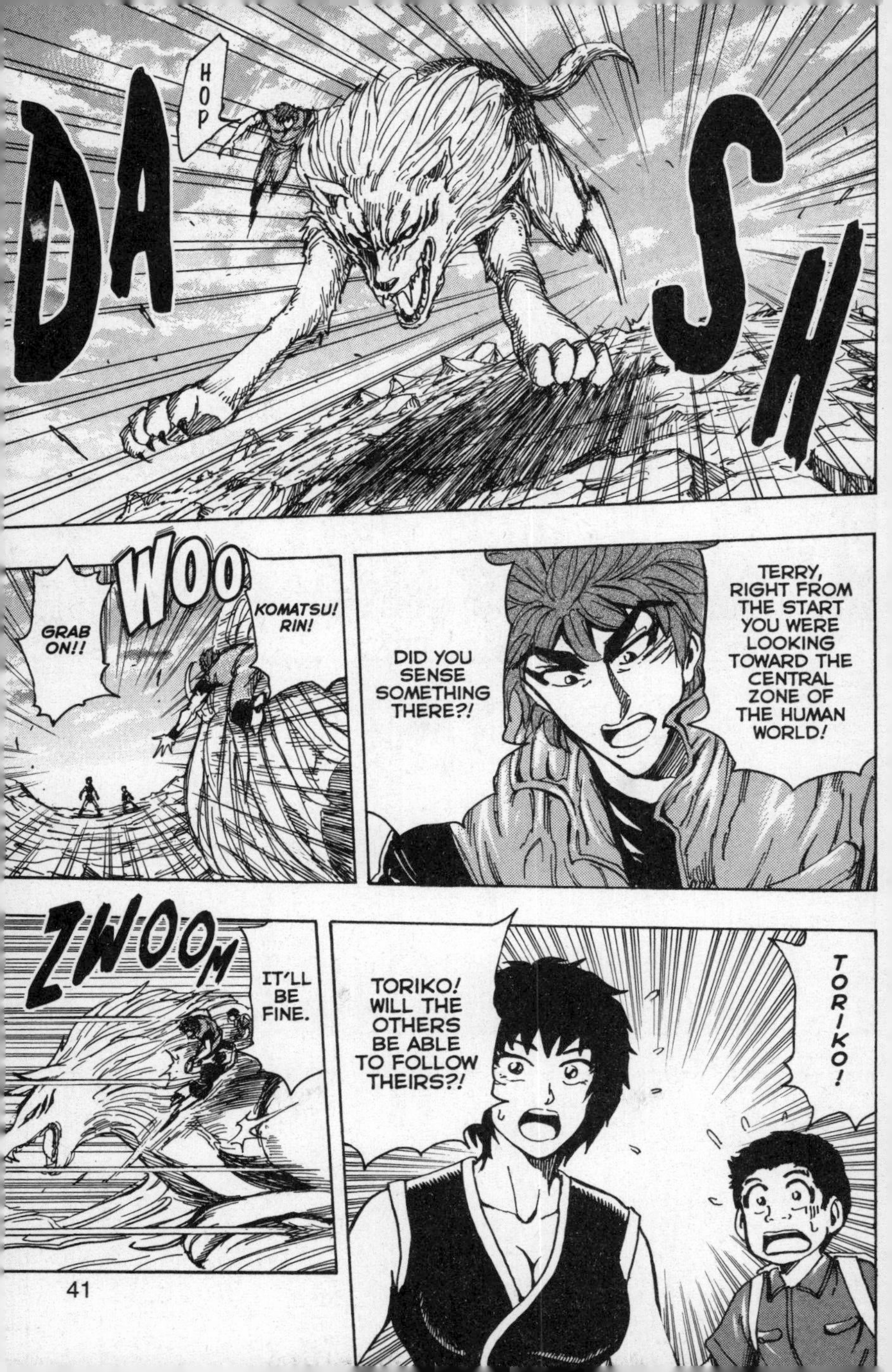
DASH
HOP
TERRY, RIGHT FROM THE START YOU WERE LOOKING TOWARD THE CENTRAL ZONE OF THE HUMAN WORLD!
DID YOU SENSE SOMETHING THERE?!
WOO
KOMATSU! RIN!
GRAB ON!!
TORIKO!
TORIKO! WILL THE OTHERS BE ABLE TO FOLLOW THEIRS?!
IT'LL BE FINE.
ZWOOM

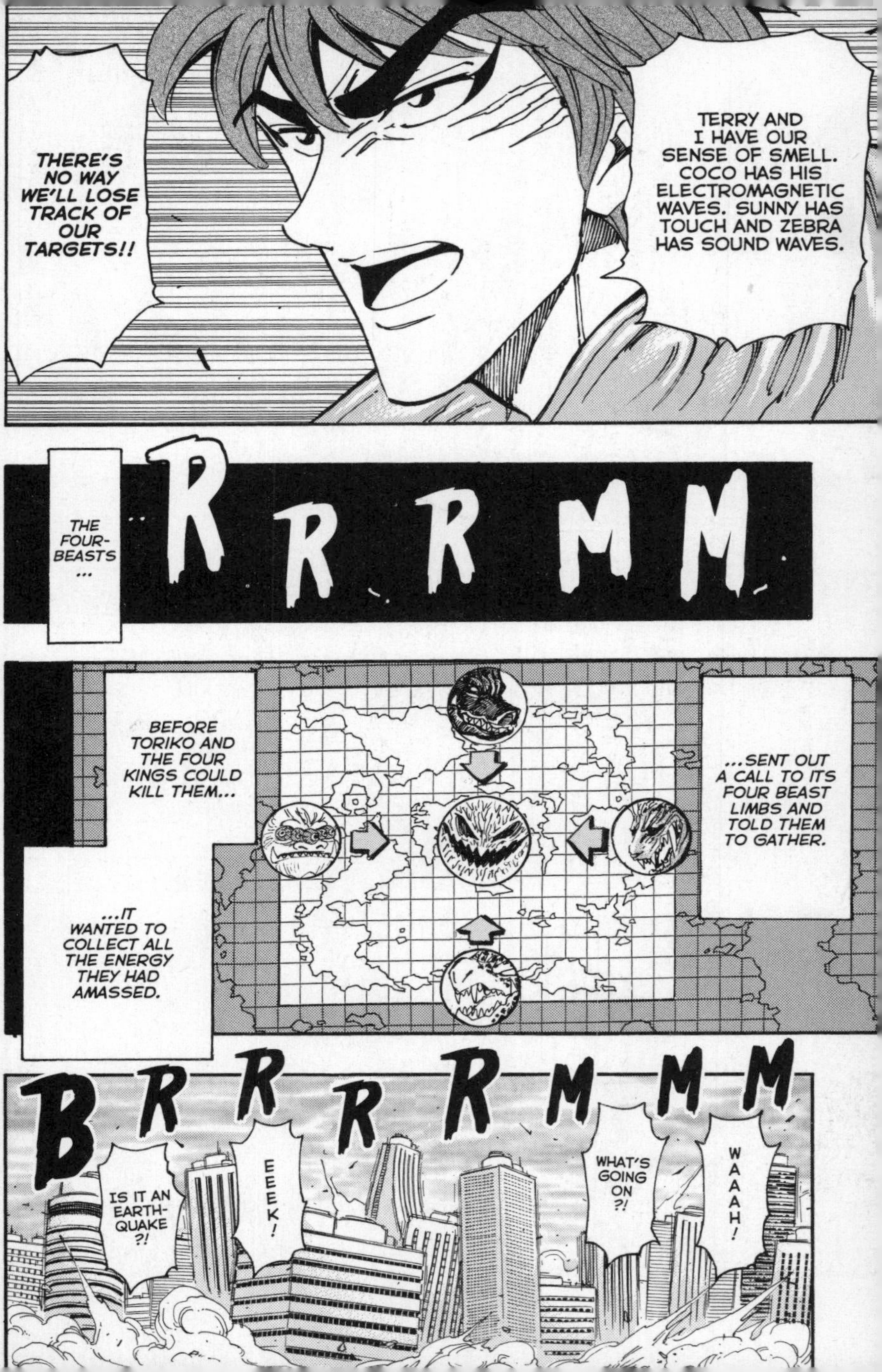
TERRY AND I HAVE OUR SENSE OF SMELL. COCO HAS HIS ELECTROMAGNETIC WAVES. SUNNY HAS TOUCH AND ZEBRA HAS SOUND WAVES.
THERE'S NO WAY WE'LL LOSE TRACK OF OUR TARGETS!!
RRRMM
THE FOUR-BEASTS...
...SENT OUT A CALL TO ITS FOUR BEAST LIMBS AND TOLD THEM TO GATHER.
BEFORE TORIKO AND THE FOUR KINGS COULD KILL THEM...
...IT WANTED TO COLLECT ALL THE ENERGY THEY HAD AMASSED.
BRRRRMMM
WAAAH!
WHAT'S GOING ON ?!
EEEK!
IS IT AN EARTH-QUAKE ?!

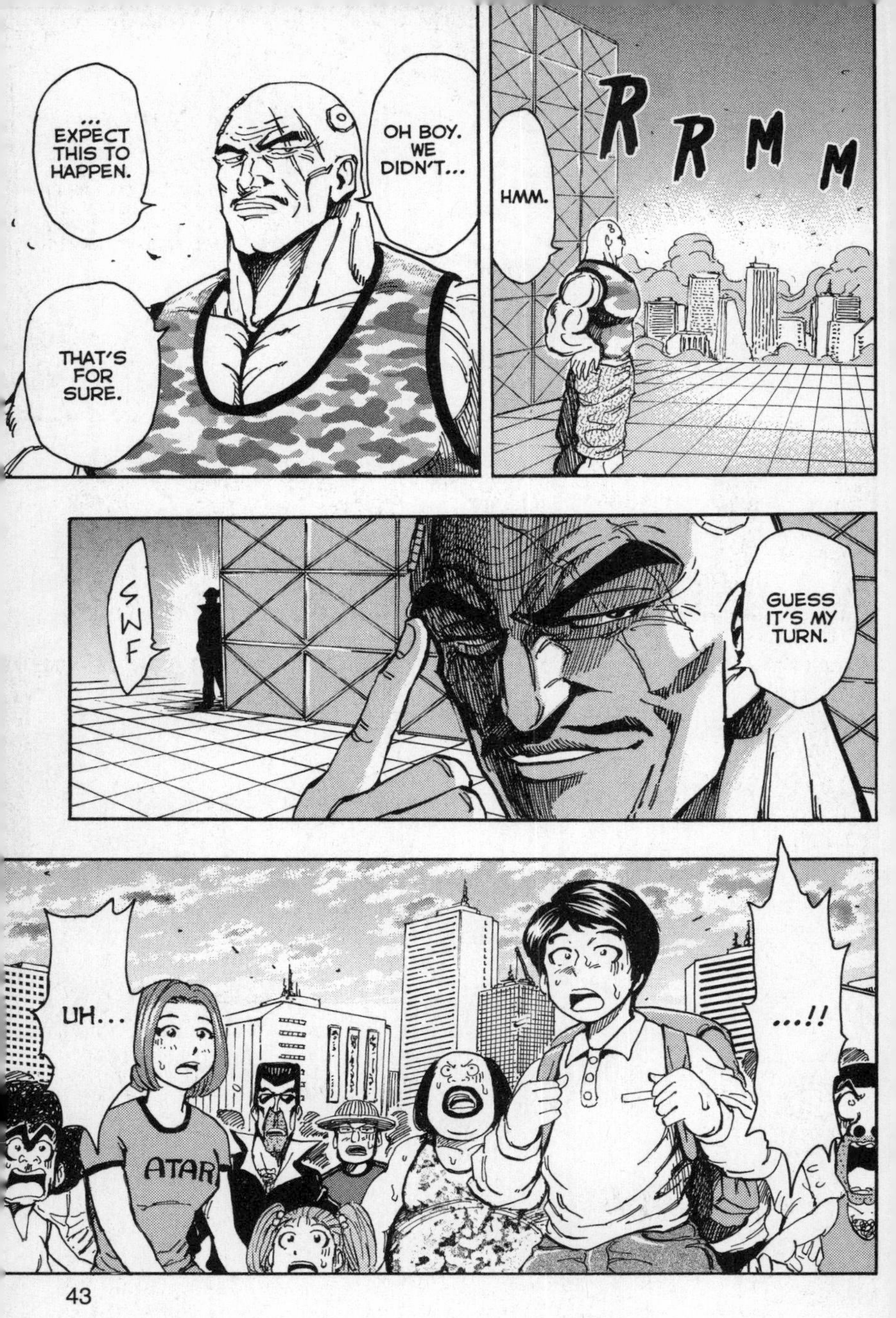
RRMM
HMM.
OH BOY. WE DIDN'T...
... EXPECT THIS TO HAPPEN.
THAT'S FOR SURE.
GUESS IT'S MY TURN.
SWF
...!!
UH...
ATAR

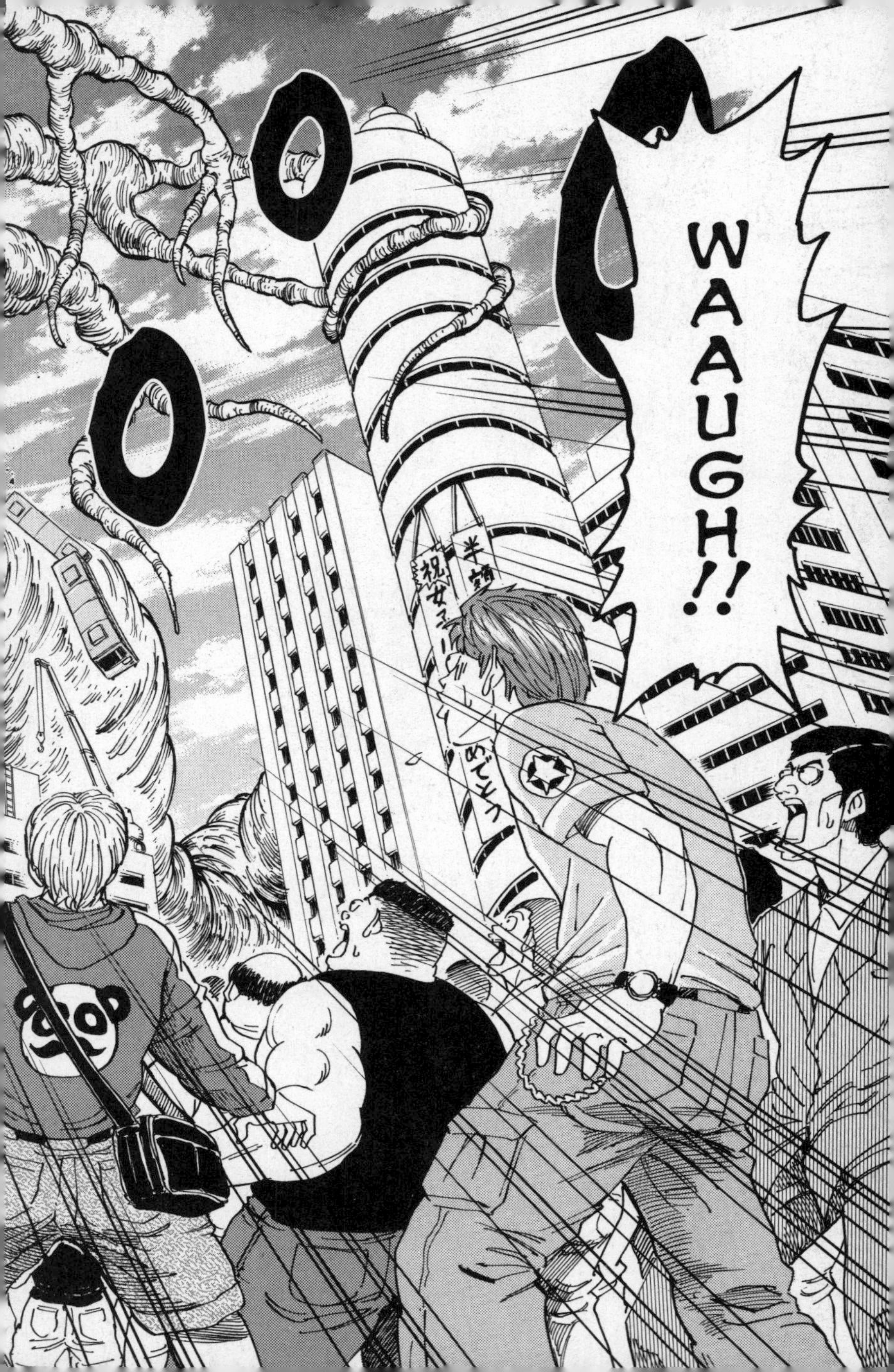
WAAUGH!!

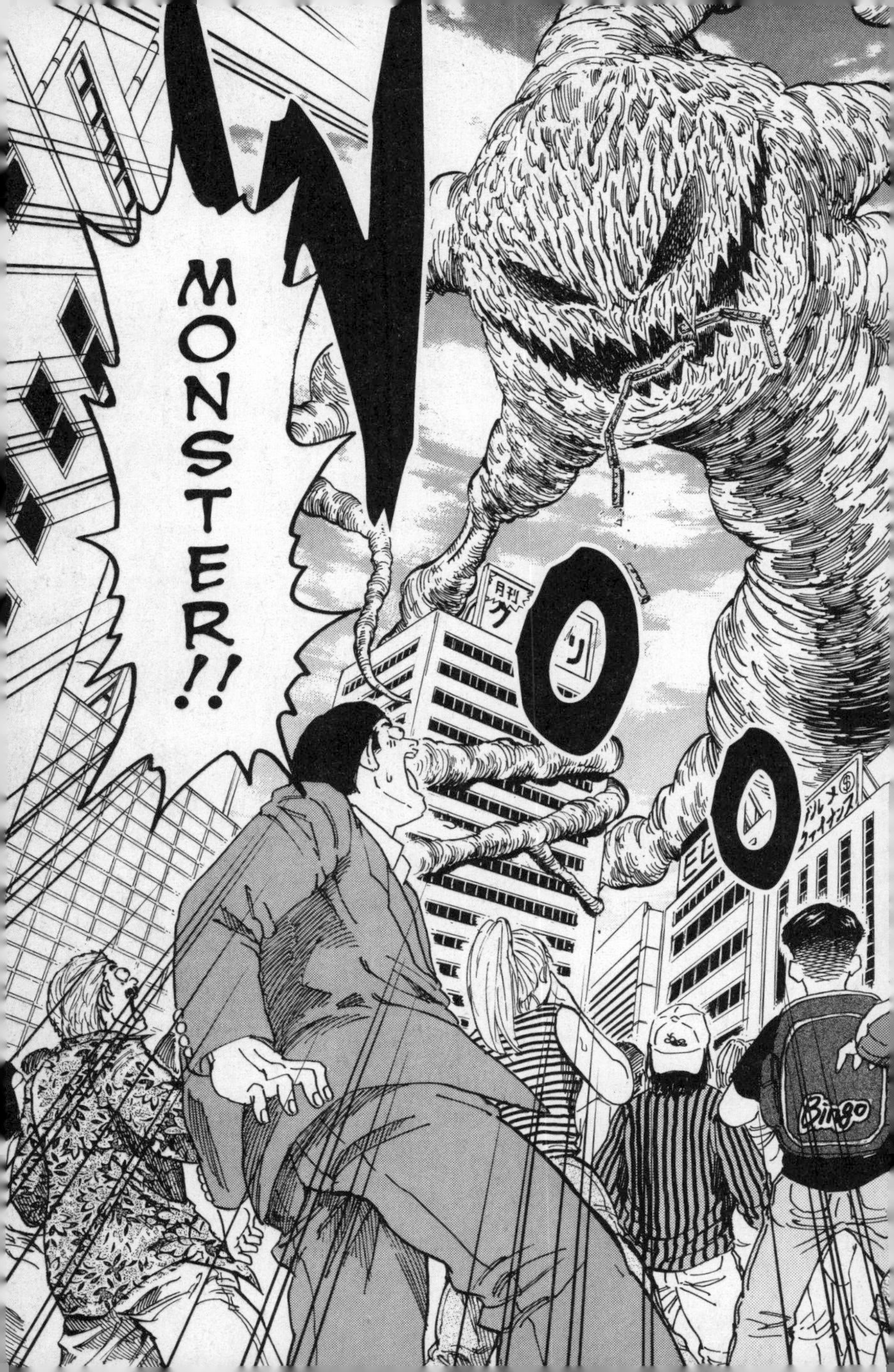
MONSTER!!
月刊グ
グルメファイナンス
Bingo

TORIKO
GOURMET CHECKLIST

Vol. 236
SLOTS TREE
(PLANT)

CAPTURE LEVEL: 6
HABITAT: GOURMET CASINO
LENGTH: ---
HEIGHT: 7 METERS
WEIGHT: ---
PRICE: 7,000,000 YEN

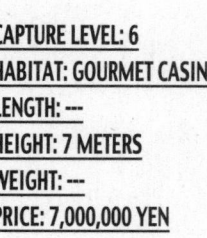

SCALE

THE CENTER OF THIS TREE HAS THREE REELS, EACH DISPLAYING THE NUMBERS ONE THROUGH SIX. WHEN YOU STRIKE THE KNOT BELOW THE NUMBERS, THEY SPIN AROUND. IF YOU MATCH THE NUMBERS ON ALL THREE REELS, THE TREE WILL BEAR FRUIT. THE STRENGTH OF THE STRIKE CHANGES THE NUMBERS, AND THE HIGHER THE NUMBERS, THE BETTER THE FRUIT TASTES. IT'S RATHER DIFFICULT FOR AN AMATEUR TO LINE UP THREE NUMBERS IN A ROW, BUT SOME PEOPLE REALLY HAVE A KNACK FOR KNOCKING THE KNOT.

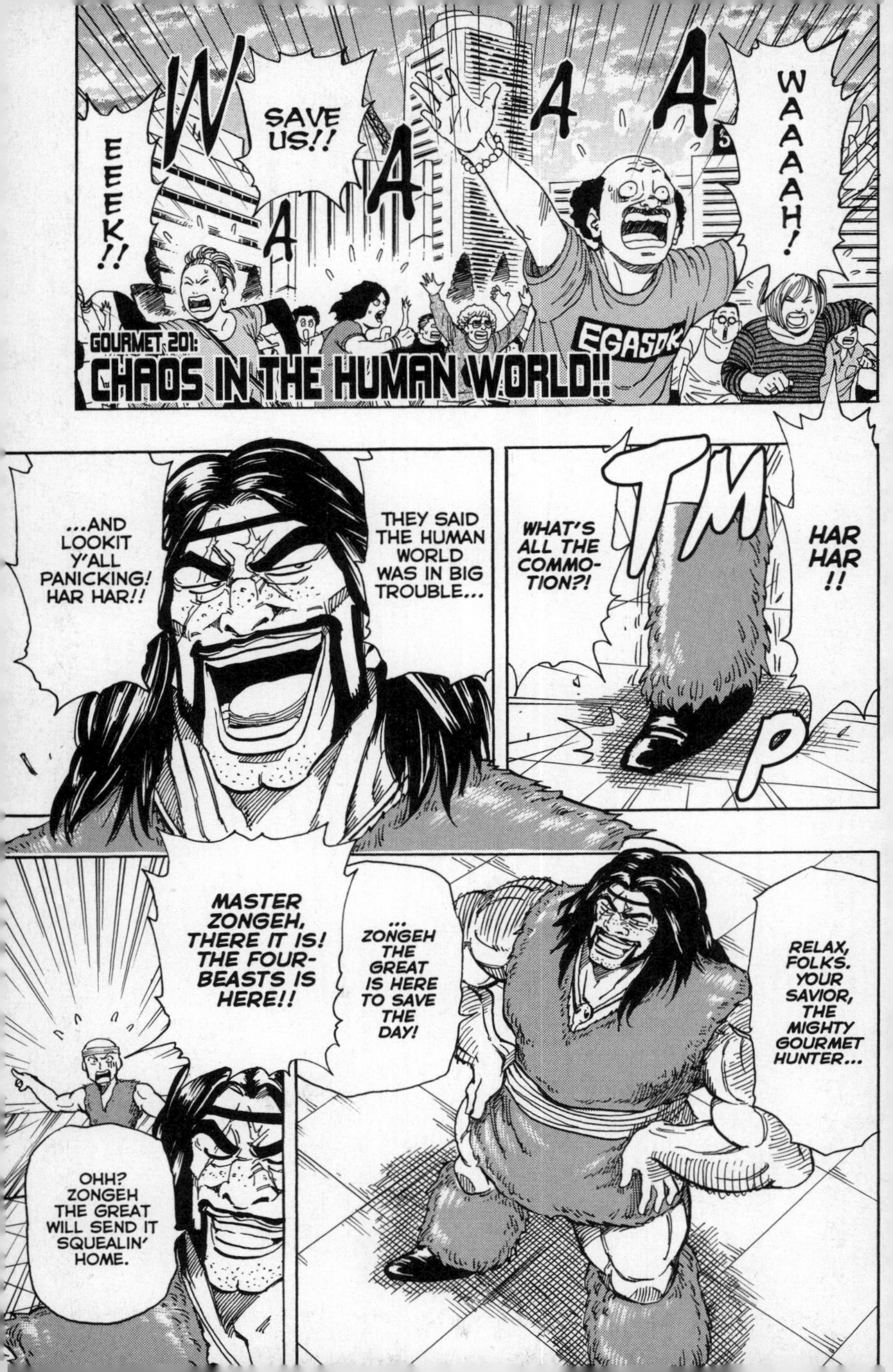
WAAAAH!
WAAAA
SAVE US!!
EEEK!!
GOURMET 201:
CHAOS IN THE HUMAN WORLD!!
TMP
HAR HAR!!
WHAT'S ALL THE COMMOTION?!
THEY SAID THE HUMAN WORLD WAS IN BIG TROUBLE...
...AND LOOKIT Y'ALL PANICKING! HAR HAR!!
RELAX, FOLKS. YOUR SAVIOR, THE MIGHTY GOURMET HUNTER...
...ZONGEH THE GREAT IS HERE TO SAVE THE DAY!
MASTER ZONGEH, THERE IT IS! THE FOUR-BEASTS IS HERE!!
OHH? ZONGEH THE GREAT WILL SEND IT SQUEALIN' HOME.

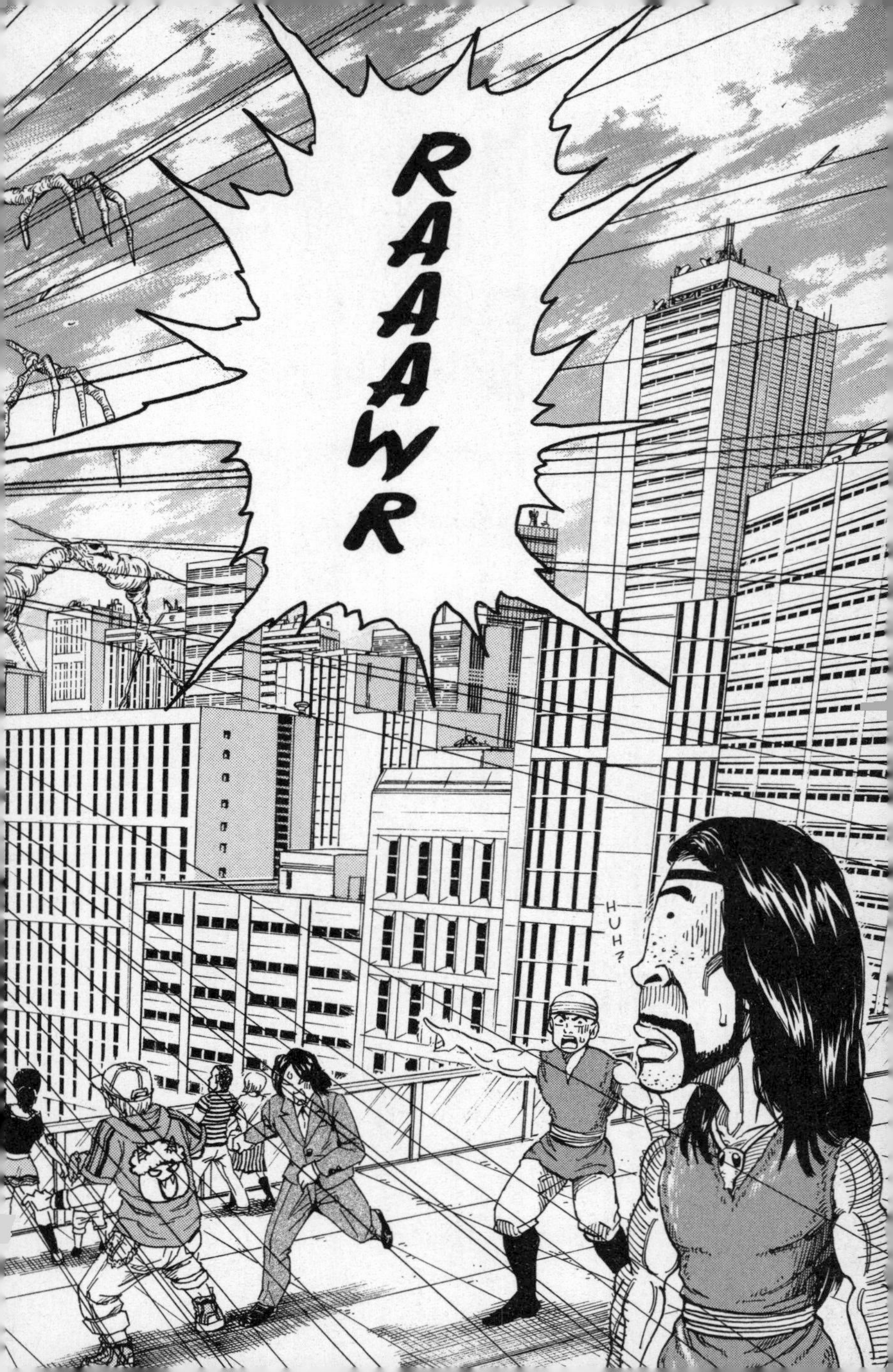
RAAAWR
HUH?

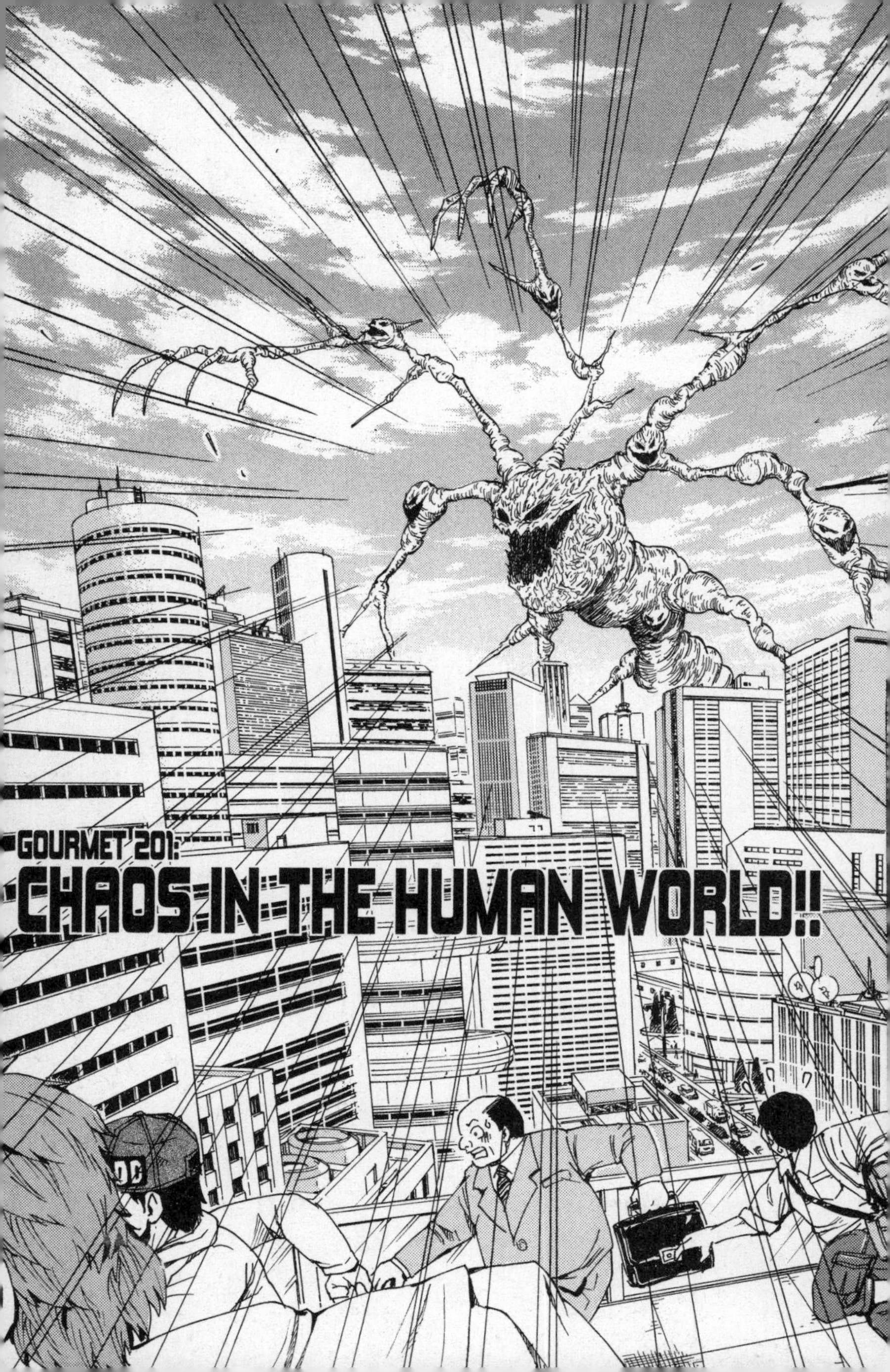
GOURMET 201:
CHAOS IN THE HUMAN WORLD!!

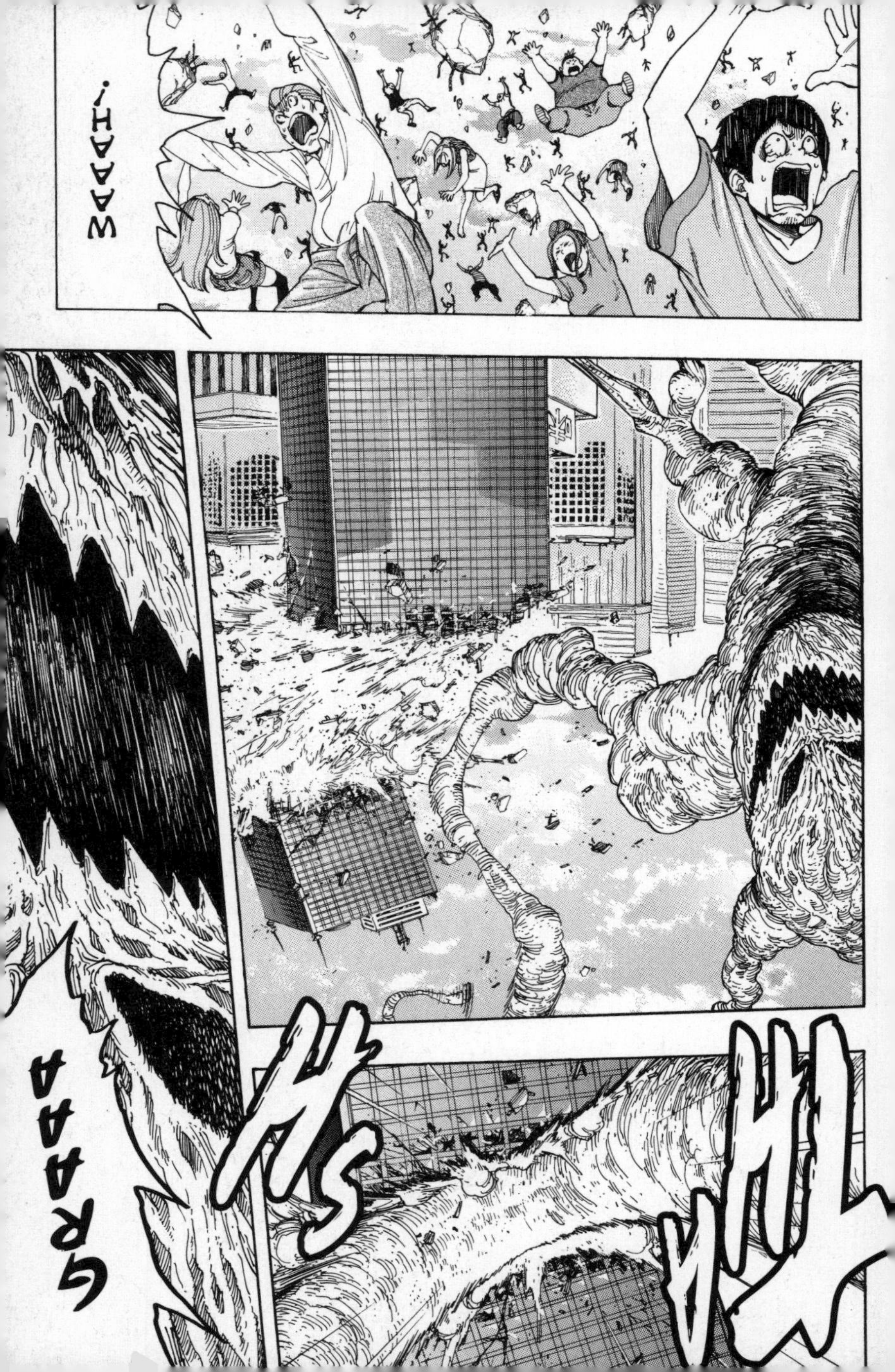
WAAAH!
GRAAAA

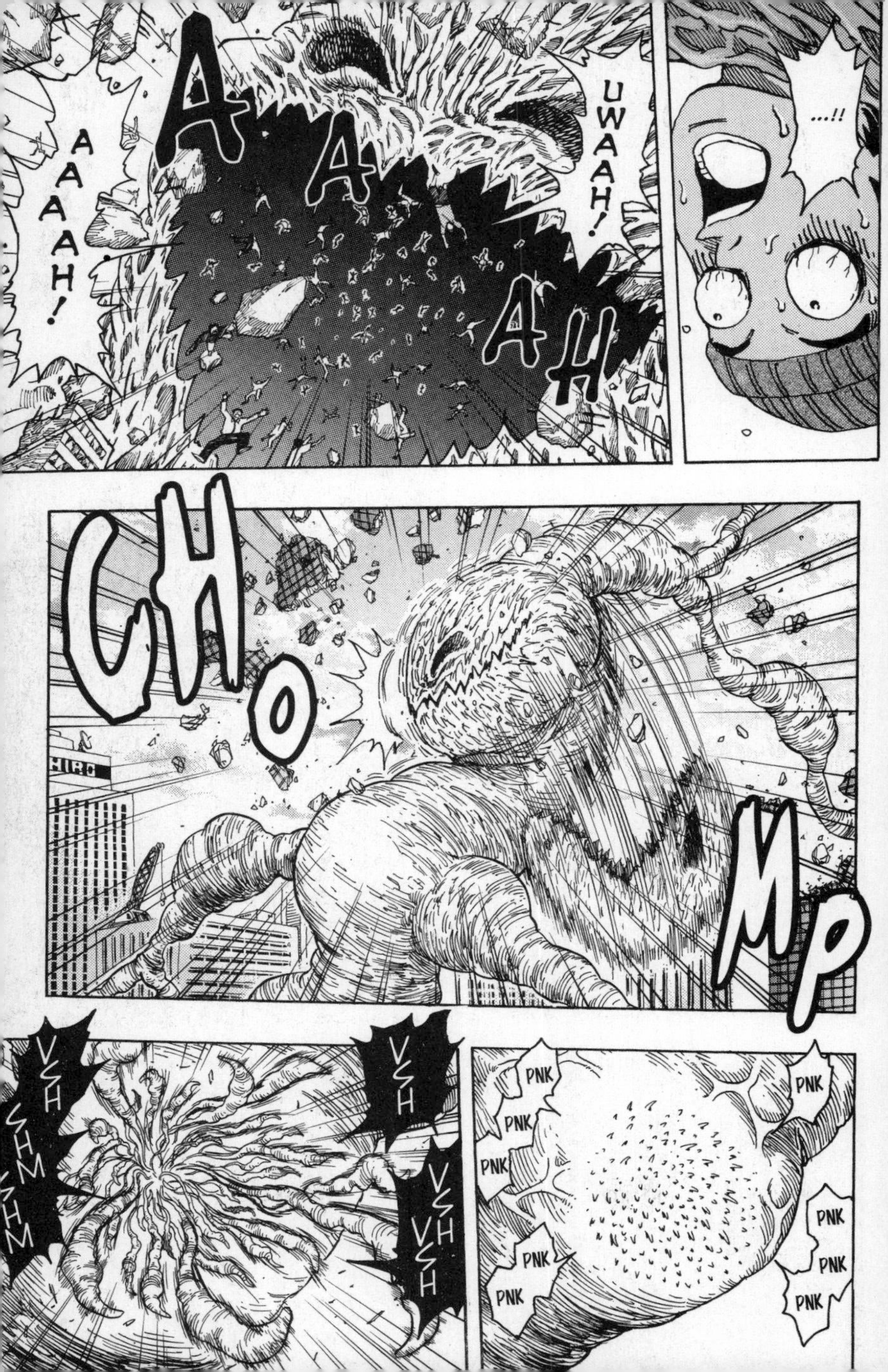
...!!
UWAAH!
AAAH
AAAAH!
CHOMP
PNK
PNK
PNK
PNK
PNK
PNK
PNK
PNK
VSH
VSH VSH
VSH
SHMSHM

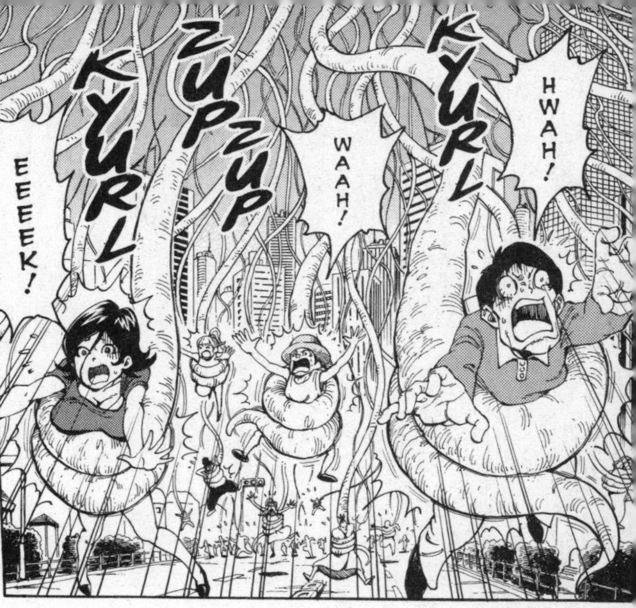
HWAH!
KYURL
WAAH!
ZUPZUP
KYURL
EEEEEK!
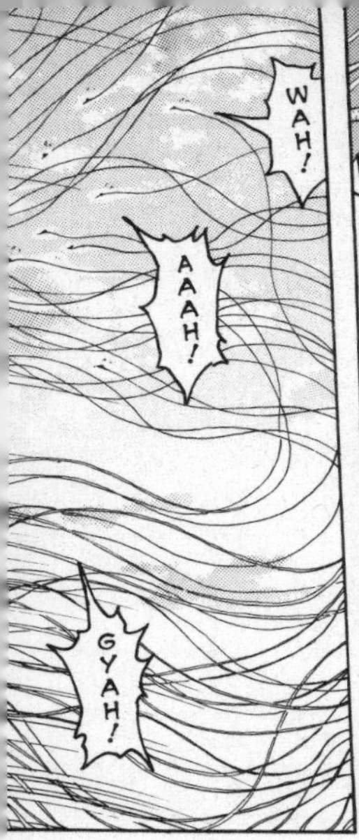
WAH!
AAAH!
GYAH!
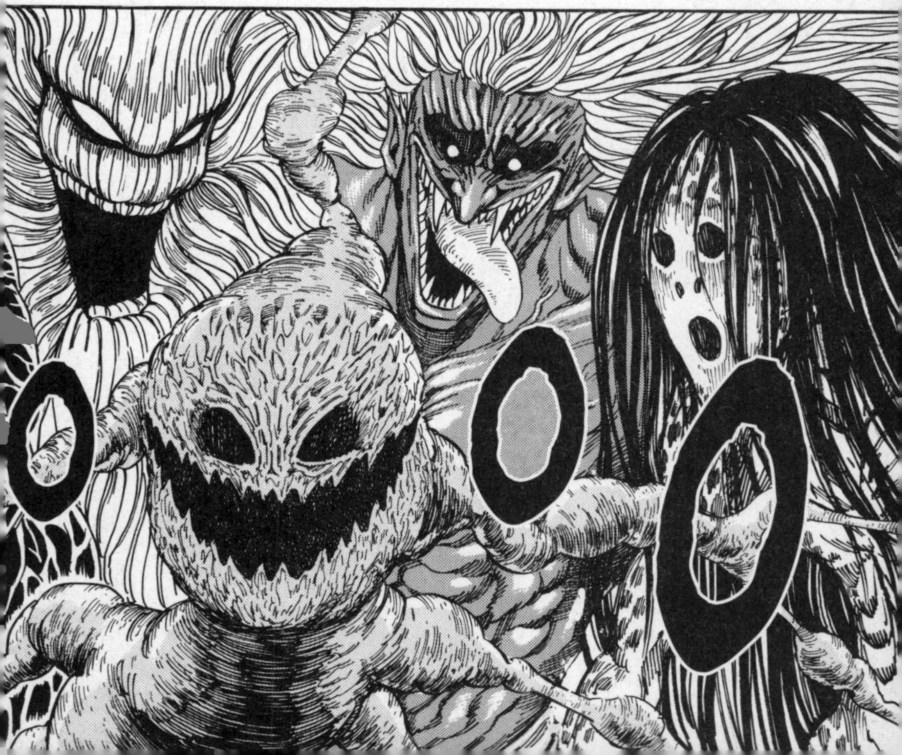

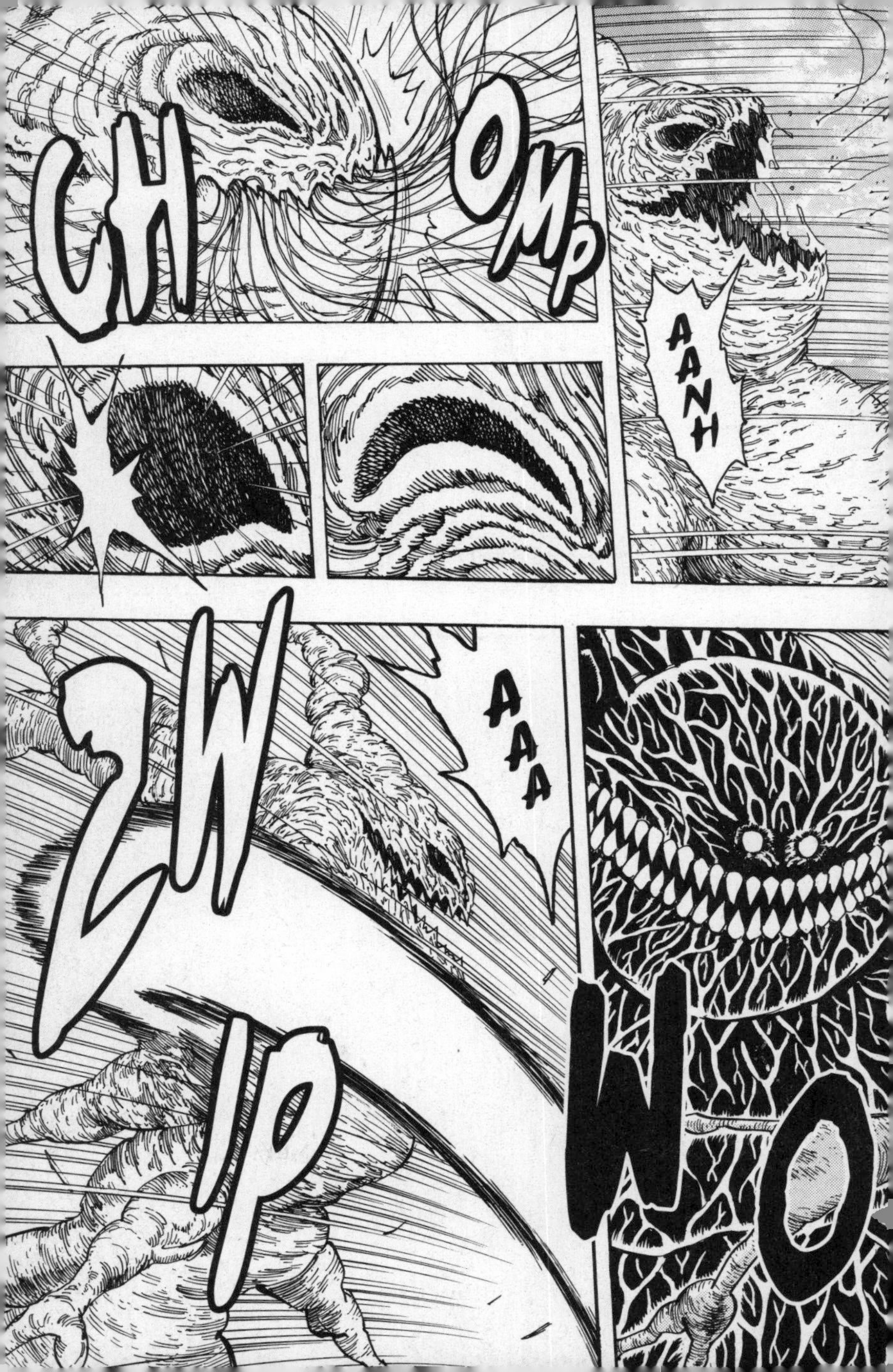
AANH
CHOMP
WO
AAA
ZWIP

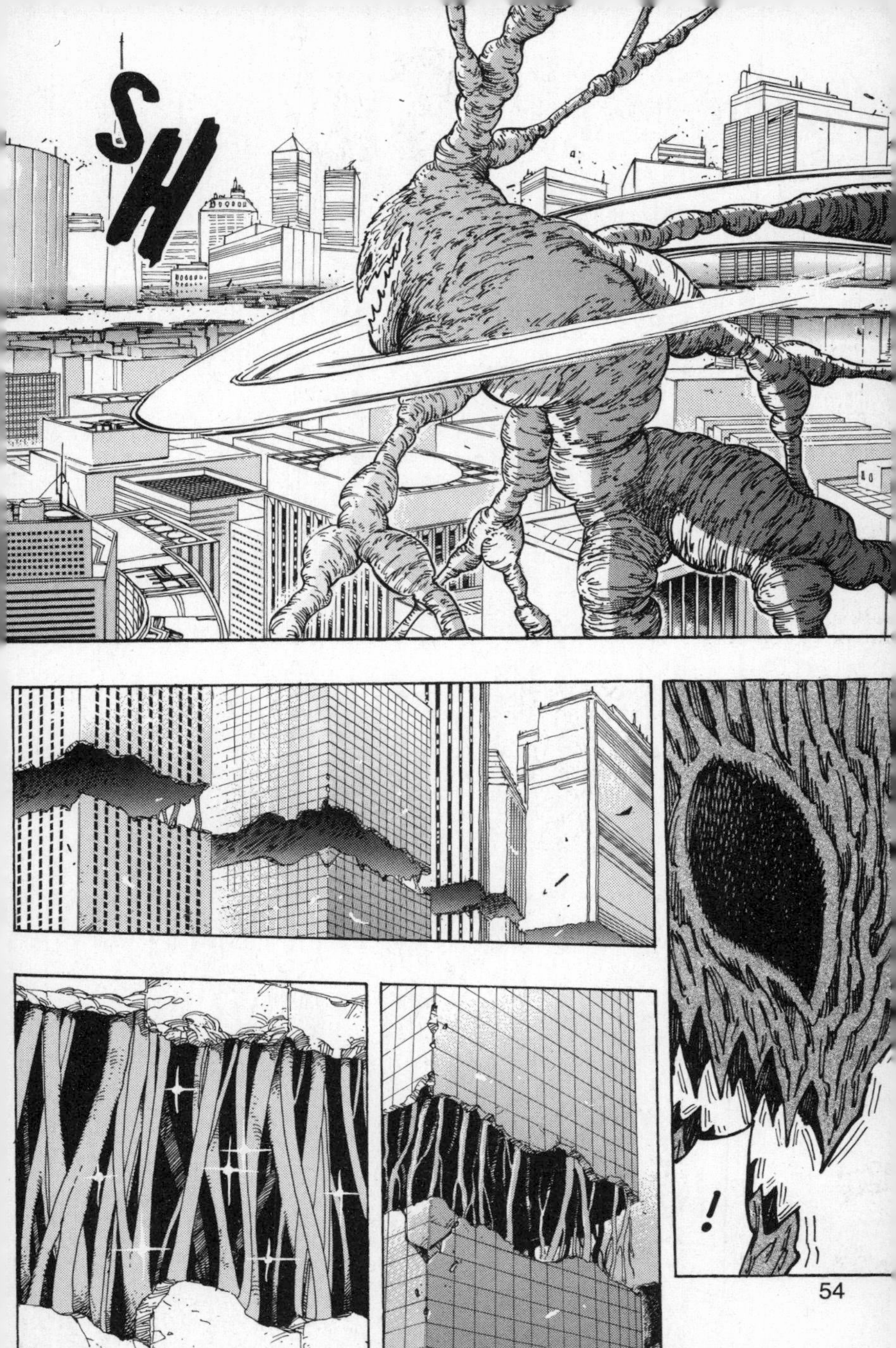
SH
!

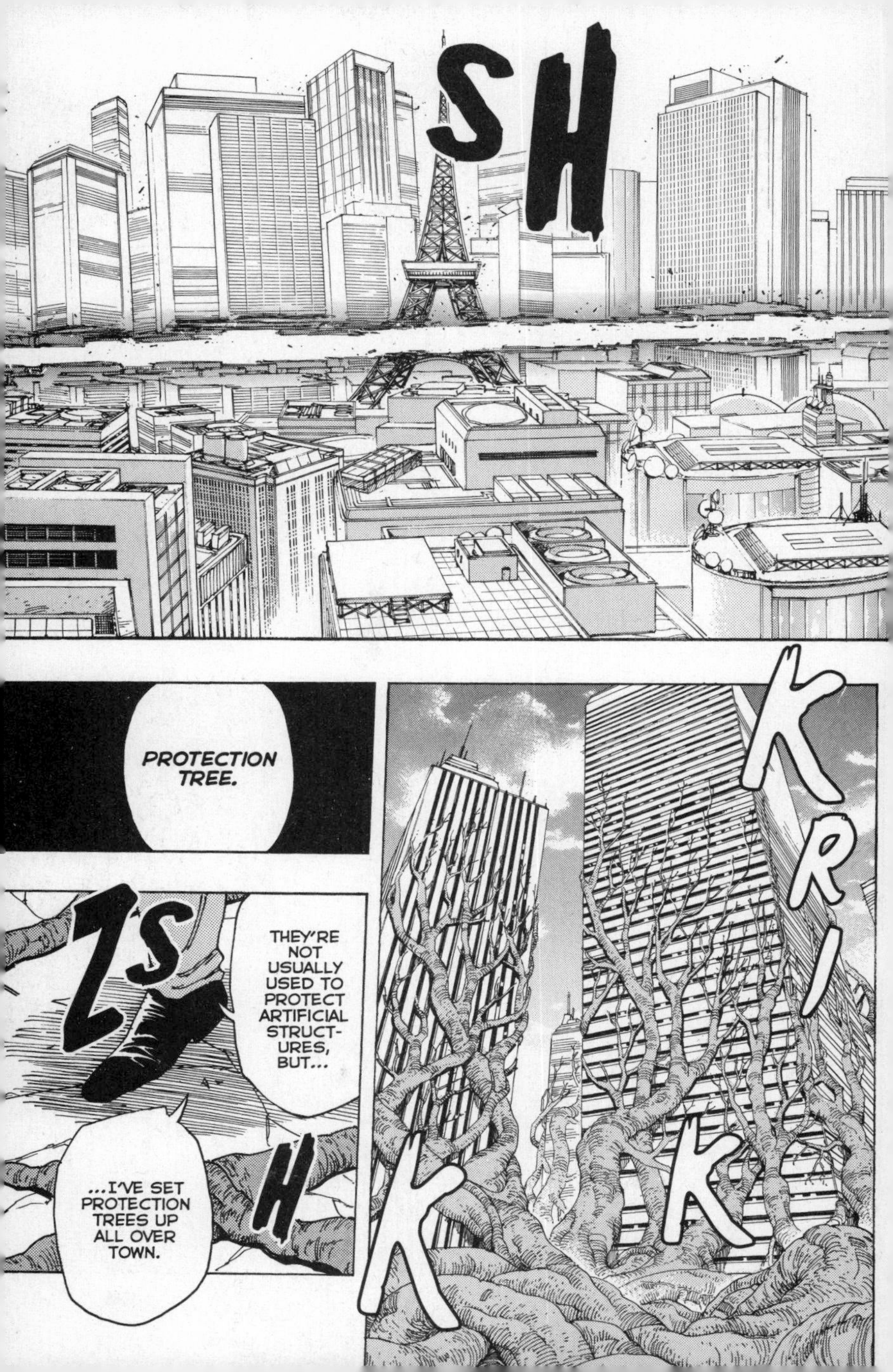
SH
KRIKK
PROTECTION TREE.
ZS
THEY'RE NOT USUALLY USED TO PROTECT ARTIFICIAL STRUCT-URES, BUT...
H
...I'VE SET PROTECTION TREES UP ALL OVER TOWN.

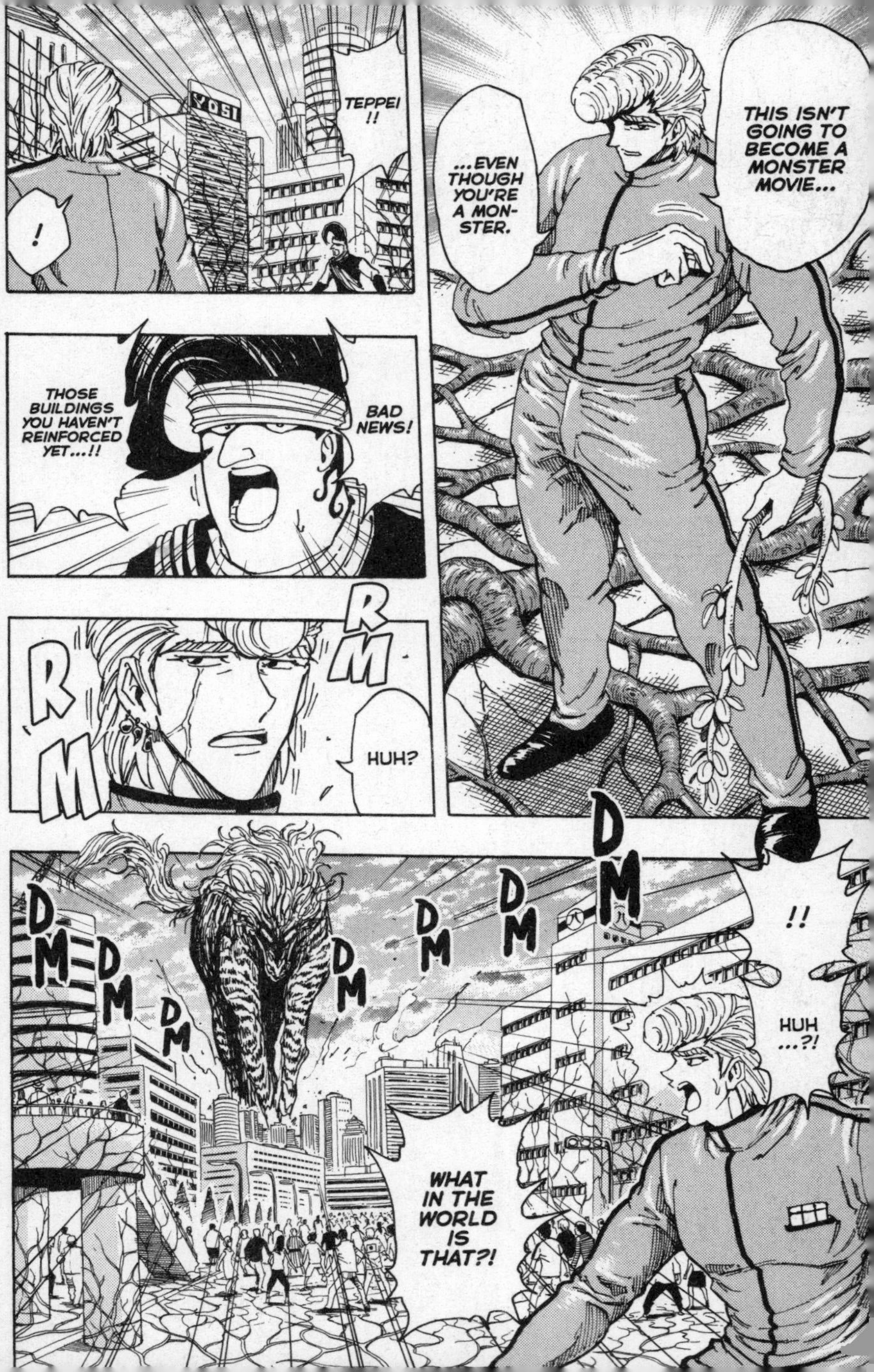
THIS ISN'T GOING TO BECOME A MONSTER MOVIE...
...EVEN THOUGH YOU'RE A MON-STER.
TEPPEI!!
!
BAD NEWS!
THOSE BUILDINGS YOU HAVEN'T REINFORCED YET...!!
RM
RM
HUH?
DM
DM
DM
DM
DM
DM
DM
DM
!!
HUH...?!
WHAT IN THE WORLD IS THAT?!

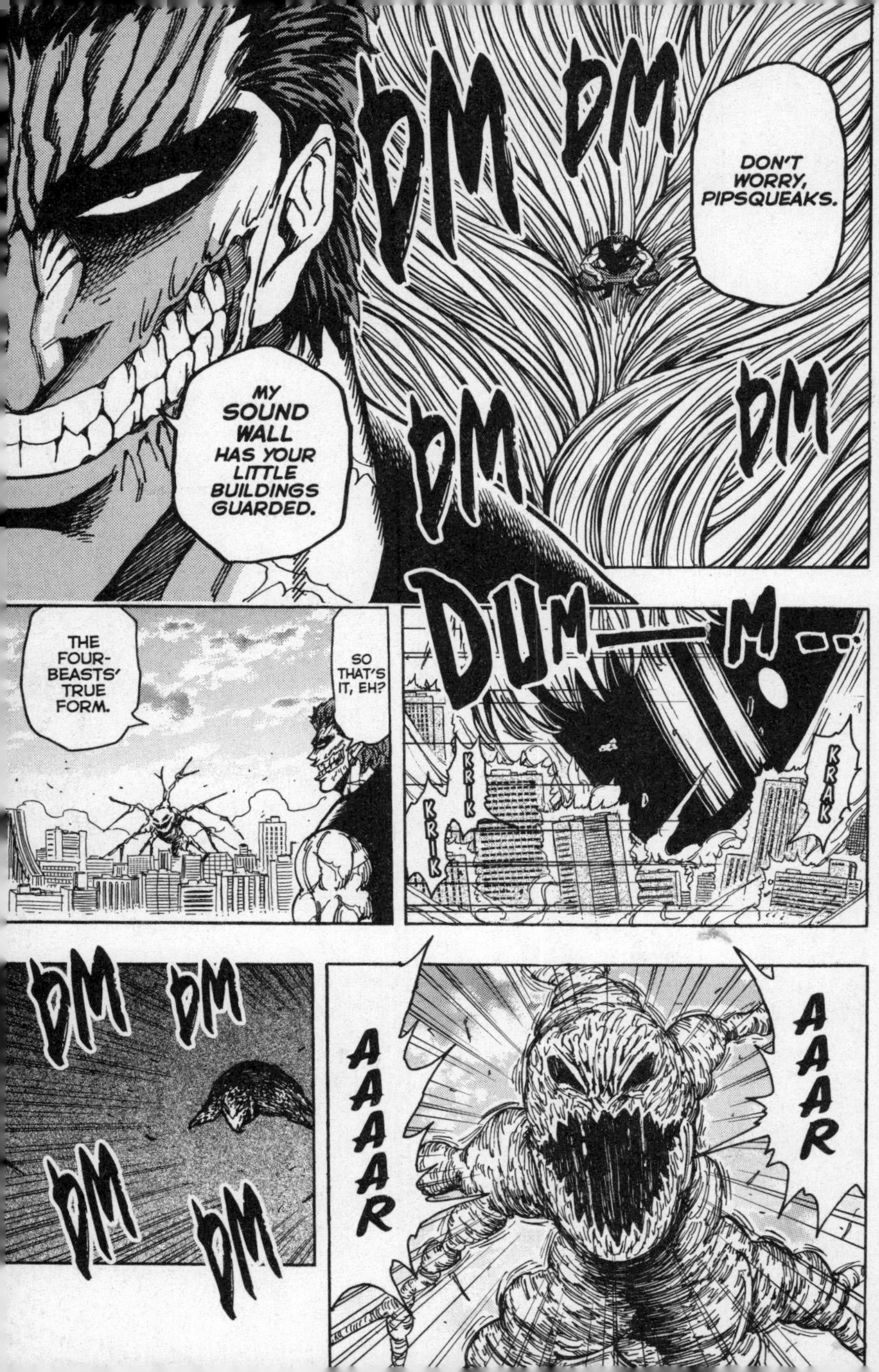
DON'T WORRY, PIPSQUEAKS.
DM DM
DM DM
MY SOUND WALL HAS YOUR LITTLE BUILDINGS GUARDED.
DUM—M...!
KRAK
KRIK
KRIK
SO THAT'S IT, EH?
THE FOUR-BEASTS' TRUE FORM.
AAAR
AAAAR
DM DM
DM DM

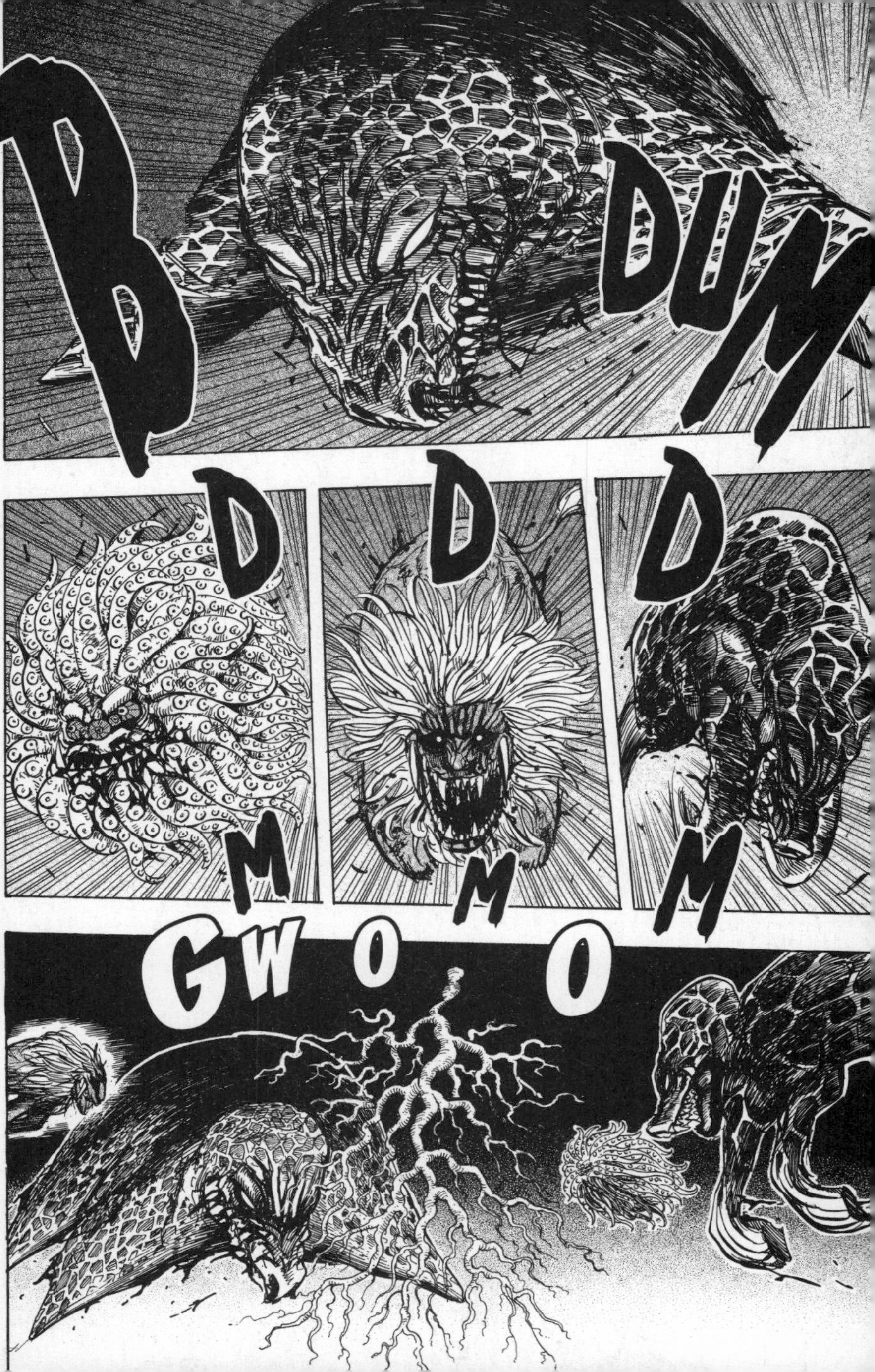
BDUM
DM
DM
DM
GWOOO

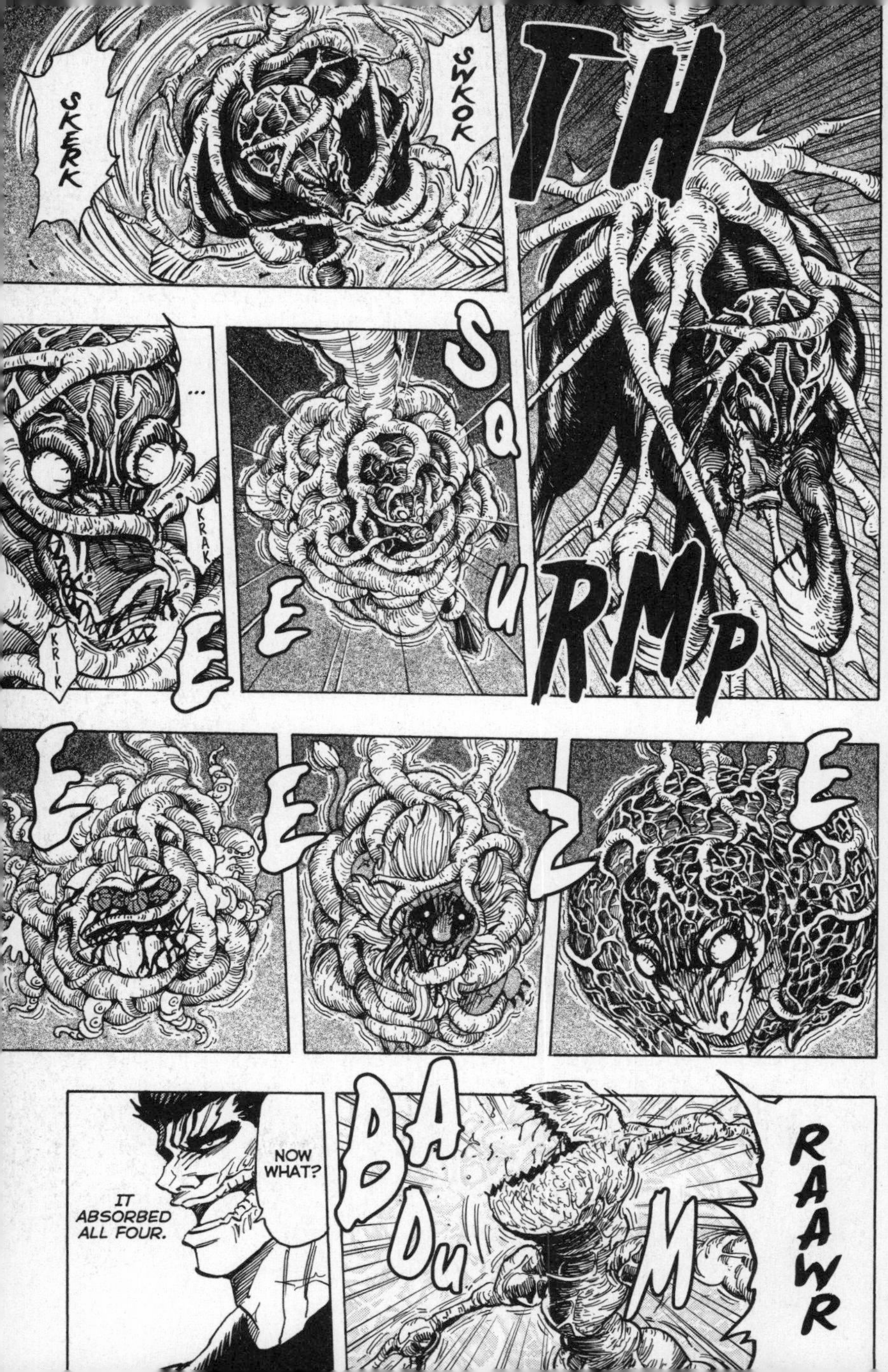
THRMP
SWKOK
SKERK
SQU
EE
...
KRAK
KRIK
E
EEZE
RAAWR
BADOUM
NOW WHAT?
IT ABSORBED ALL FOUR.

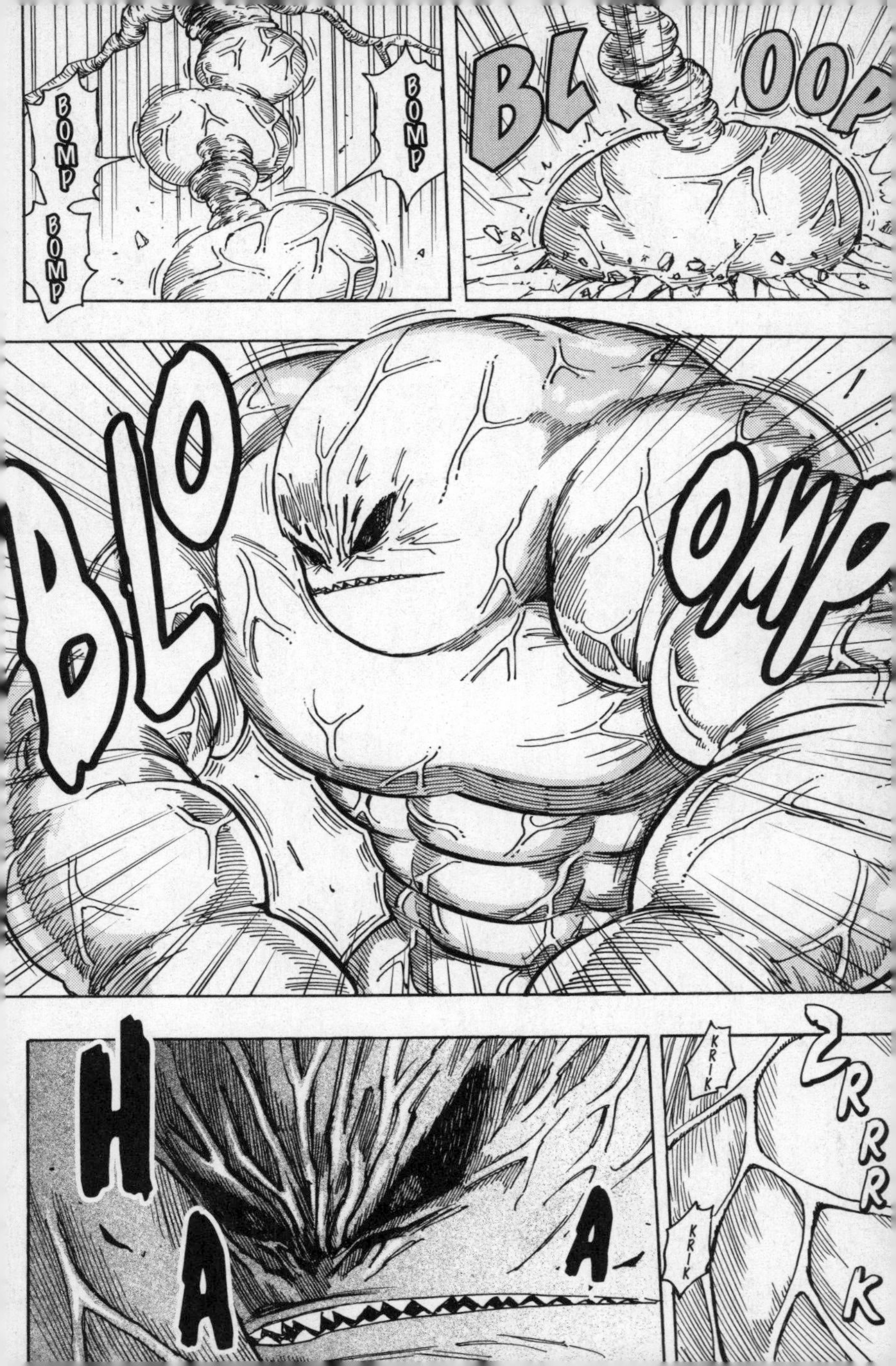
BLOOP
BOMP
BOMP BOMP
BLO
OMP
ZRRRK
KRIK
KRIK
H
A
A

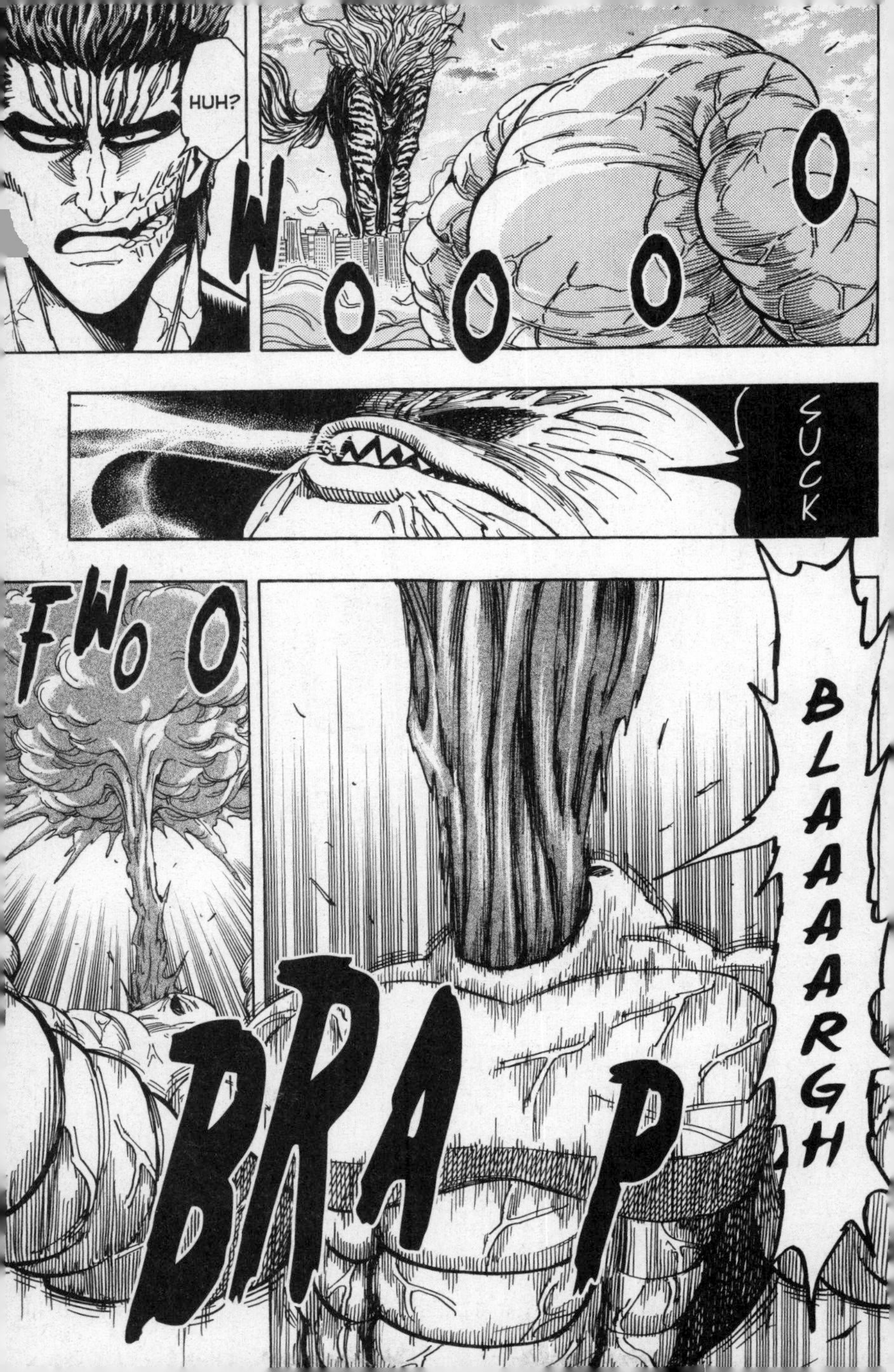
WOOOOO
HUH?
SUCK
BLAAAAARGH
BRAP
FWOO

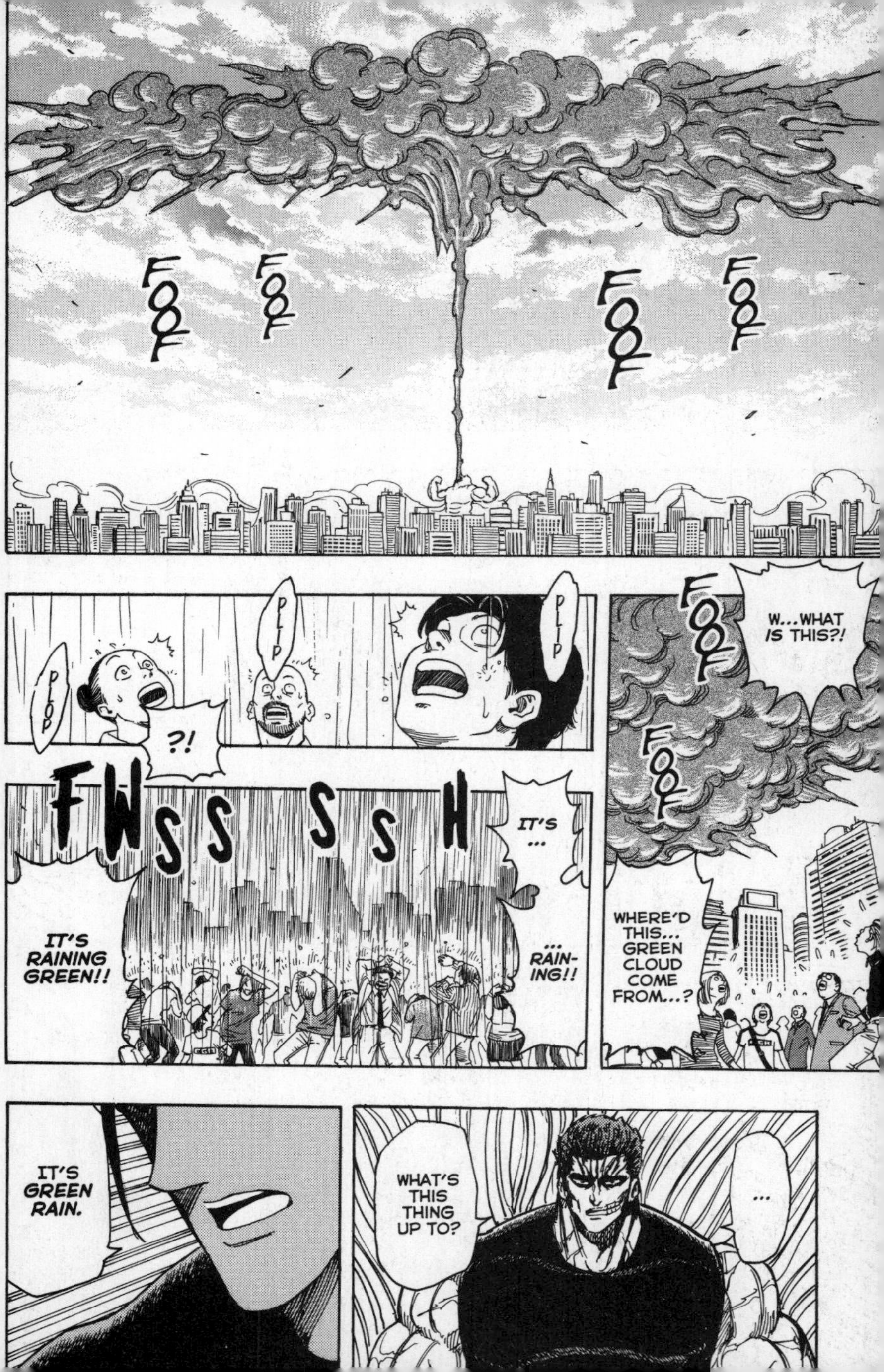
FOOF
FOOF
FOOF
FOOF
W...WHAT IS THIS?!
FOOF
FOOF
WHERE'D THIS... GREEN CLOUD COME FROM...?
PLIP
PLIP
PLOP
?!
FWSSSH
IT'S ...
...RAINING!!
IT'S RAINING GREEN!!
...
WHAT'S THIS THING UP TO?
IT'S GREEN RAIN.

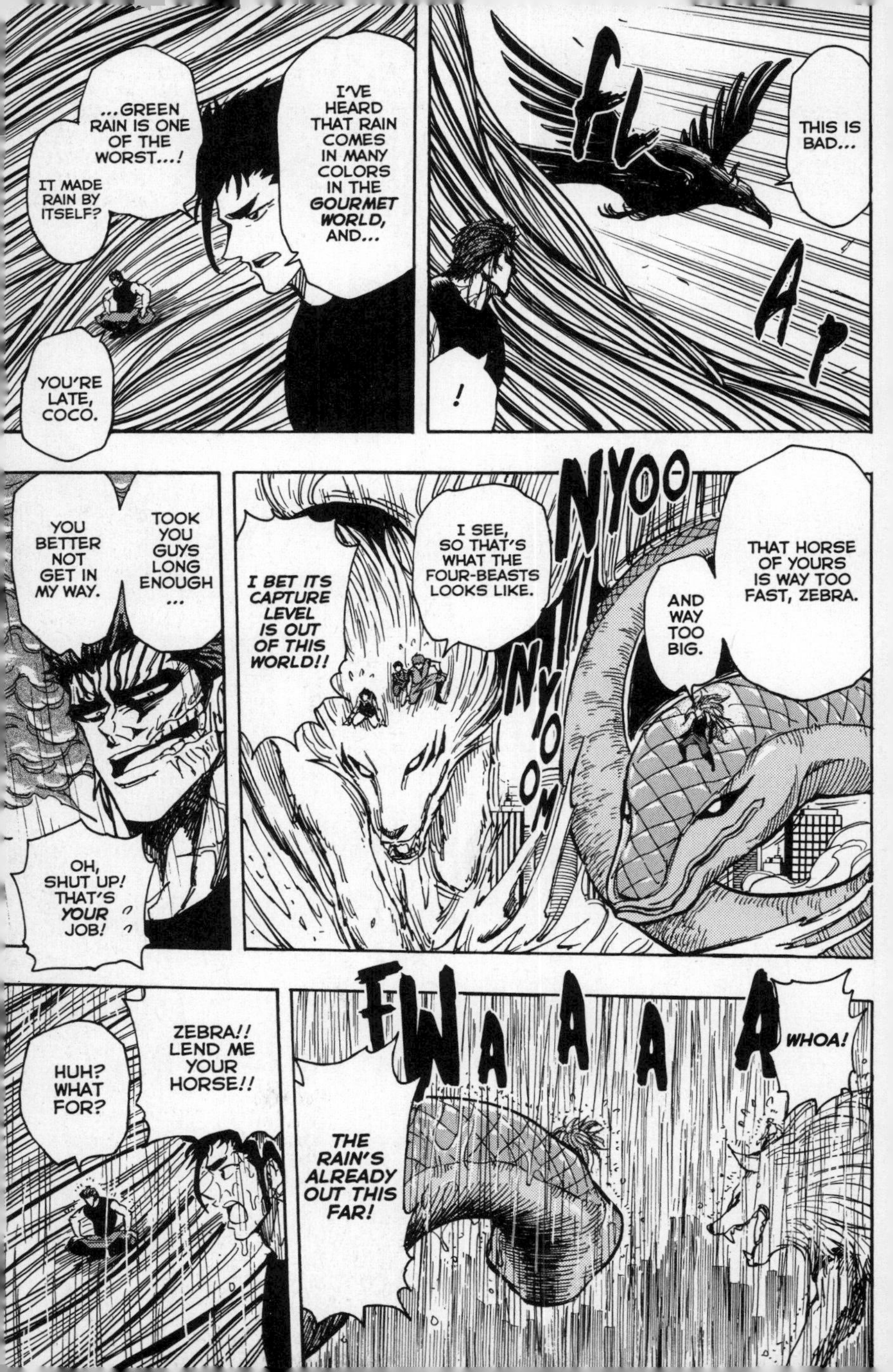
THIS IS BAD...
FLAP
!
I'VE HEARD THAT RAIN COMES IN MANY COLORS IN THE *GOURMET WORLD,* AND...
...GREEN RAIN IS ONE OF THE WORST...!
IT MADE RAIN BY ITSELF?
YOU'RE LATE, COCO.
THAT HORSE OF YOURS IS WAY TOO FAST, ZEBRA.
AND WAY TOO BIG.
NYOO NYOOOM
I SEE, SO THAT'S WHAT THE FOUR-BEASTS LOOKS LIKE.
I BET ITS CAPTURE LEVEL IS OUT OF THIS WORLD!!
TOOK YOU GUYS LONG ENOUGH...
YOU BETTER NOT GET IN MY WAY.
OH, SHUT UP! THAT'S *YOUR* JOB!
WHOA!
FWAAAA
THE RAIN'S ALREADY OUT THIS FAR!
ZEBRA!! LEND ME YOUR HORSE!!
HUH? WHAT FOR?

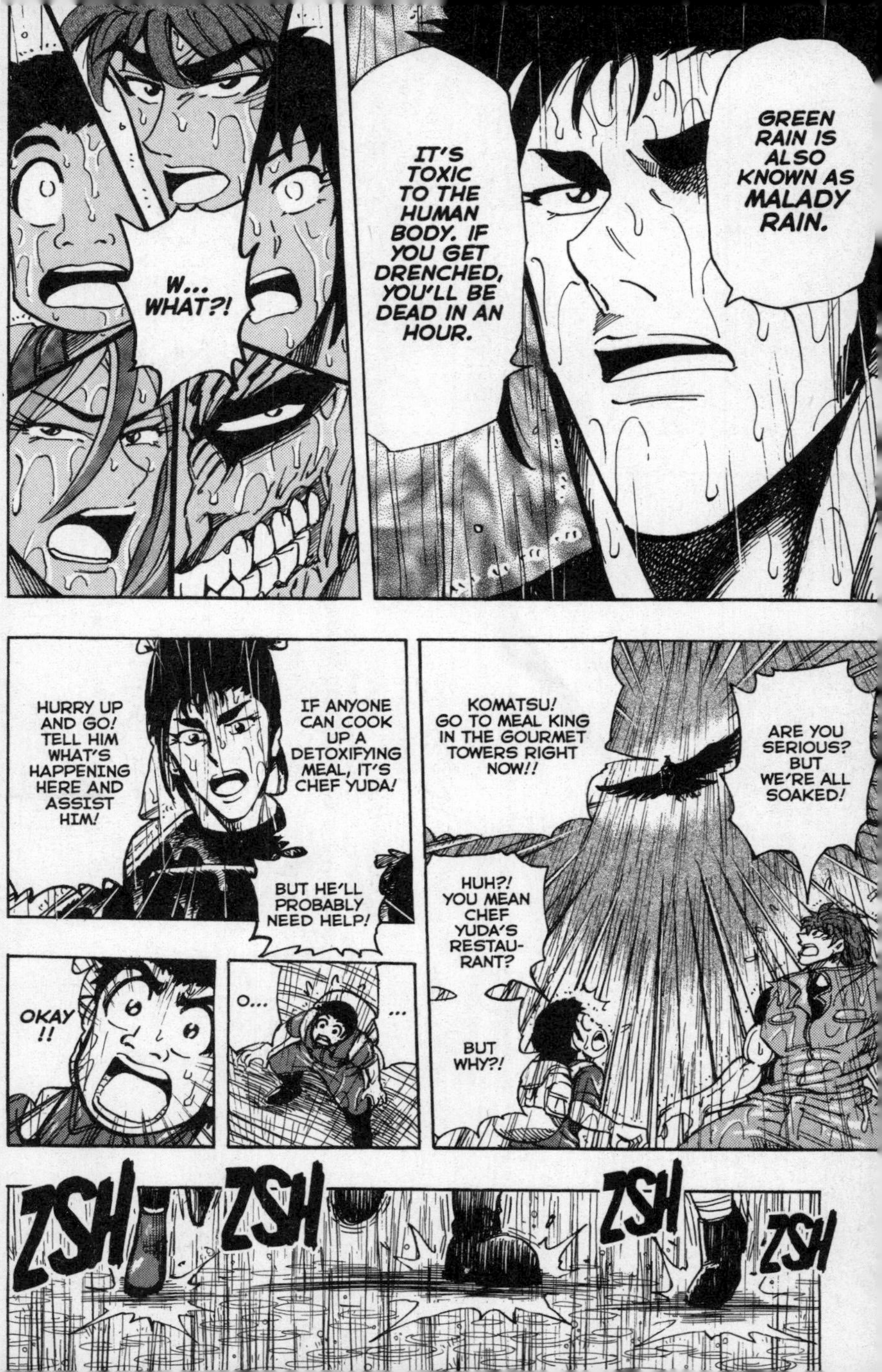
GREEN RAIN IS ALSO KNOWN AS MALADY RAIN.
IT'S TOXIC TO THE HUMAN BODY. IF YOU GET DRENCHED, YOU'LL BE DEAD IN AN HOUR.
W... WHAT?!
ARE YOU SERIOUS? BUT WE'RE ALL SOAKED!
KOMATSU! GO TO MEAL KING IN THE GOURMET TOWERS RIGHT NOW!!
HUH?! YOU MEAN CHEF YUDA'S RESTAU-RANT?
BUT WHY?!
IF ANYONE CAN COOK UP A DETOXIFYING MEAL, IT'S CHEF YUDA!
BUT HE'LL PROBABLY NEED HELP!
HURRY UP AND GO! TELL HIM WHAT'S HAPPENING HERE AND ASSIST HIM!
...
O...
OKAY !!
ZSH
ZSH
ZSH
ZSH

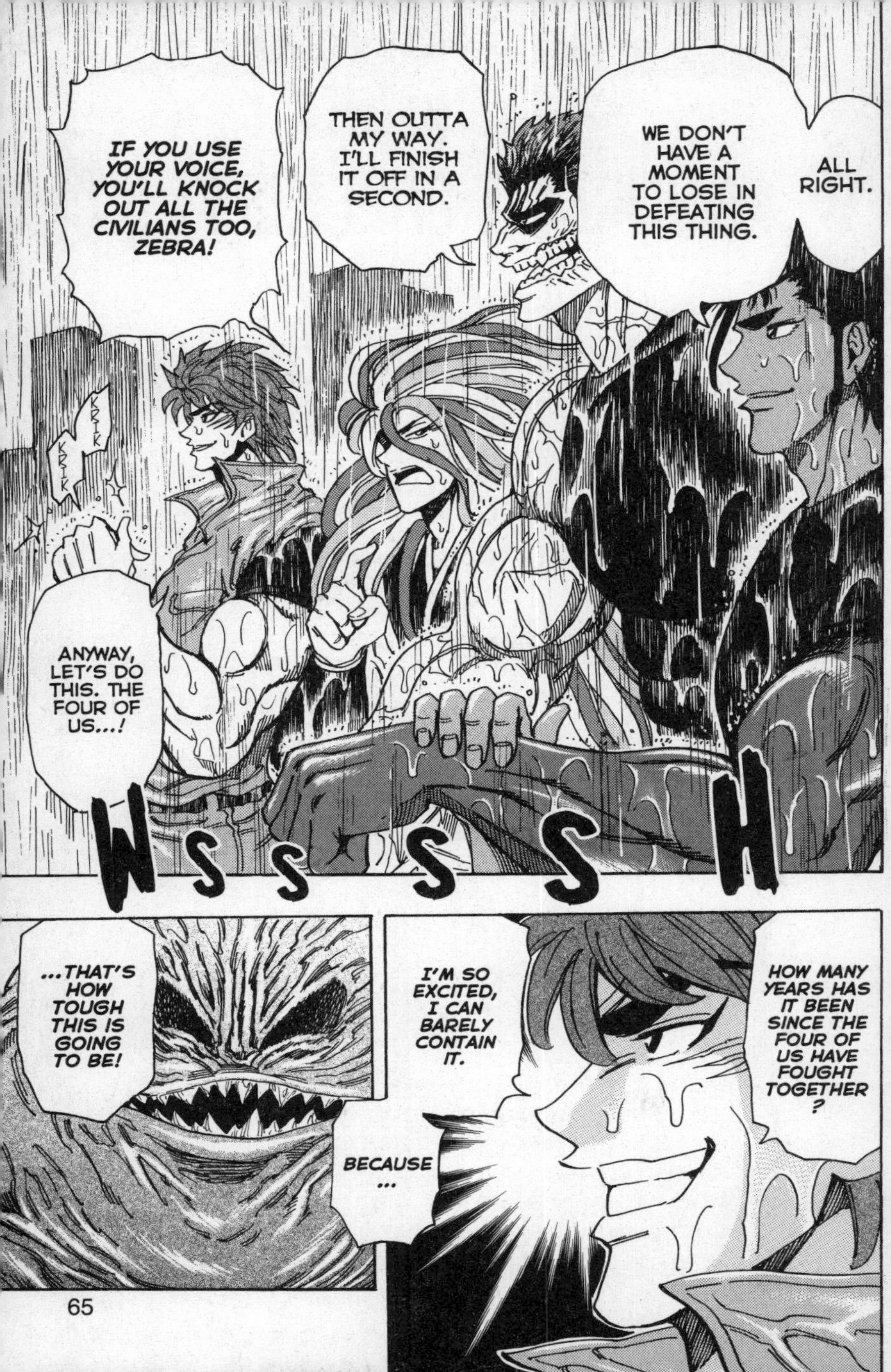
ALL RIGHT.
WE DON'T HAVE A MOMENT TO LOSE IN DEFEATING THIS THING.
THEN OUTTA MY WAY. I'LL FINISH IT OFF IN A SECOND.
IF YOU USE YOUR VOICE, YOU'LL KNOCK OUT ALL THE CIVILIANS TOO, ZEBRA!
KRIK KRIK
ANYWAY, LET'S DO THIS. THE FOUR OF US...!
WSSSSH
HOW MANY YEARS HAS IT BEEN SINCE THE FOUR OF US HAVE FOUGHT TOGETHER?
I'M SO EXCITED, I CAN BARELY CONTAIN IT.
BECAUSE...
...THAT'S HOW TOUGH THIS IS GOING TO BE!

TORIKO

GOURMET CHECKLIST

Vol.237

GAMBLE BERRY
(FRUIT)

CAPTURE LEVEL: 2
HABITAT: DEEP FOREST
LENGTH: 2 CM
HEIGHT: ---
WEIGHT: 12 G PER BERRY
PRICE: 420,000 YEN PER CLUSTER

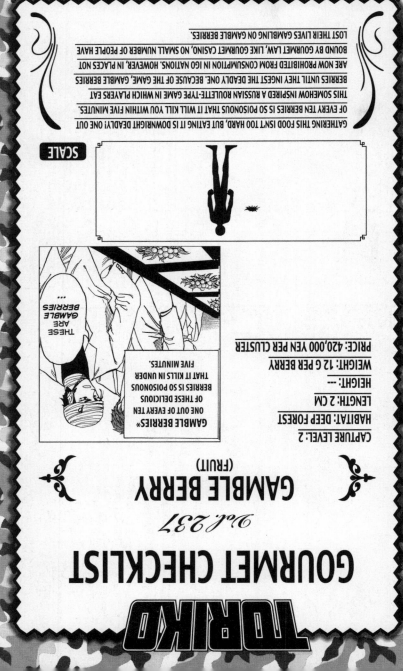

GAMBLE BERRIES*
ONE OUT OF EVERY TEN
OF THESE DELICIOUS
BERRIES IS SO POISONOUS
THAT IT KILLS IN UNDER
FIVE MINUTES.

...
THESE
ARE
GAMBLE
BERRIES

SCALE

GATHERING THIS FOOD ISN'T TOO HARD, BUT EATING IT IS DOWNRIGHT DEADLY! ONE OUT
OF EVERY TEN BERRIES IS SO POISONOUS THAT IT WILL KILL YOU WITHIN FIVE MINUTES.
THIS SOMEHOW INSPIRED A RUSSIAN ROULETTE-TYPE GAME IN WHICH PLAYERS EAT
BERRIES UNTIL THEY INGEST THE DEADLY ONE. BECAUSE OF THE GAME, GAMBLE BERRIES
ARE NOW PROHIBITED FROM CONSUMPTION IN IGO NATIONS. HOWEVER, IN PLACES NOT
BOUND BY GOURMET LAW, LIKE GOURMET CASINO, NO SMALL NUMBER OF PEOPLE HAVE
LOST THEIR LIVES GAMBLING ON GAMBLE BERRIES.

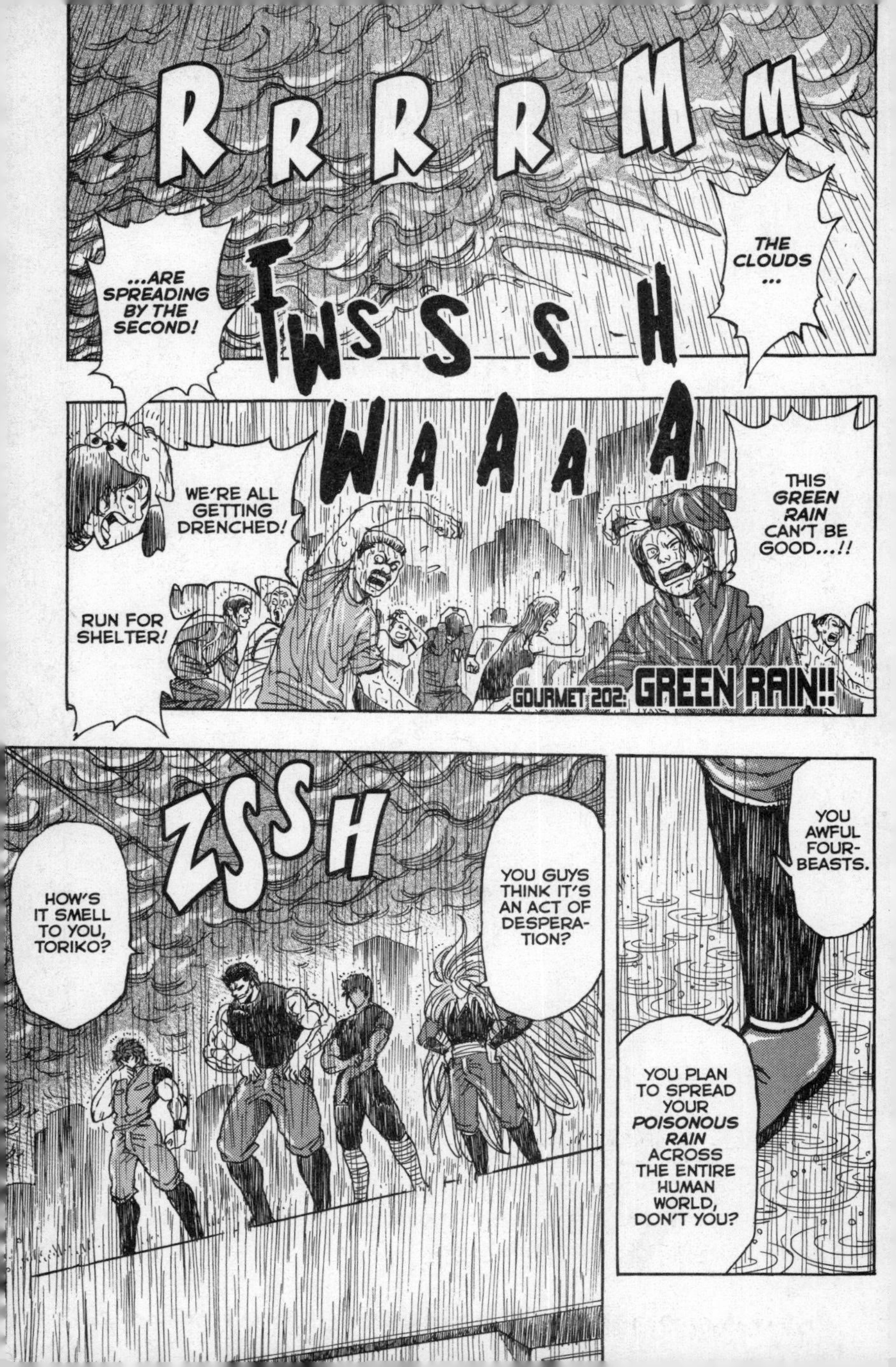
RRRRMM
THE CLOUDS ...
FWSSSH
...ARE SPREADING BY THE SECOND!
WAAAA
THIS GREEN RAIN CAN'T BE GOOD...!!
WE'RE ALL GETTING DRENCHED!
RUN FOR SHELTER!
GOURMET 202: GREEN RAIN!!
YOU AWFUL FOUR-BEASTS.
YOU PLAN TO SPREAD YOUR POISONOUS RAIN ACROSS THE ENTIRE HUMAN WORLD, DON'T YOU?
ZSSH
YOU GUYS THINK IT'S AN ACT OF DESPERA-TION?
HOW'S IT SMELL TO YOU, TORIKO?

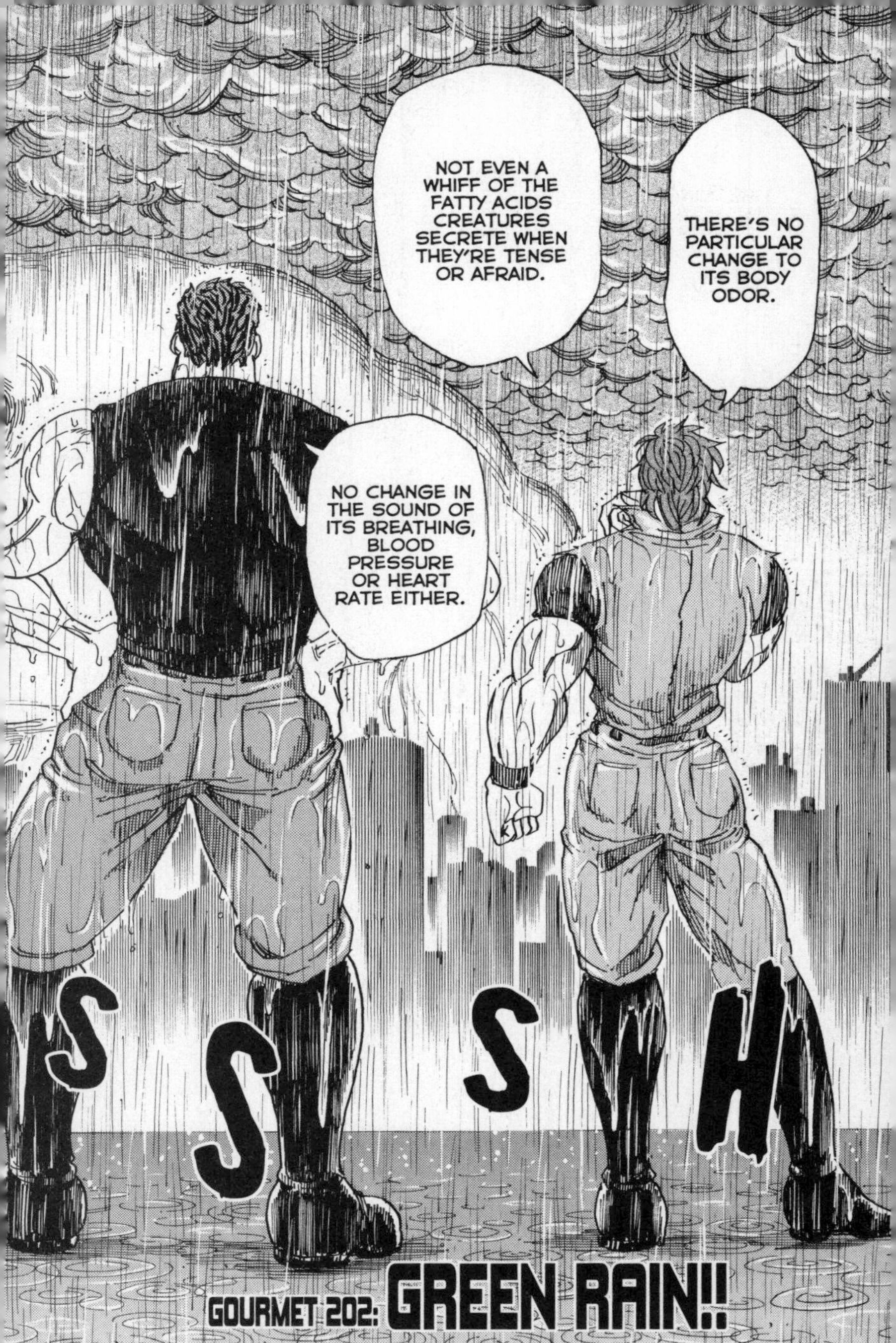
THERE'S NO PARTICULAR CHANGE TO ITS BODY ODOR.
NOT EVEN A WHIFF OF THE FATTY ACIDS CREATURES SECRETE WHEN THEY'RE TENSE OR AFRAID.
NO CHANGE IN THE SOUND OF ITS BREATHING, BLOOD PRESSURE OR HEART RATE EITHER.
SSSH

GOURMET 202: GREEN RAIN!!

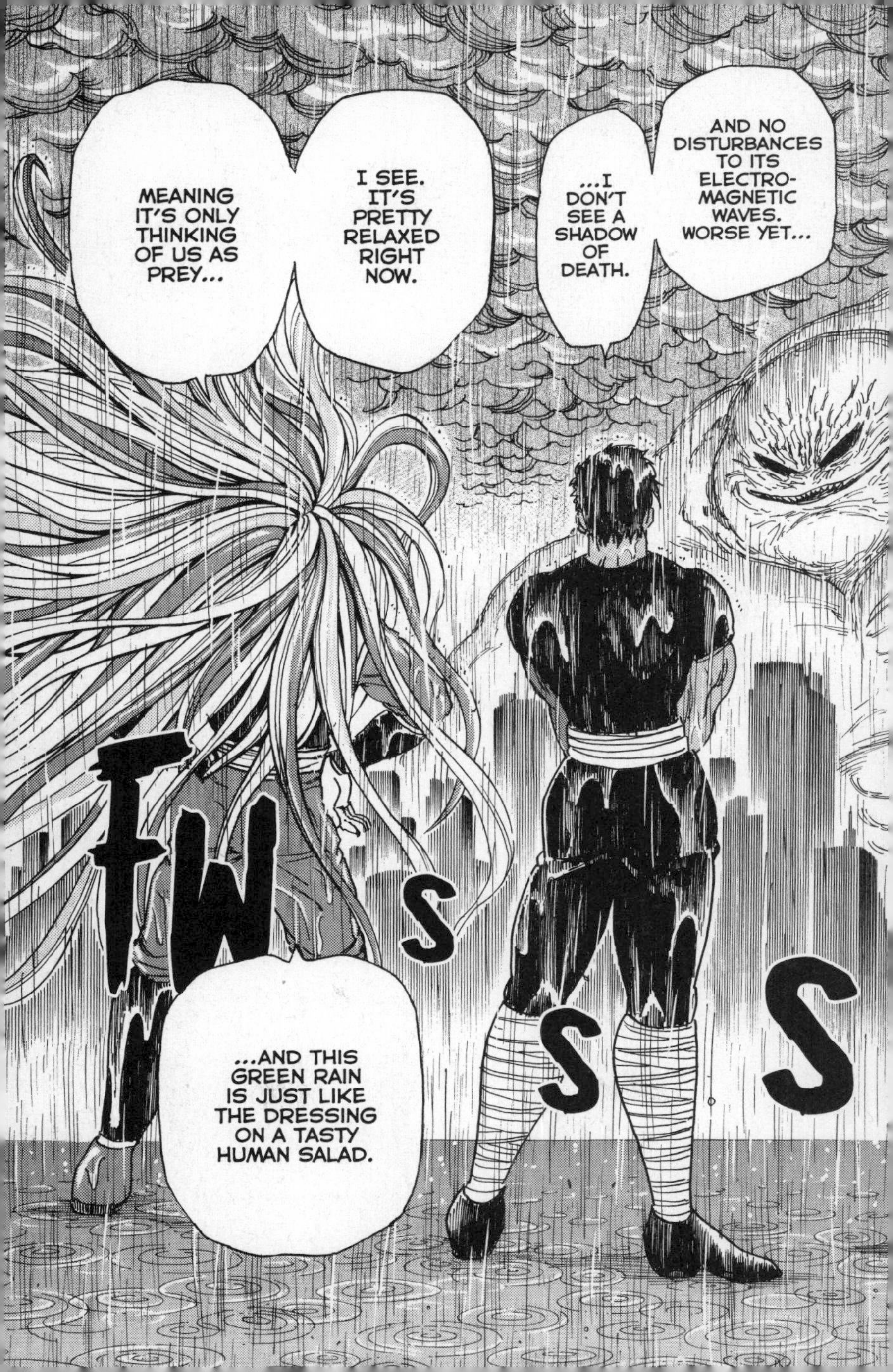
AND NO DISTURBANCES TO ITS ELECTRO-MAGNETIC WAVES. WORSE YET...
...I DON'T SEE A SHADOW OF DEATH.
I SEE. IT'S PRETTY RELAXED RIGHT NOW.
MEANING IT'S ONLY THINKING OF US AS PREY...
FWSSSS
...AND THIS GREEN RAIN IS JUST LIKE THE DRESSING ON A TASTY HUMAN SALAD.

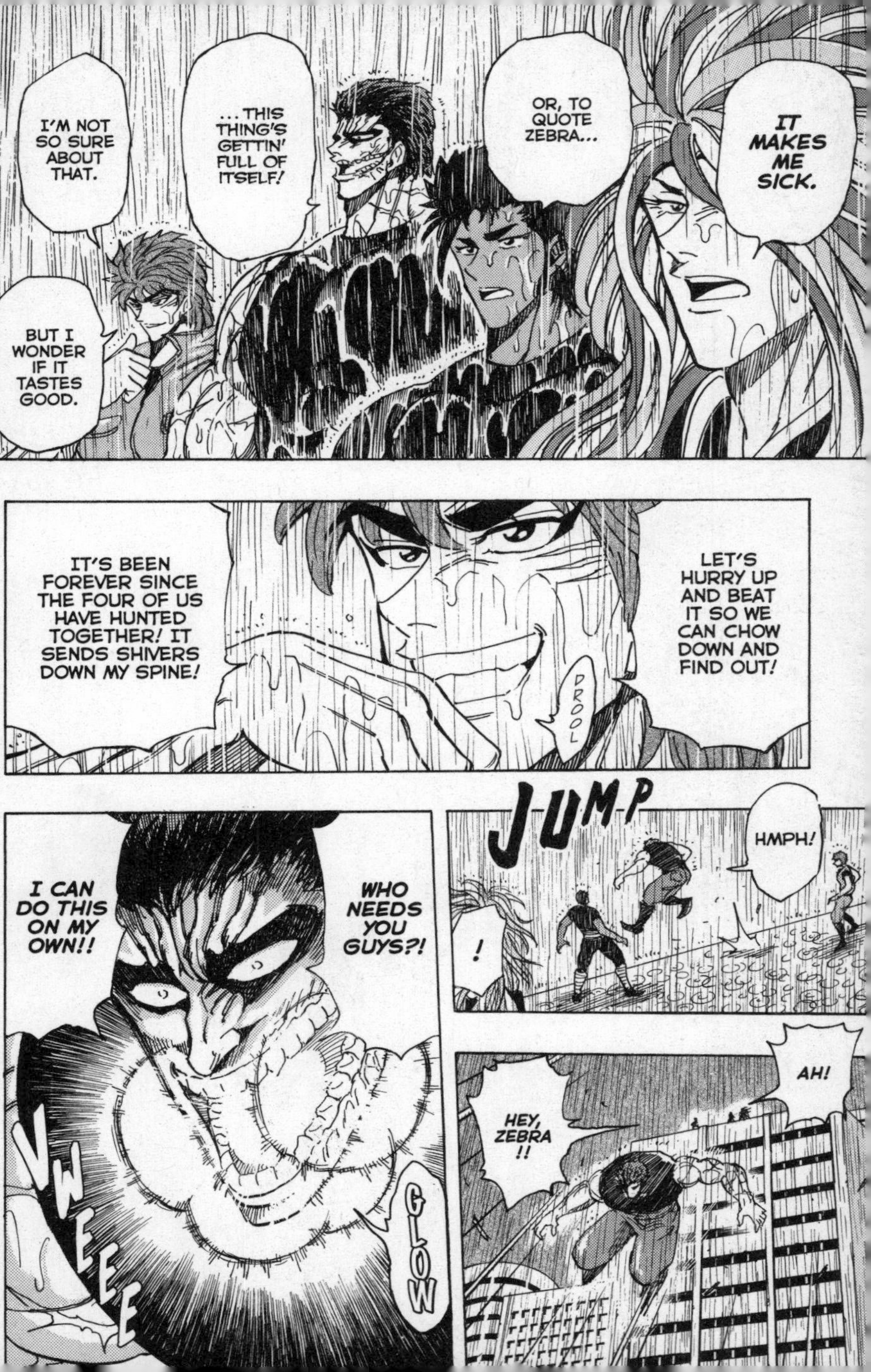
IT MAKES ME SICK.
OR, TO QUOTE ZEBRA...
...THIS THING'S GETTIN' FULL OF ITSELF!
I'M NOT SO SURE ABOUT THAT.
BUT I WONDER IF IT TASTES GOOD.
LET'S HURRY UP AND BEAT IT SO WE CAN CHOW DOWN AND FIND OUT!
DROOL
IT'S BEEN FOREVER SINCE THE FOUR OF US HAVE HUNTED TOGETHER! IT SENDS SHIVERS DOWN MY SPINE!
HMPH!
JUMP
!
AH!
HEY, ZEBRA!!
WHO NEEDS YOU GUYS?!
I CAN DO THIS ON MY OWN!!
GLOW
VWEEEE

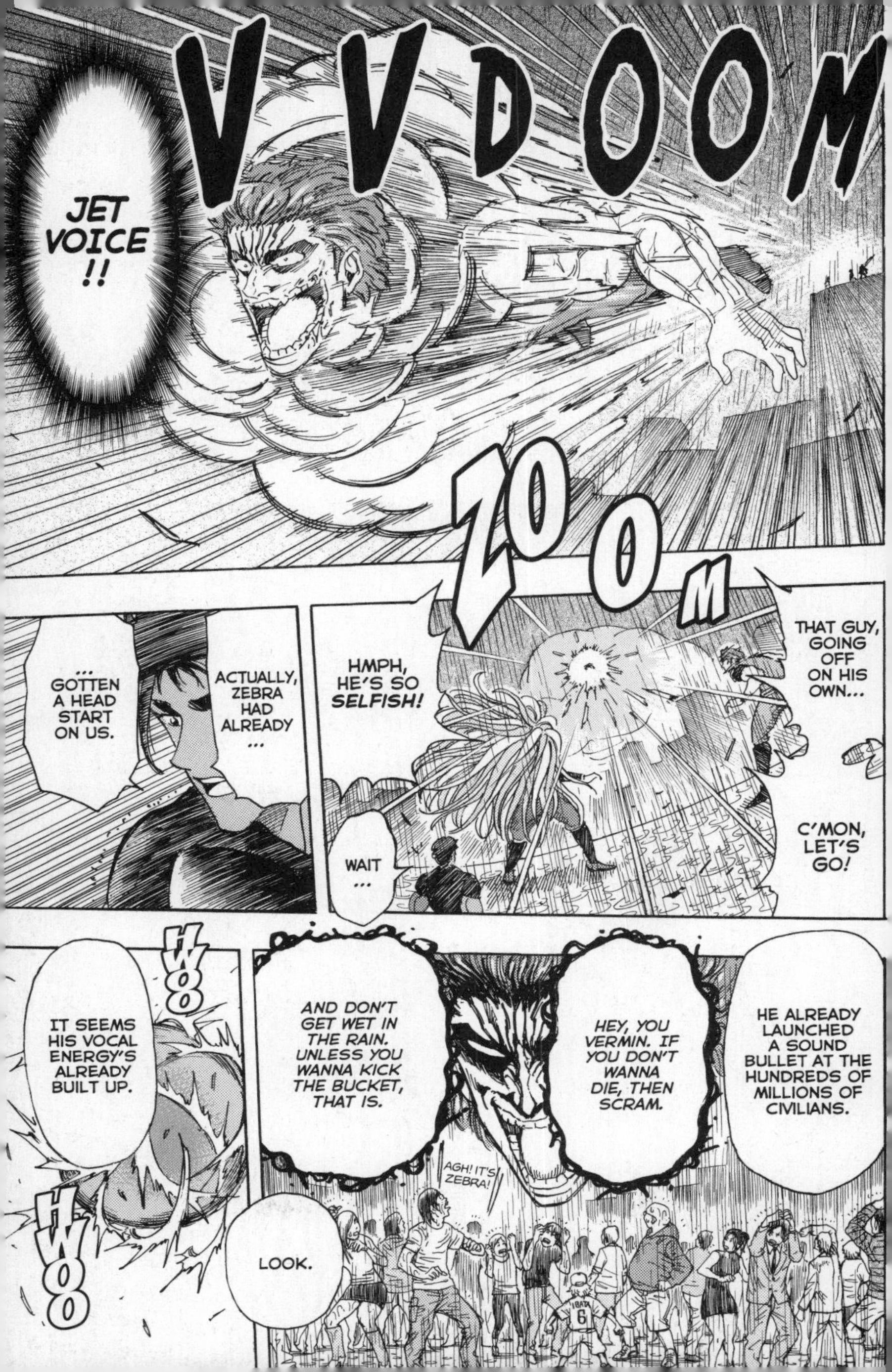
VVDOOM
JET VOICE!!
ZOOOM
THAT GUY, GOING OFF ON HIS OWN...
C'MON, LET'S GO!
HMPH, HE'S SO SELFISH!
WAIT...
ACTUALLY, ZEBRA HAD ALREADY...
... GOTTEN A HEAD START ON US.
HE ALREADY LAUNCHED A SOUND BULLET AT THE HUNDREDS OF MILLIONS OF CIVILIANS.
HEY, YOU VERMIN. IF YOU DON'T WANNA DIE, THEN SCRAM.
AGH! IT'S ZEBRA!
AND DON'T GET WET IN THE RAIN. UNLESS YOU WANNA KICK THE BUCKET, THAT IS.
LOOK.
HWOO
IT SEEMS HIS VOCAL ENERGY'S ALREADY BUILT UP.
HWOO

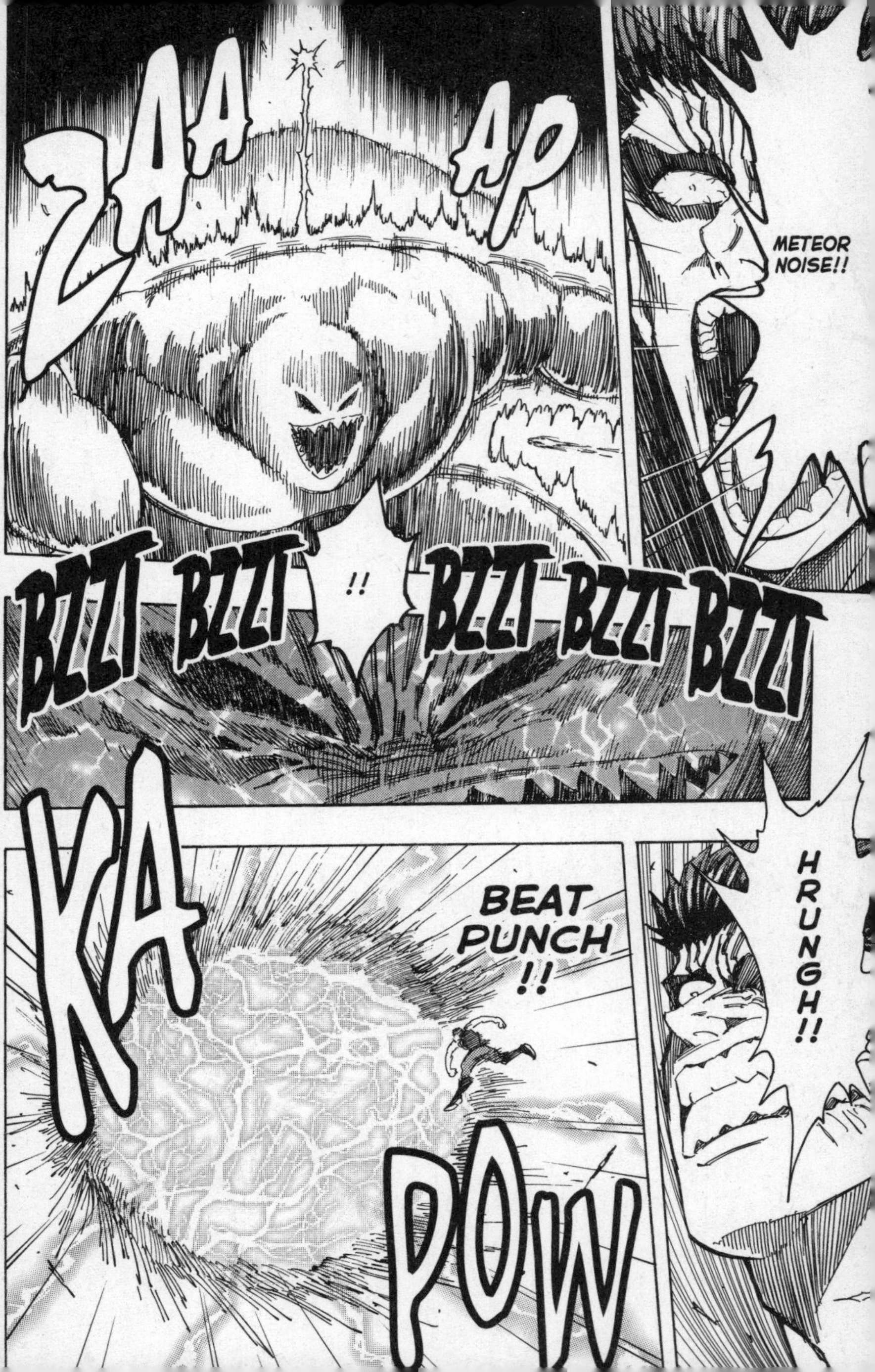
METEOR NOISE!!
ZAAAP
BZZT BZZT BZZT
!!
BZZT BZZT
HRUNGH!!
BEAT PUNCH!!
KA
POW

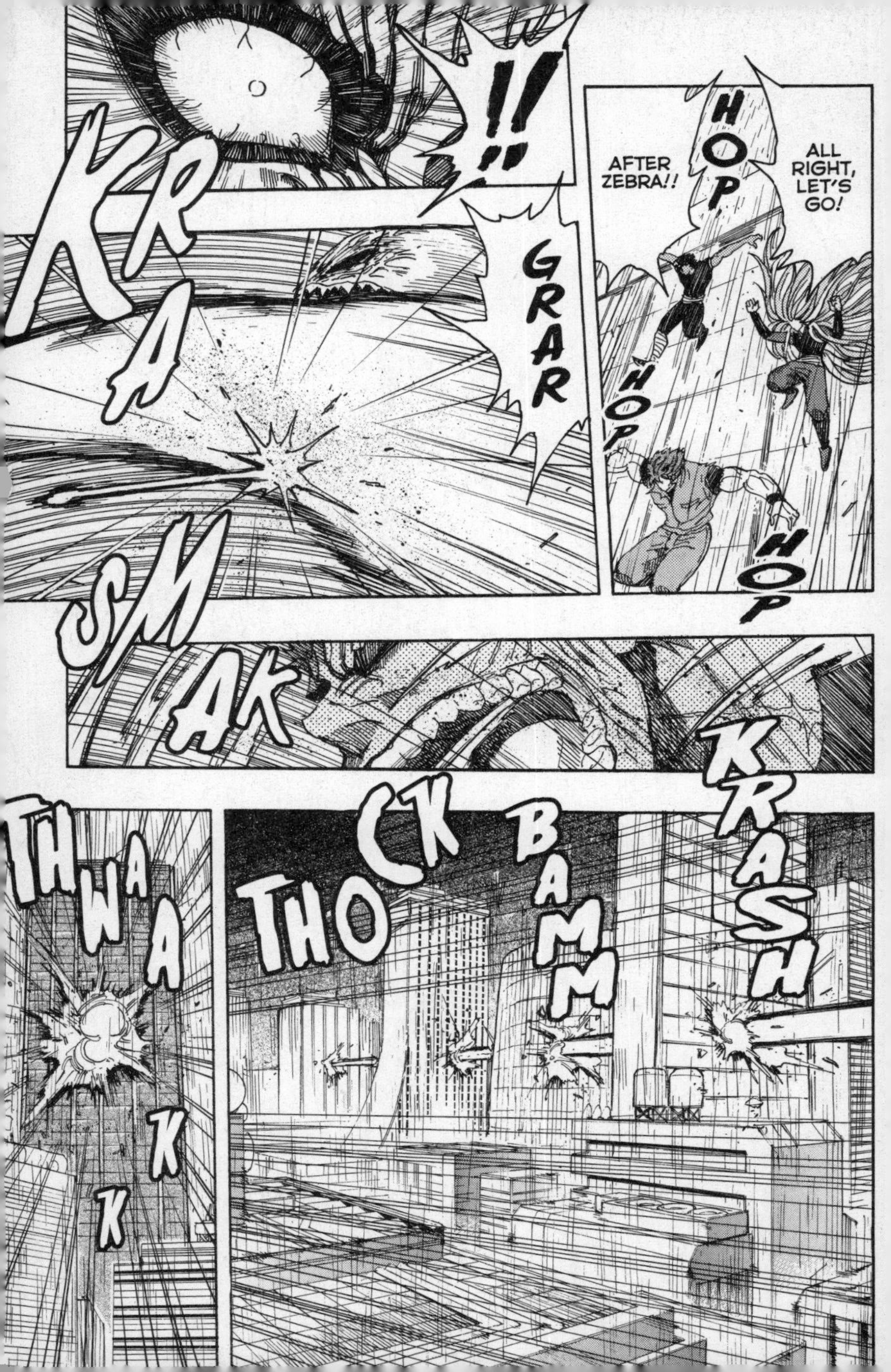
ALL RIGHT, LET'S GO!
HOP
AFTER ZEBRA!!
HOP
HOP
!!
GRAR
KRAA
SMAK
KRASH
BAMM
THOCK
THWAAKK

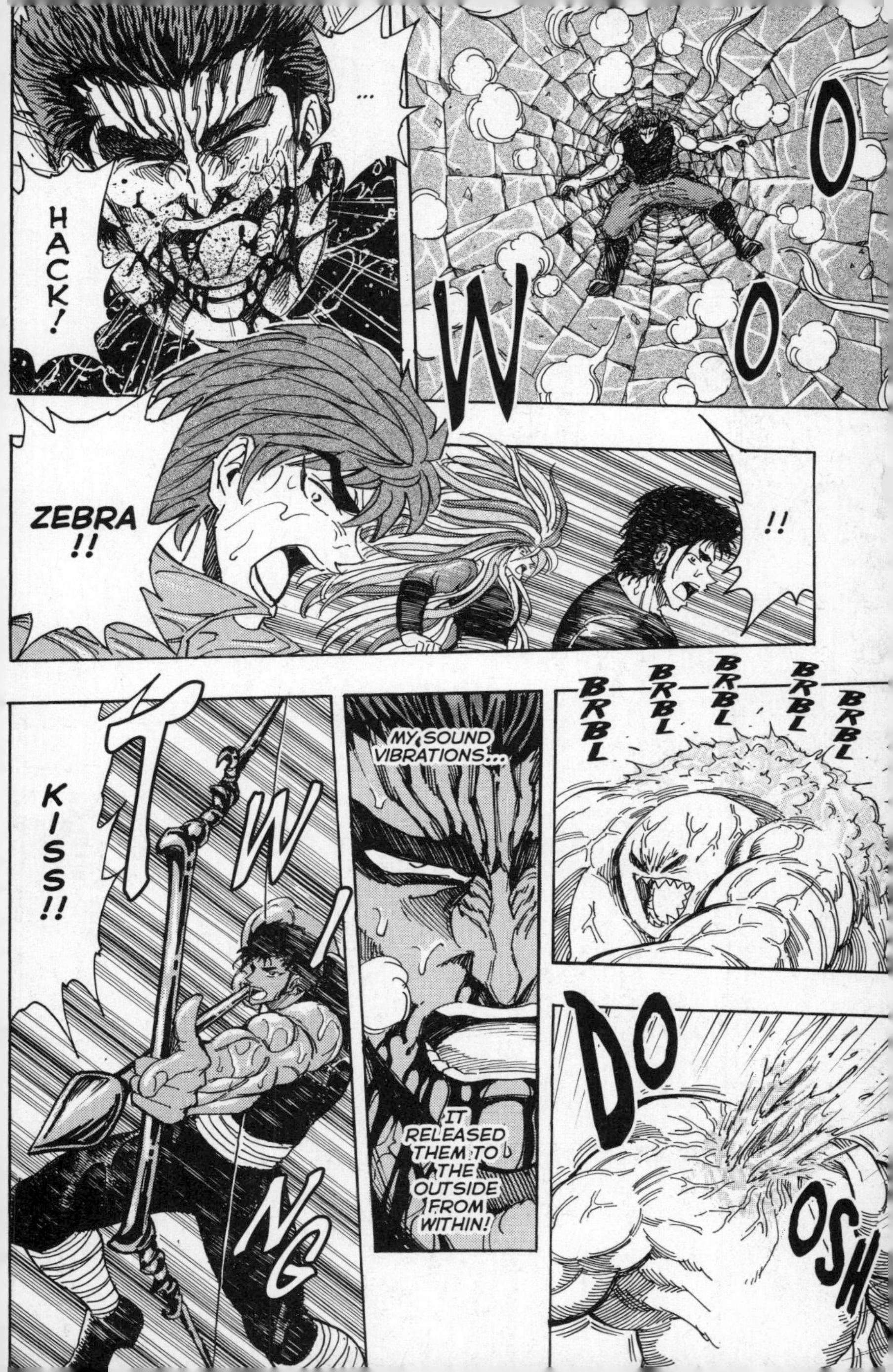
WOOO
...
HACK!
!!
ZEBRA !!
BRBL BRBL BRBL BRBL BRBL
DOOSH
MY SOUND VIBRATIONS...
IT RELEASED THEM TO THE OUTSIDE FROM WITHIN!
TWING
KISS!!

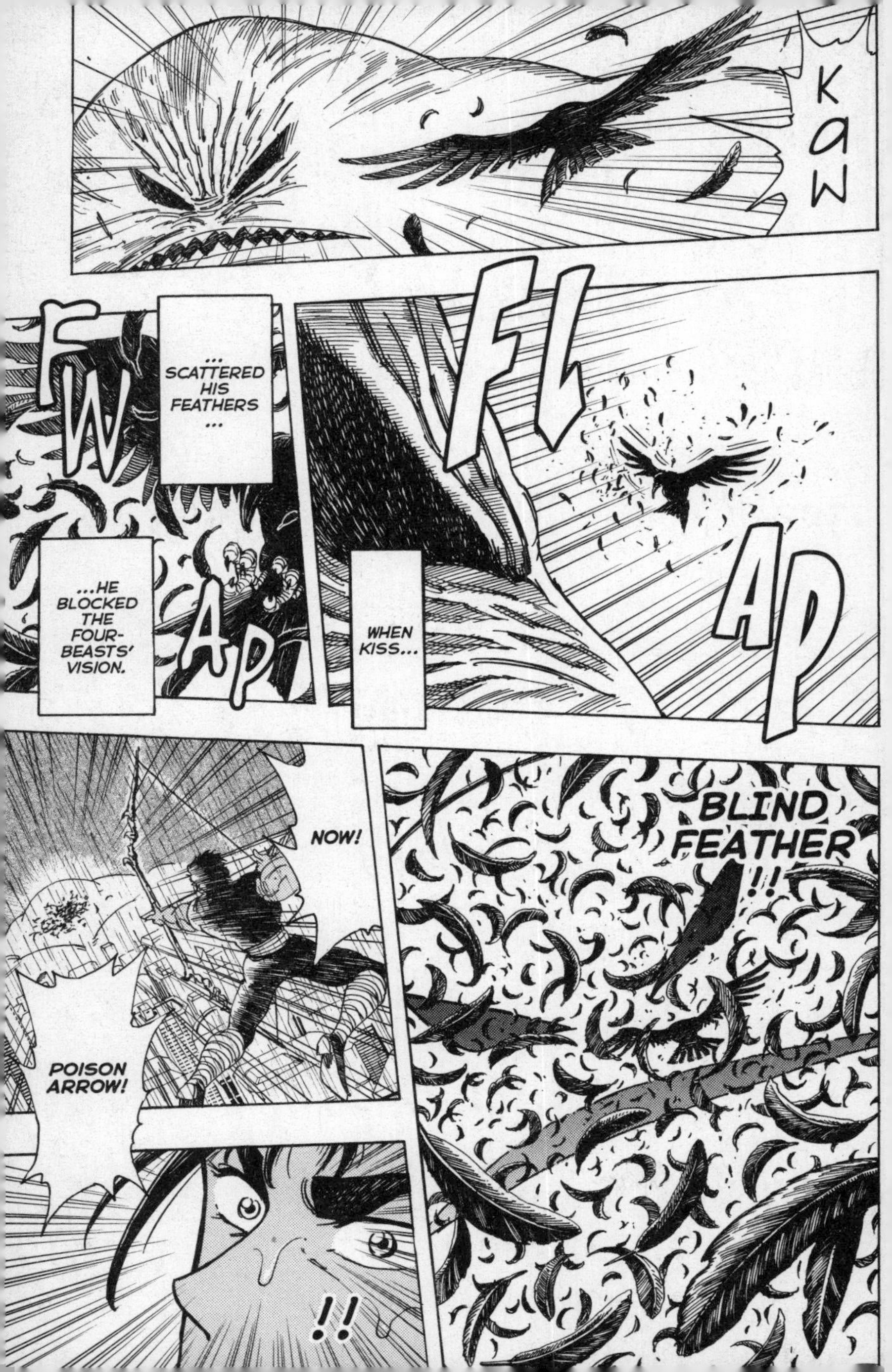
KAW
FLAP
WHEN KISS...
...SCATTERED HIS FEATHERS...
...HE BLOCKED THE FOUR-BEASTS' VISION.
FWAP
BLIND FEATHER!!
NOW!
POISON ARROW!
!!

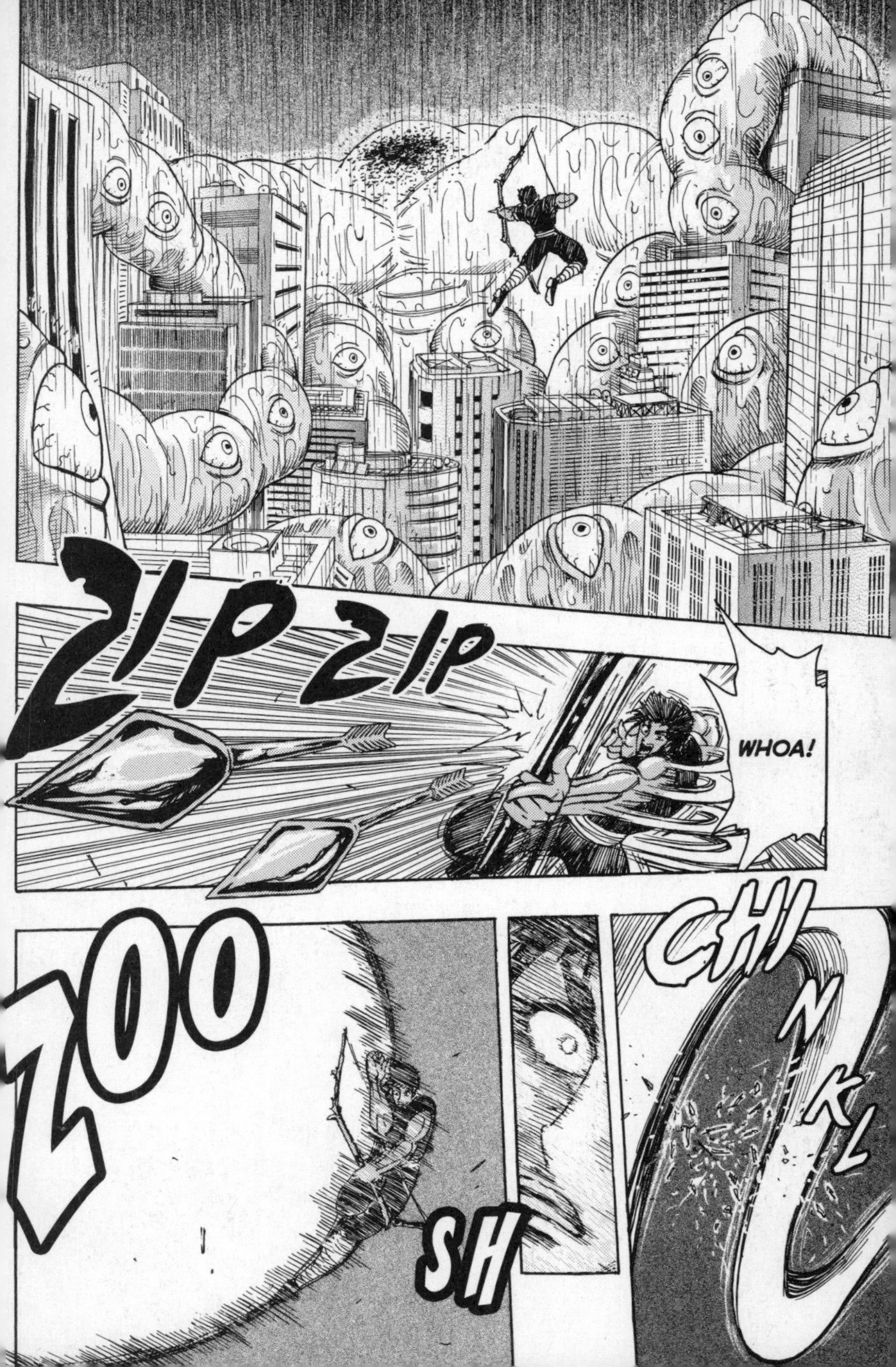
WHOA!
ZIP ZIP
CHINKL
SH
ZOO

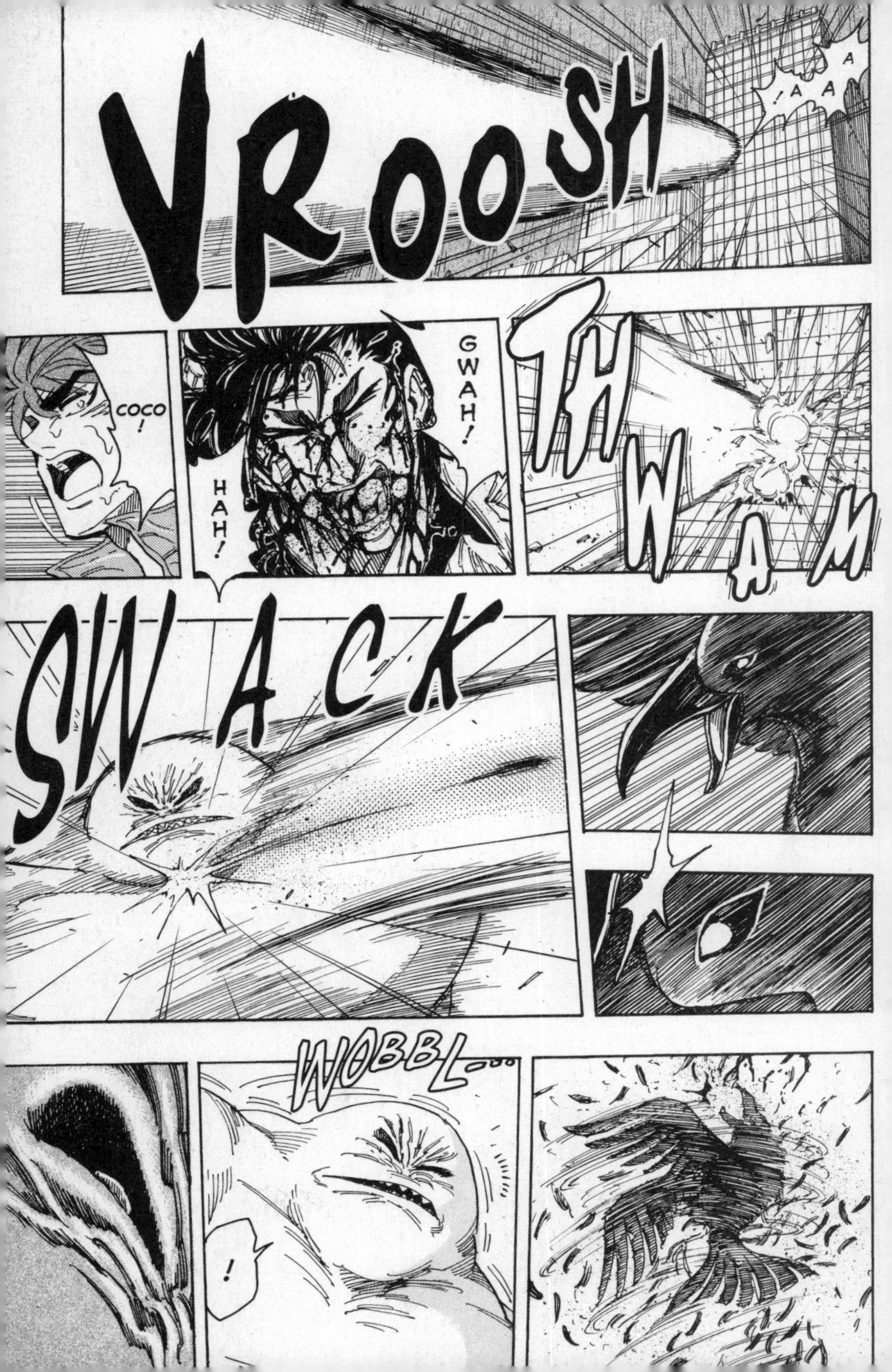
A A A!
VROOSH
THWAM
GWAH!
HAH!
COCO!
SWACK
WOBBL...
!

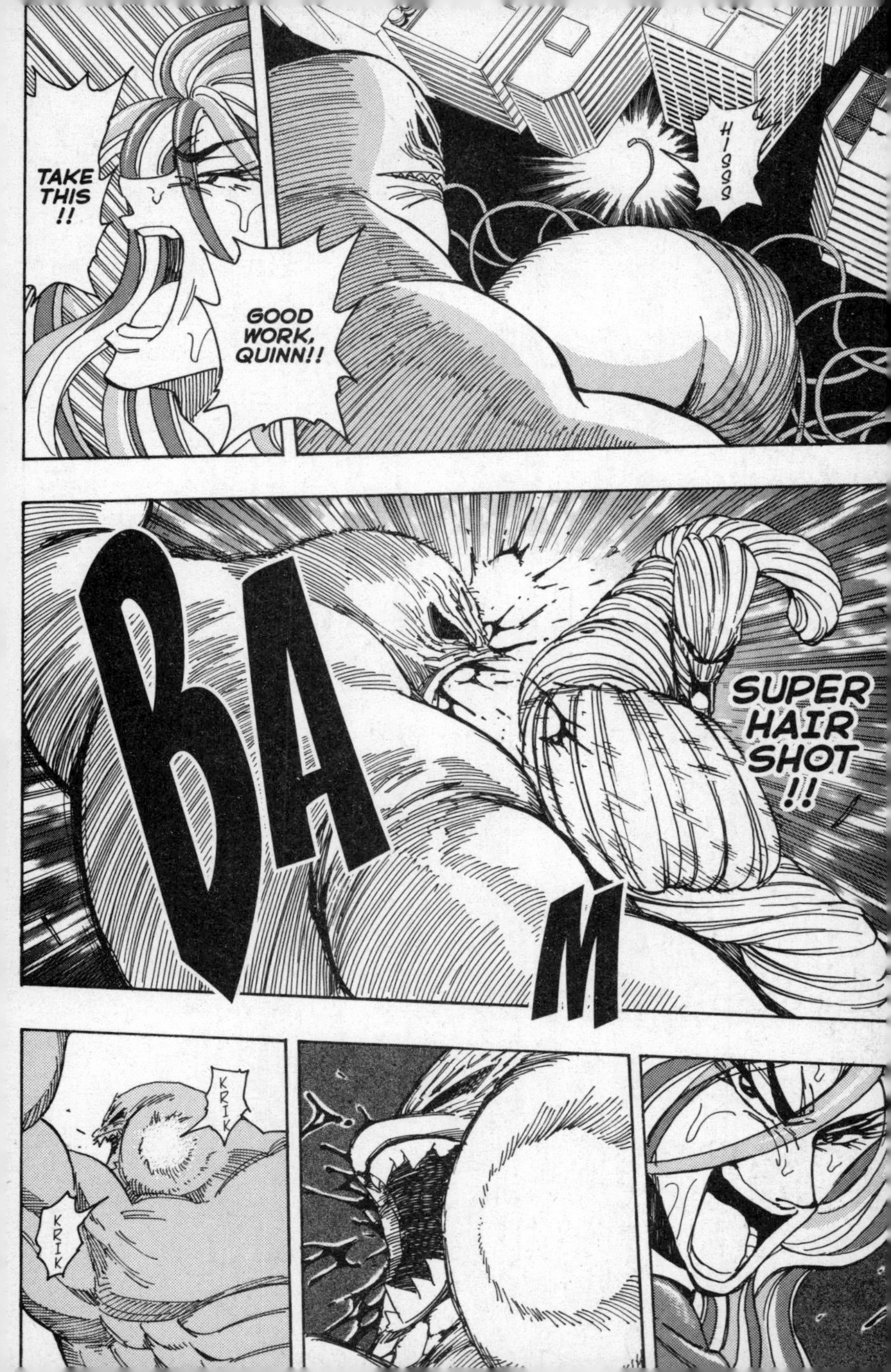
HISSS
GOOD WORK, QUINN!!
TAKE THIS!!
SUPER HAIR SHOT!!
BAM
KRIK
KRIK

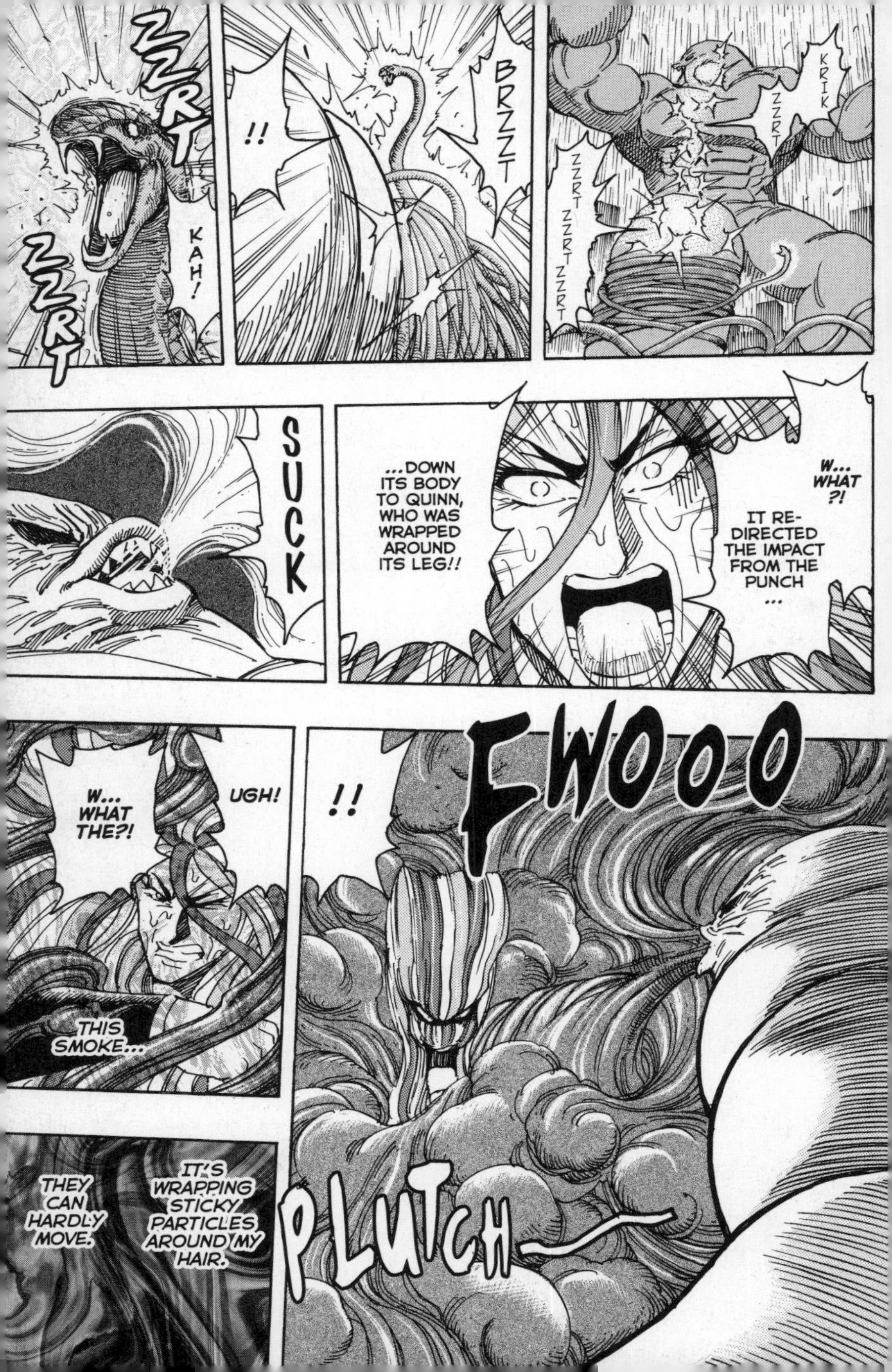
KRIK
ZZRT
ZZRT
ZZRT
ZZRT
BRZZZT
!!
ZZRT
KAH!
ZZRT
W... WHAT ?!
IT RE-DIRECTED THE IMPACT FROM THE PUNCH ...
...DOWN ITS BODY TO QUINN, WHO WAS WRAPPED AROUND ITS LEG!!
SUCK
FWOOO
!!
PLUTCH
UGH!
W... WHAT THE?!
THIS SMOKE...
IT'S WRAPPING STICKY PARTICLES AROUND MY HAIR.
THEY CAN HARDLY MOVE.

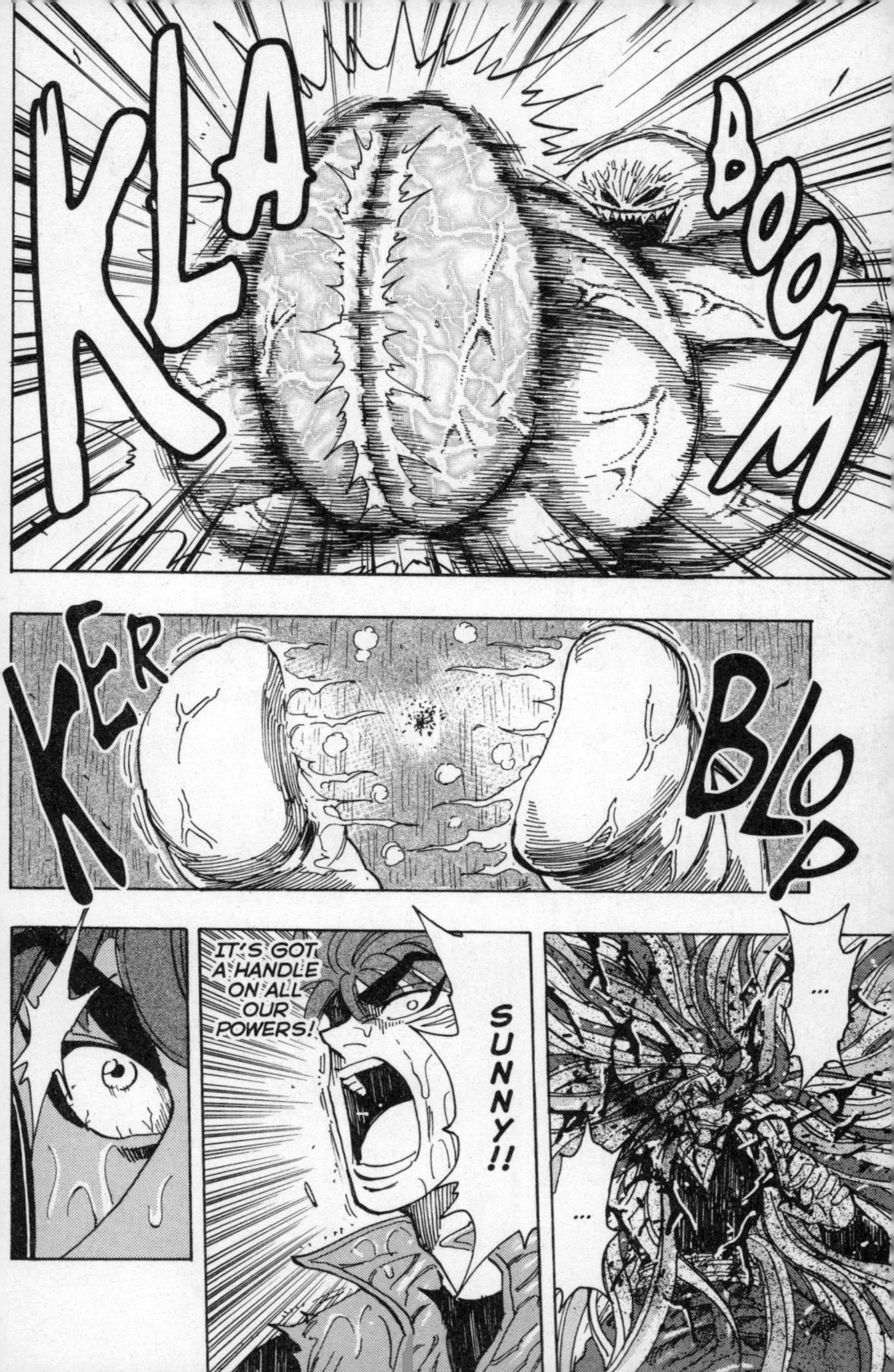
KLA
BOOM
KER
BLOP
...
...
SUNNY!!
IT'S GOT A HANDLE ON ALL OUR POWERS!

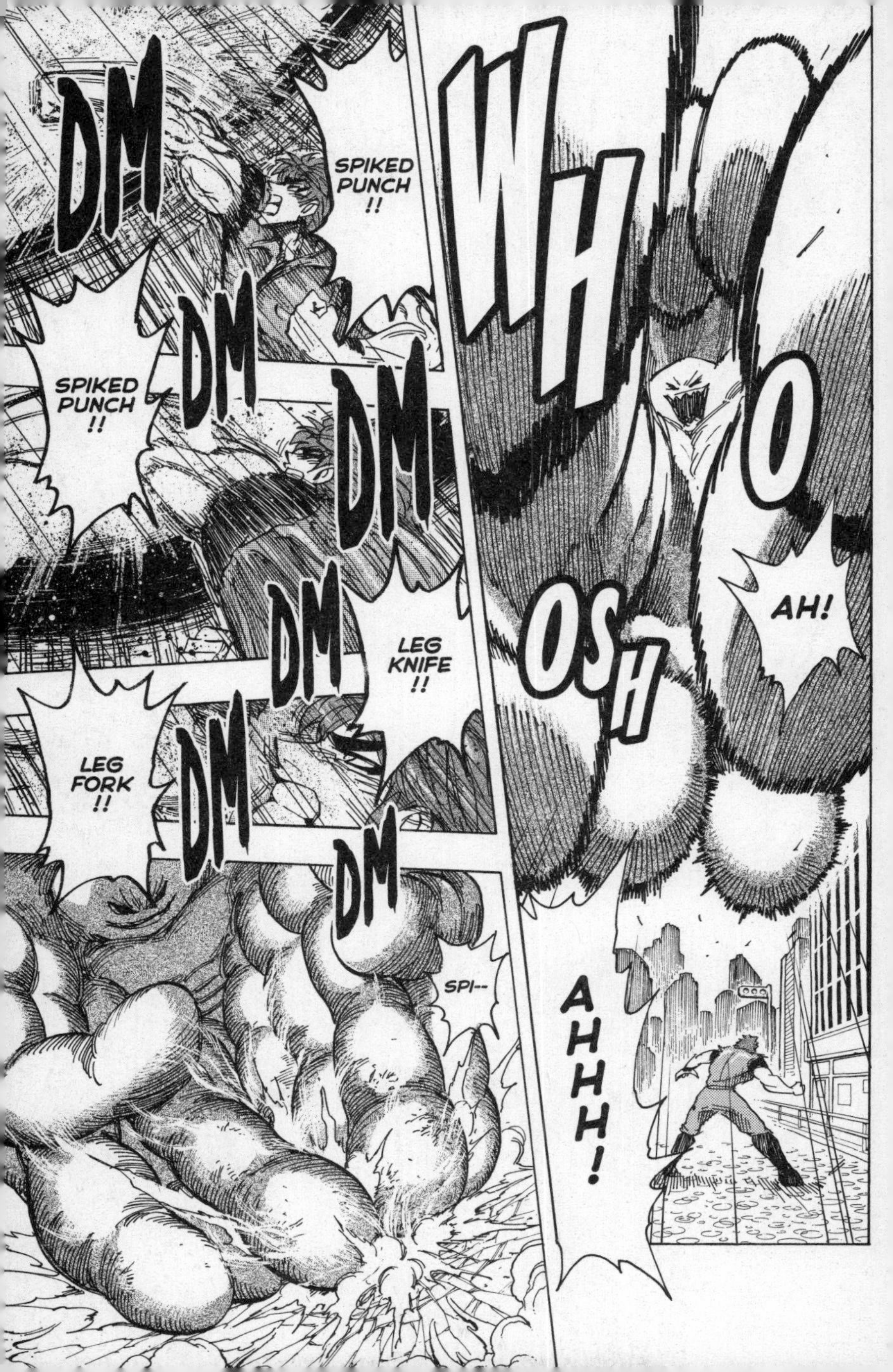
WHOOSH
AH!
AHHH!
DM
SPIKED PUNCH !!
DM
SPIKED PUNCH !!
DM
DM
LEG KNIFE !!
DM
LEG FORK !!
DM
SPI--

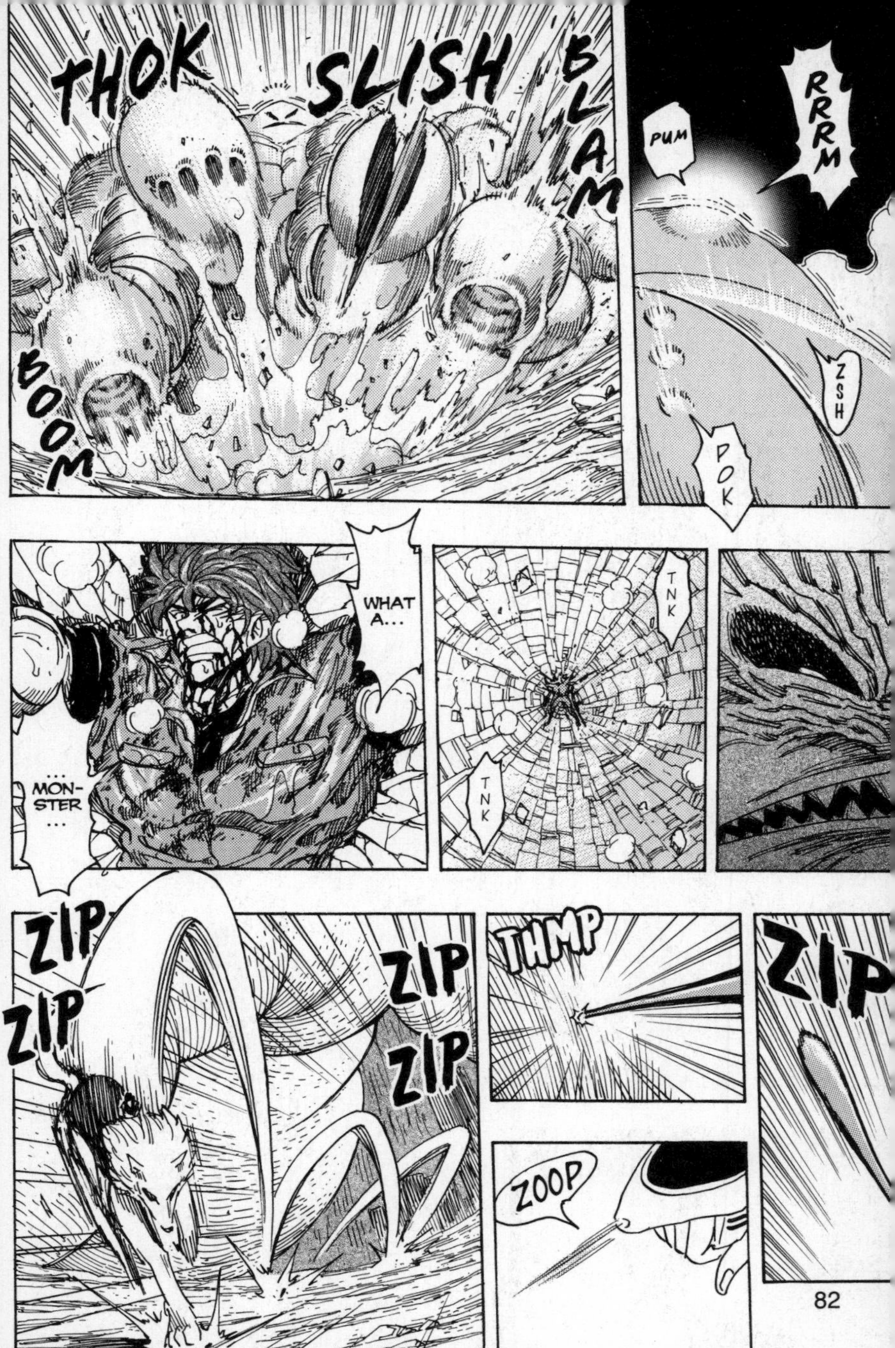
RRRM
PUM
ZSH
POK
THOK
SLISH
BLAM
BOOM
TNK
TNK
WHAT A...
...MON-STER...
ZIP
THMP
ZOOP
ZIP
ZIP
ZIP
ZIP

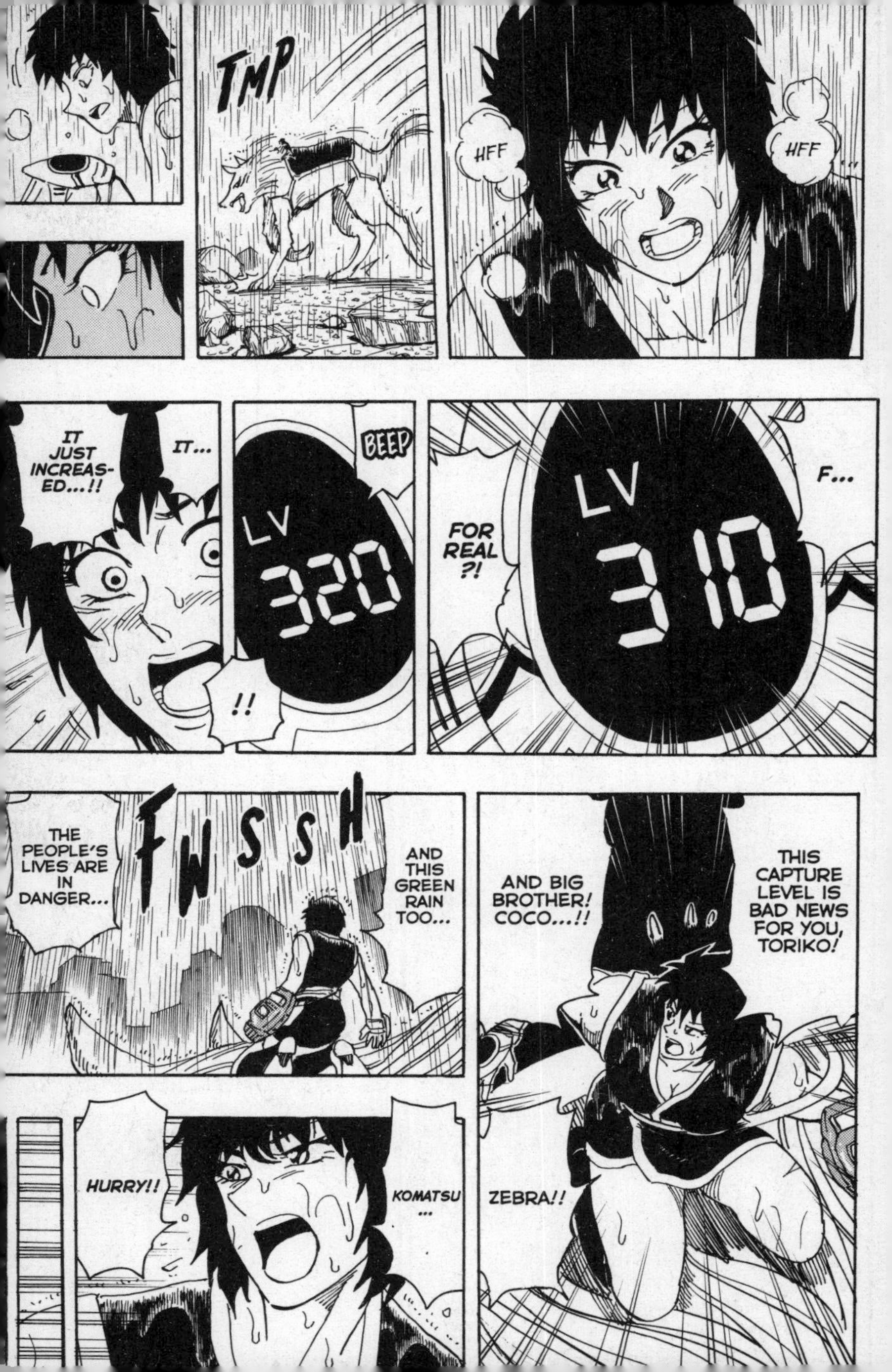
HFF
HFF
TMP
F...
LV 310
FOR REAL?!
BEEP
LV 320
!!
IT...
IT JUST INCREASED...!!
THIS CAPTURE LEVEL IS BAD NEWS FOR YOU, TORIKO!
AND BIG BROTHER! COCO...!!
AND THIS GREEN RAIN TOO...
FWSSH
THE PEOPLE'S LIVES ARE IN DANGER...
ZEBRA!!
KOMATSU...
HURRY!!

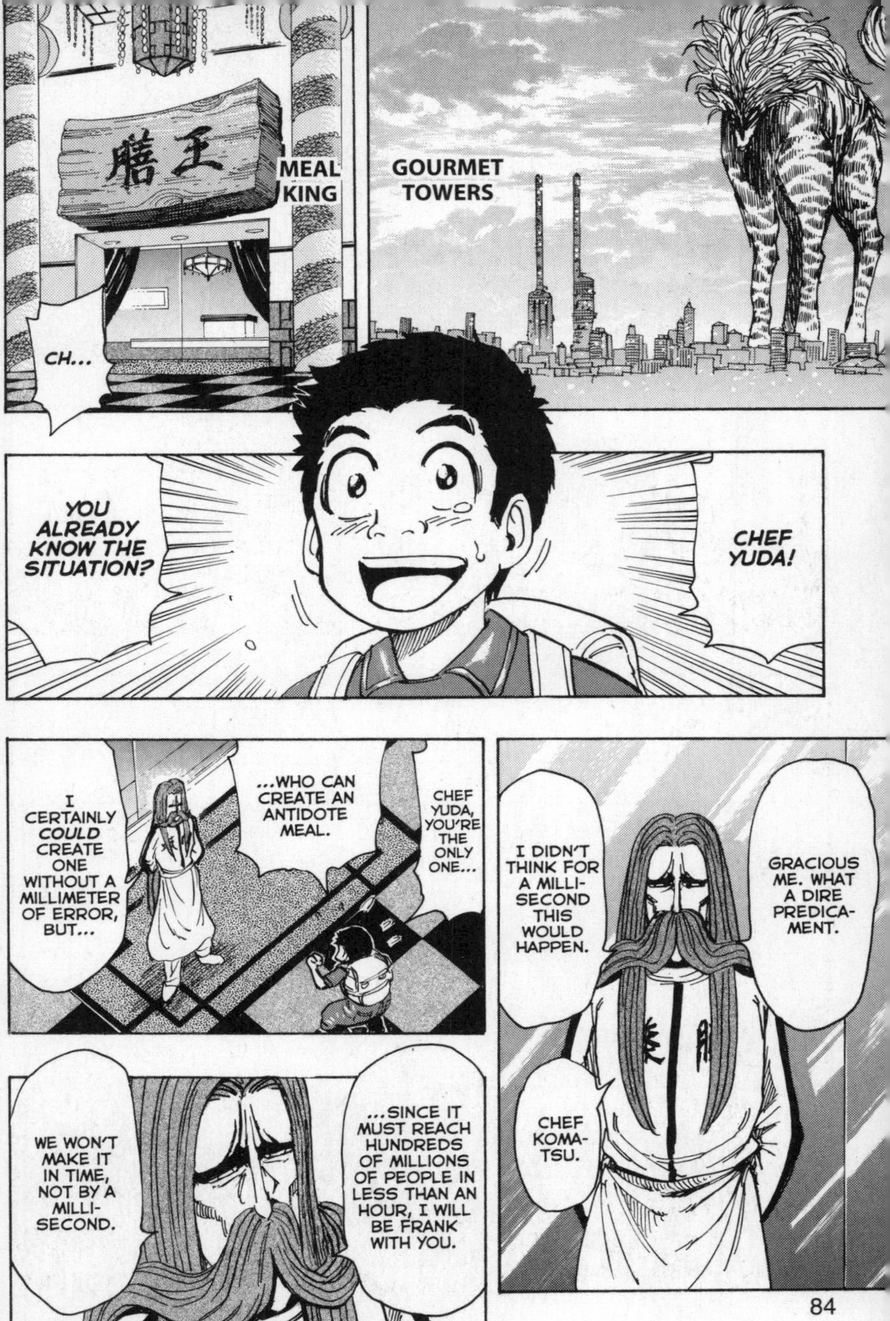
GOURMET TOWERS
MEAL KING
CH...
CHEF YUDA!
YOU ALREADY KNOW THE SITUATION?
GRACIOUS ME. WHAT A DIRE PREDICAMENT.
I DIDN'T THINK FOR A MILLISECOND THIS WOULD HAPPEN.
CHEF KOMATSU.
CHEF YUDA, YOU'RE THE ONLY ONE...
...WHO CAN CREATE AN ANTIDOTE MEAL.
I CERTAINLY COULD CREATE ONE WITHOUT A MILLIMETER OF ERROR, BUT...
...SINCE IT MUST REACH HUNDREDS OF MILLIONS OF PEOPLE IN LESS THAN AN HOUR, I WILL BE FRANK WITH YOU.
WE WON'T MAKE IT IN TIME, NOT BY A MILLISECOND.

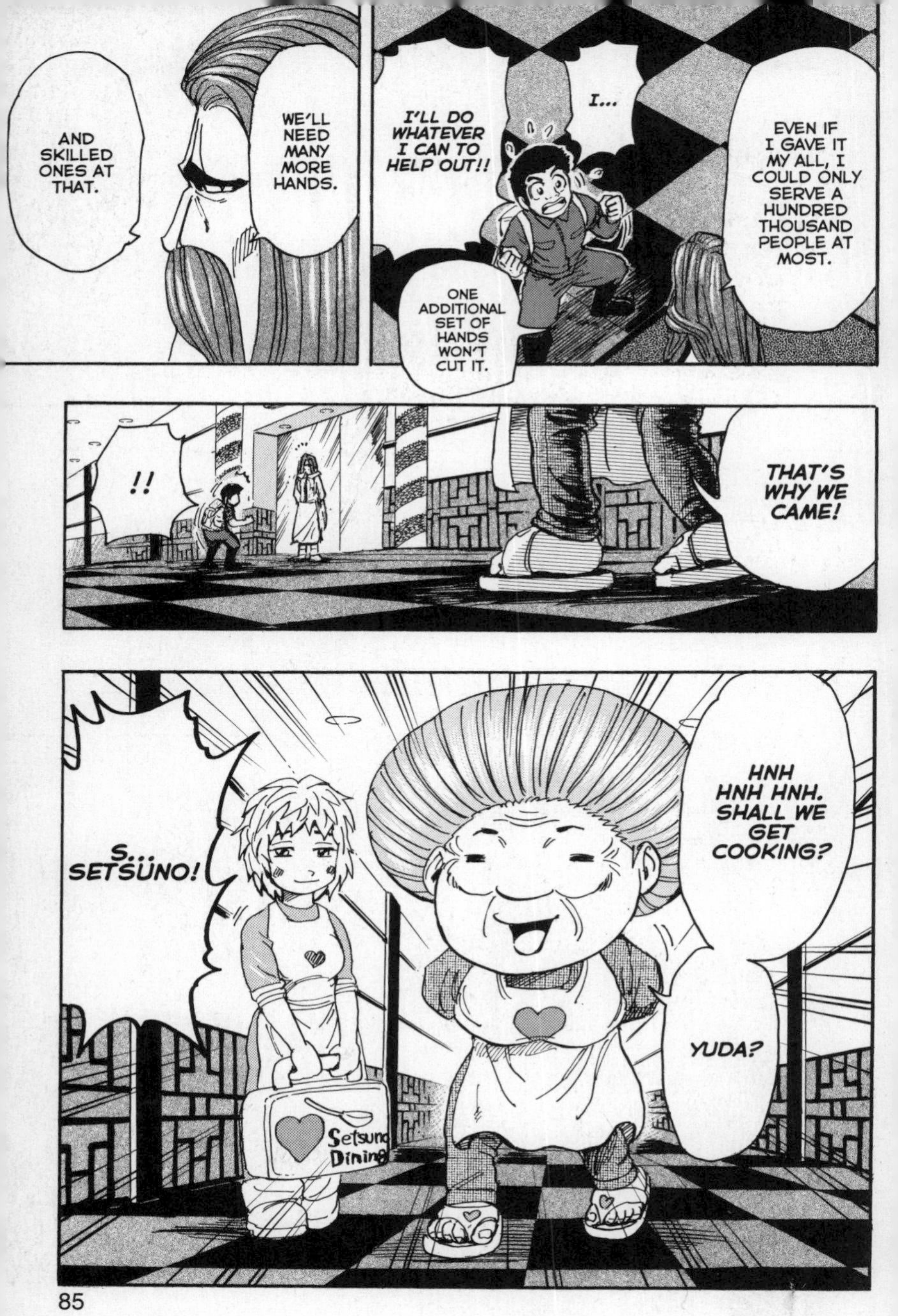
EVEN IF I GAVE IT MY ALL, I COULD ONLY SERVE A HUNDRED THOUSAND PEOPLE AT MOST.
I...
I'LL DO WHATEVER I CAN TO HELP OUT!!
ONE ADDITIONAL SET OF HANDS WON'T CUT IT.
WE'LL NEED MANY MORE HANDS.
AND SKILLED ONES AT THAT.
THAT'S WHY WE CAME!
!!
HNH HNH HNH. SHALL WE GET COOKING?
YUDA?
S... SETSŪNO!
Setsuno Dining

TORIKO

GOURMET CHECKLIST

Vol. 238

CHERRY APPLES

(FRUIT)

CAPTURE LEVEL: 1

HABITAT: WIDELY DISTRIBUTED

LENGTH: 2.5 CM

HEIGHT: ---

WEIGHT: 15 G

PRICE: 1,500 YEN

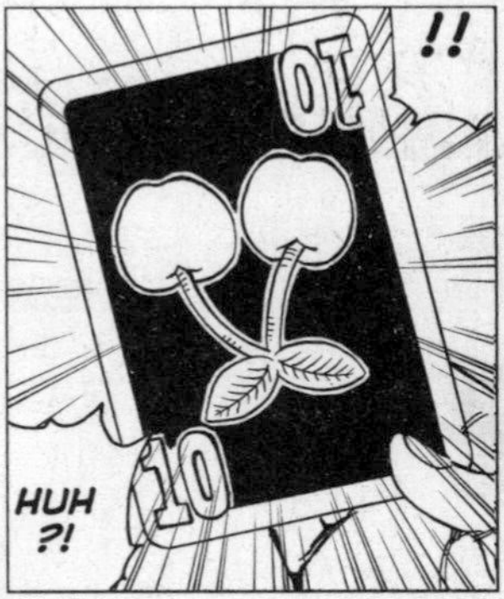
!!
10
10
HUH ?!

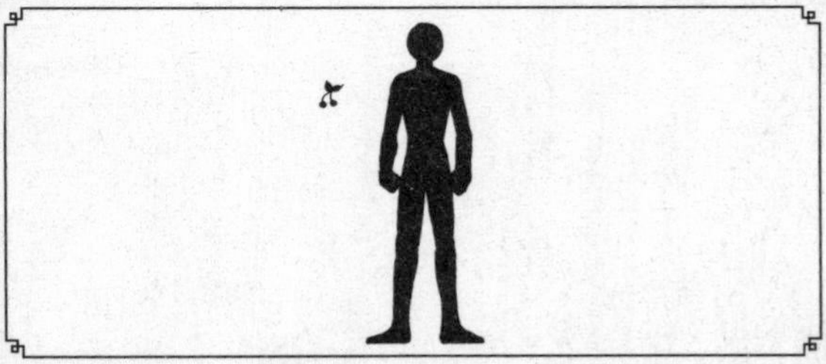

SCALE

A STRANGE CHERRY IN THE ROSACEAE FAMILY. THIS HIGH-END FOOD HAS A REFRESHING SOURNESS AND DELICATE FLAVOR. THE FRUIT IS RED, ROUND AND LOOKS LIKE AN APPLE AT FIRST GLANCE, BUT IT IS THE SIZE OF A CHERRY. IT CAN BE EATEN RAW AND WITHOUT ANY REAL PREPARATION, BUT DELECTABLY SWEET GRILLED CHERRY APPLE PAIRS ESPECIALLY WELL WITH A MEAT DISH.

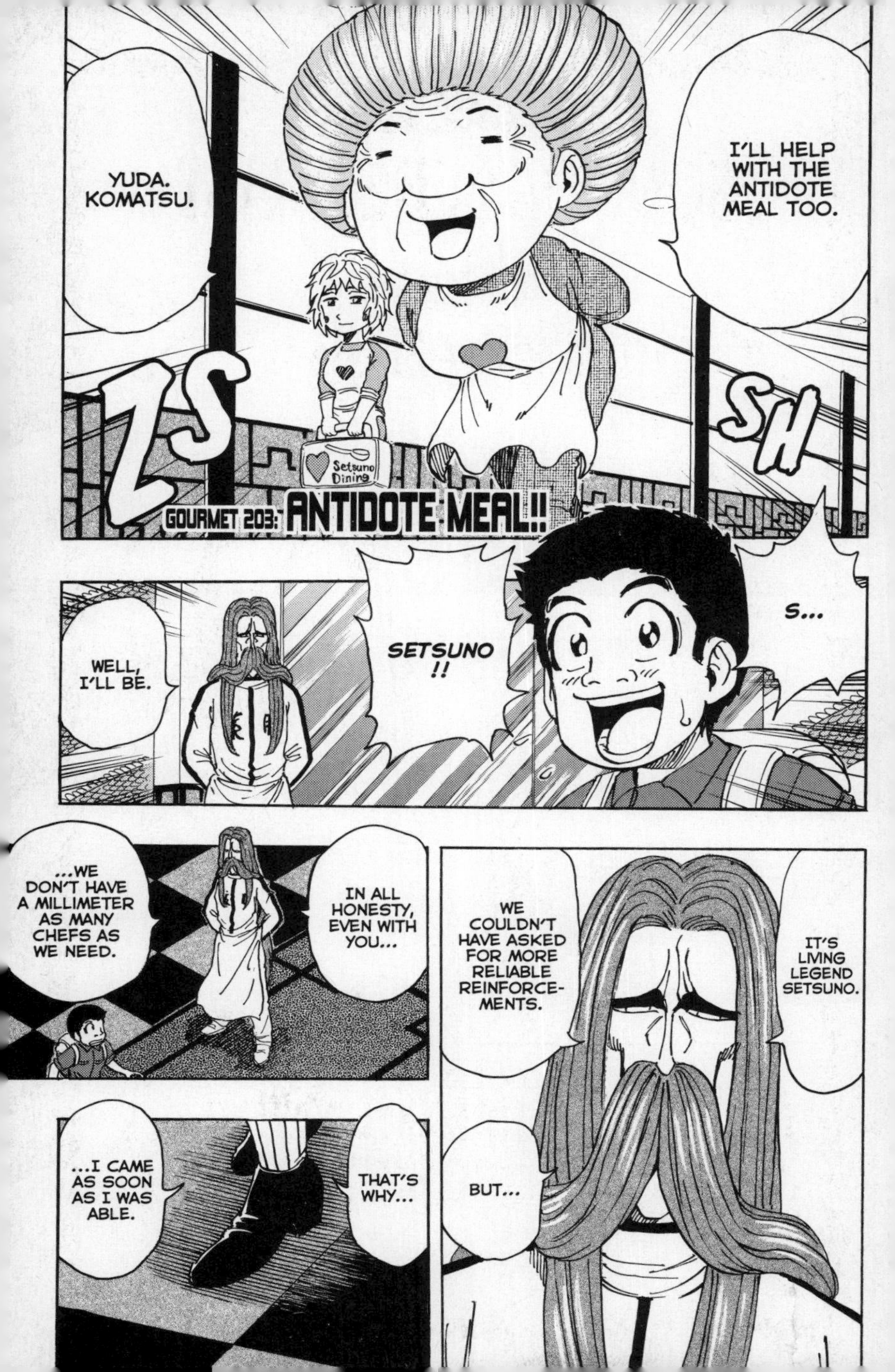
I'LL HELP WITH THE ANTIDOTE MEAL TOO.
YUDA. KOMATSU.
SH
ZS
Setsuno Dining
GOURMET 203: ANTIDOTE MEAL!!
S...
SETSUNO !!
WELL, I'LL BE.
IT'S LIVING LEGEND SETSUNO.
WE COULDN'T HAVE ASKED FOR MORE RELIABLE REINFORCE-MENTS.
BUT...
IN ALL HONESTY, EVEN WITH YOU...
...WE DON'T HAVE A MILLIMETER AS MANY CHEFS AS WE NEED.
THAT'S WHY...
...I CAME AS SOON AS I WAS ABLE.

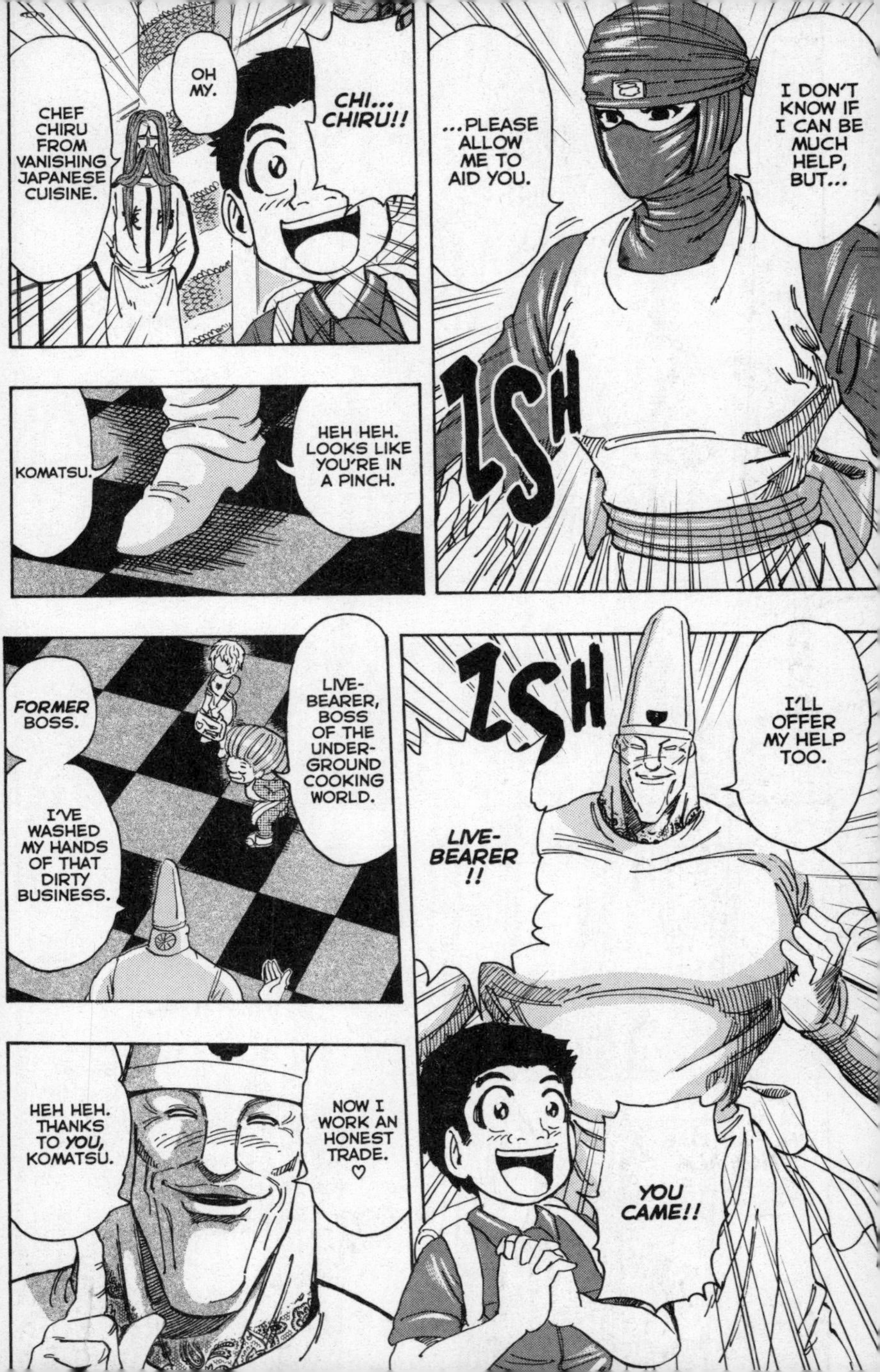
I DON'T KNOW IF I CAN BE MUCH HELP, BUT...
...PLEASE ALLOW ME TO AID YOU.
ZSH
CHI... CHIRU!!
OH MY.
CHEF CHIRU FROM VANISHING JAPANESE CUISINE.
HEH HEH. LOOKS LIKE YOU'RE IN A PINCH.
KOMATSU.
ZSH
I'LL OFFER MY HELP TOO.
LIVE-BEARER!!
YOU CAME!!
LIVE-BEARER, BOSS OF THE UNDERGROUND COOKING WORLD.
FORMER BOSS.
I'VE WASHED MY HANDS OF THAT DIRTY BUSINESS.
NOW I WORK AN HONEST TRADE. ♡
HEH HEH. THANKS TO *YOU*, KOMATSU.

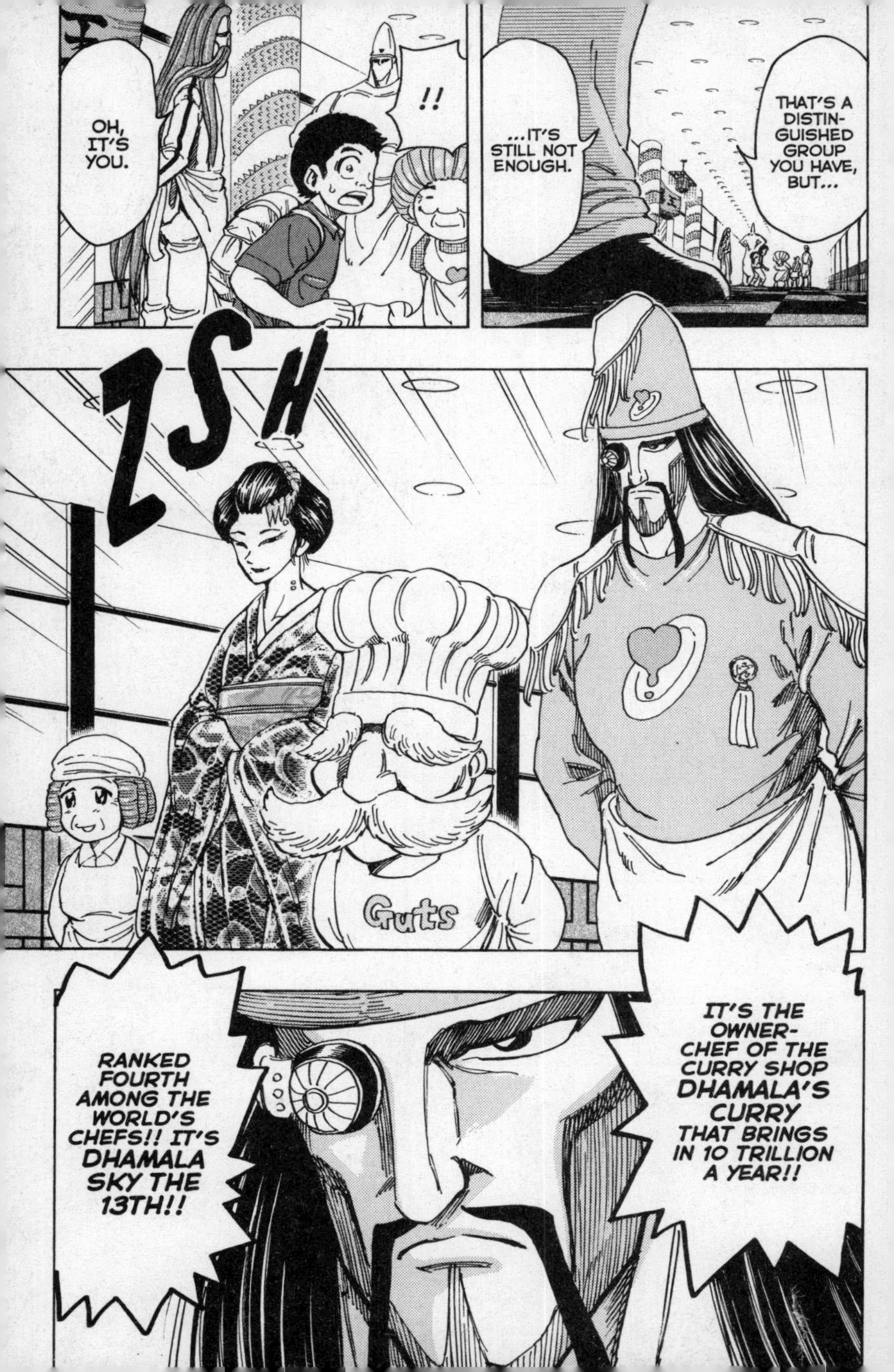
THAT'S A DISTIN-GUISHED GROUP YOU HAVE, BUT...
...IT'S STILL NOT ENOUGH.
OH, IT'S YOU.
!!
ZSH
Guts
IT'S THE OWNER-CHEF OF THE CURRY SHOP DHAMALA'S CURRY THAT BRINGS IN 10 TRILLION A YEAR!!
RANKED FOURTH AMONG THE WORLD'S CHEFS!! IT'S DHAMALA SKY THE 13TH!!

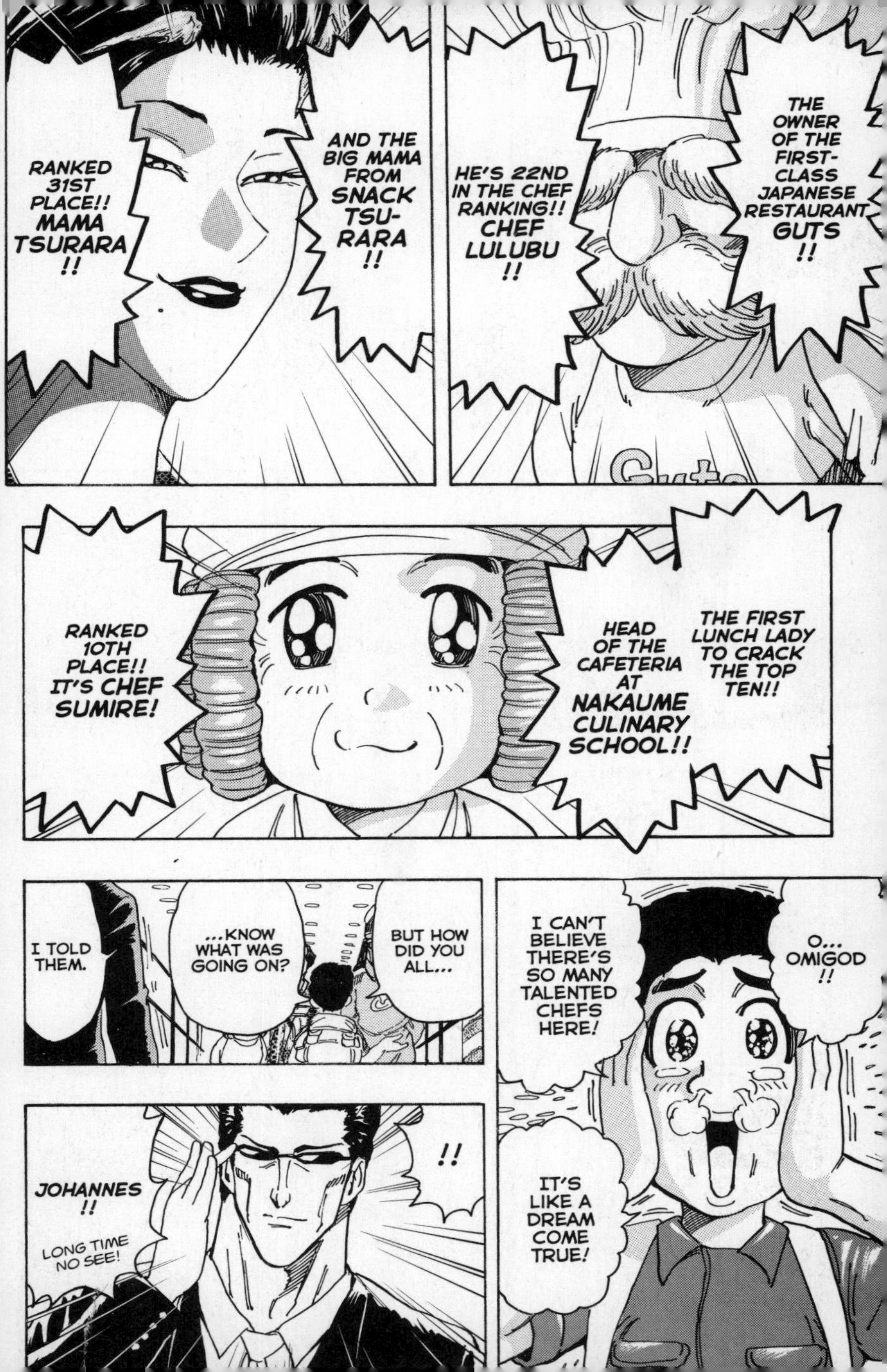
THE OWNER OF THE FIRST-CLASS JAPANESE RESTAURANT GUTS!!
HE'S 22ND IN THE CHEF RANKING!! CHEF LULUBU!!
Guts
AND THE BIG MAMA FROM SNACK TSU-RARA!!
RANKED 31ST PLACE!! MAMA TSURARA!!
THE FIRST LUNCH LADY TO CRACK THE TOP TEN!!
HEAD OF THE CAFETERIA AT NAKAUME CULINARY SCHOOL!!
RANKED 10TH PLACE!! IT'S CHEF SUMIRE!
O... OMIGOD!!
I CAN'T BELIEVE THERE'S SO MANY TALENTED CHEFS HERE!
IT'S LIKE A DREAM COME TRUE!
BUT HOW DID YOU ALL...
...KNOW WHAT WAS GOING ON?
I TOLD THEM.
!!
JOHANNES!!
LONG TIME NO SEE!

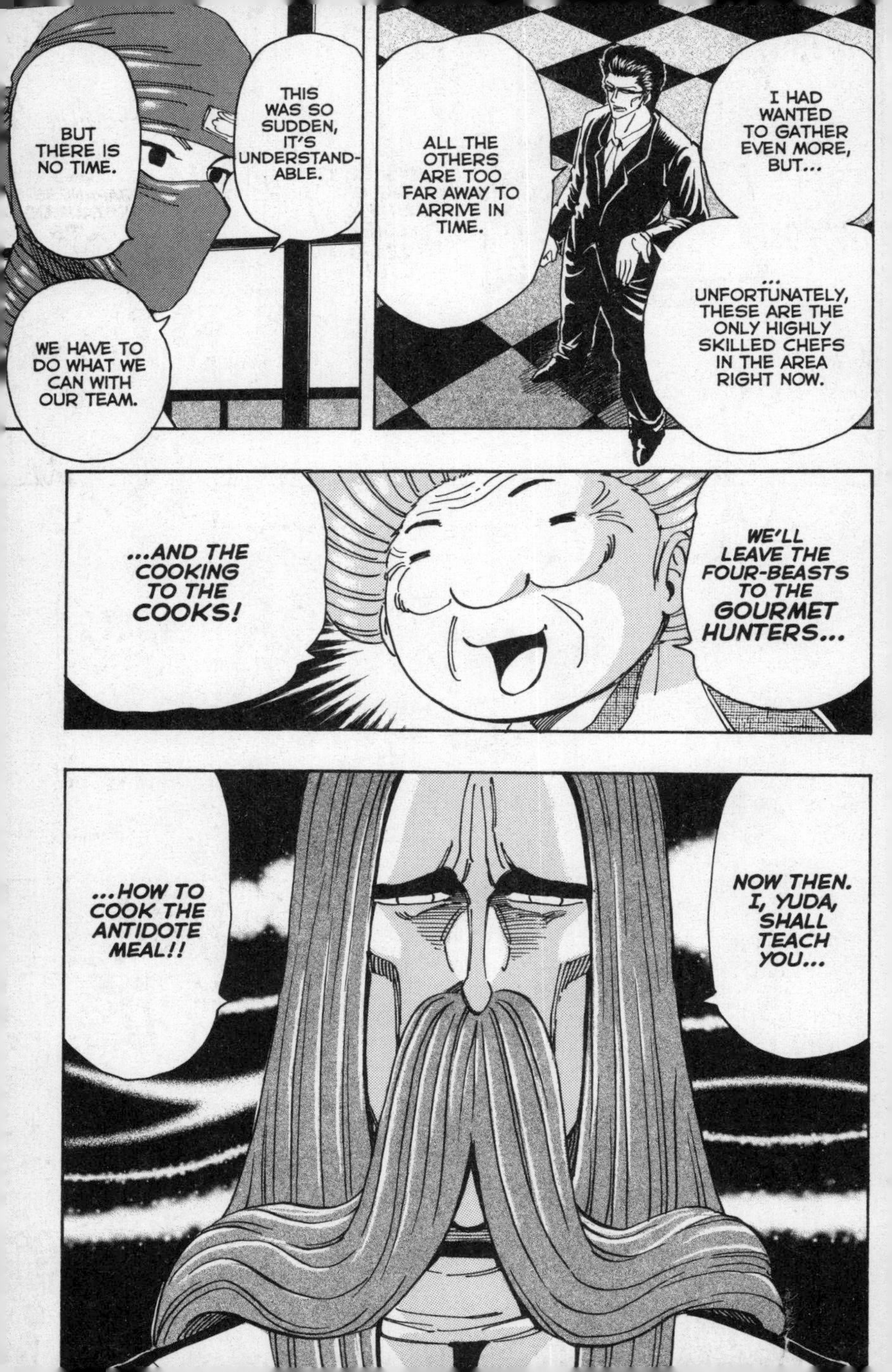
I HAD WANTED TO GATHER EVEN MORE, BUT...
...UNFORTUNATELY, THESE ARE THE ONLY HIGHLY SKILLED CHEFS IN THE AREA RIGHT NOW.
ALL THE OTHERS ARE TOO FAR AWAY TO ARRIVE IN TIME.
THIS WAS SO SUDDEN, IT'S UNDERSTAND-ABLE.
BUT THERE IS NO TIME.
WE HAVE TO DO WHAT WE CAN WITH OUR TEAM.
WE'LL LEAVE THE FOUR-BEASTS TO THE GOURMET HUNTERS...
...AND THE COOKING TO THE COOKS!
NOW THEN. I, YUDA, SHALL TEACH YOU...
...HOW TO COOK THE ANTIDOTE MEAL!!

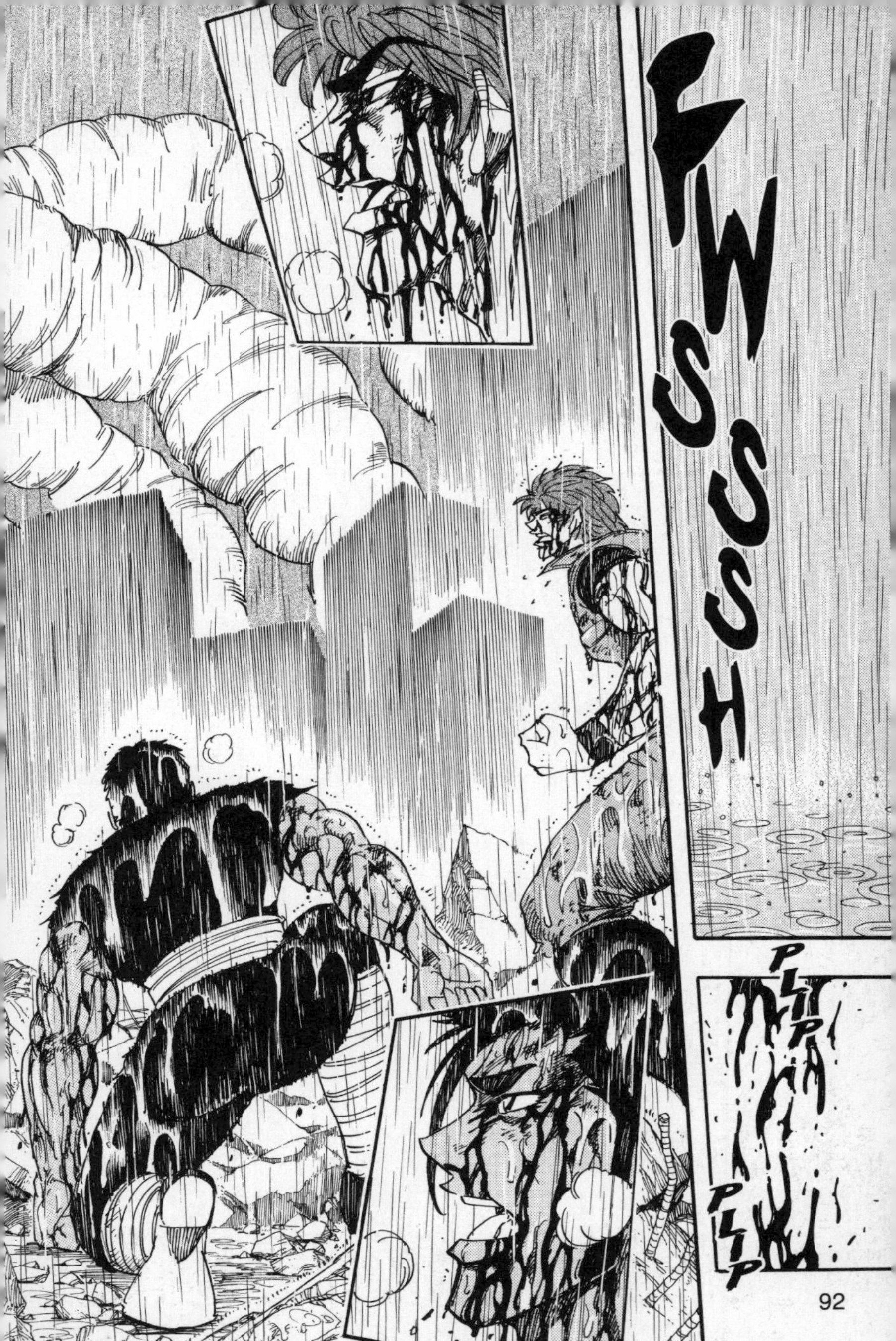
FWSSSH
PLIP PLIP
PLIP

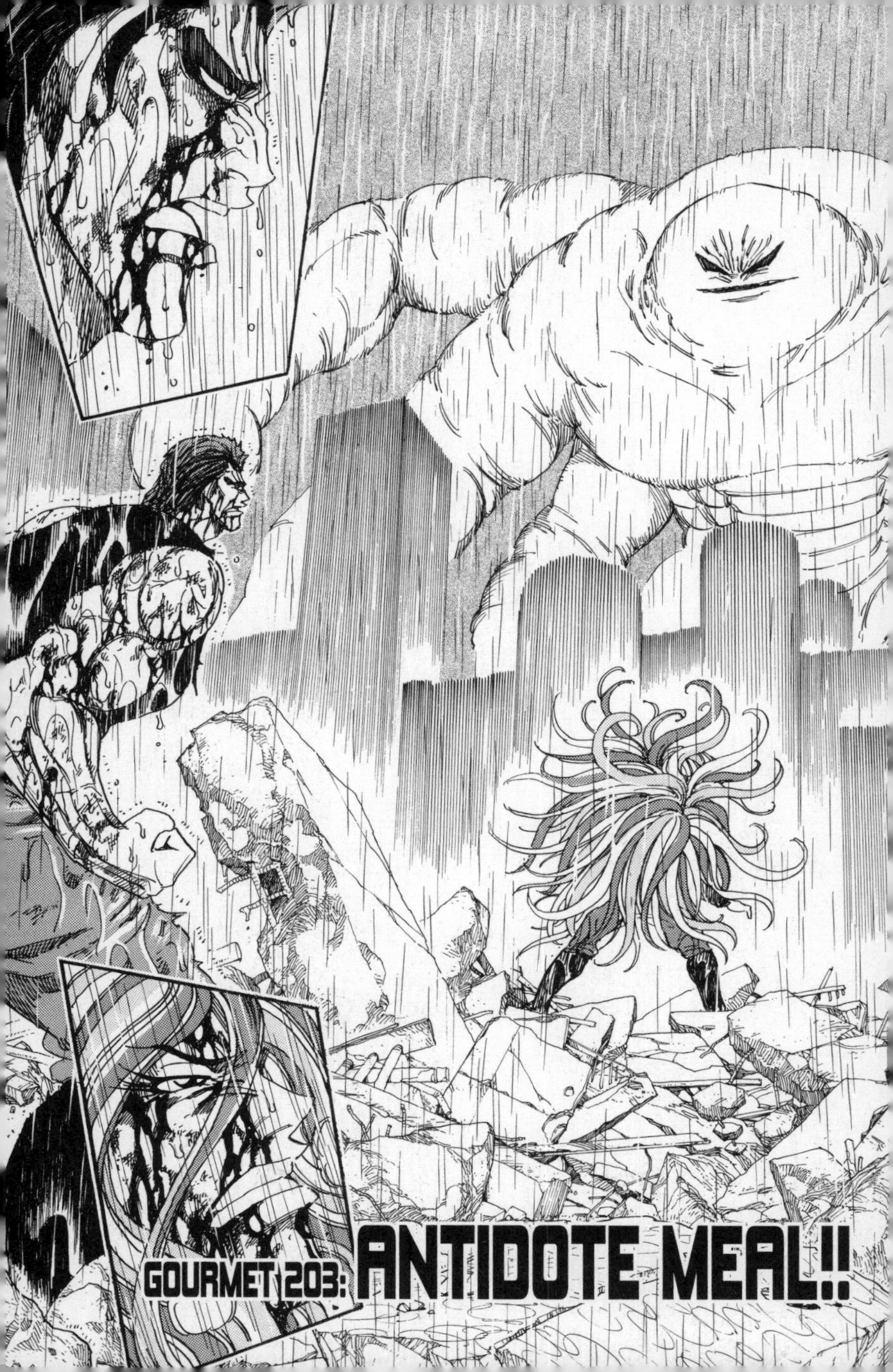
GOURMET 203: ANTIDOTE MEAL!!

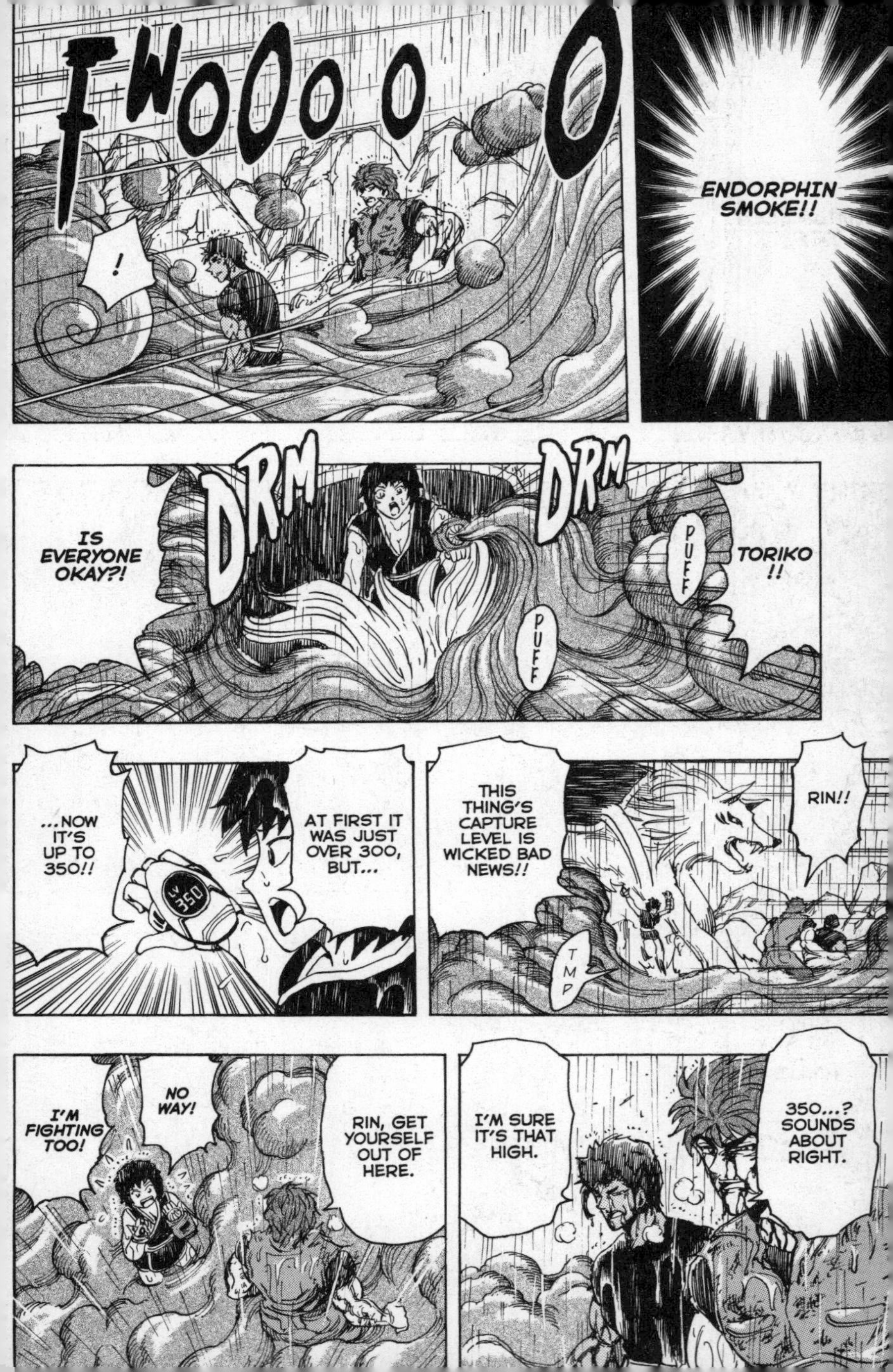
ENDORPHIN SMOKE!!
FWOOO O O
!
TORIKO!!
PUFF
PUFF
DRM
DRM
IS EVERYONE OKAY?!
RIN!!
THIS THING'S CAPTURE LEVEL IS WICKED BAD NEWS!!
TMP
AT FIRST IT WAS JUST OVER 300, BUT...
...NOW IT'S UP TO 350!!
LV 350
350...? SOUNDS ABOUT RIGHT.
I'M SURE IT'S THAT HIGH.
RIN, GET YOURSELF OUT OF HERE.
NO WAY!
I'M FIGHTING TOO!

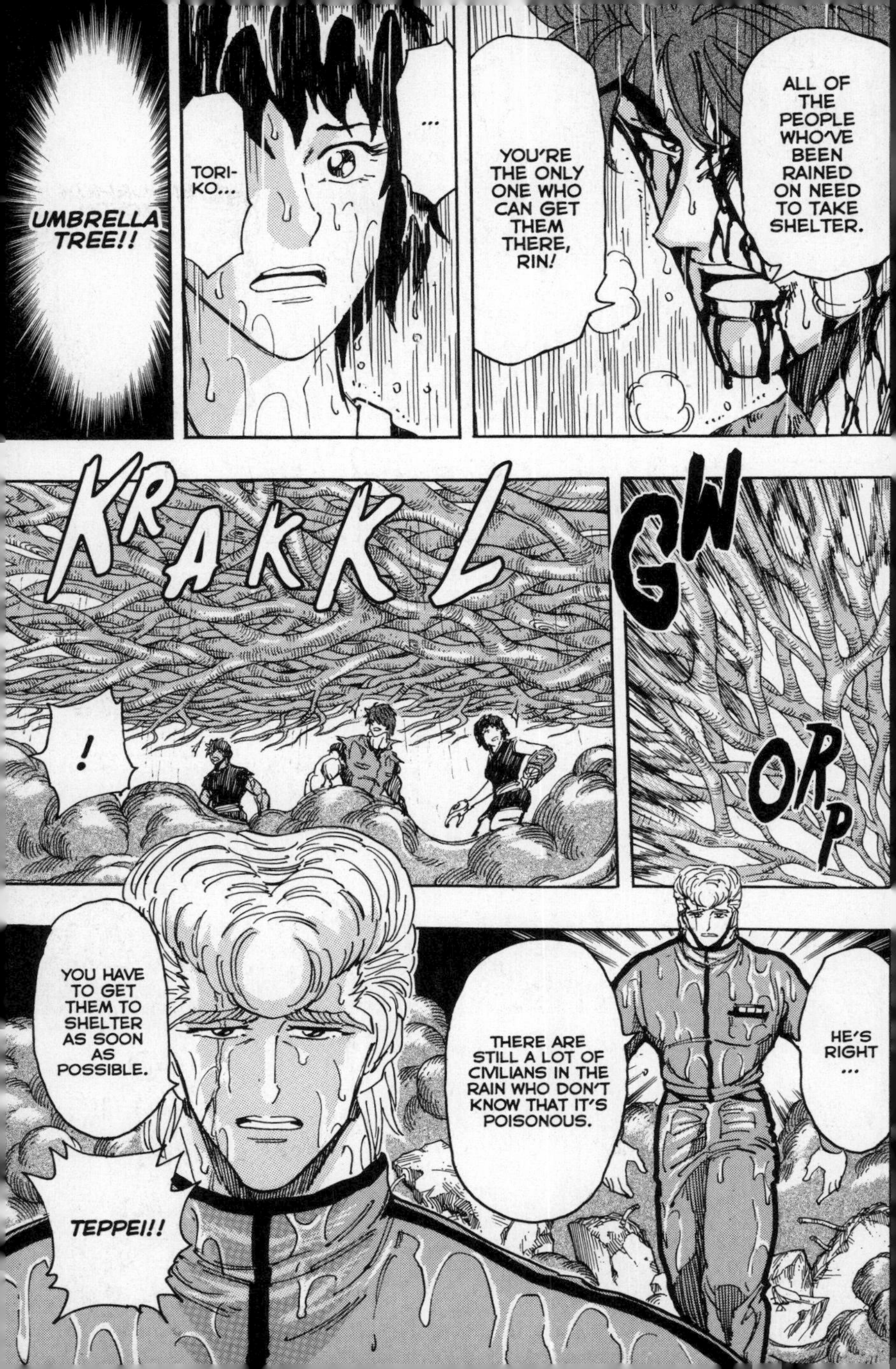
ALL OF THE PEOPLE WHO'VE BEEN RAINED ON NEED TO TAKE SHELTER.
YOU'RE THE ONLY ONE WHO CAN GET THEM THERE, RIN!
...
TORI-KO...
UMBRELLA TREE!!
GWORP
KRAKKL
!
HE'S RIGHT ...
THERE ARE STILL A LOT OF CIVILIANS IN THE RAIN WHO DON'T KNOW THAT IT'S POISONOUS.
YOU HAVE TO GET THEM TO SHELTER AS SOON AS POSSIBLE.
TEPPEI!!

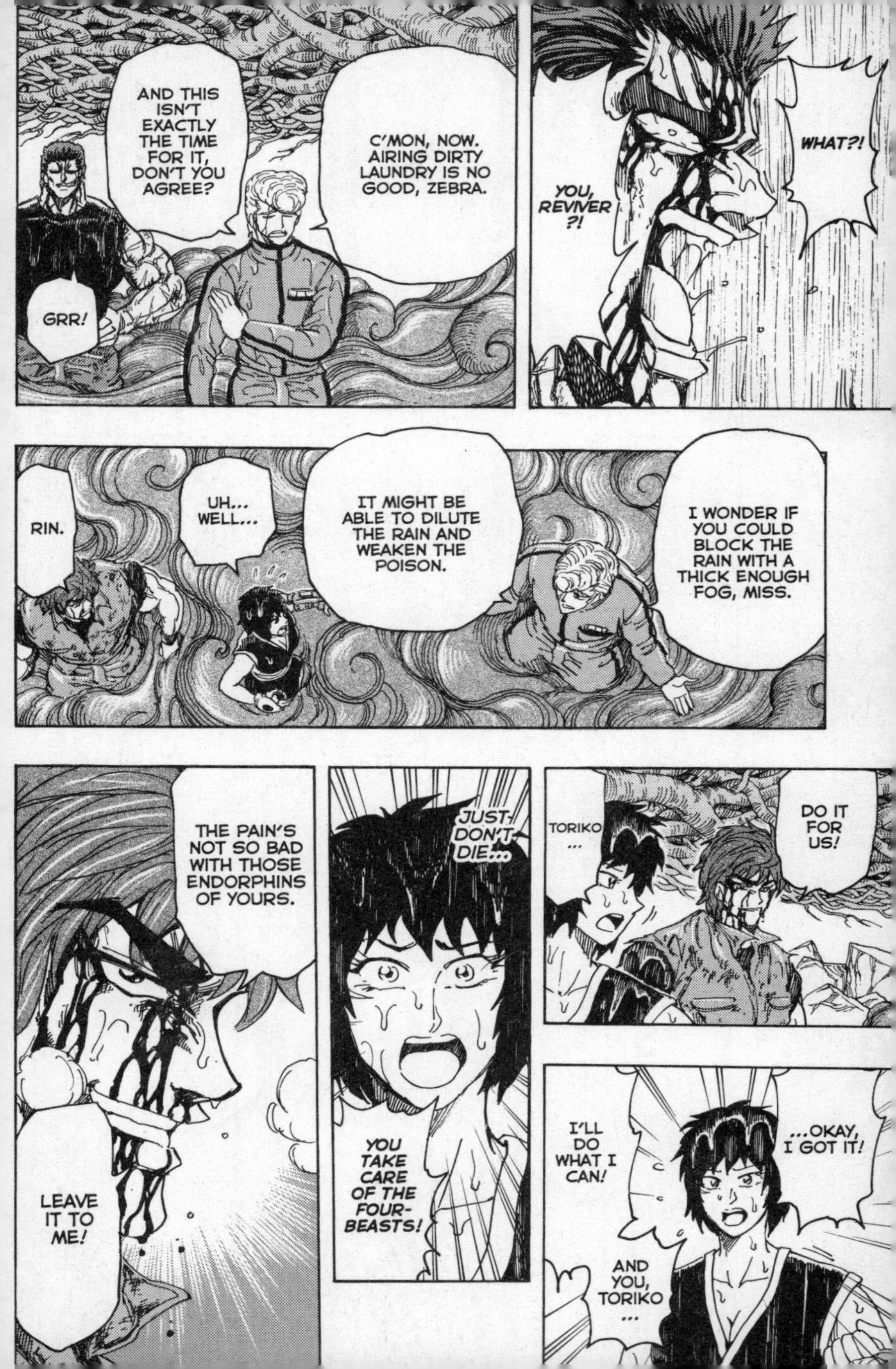
WHAT?!
YOU, REVIVER?!
C'MON, NOW. AIRING DIRTY LAUNDRY IS NO GOOD, ZEBRA.
AND THIS ISN'T EXACTLY THE TIME FOR IT, DON'T YOU AGREE?
GRR!
I WONDER IF YOU COULD BLOCK THE RAIN WITH A THICK ENOUGH FOG, MISS.
IT MIGHT BE ABLE TO DILUTE THE RAIN AND WEAKEN THE POISON.
UH... WELL...
RIN.
DO IT FOR US!
TORIKO...
...OKAY, I GOT IT!
I'LL DO WHAT I CAN!
AND YOU, TORIKO...
JUST DON'T DIE...
YOU TAKE CARE OF THE FOUR-BEASTS!
THE PAIN'S NOT SO BAD WITH THOSE ENDORPHINS OF YOURS.
LEAVE IT TO ME!

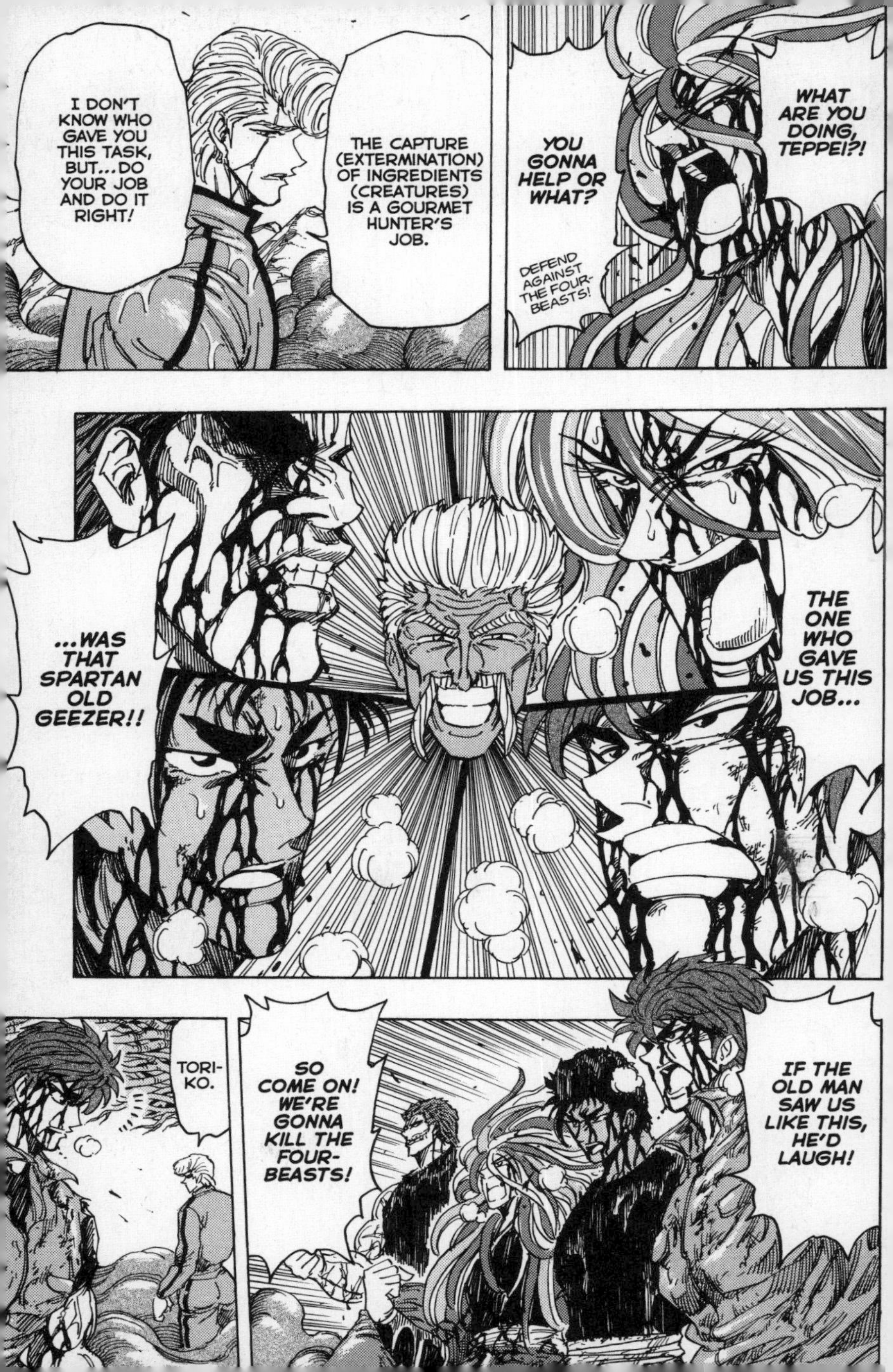
WHAT ARE YOU DOING, TEPPEI?!
YOU GONNA HELP OR WHAT?
DEFEND AGAINST THE FOUR-BEASTS!
THE CAPTURE (EXTERMINATION) OF INGREDIENTS (CREATURES) IS A GOURMET HUNTER'S JOB.
I DON'T KNOW WHO GAVE YOU THIS TASK, BUT...DO YOUR JOB AND DO IT RIGHT!
THE ONE WHO GAVE US THIS JOB...
...WAS THAT SPARTAN OLD GEEZER!!
IF THE OLD MAN SAW US LIKE THIS, HE'D LAUGH!
SO COME ON! WE'RE GONNA KILL THE FOUR-BEASTS!
TORI-KO.

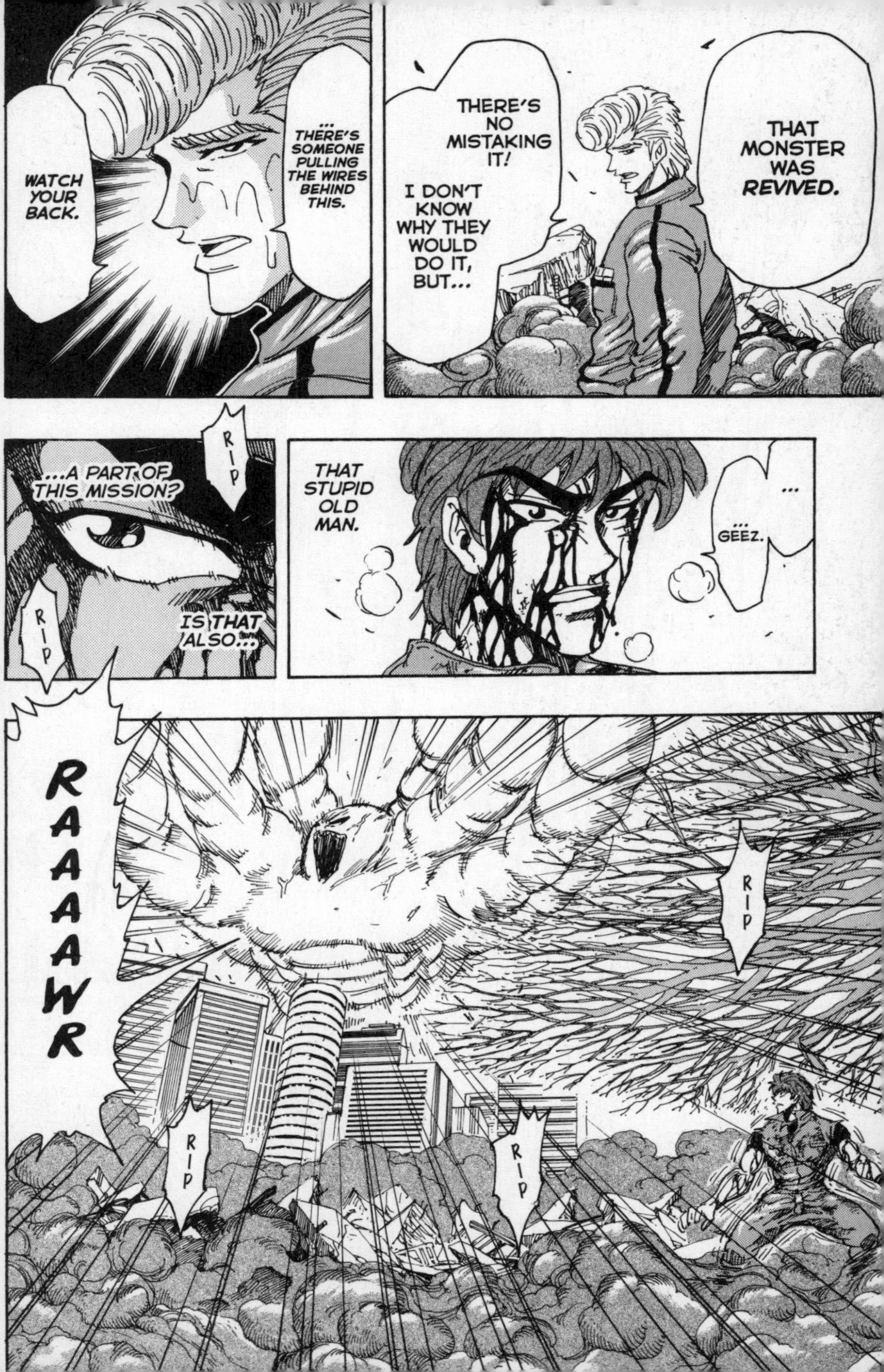
THAT MONSTER WAS REVIVED.
THERE'S NO MISTAKING IT!
I DON'T KNOW WHY THEY WOULD DO IT, BUT...
...THERE'S SOMEONE PULLING THE WIRES BEHIND THIS.
WATCH YOUR BACK.
...
...GEEZ.
THAT STUPID OLD MAN.
RIP
...A PART OF THIS MISSION?
RIP
IS THAT ALSO...
RIP
RAAAAAWR
RIP
RIP

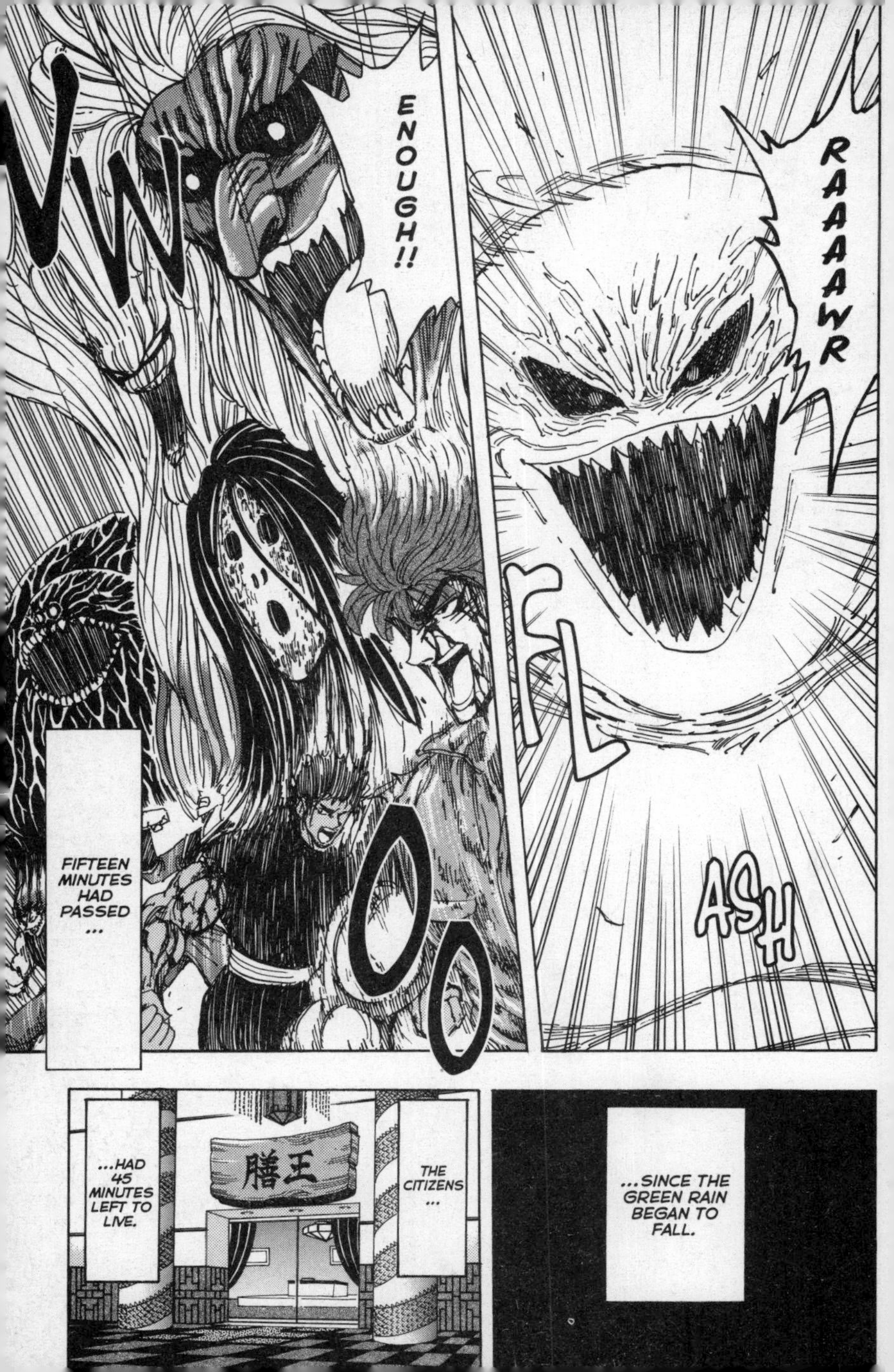
RAAAAAWR
FL
ASH
VW
ENOUGH!!
OO
FIFTEEN MINUTES HAD PASSED ...
...SINCE THE GREEN RAIN BEGAN TO FALL.
THE CITIZENS ...
膳王
...HAD 45 MINUTES LEFT TO LIVE.

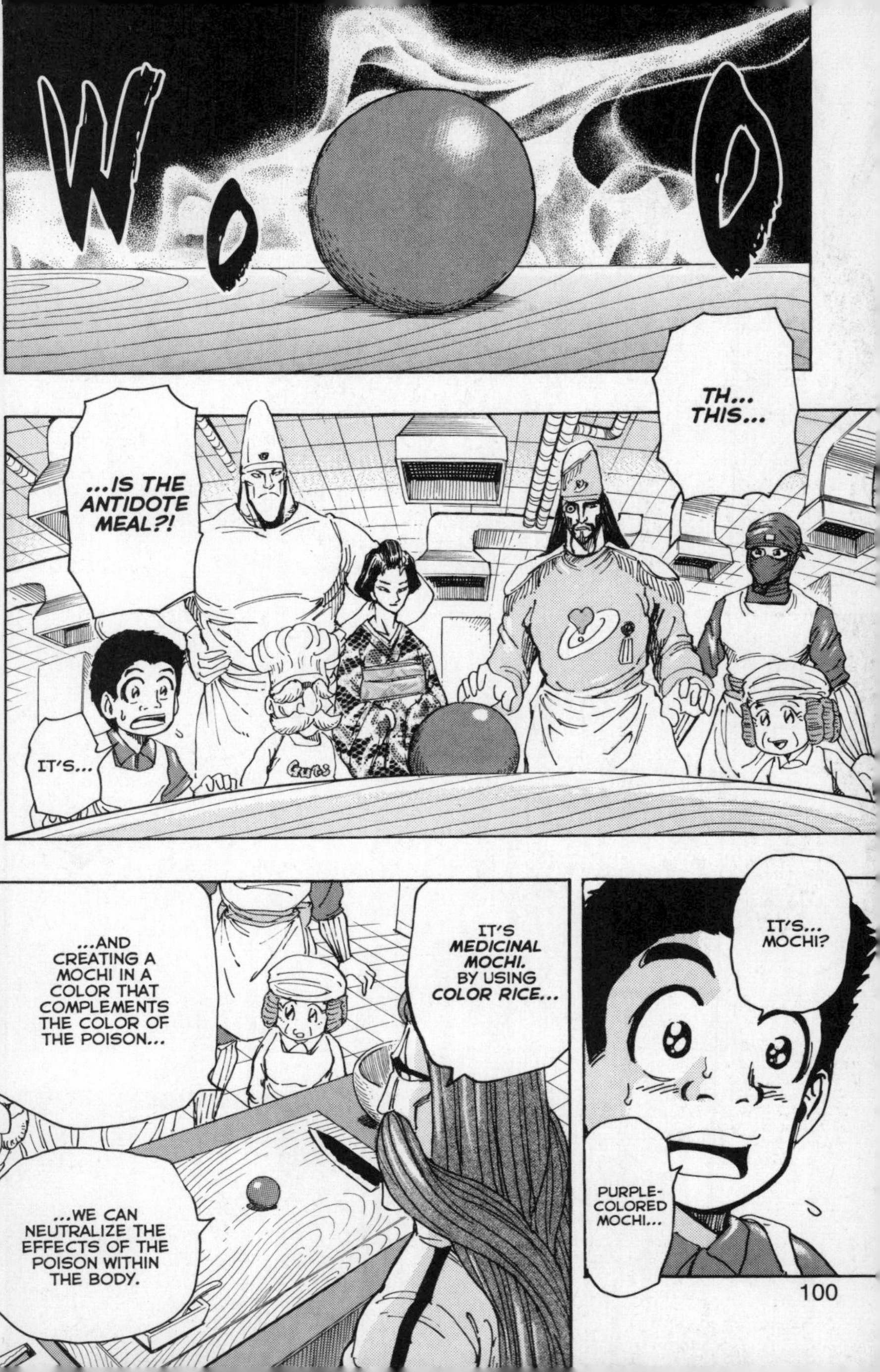
WOO
TH... THIS...
...IS THE ANTIDOTE MEAL?!
IT'S...
IT'S... MOCHI?
PURPLE-COLORED MOCHI...
IT'S MEDICINAL MOCHI. BY USING COLOR RICE...
...AND CREATING A MOCHI IN A COLOR THAT COMPLEMENTS THE COLOR OF THE POISON...
...WE CAN NEUTRALIZE THE EFFECTS OF THE POISON WITHIN THE BODY.

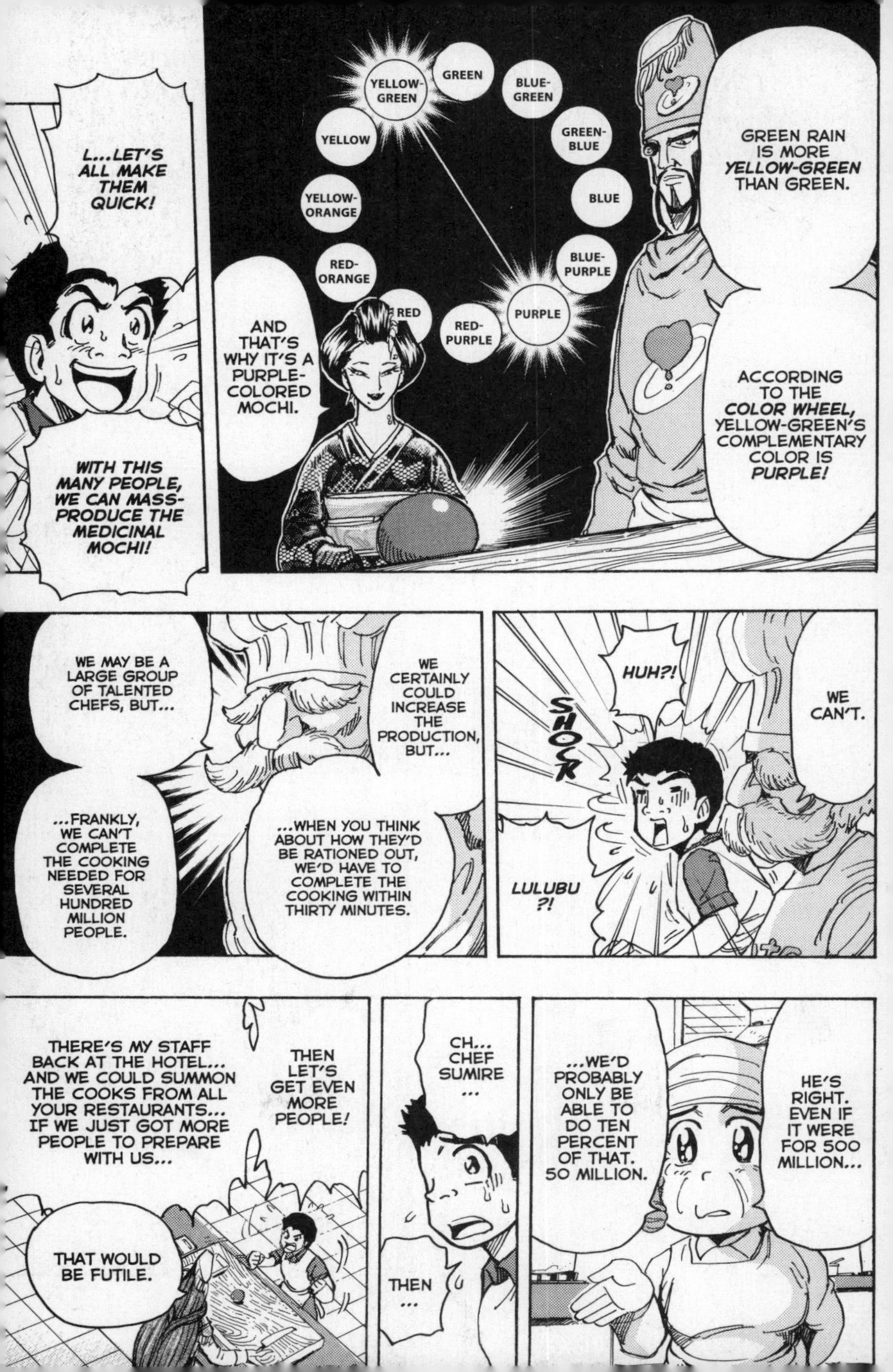
GREEN RAIN IS MORE *YELLOW-GREEN* THAN GREEN.
ACCORDING TO THE *COLOR WHEEL*, YELLOW-GREEN'S COMPLEMENTARY COLOR IS *PURPLE!*
YELLOW-GREEN
GREEN
BLUE-GREEN
GREEN-BLUE
BLUE
BLUE-PURPLE
PURPLE
RED-PURPLE
RED
RED-ORANGE
YELLOW-ORANGE
YELLOW
AND THAT'S WHY IT'S A PURPLE-COLORED MOCHI.
L...LET'S ALL MAKE THEM QUICK!
WITH THIS MANY PEOPLE, WE CAN MASS-PRODUCE THE MEDICINAL MOCHI!
WE CAN'T.
HUH?!
SHOCK
LULUBU ?!
WE CERTAINLY COULD INCREASE THE PRODUCTION, BUT...
...WHEN YOU THINK ABOUT HOW THEY'D BE RATIONED OUT, WE'D HAVE TO COMPLETE THE COOKING WITHIN THIRTY MINUTES.
WE MAY BE A LARGE GROUP OF TALENTED CHEFS, BUT...
...FRANKLY, WE CAN'T COMPLETE THE COOKING NEEDED FOR SEVERAL HUNDRED MILLION PEOPLE.
HE'S RIGHT. EVEN IF IT WERE FOR 500 MILLION...
...WE'D PROBABLY ONLY BE ABLE TO DO TEN PERCENT OF THAT. 50 MILLION.
CH... CHEF SUMIRE ...
THEN ...
THEN LET'S GET EVEN MORE PEOPLE!
THERE'S MY STAFF BACK AT THE HOTEL... AND WE COULD SUMMON THE COOKS FROM ALL YOUR RESTAURANTS... IF WE JUST GOT MORE PEOPLE TO PREPARE WITH US...
THAT WOULD BE FUTILE.

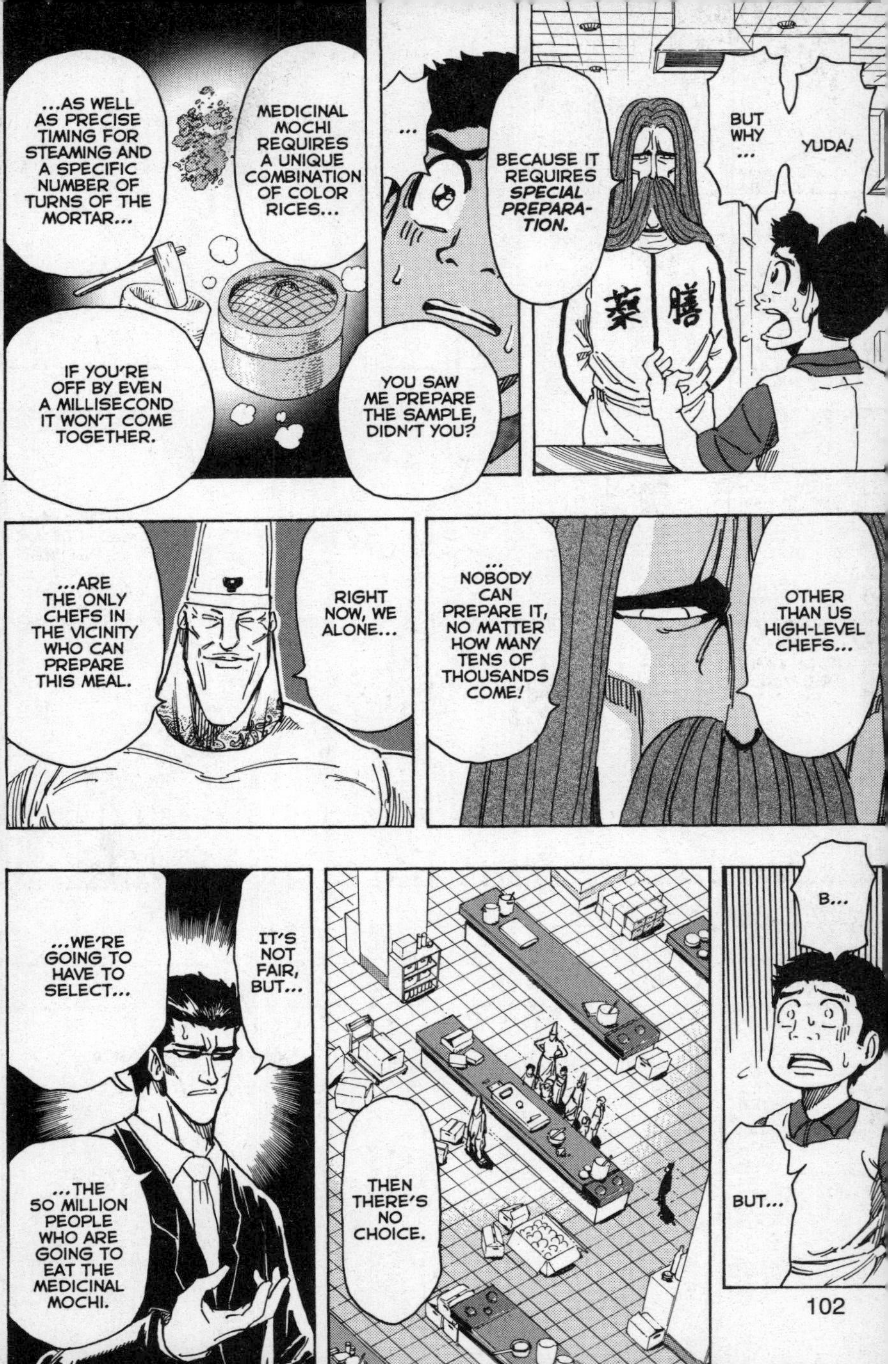
BUT WHY ...
YUDA!
BECAUSE IT REQUIRES *SPECIAL PREPARATION.*
...
YOU SAW ME PREPARE THE SAMPLE, DIDN'T YOU?
MEDICINAL MOCHI REQUIRES A UNIQUE COMBINATION OF COLOR RICES...
...AS WELL AS PRECISE TIMING FOR STEAMING AND A SPECIFIC NUMBER OF TURNS OF THE MORTAR...
IF YOU'RE OFF BY EVEN A MILLISECOND IT WON'T COME TOGETHER.
OTHER THAN US HIGH-LEVEL CHEFS...
... NOBODY CAN PREPARE IT, NO MATTER HOW MANY TENS OF THOUSANDS COME!
RIGHT NOW, WE ALONE...
...ARE THE ONLY CHEFS IN THE VICINITY WHO CAN PREPARE THIS MEAL.
B...
BUT...
THEN THERE'S NO CHOICE.
IT'S NOT FAIR, BUT...
...WE'RE GOING TO HAVE TO SELECT...
...THE 50 MILLION PEOPLE WHO ARE GOING TO EAT THE MEDICINAL MOCHI.

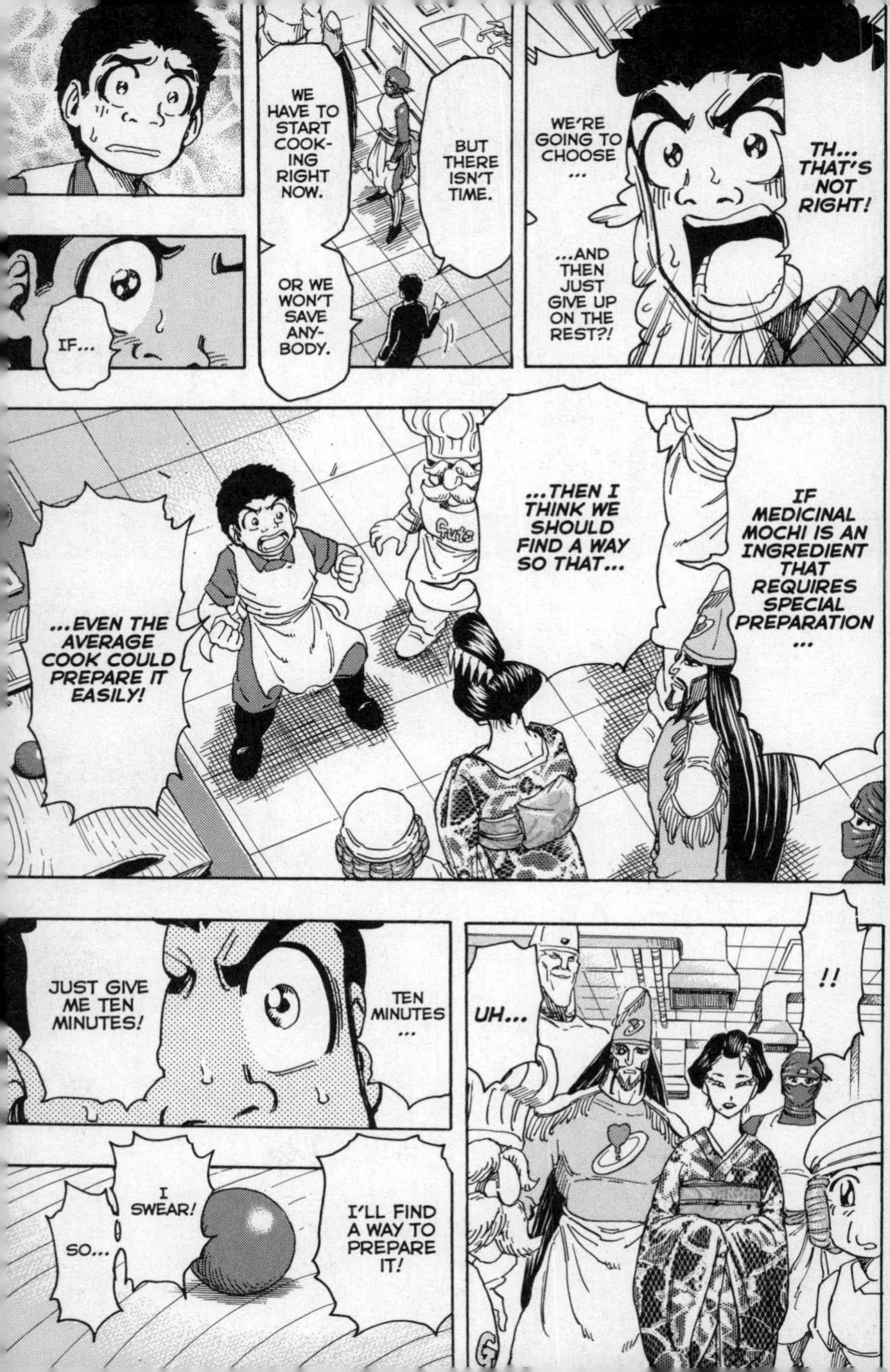
WE'RE GOING TO CHOOSE ...
...AND THEN JUST GIVE UP ON THE REST?!
TH... THAT'S NOT RIGHT!
WE HAVE TO START COOK-ING RIGHT NOW.
BUT THERE ISN'T TIME.
OR WE WON'T SAVE ANY-BODY.
IF...
IF MEDICINAL MOCHI IS AN INGREDIENT THAT REQUIRES SPECIAL PREPARATION ...
...THEN I THINK WE SHOULD FIND A WAY SO THAT...
...EVEN THE AVERAGE COOK COULD PREPARE IT EASILY!
!!
UH...
TEN MINUTES ...
JUST GIVE ME TEN MINUTES!
I'LL FIND A WAY TO PREPARE IT!
I SWEAR!
SO...

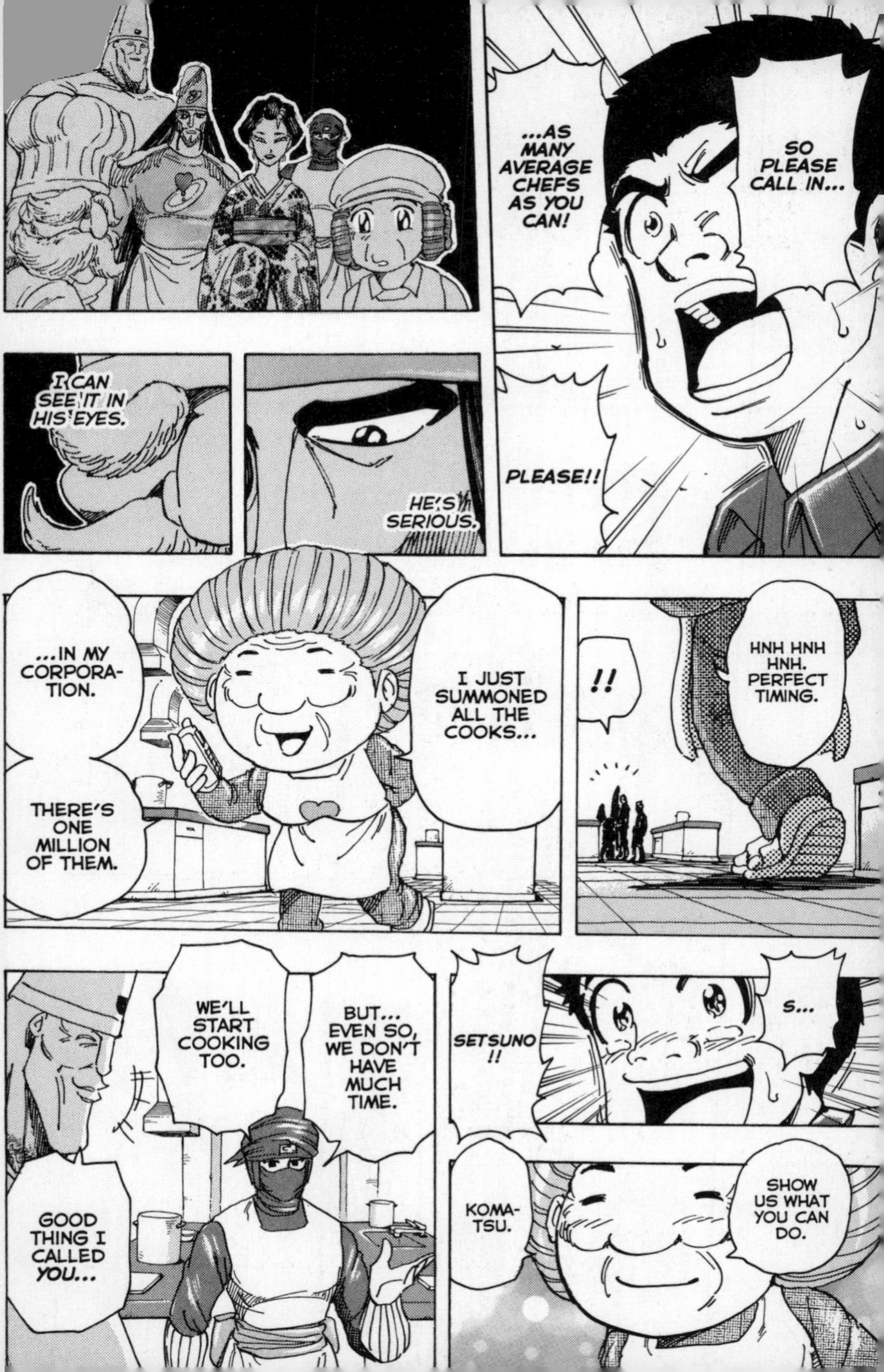
SO PLEASE CALL IN...
...AS MANY AVERAGE CHEFS AS YOU CAN!
PLEASE!!
HE'S SERIOUS.
I CAN SEE IT IN HIS EYES.
HNH HNH HNH. PERFECT TIMING.
!!
I JUST SUMMONED ALL THE COOKS...
...IN MY CORPORATION.
THERE'S ONE MILLION OF THEM.
S...
SETSUNO!!
SHOW US WHAT YOU CAN DO.
KOMATSU.
BUT... EVEN SO, WE DON'T HAVE MUCH TIME.
WE'LL START COOKING TOO.
GOOD THING I CALLED YOU...

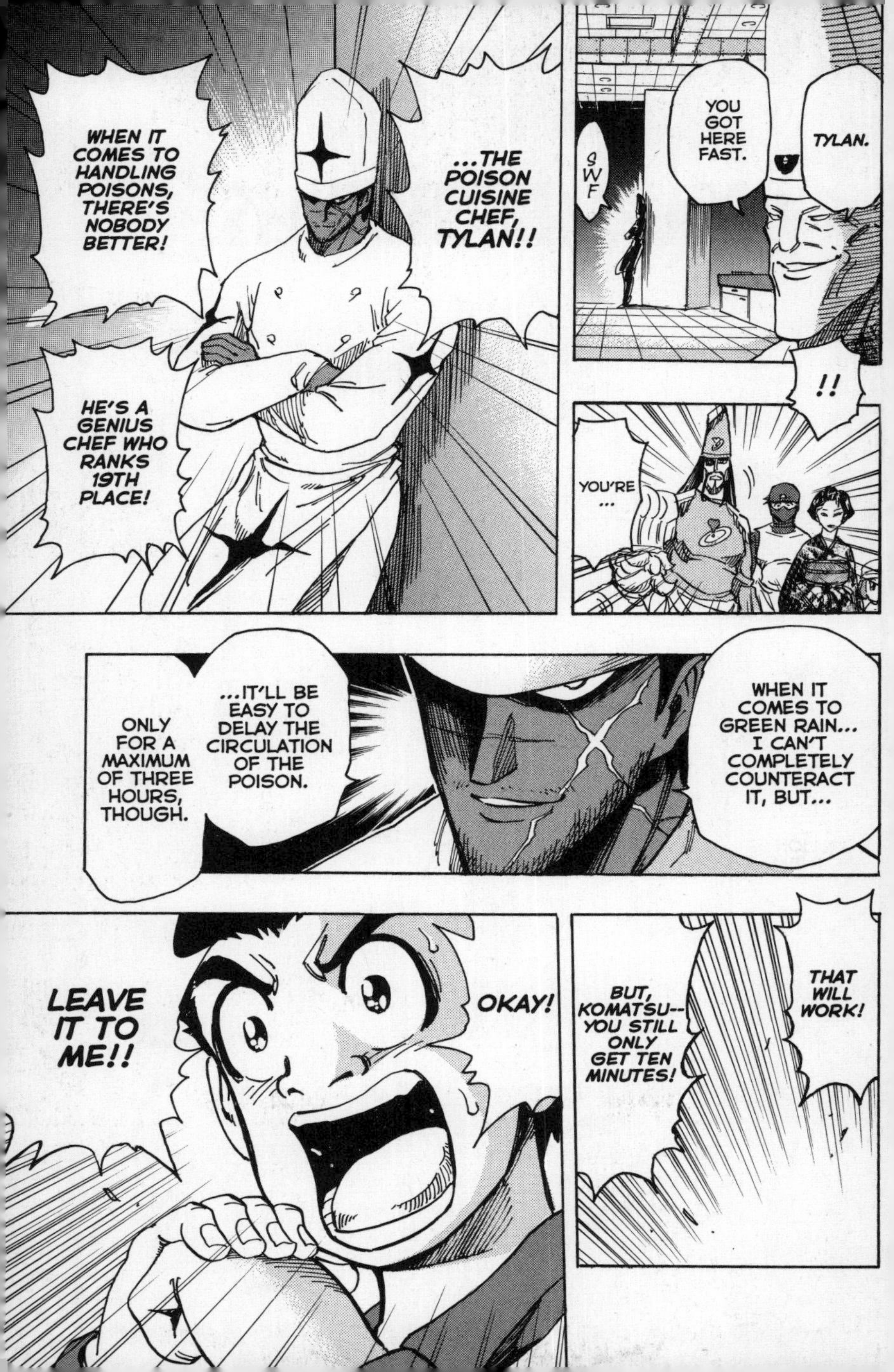
TYLAN.
YOU GOT HERE FAST.
SWF
!!
YOU'RE ...
...THE POISON CUISINE CHEF, TYLAN!!
WHEN IT COMES TO HANDLING POISONS, THERE'S NOBODY BETTER!
HE'S A GENIUS CHEF WHO RANKS 19TH PLACE!
WHEN IT COMES TO GREEN RAIN... I CAN'T COMPLETELY COUNTERACT IT, BUT...
...IT'LL BE EASY TO DELAY THE CIRCULATION OF THE POISON.
ONLY FOR A MAXIMUM OF THREE HOURS, THOUGH.
THAT WILL WORK!
BUT, KOMATSU-- YOU STILL ONLY GET TEN MINUTES!
OKAY!
LEAVE IT TO ME!!

TORIKO

GOURMET CHECKLIST

Vol. 239

SMASHROOM
(MUSHROOM)

CAPTURE LEVEL: 15
HABITAT: TROPICAL RAINFORESTS
LENGTH: 15 CM
HEIGHT: ---
WEIGHT: 180 G
PRICE: 20,000 YEN

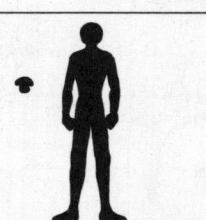

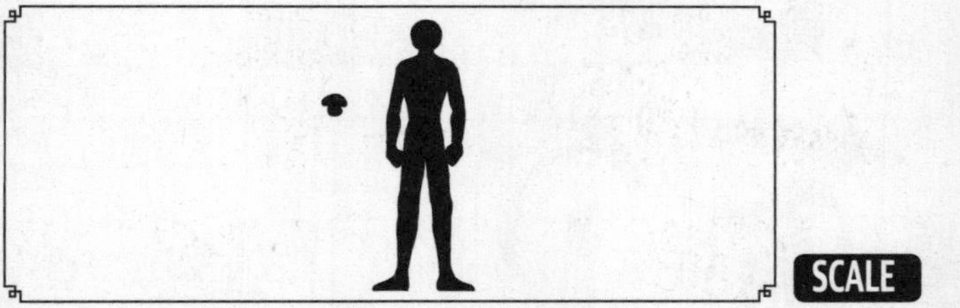

SCALE

A FUNGUS THAT RELEASES SPICE SPORES WHEN STRUCK. A MATURE SHROOM DISPLAYS A POLKA DOT PATTERN ON ITS CAP. THE NUMBER OF DOTS INDICATE HOW MANY SPICE SPORES IT WILL RELEASE. THE MORE SPICE SPORES, THE BETTER THE TASTE THAT WILL ACCOMPANY THE CHEWY TEXTURE! HOWEVER, BECAUSE THE EXTERIOR IS SO TOUGH, IT TAKES A POWERFUL BLOW TO MAKE A SIZABLE AMOUNT OF SPICE SPORES RELEASE.

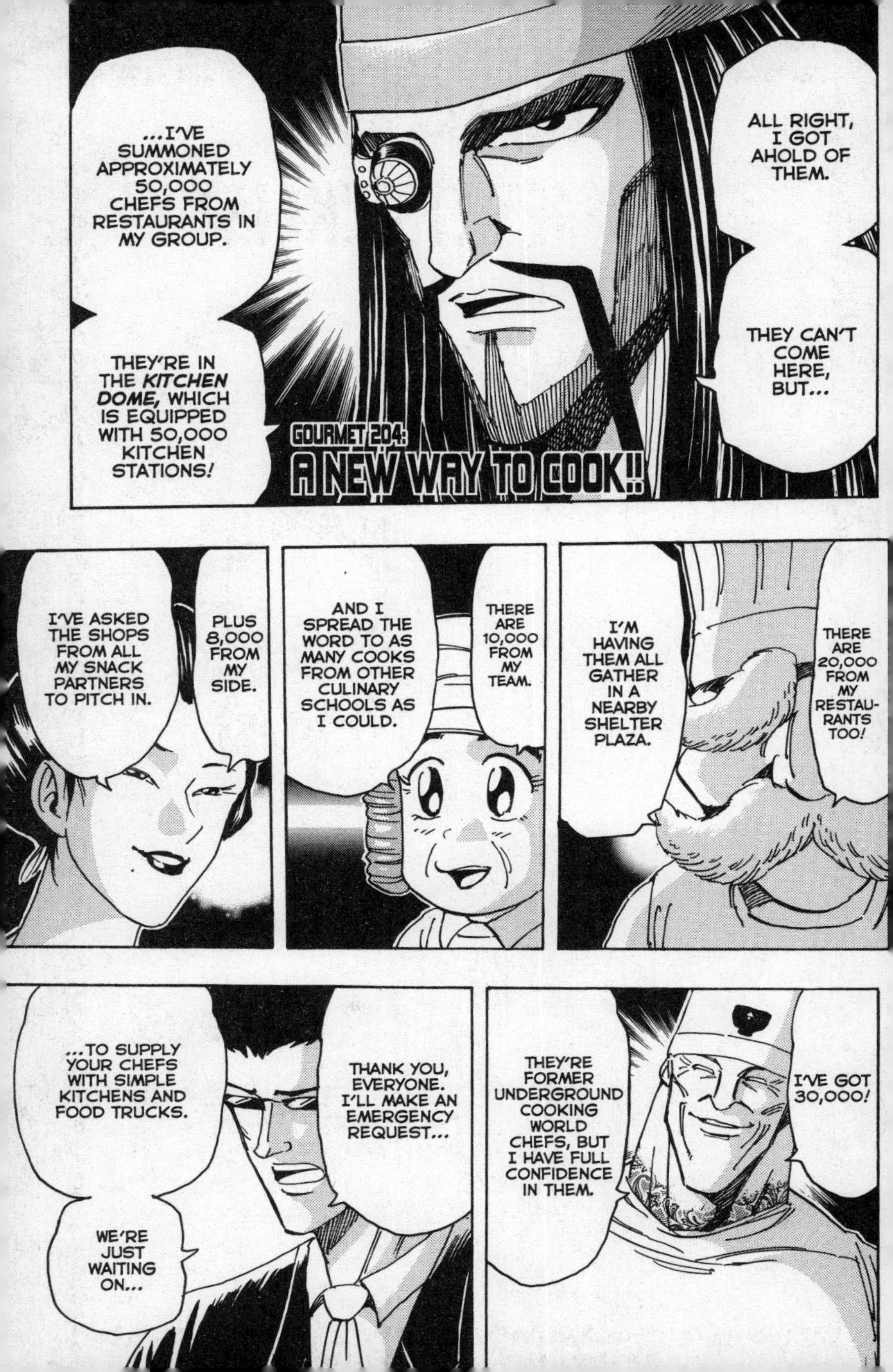
ALL RIGHT, I GOT AHOLD OF THEM.
THEY CAN'T COME HERE, BUT...
...I'VE SUMMONED APPROXIMATELY 50,000 CHEFS FROM RESTAURANTS IN MY GROUP.
THEY'RE IN THE *KITCHEN DOME,* WHICH IS EQUIPPED WITH 50,000 KITCHEN STATIONS!
GOURMET 204:
A NEW WAY TO COOK!!
THERE ARE 20,000 FROM MY RESTAU-RANTS TOO!
I'M HAVING THEM ALL GATHER IN A NEARBY SHELTER PLAZA.
THERE ARE 10,000 FROM MY TEAM.
AND I SPREAD THE WORD TO AS MANY COOKS FROM OTHER CULINARY SCHOOLS AS I COULD.
PLUS 8,000 FROM MY SIDE.
I'VE ASKED THE SHOPS FROM ALL MY SNACK PARTNERS TO PITCH IN.
I'VE GOT 30,000!
THEY'RE FORMER UNDERGROUND COOKING WORLD CHEFS, BUT I HAVE FULL CONFIDENCE IN THEM.
THANK YOU, EVERYONE. I'LL MAKE AN EMERGENCY REQUEST...
...TO SUPPLY YOUR CHEFS WITH SIMPLE KITCHENS AND FOOD TRUCKS.
WE'RE JUST WAITING ON...

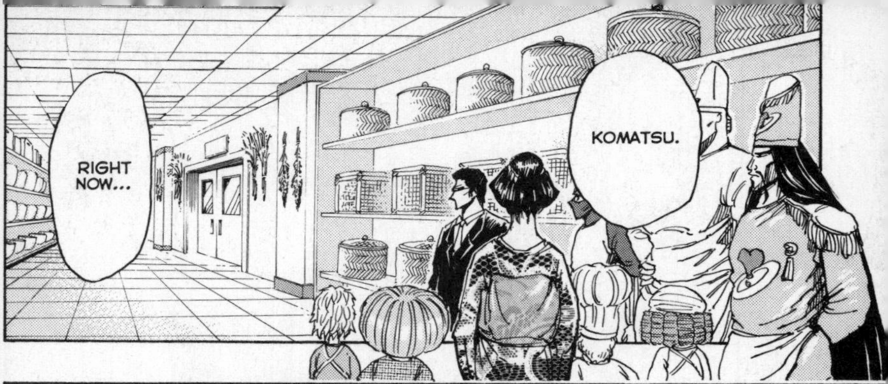
KOMATSU.
RIGHT NOW...

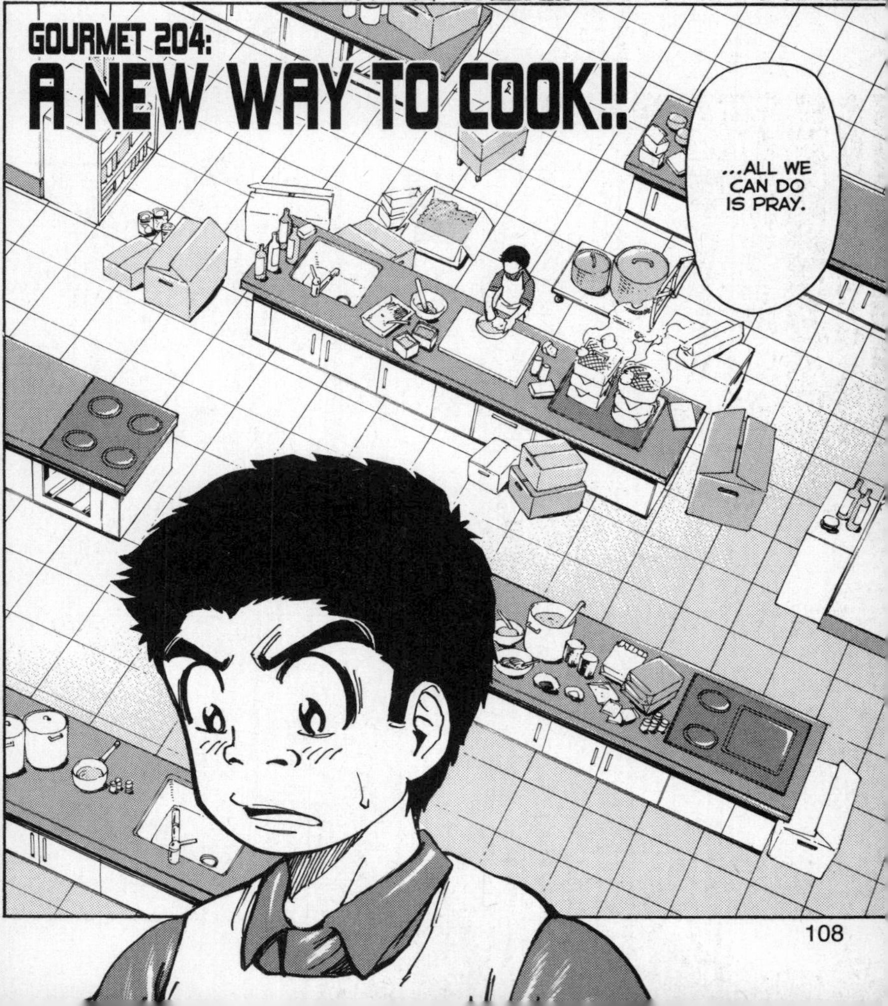
GOURMET 204:
A NEW WAY TO COOK!!
...ALL WE CAN DO IS PRAY.

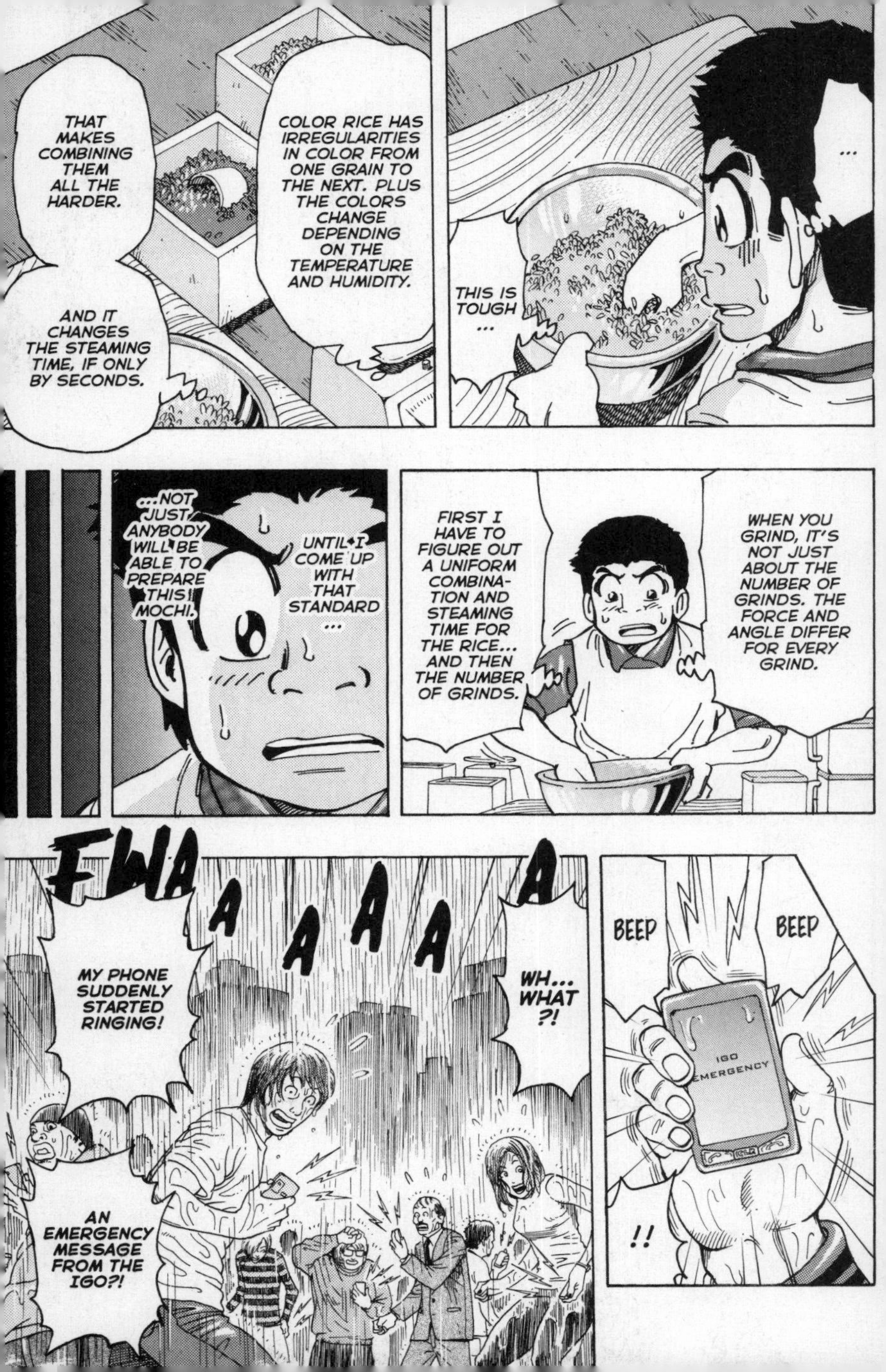
...
THIS IS TOUGH...
COLOR RICE HAS IRREGULARITIES IN COLOR FROM ONE GRAIN TO THE NEXT. PLUS THE COLORS CHANGE DEPENDING ON THE TEMPERATURE AND HUMIDITY.
THAT MAKES COMBINING THEM ALL THE HARDER.
AND IT CHANGES THE STEAMING TIME, IF ONLY BY SECONDS.
WHEN YOU GRIND, IT'S NOT JUST ABOUT THE NUMBER OF GRINDS. THE FORCE AND ANGLE DIFFER FOR EVERY GRIND.
FIRST I HAVE TO FIGURE OUT A UNIFORM COMBINATION AND STEAMING TIME FOR THE RICE... AND THEN THE NUMBER OF GRINDS.
UNTIL I COME UP WITH THAT STANDARD...
...NOT JUST ANYBODY WILL BE ABLE TO PREPARE THIS MOCHI.
BEEP
BEEP
IGO EMERGENCY
!!
EWAAAAAA
WH... WHAT?!
MY PHONE SUDDENLY STARTED RINGING!
AN EMERGENCY MESSAGE FROM THE IGO?!

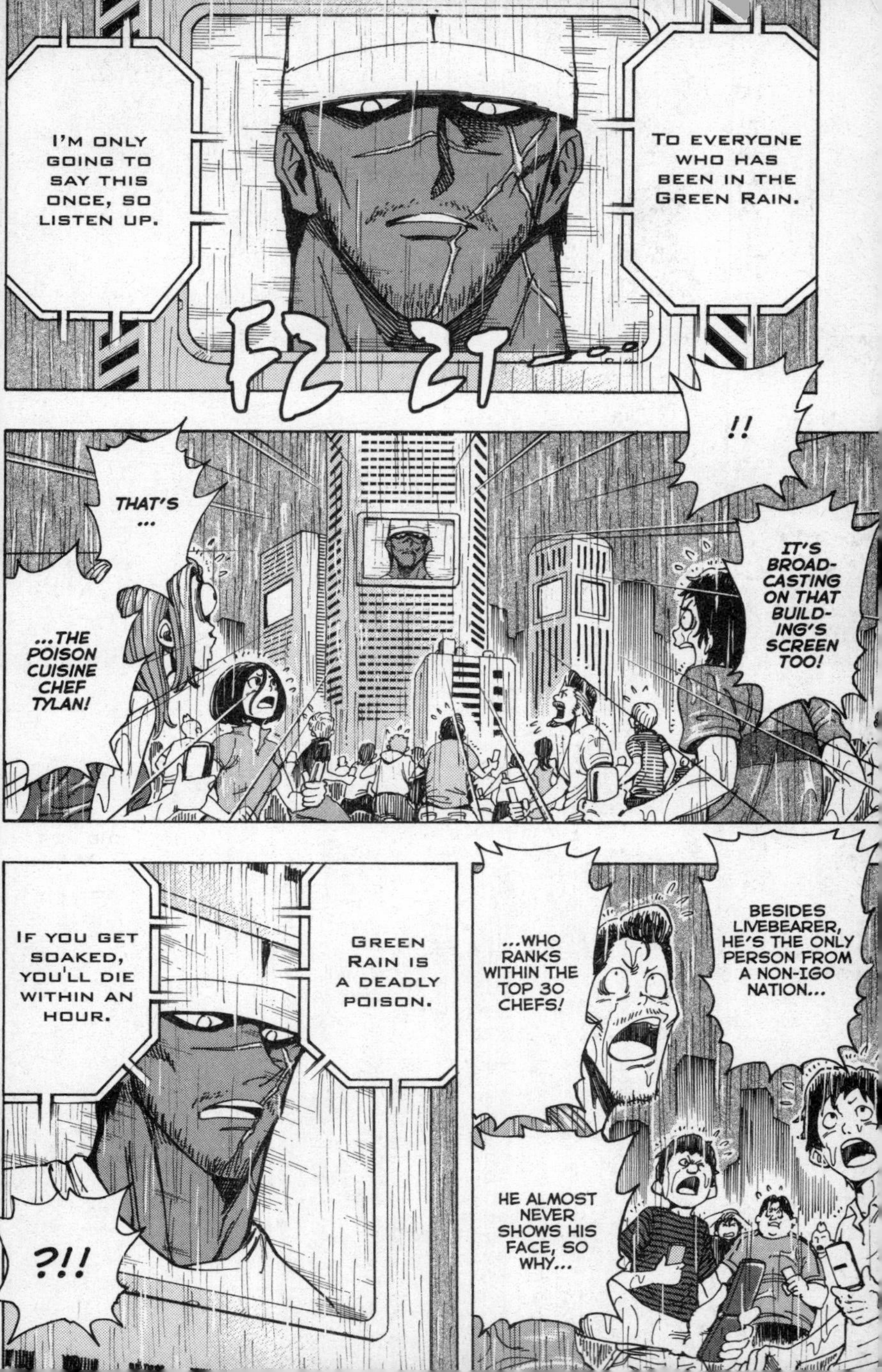
TO EVERYONE WHO HAS BEEN IN THE GREEN RAIN.
I'M ONLY GOING TO SAY THIS ONCE, SO LISTEN UP.
!!
IT'S BROAD-CASTING ON THAT BUILD-ING'S SCREEN TOO!
THAT'S ...
...THE POISON CUISINE CHEF TYLAN!
BESIDES LIVEBEARER, HE'S THE ONLY PERSON FROM A NON-IGO NATION...
...WHO RANKS WITHIN THE TOP 30 CHEFS!
HE ALMOST NEVER SHOWS HIS FACE, SO WHY...
GREEN RAIN IS A DEADLY POISON.
IF YOU GET SOAKED, YOU'LL DIE WITHIN AN HOUR.
?!!

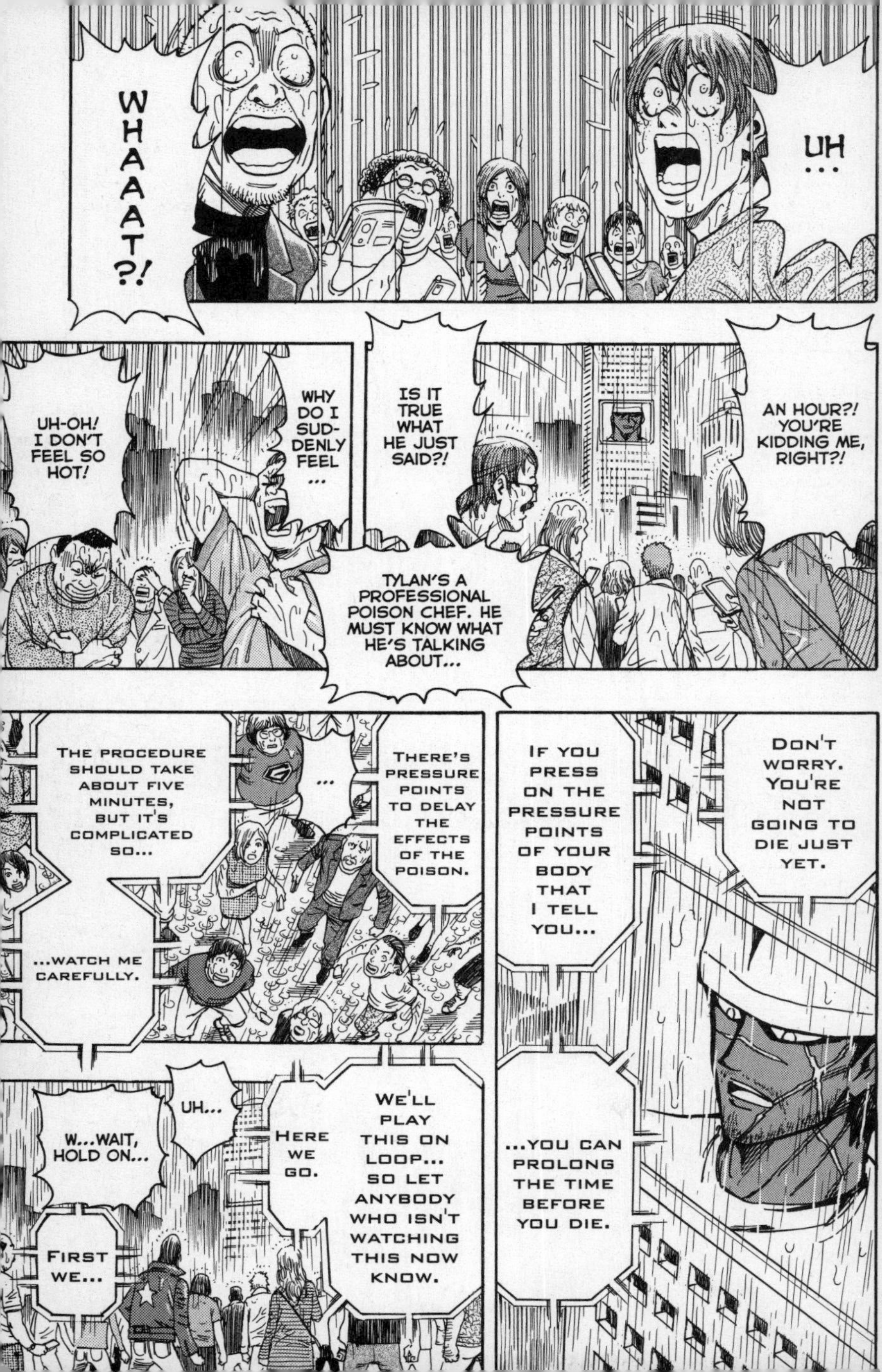
UH...
WHAAAT?!
AN HOUR?! YOU'RE KIDDING ME, RIGHT?!
IS IT TRUE WHAT HE JUST SAID?!
TYLAN'S A PROFESSIONAL POISON CHEF. HE MUST KNOW WHAT HE'S TALKING ABOUT...
WHY DO I SUD-DENLY FEEL...
UH-OH! I DON'T FEEL SO HOT!
DON'T WORRY. YOU'RE NOT GOING TO DIE JUST YET.
IF YOU PRESS ON THE PRESSURE POINTS OF YOUR BODY THAT I TELL YOU...
...YOU CAN PROLONG THE TIME BEFORE YOU DIE.
THERE'S PRESSURE POINTS TO DELAY THE EFFECTS OF THE POISON.
...
THE PROCEDURE SHOULD TAKE ABOUT FIVE MINUTES, BUT IT'S COMPLICATED SO...
...WATCH ME CAREFULLY.
WE'LL PLAY THIS ON LOOP... SO LET ANYBODY WHO ISN'T WATCHING THIS NOW KNOW.
HERE WE GO.
UH...
W...WAIT, HOLD ON...
FIRST WE...

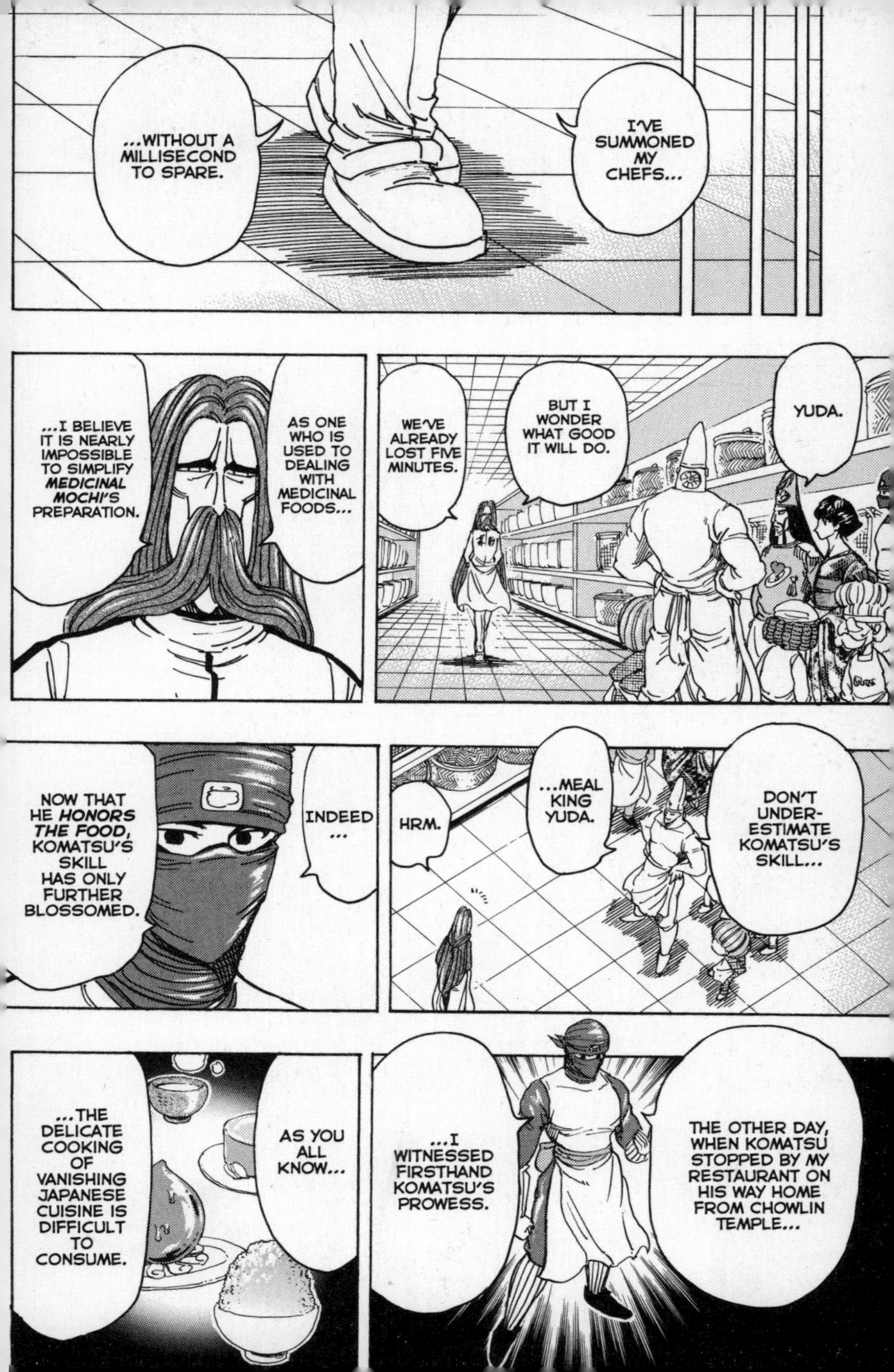
I'VE SUMMONED MY CHEFS...
...WITHOUT A MILLISECOND TO SPARE.
YUDA.
BUT I WONDER WHAT GOOD IT WILL DO.
WE'VE ALREADY LOST FIVE MINUTES.
AS ONE WHO IS USED TO DEALING WITH MEDICINAL FOODS...
...I BELIEVE IT IS NEARLY IMPOSSIBLE TO SIMPLIFY *MEDICINAL MOCHI*'S PREPARATION.
DON'T UNDER-ESTIMATE KOMATSU'S SKILL...
...MEAL KING YUDA.
HRM.
INDEED...
NOW THAT HE *HONORS THE FOOD*, KOMATSU'S SKILL HAS ONLY FURTHER BLOSSOMED.
THE OTHER DAY, WHEN KOMATSU STOPPED BY MY RESTAURANT ON HIS WAY HOME FROM CHOWLIN TEMPLE...
...I WITNESSED FIRSTHAND KOMATSU'S PROWESS.
AS YOU ALL KNOW...
...THE DELICATE COOKING OF VANISHING JAPANESE CUISINE IS DIFFICULT TO CONSUME.

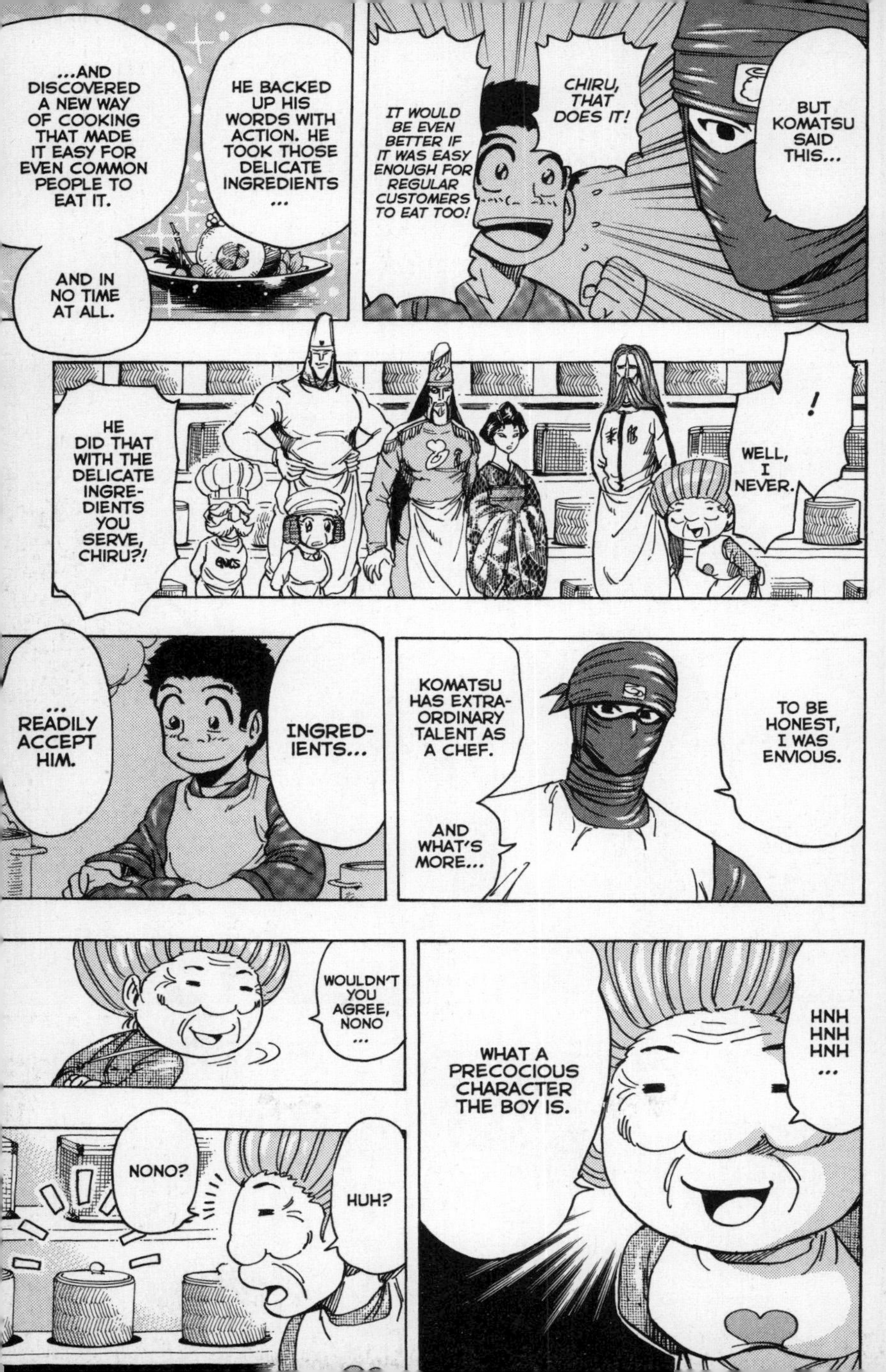
BUT KOMATSU SAID THIS...
CHIRU, THAT DOES IT!
IT WOULD BE EVEN BETTER IF IT WAS EASY ENOUGH FOR REGULAR CUSTOMERS TO EAT TOO!
HE BACKED UP HIS WORDS WITH ACTION. HE TOOK THOSE DELICATE INGREDIENTS ...
...AND DISCOVERED A NEW WAY OF COOKING THAT MADE IT EASY FOR EVEN COMMON PEOPLE TO EAT IT.
AND IN NO TIME AT ALL.
!
WELL, I NEVER.
HE DID THAT WITH THE DELICATE INGRE-DIENTS YOU SERVE, CHIRU?!
TO BE HONEST, I WAS ENVIOUS.
KOMATSU HAS EXTRA-ORDINARY TALENT AS A CHEF.
AND WHAT'S MORE...
INGRED-IENTS...
... READILY ACCEPT HIM.
HNH HNH HNH ...
WHAT A PRECOCIOUS CHARACTER THE BOY IS.
WOULDN'T YOU AGREE, NONO ...
HUH?
NONO?

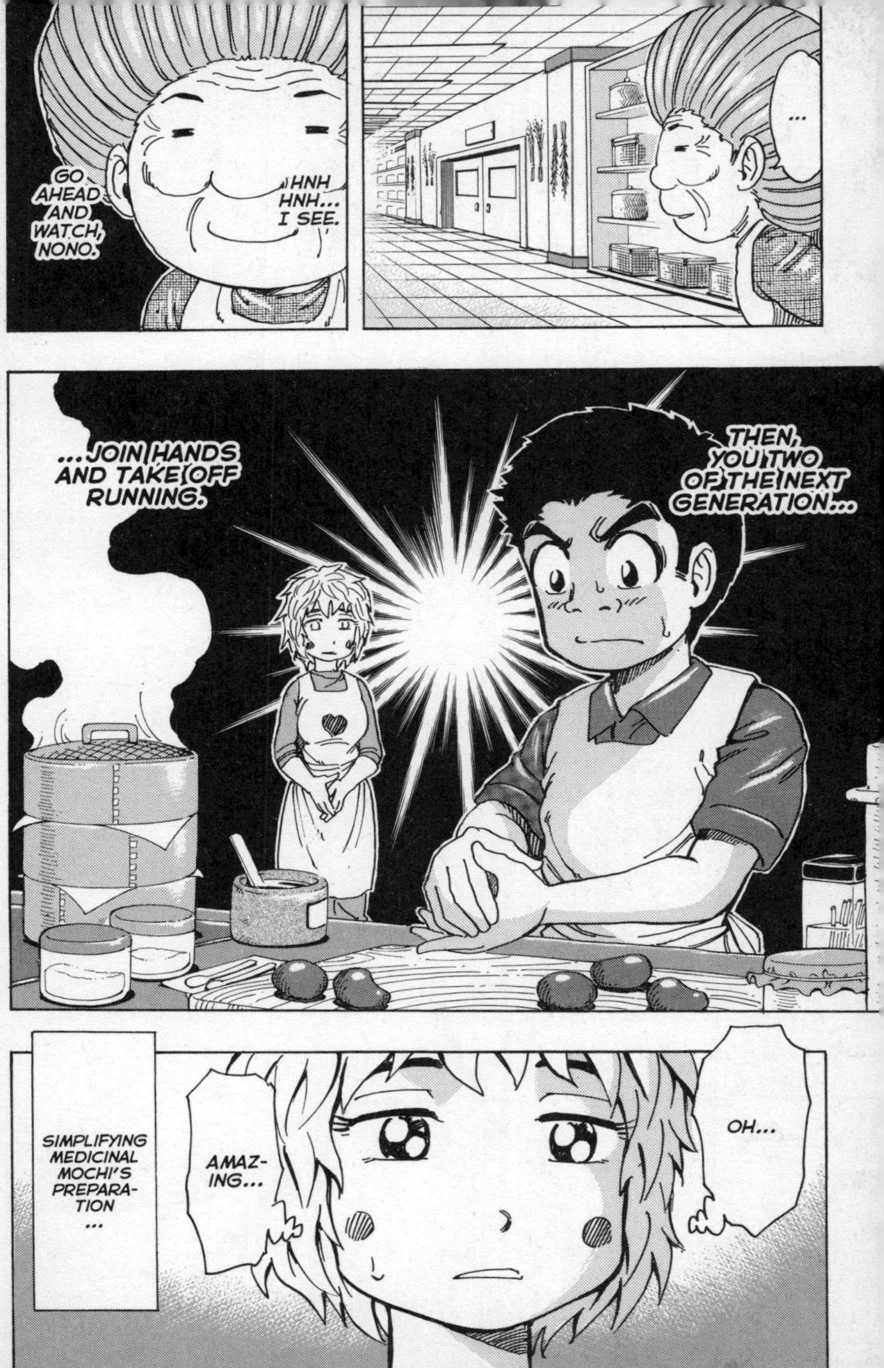
...
HNH HNH... I SEE.
GO AHEAD AND WATCH, NONO.
THEN, YOU TWO OF THE NEXT GENERATION...
...JOIN HANDS AND TAKE OFF RUNNING.
OH...
AMAZ-ING...
SIMPLIFYING MEDICINAL MOCHI'S PREPARA-TION ...

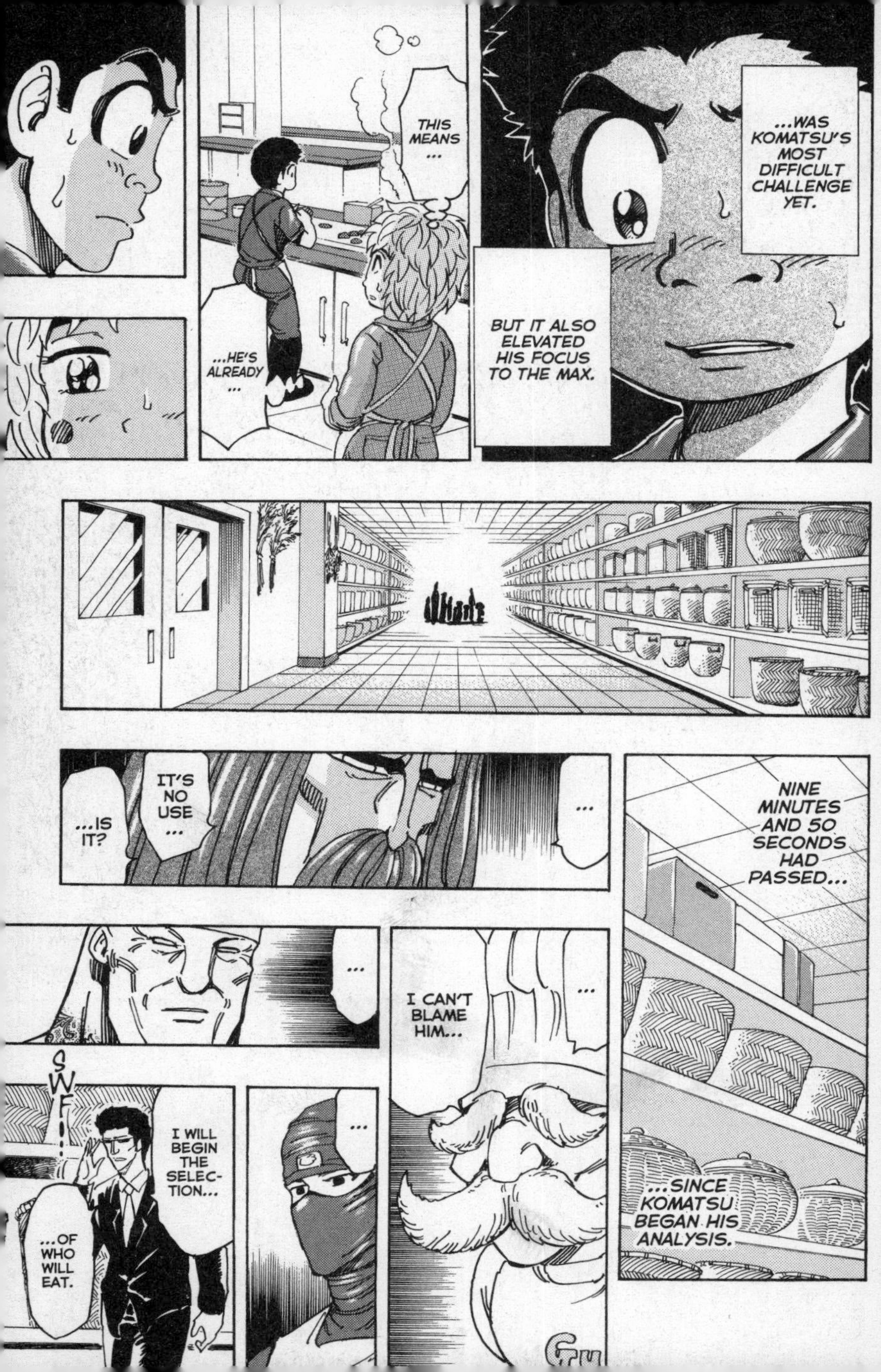
...WAS KOMATSU'S MOST DIFFICULT CHALLENGE YET.
BUT IT ALSO ELEVATED HIS FOCUS TO THE MAX.
THIS MEANS ...
...HE'S ALREADY ...
NINE MINUTES AND 50 SECONDS HAD PASSED...
...SINCE KOMATSU BEGAN HIS ANALYSIS.
...
IT'S NO USE ...
...IS IT?
...
I CAN'T BLAME HIM...
...
...
SWF
I WILL BEGIN THE SELECTION...
...OF WHO WILL EAT.

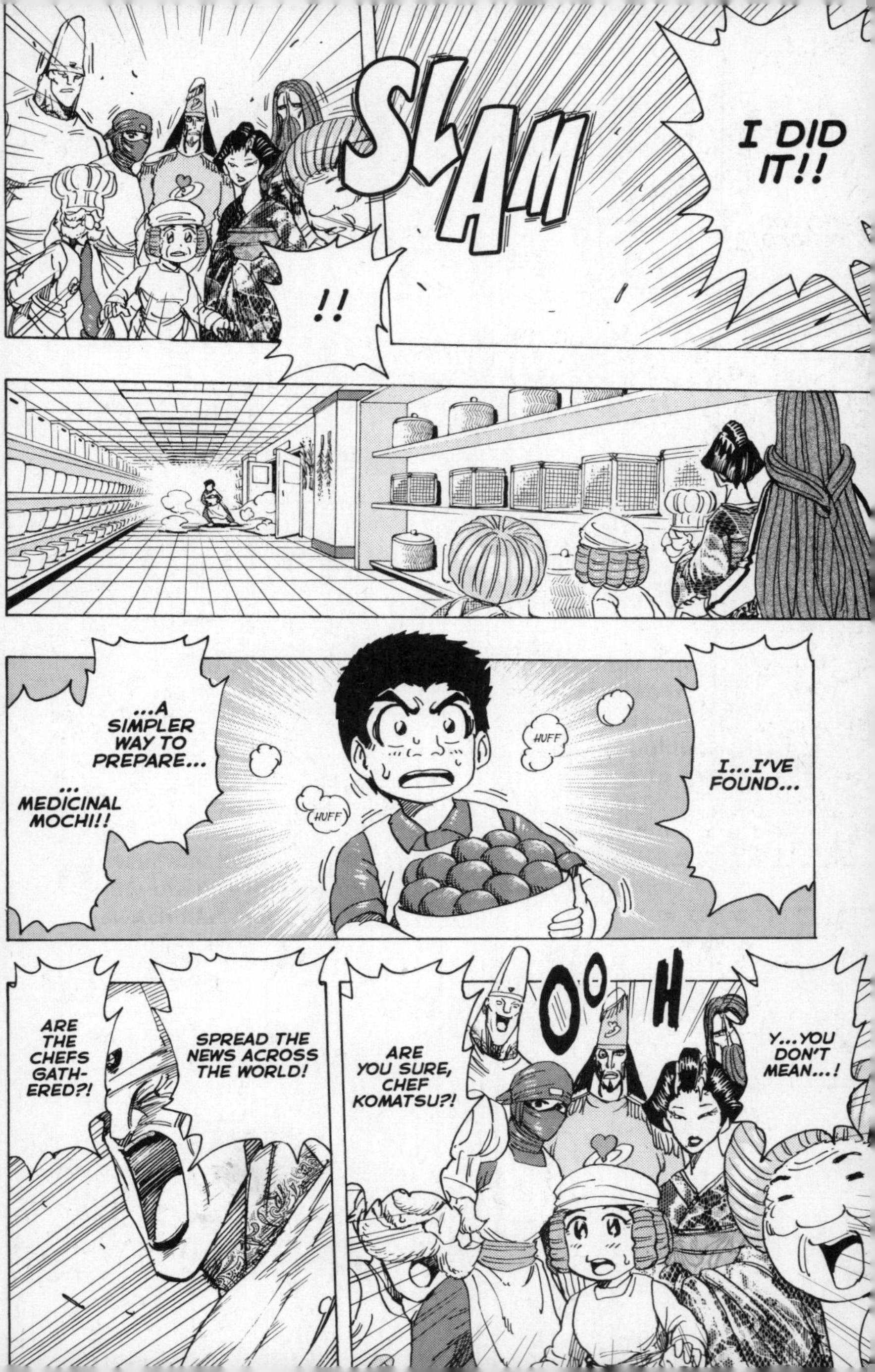
I DID IT!!
SLAM
!!
I...I'VE FOUND...
...A SIMPLER WAY TO PREPARE...
... MEDICINAL MOCHI!!
HUFF
HUFF
Y...YOU DON'T MEAN...!
OOH
ARE YOU SURE, CHEF KOMATSU?!
SPREAD THE NEWS ACROSS THE WORLD!
ARE THE CHEFS GATH-ERED?!

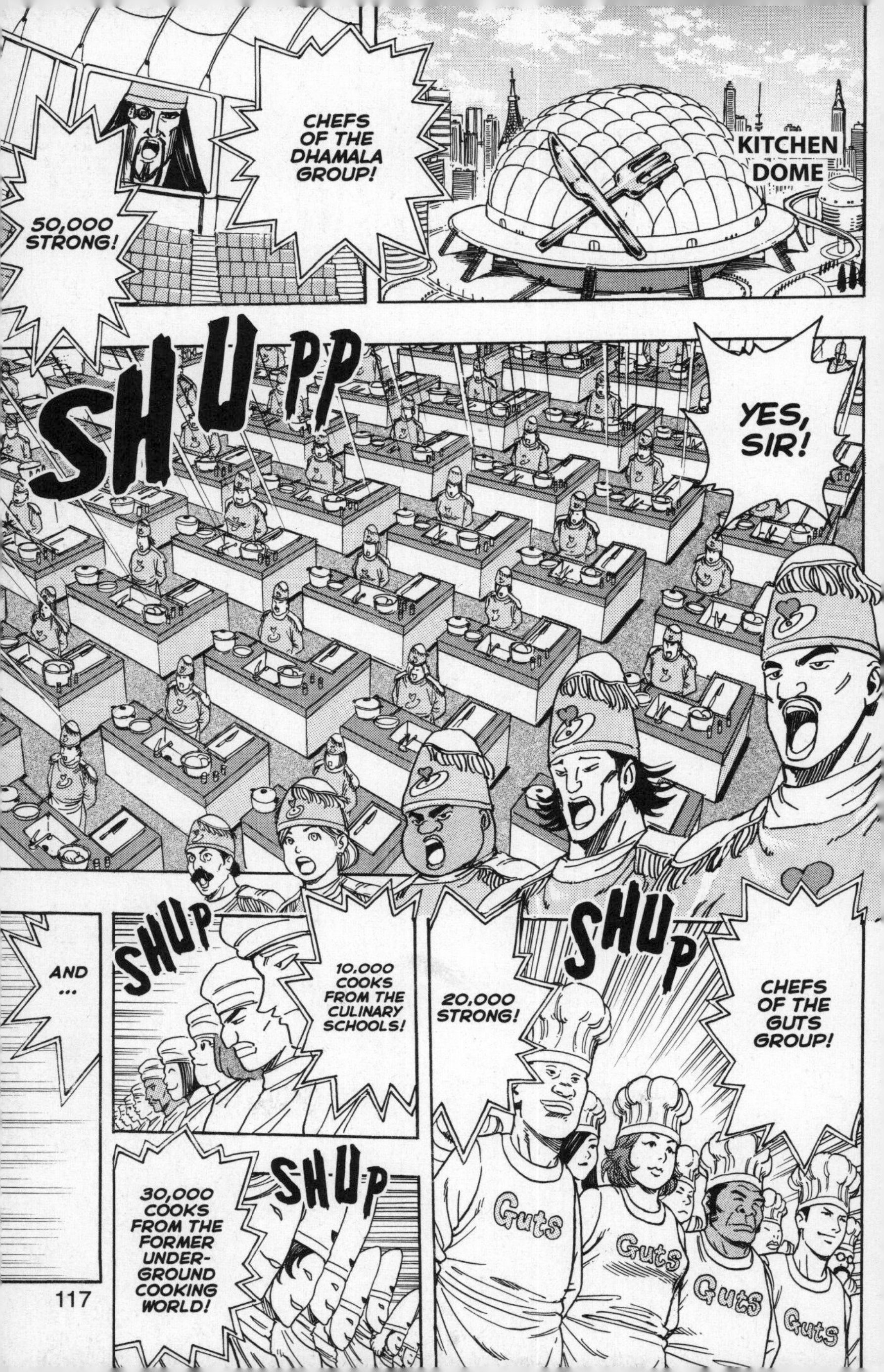
KITCHEN DOME
CHEFS OF THE DHAMALA GROUP!
50,000 STRONG!
YES, SIR!
SHUPP
CHEFS OF THE GUTS GROUP!
20,000 STRONG!
SHUP
10,000 COOKS FROM THE CULINARY SCHOOLS!
SHUP
AND ...
SHUP
30,000 COOKS FROM THE FORMER UNDER-GROUND COOKING WORLD!
Guts
Guts
Guts
Guts

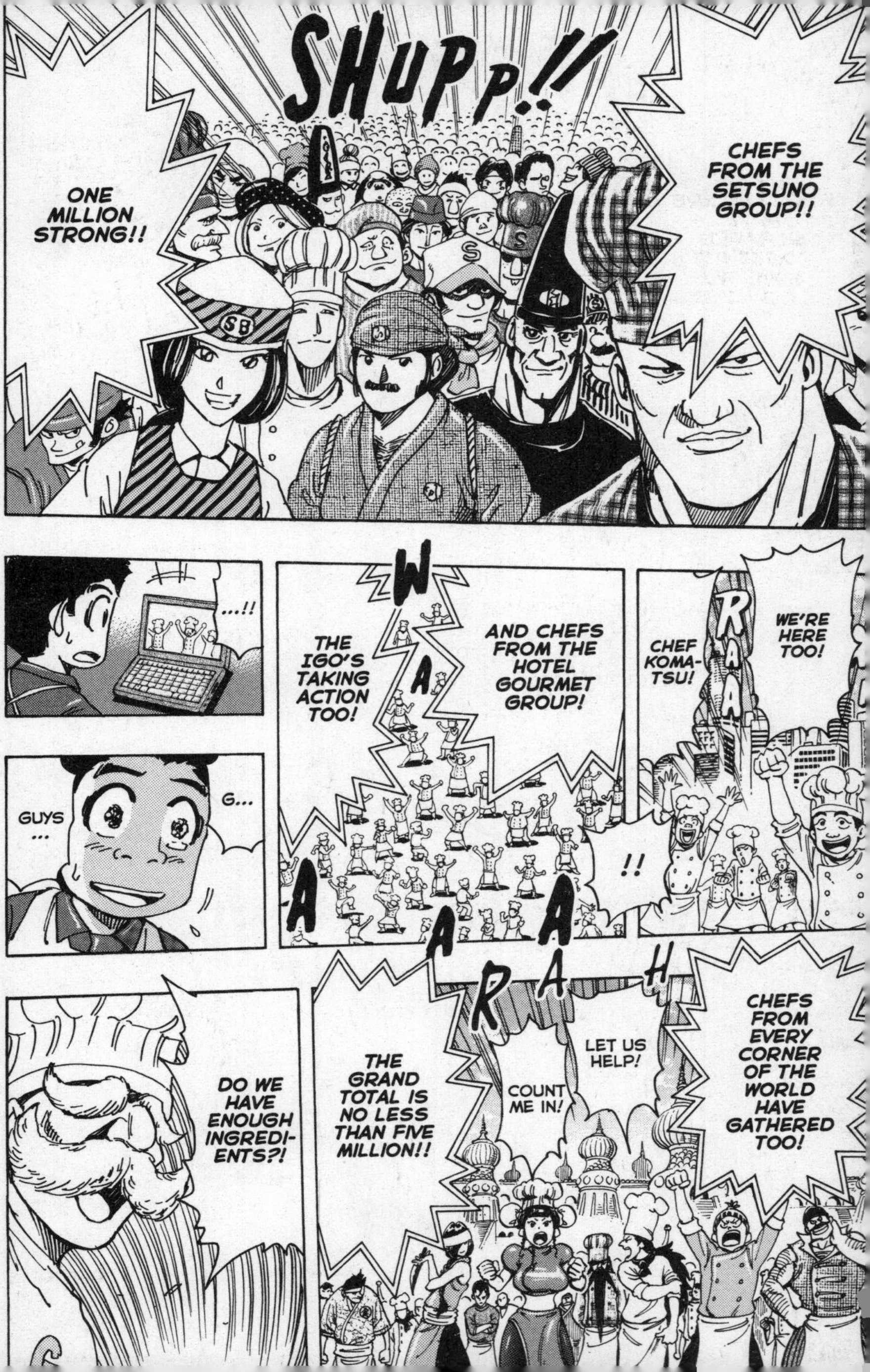
SHUPP!!
CHEFS FROM THE SETSUNO GROUP!!
ONE MILLION STRONG!!
WE'RE HERE TOO!
CHEF KOMATSU!
RAA
!!
AND CHEFS FROM THE HOTEL GOURMET GROUP!
THE IGO'S TAKING ACTION TOO!
WAA
...!!
G...
GUYS ...
AARAH
CHEFS FROM EVERY CORNER OF THE WORLD HAVE GATHERED TOO!
LET US HELP!
COUNT ME IN!
THE GRAND TOTAL IS NO LESS THAN FIVE MILLION!!
DO WE HAVE ENOUGH INGREDI-ENTS?!

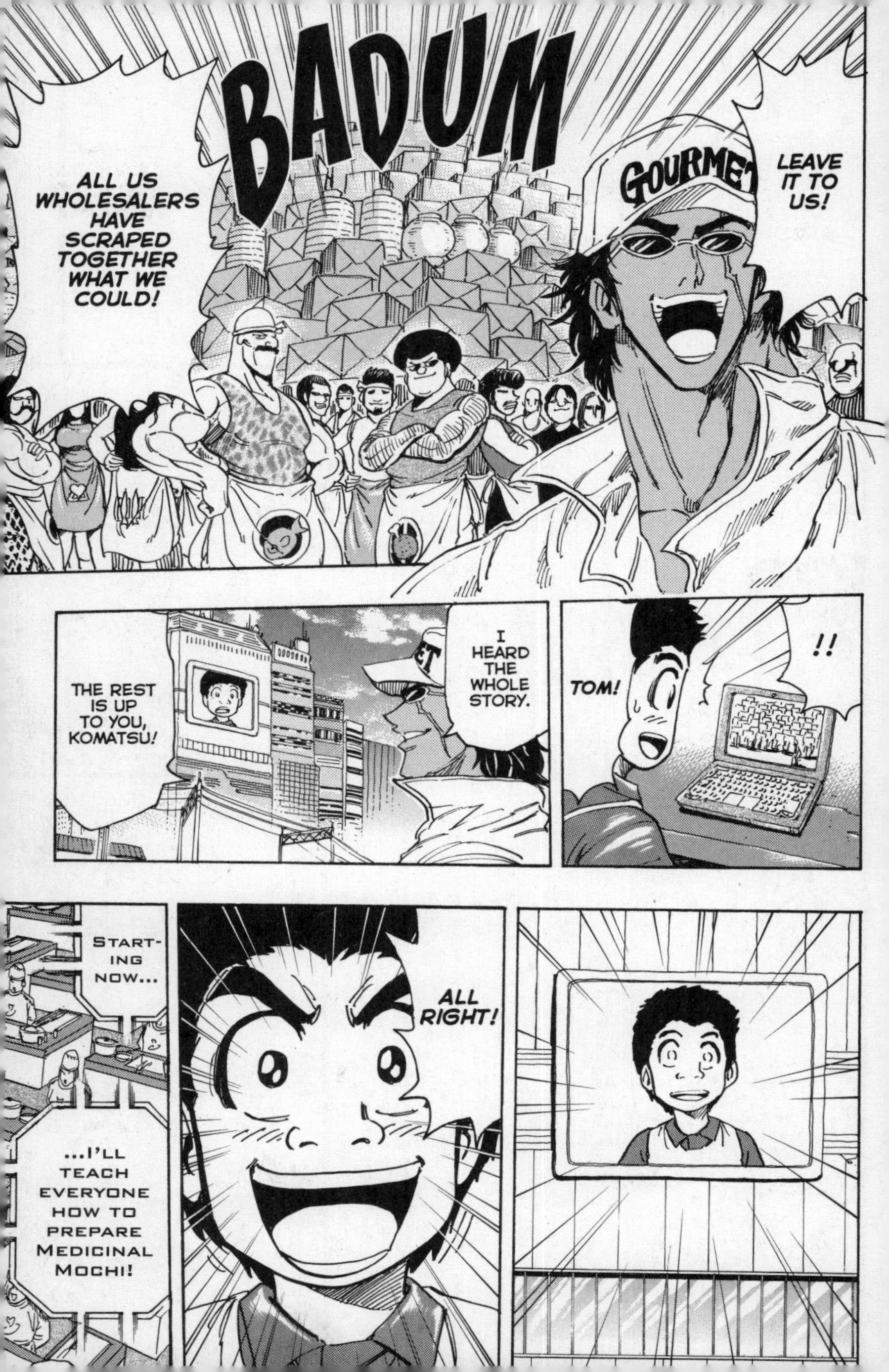
LEAVE IT TO US!
GOURMET
BADUM
ALL US WHOLESALERS HAVE SCRAPED TOGETHER WHAT WE COULD!
!!
TOM!
I HEARD THE WHOLE STORY.
THE REST IS UP TO YOU, KOMATSU!
ALL RIGHT!
START-ING NOW...
...I'LL TEACH EVERYONE HOW TO PREPARE MEDICINAL MOCHI!

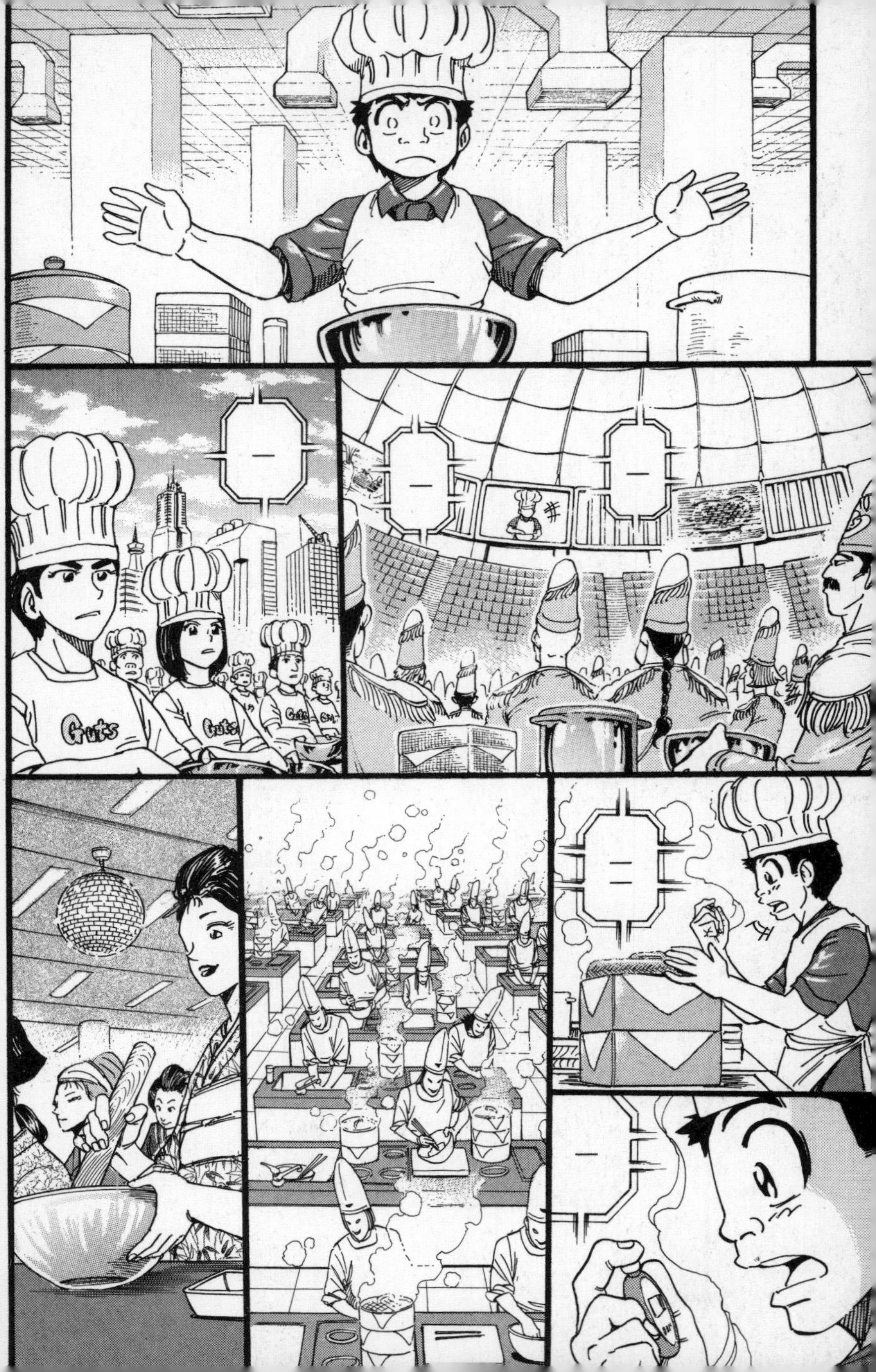
Guts
Guts

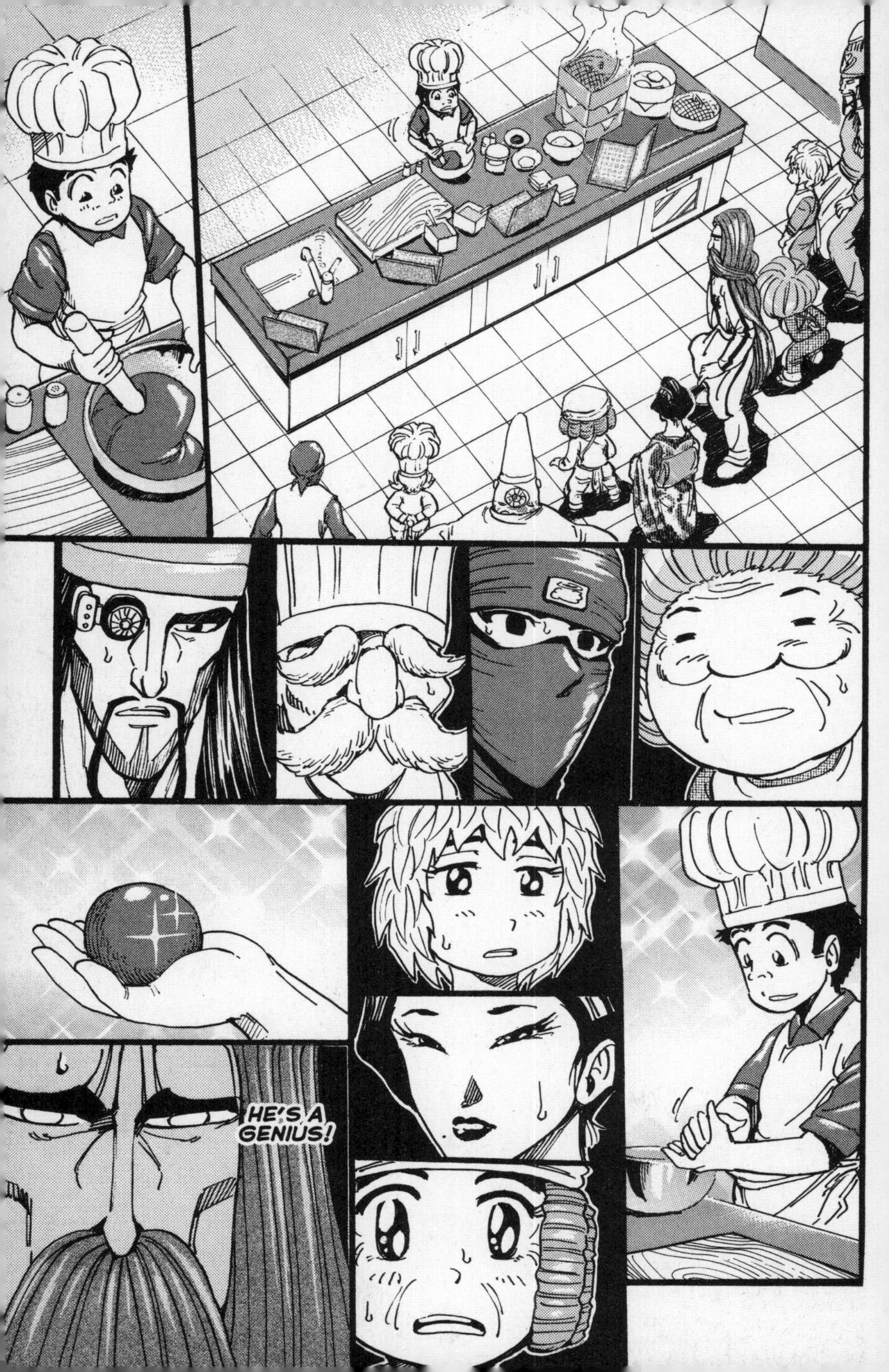
HE'S A GENIUS!

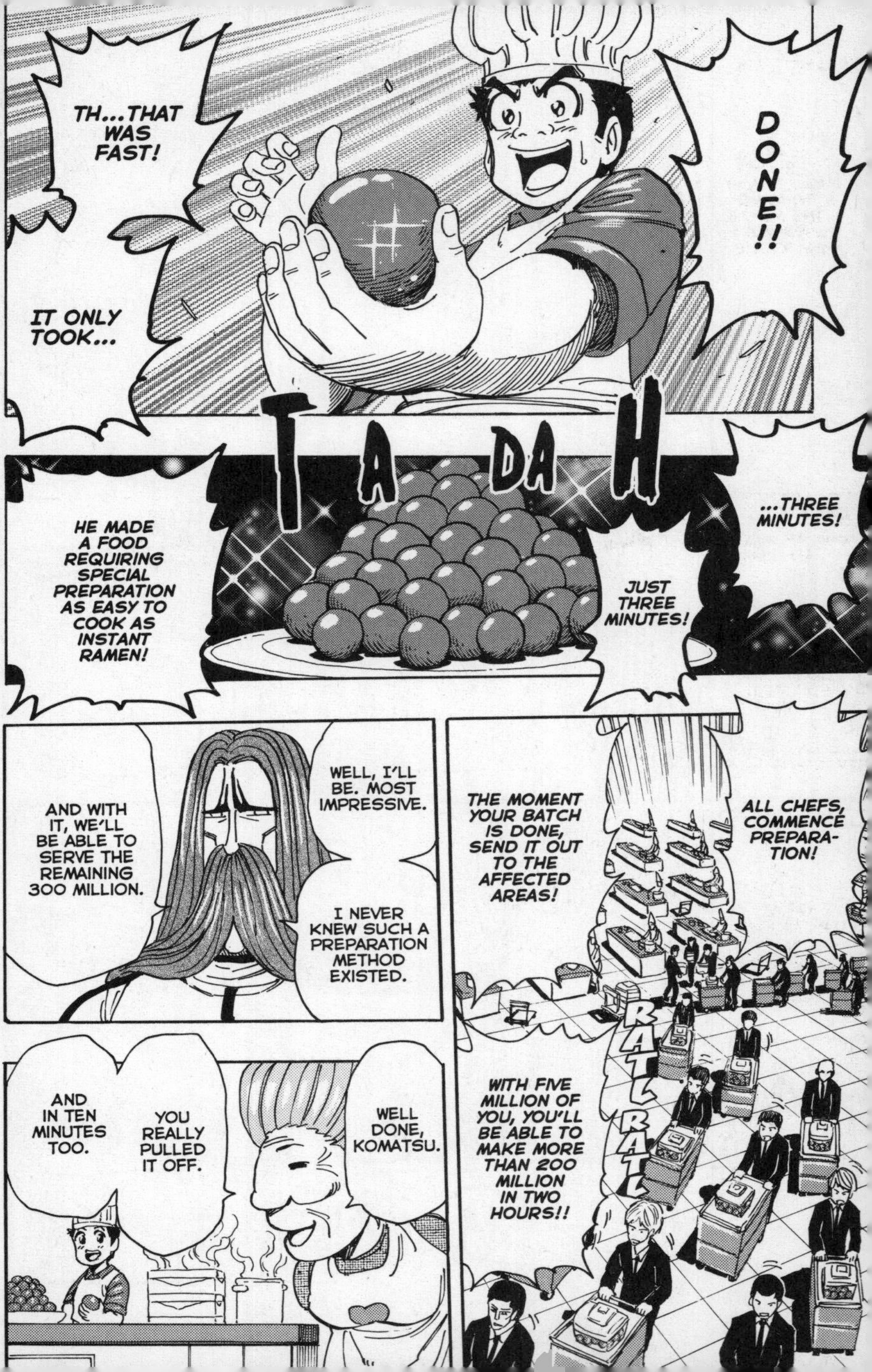
DONE!!
TH...THAT WAS FAST!
IT ONLY TOOK...
TADAH
...THREE MINUTES!
JUST THREE MINUTES!
HE MADE A FOOD REQUIRING SPECIAL PREPARATION AS EASY TO COOK AS INSTANT RAMEN!
ALL CHEFS, COMMENCE PREPARA-TION!
THE MOMENT YOUR BATCH IS DONE, SEND IT OUT TO THE AFFECTED AREAS!
RATL RATL
WITH FIVE MILLION OF YOU, YOU'LL BE ABLE TO MAKE MORE THAN 200 MILLION IN TWO HOURS!!
WELL, I'LL BE. MOST IMPRESSIVE.
I NEVER KNEW SUCH A PREPARATION METHOD EXISTED.
AND WITH IT, WE'LL BE ABLE TO SERVE THE REMAINING 300 MILLION.
WELL DONE, KOMATSU.
YOU REALLY PULLED IT OFF.
AND IN TEN MINUTES TOO.

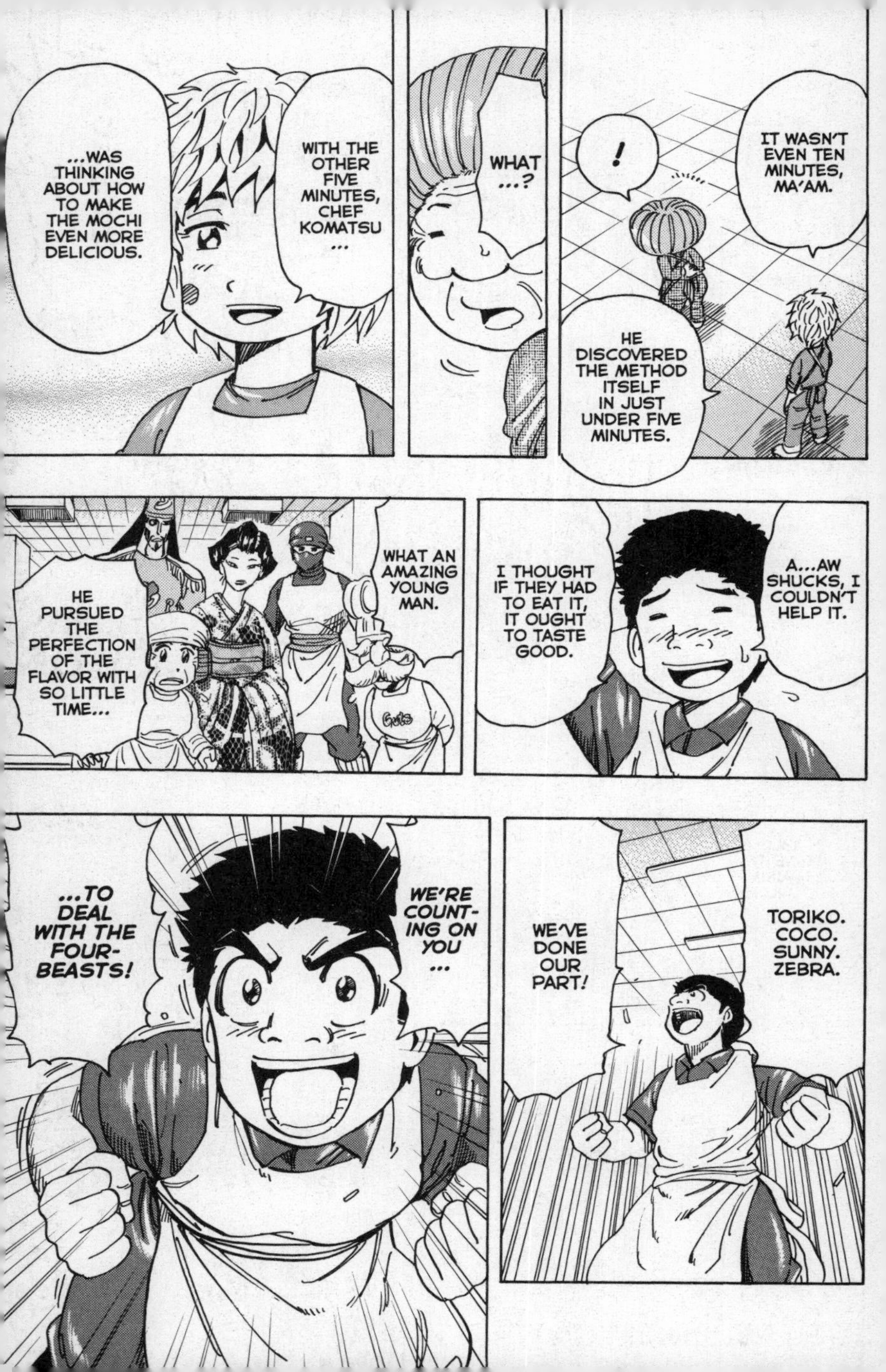
IT WASN'T EVEN TEN MINUTES, MA'AM.
HE DISCOVERED THE METHOD ITSELF IN JUST UNDER FIVE MINUTES.
!
WHAT ...?
WITH THE OTHER FIVE MINUTES, CHEF KOMATSU ...
...WAS THINKING ABOUT HOW TO MAKE THE MOCHI EVEN MORE DELICIOUS.
A...AW SHUCKS, I COULDN'T HELP IT.
I THOUGHT IF THEY HAD TO EAT IT, IT OUGHT TO TASTE GOOD.
WHAT AN AMAZING YOUNG MAN.
HE PURSUED THE PERFECTION OF THE FLAVOR WITH SO LITTLE TIME...
TORIKO. COCO. SUNNY. ZEBRA.
WE'VE DONE OUR PART!
WE'RE COUNT-ING ON YOU ...
...TO DEAL WITH THE FOUR-BEASTS!

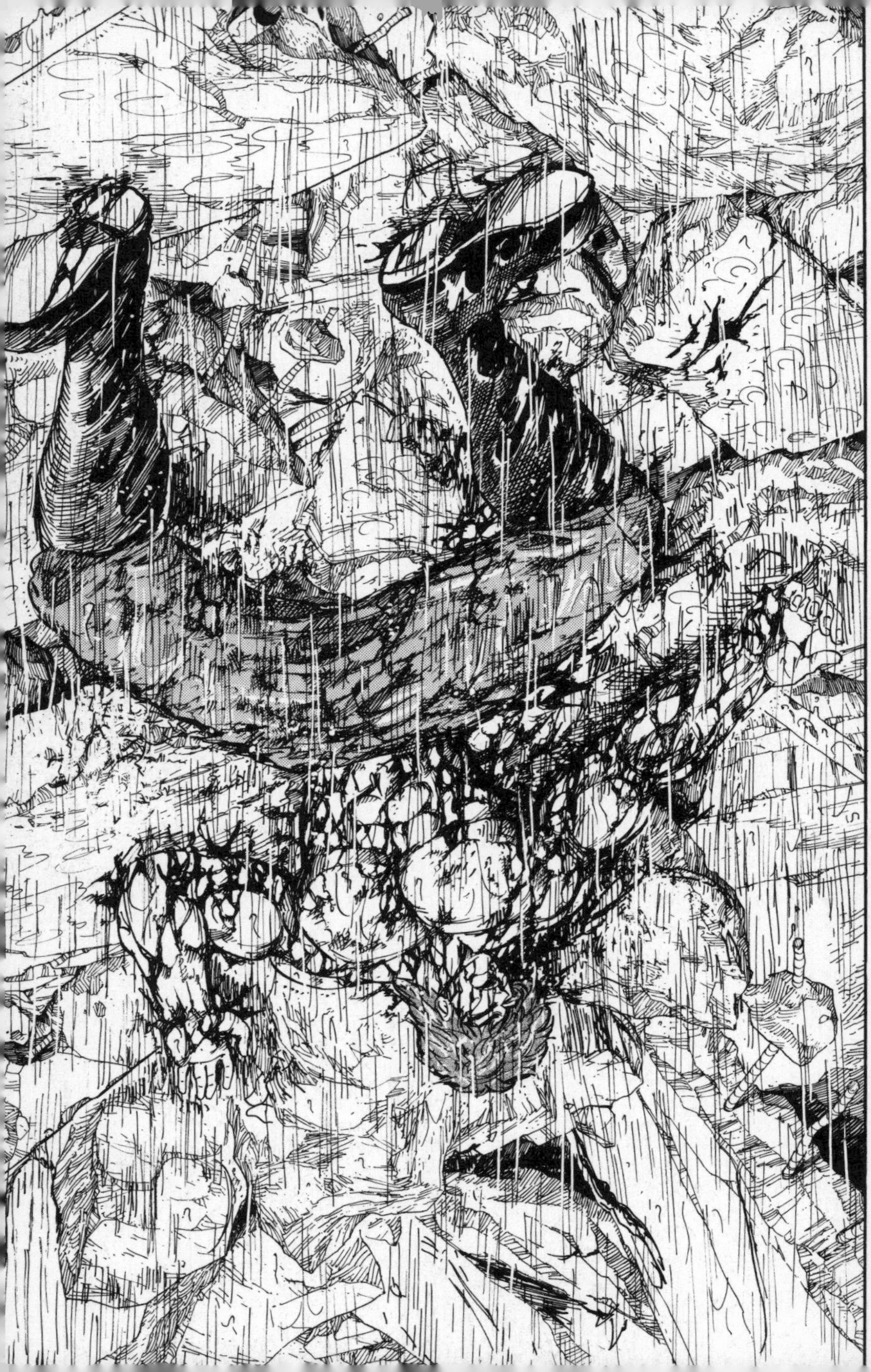

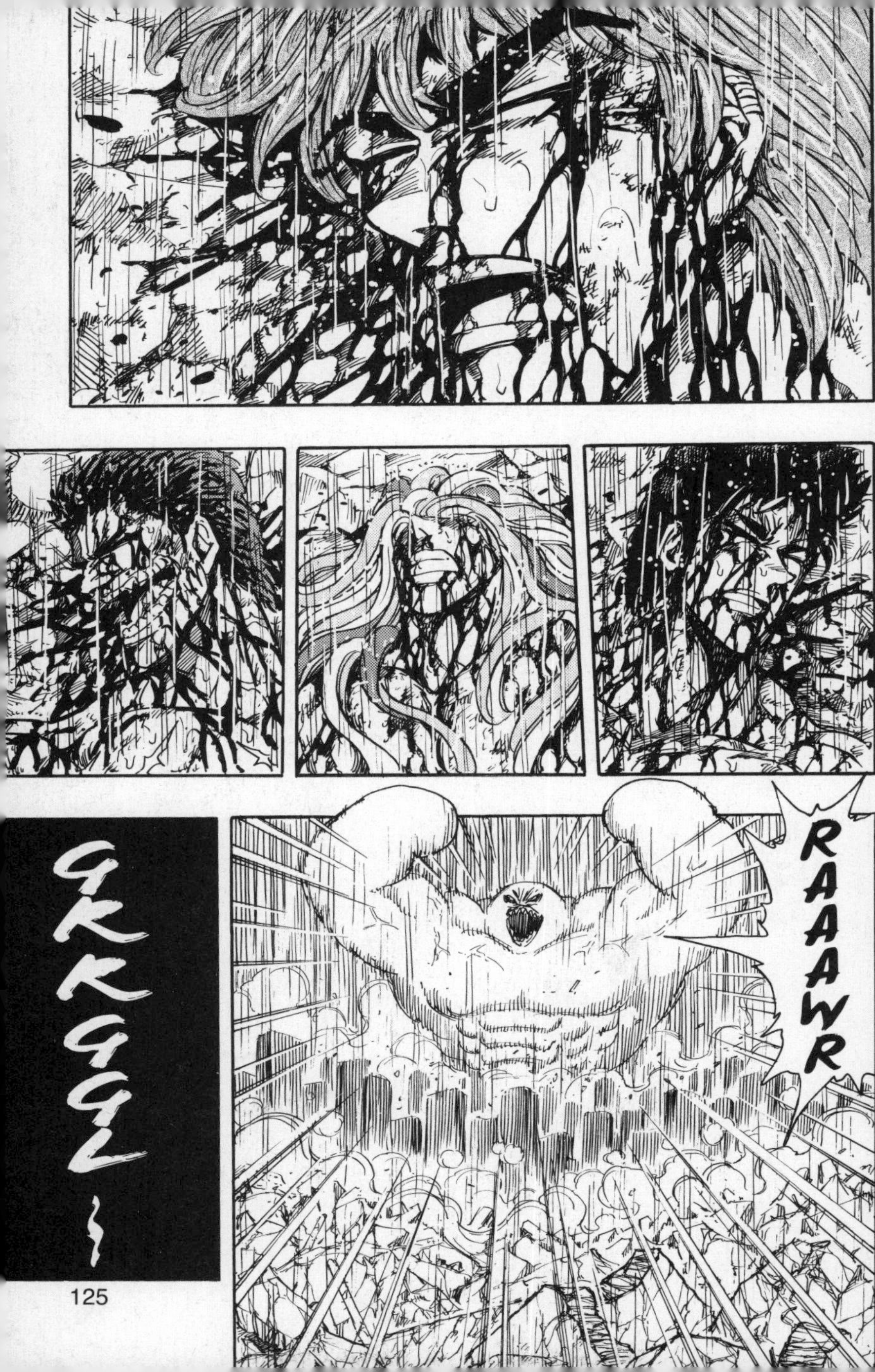
RAAAWR
GKRGGL~

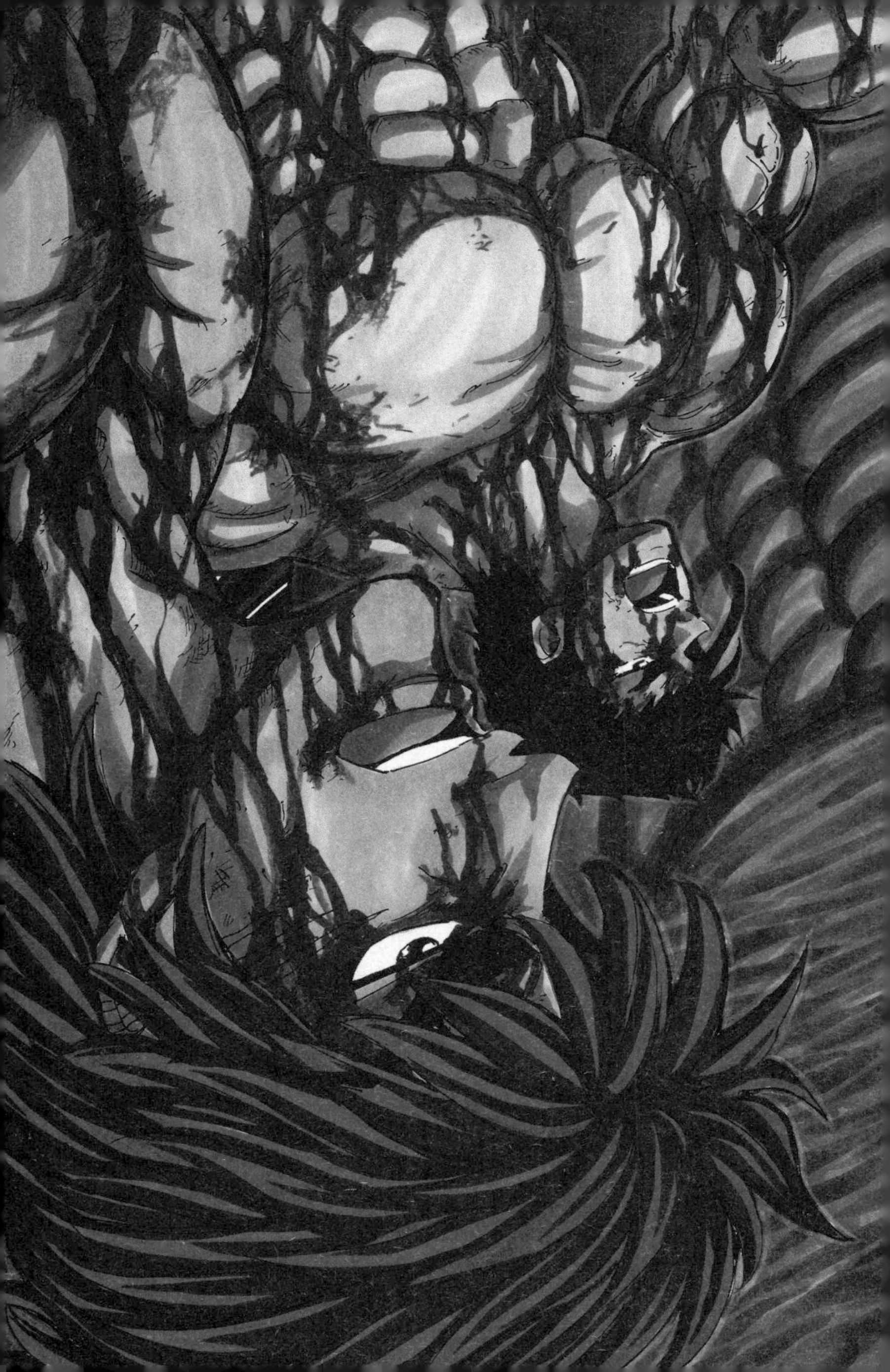

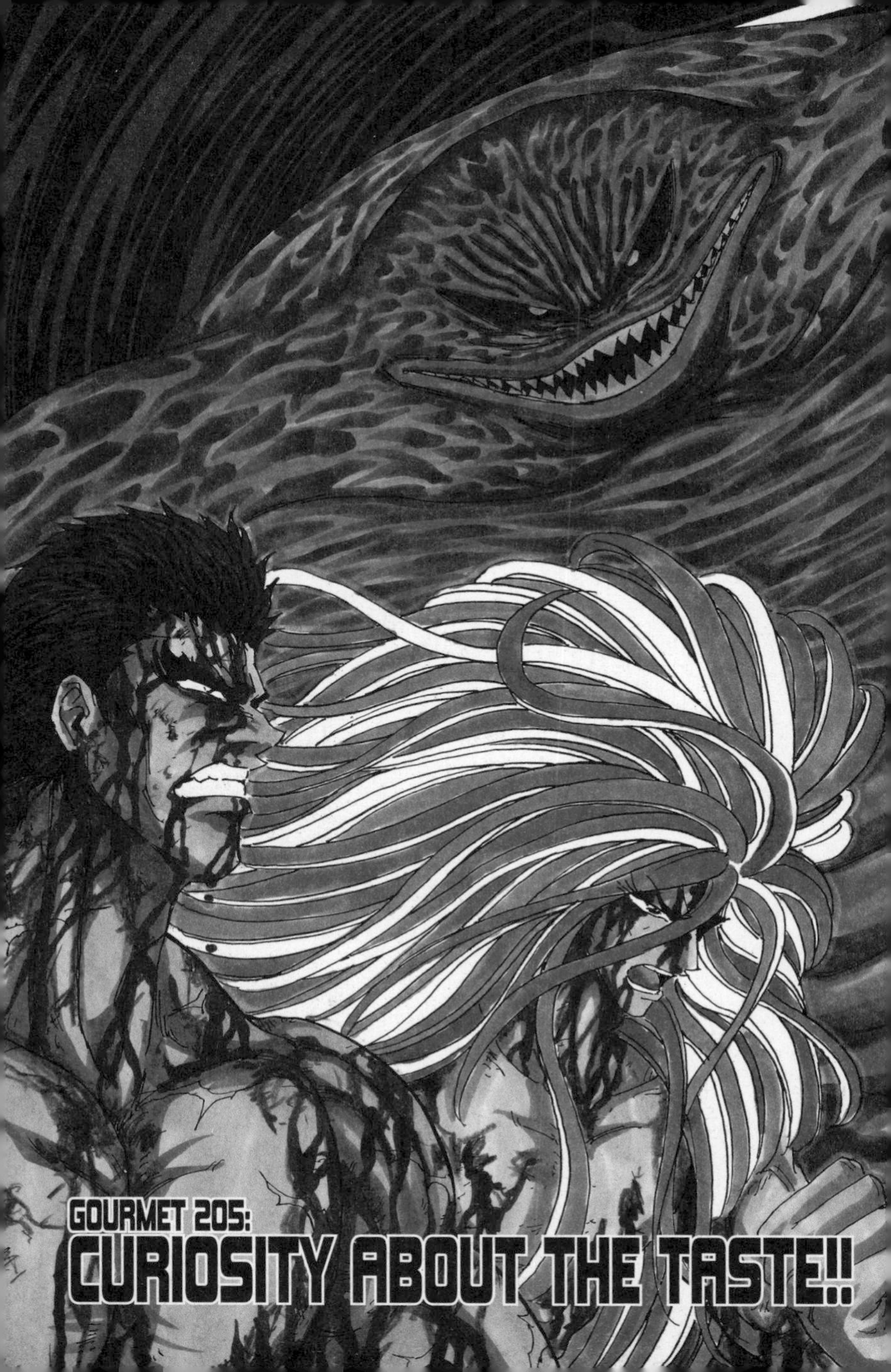
GOURMET 205:
CURIOSITY ABOUT THE TASTE!!

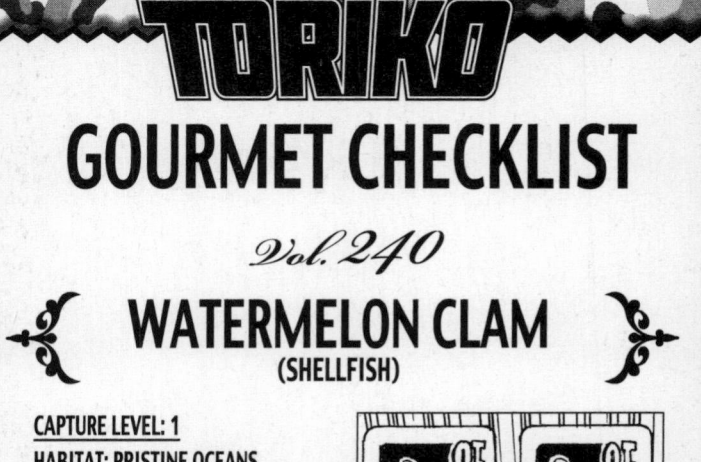

TORIKO

GOURMET CHECKLIST

Vol. 240

❦ WATERMELON CLAM ❧
(SHELLFISH)

CAPTURE LEVEL: 1
HABITAT: PRISTINE OCEANS
LENGTH: 22 CM
HEIGHT: ---
WEIGHT: 1.5 KG
PRICE: WATERMELON CLAM /
30,000 YEN; BLACK PEARL /
300,000 YEN

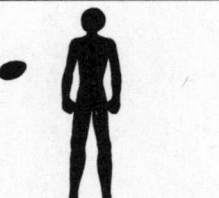

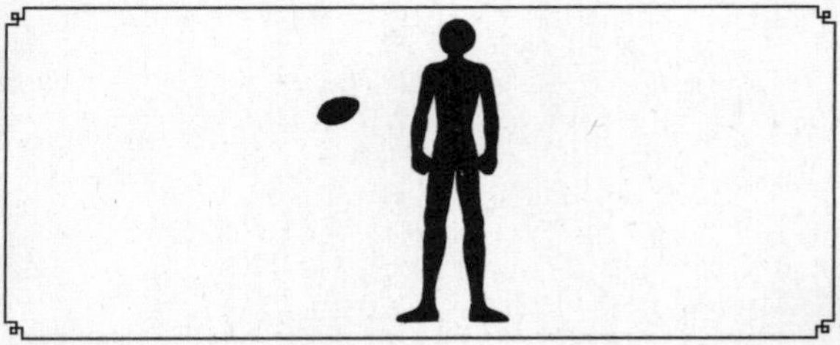

SCALE

A CLAM SHAPED LIKE A WATERMELON THAT ONLY LIVES IN PRISTINE OCEAN WATERS.
ITS FLESH IS FRESH, JUICY AND TASTES LIKE A SWEET, RIPE WATERMELON. ALSO, THE
LIVING MINERAL THAT GROWS WITHIN THE BODY OF THE WATERMELON CLAM, A BLACK
PEARL, IS HIGHLY VALUED AS A JEWEL. WATERMELON CLAM IS HARVESTED FOR ITS
BLACK PEARL MORE OFTEN THAN ITS FLESH.

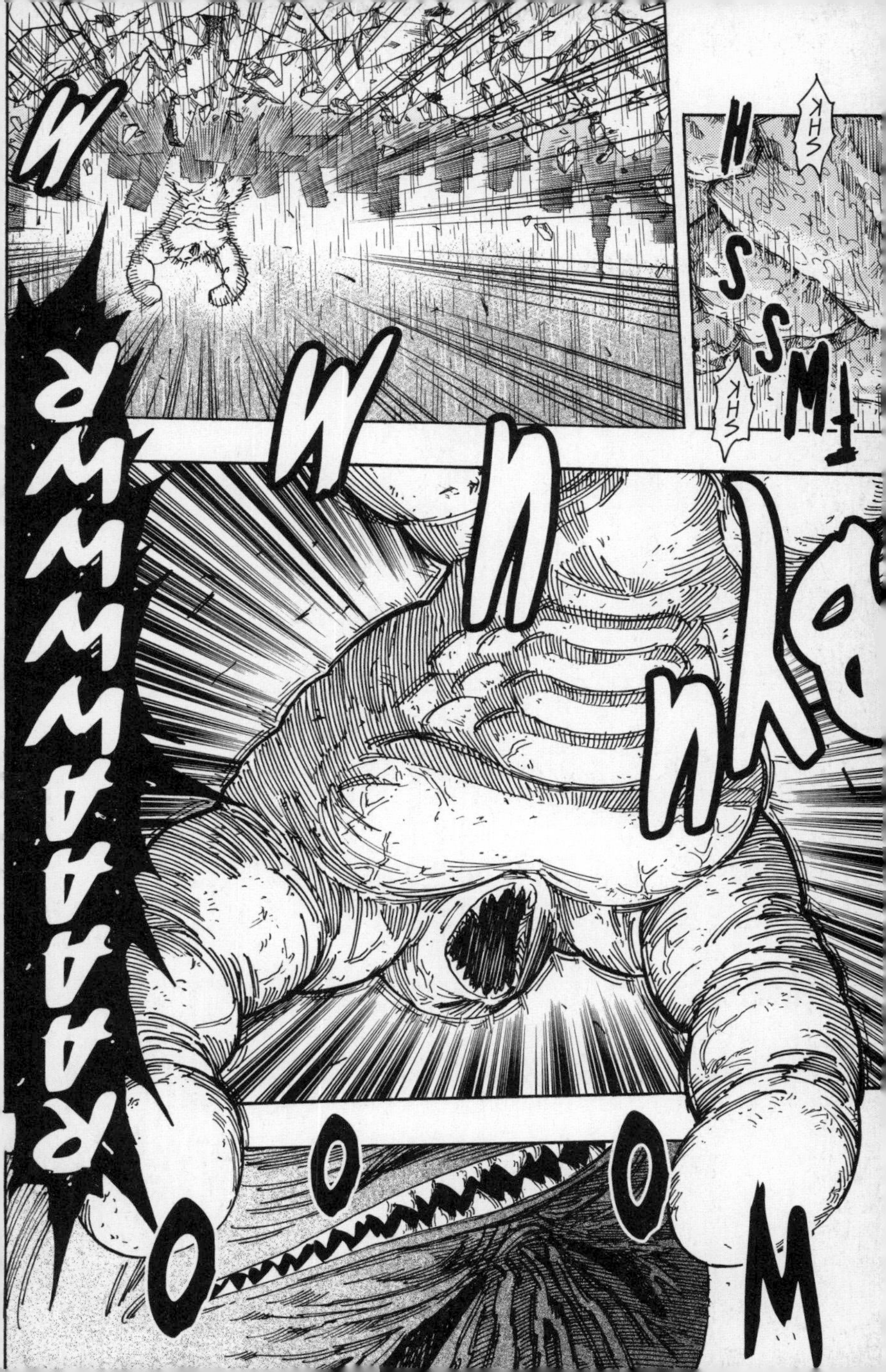

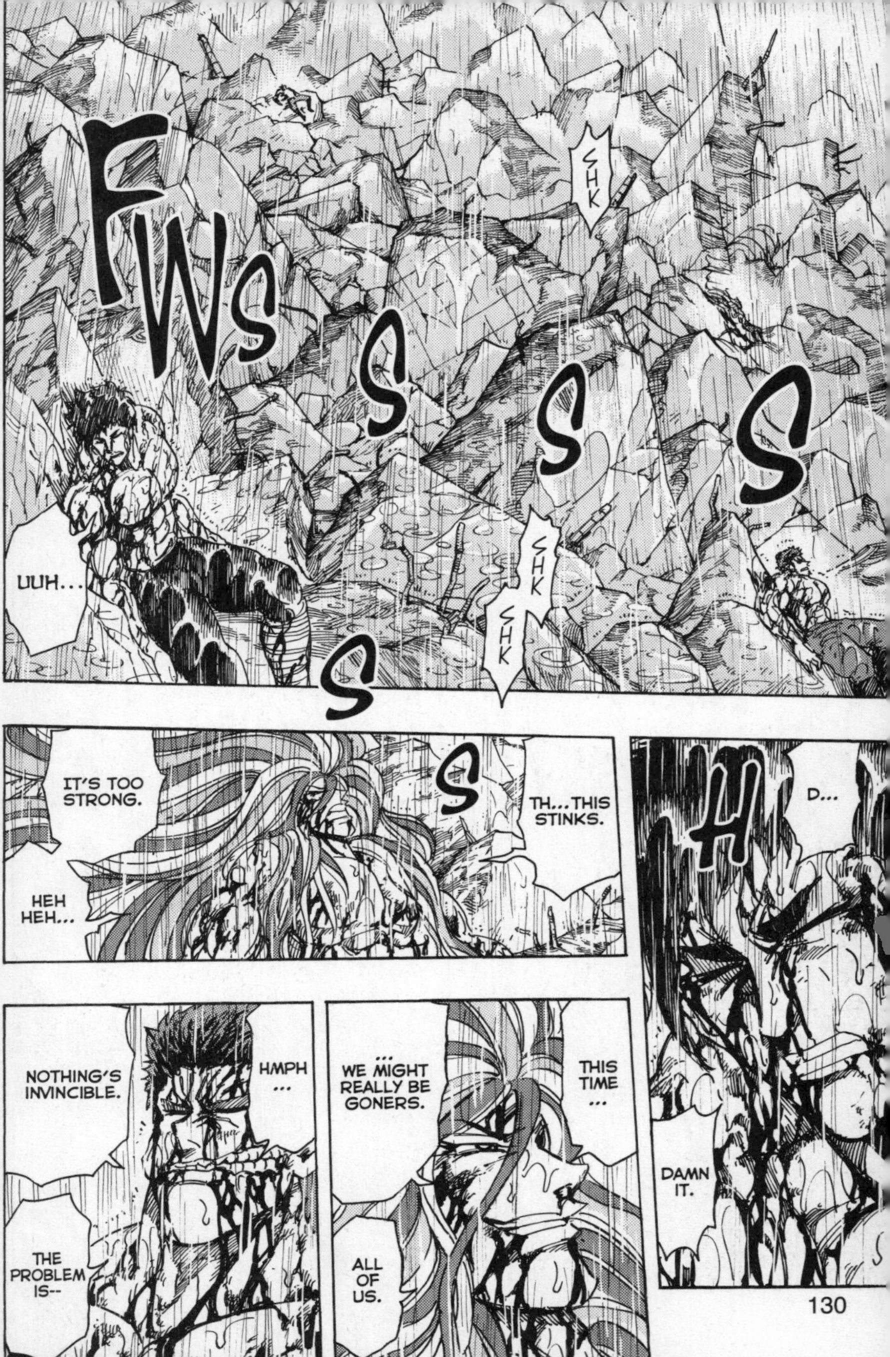
SHK
FWSSSSS
SHK
SHK
UUH...
D...
H
DAMN IT.
TH...THIS STINKS.
S
IT'S TOO STRONG.
HEH HEH...
THIS TIME...
...WE MIGHT REALLY BE GONERS.
ALL OF US.
HMPH...
NOTHING'S INVINCIBLE.
THE PROBLEM IS--

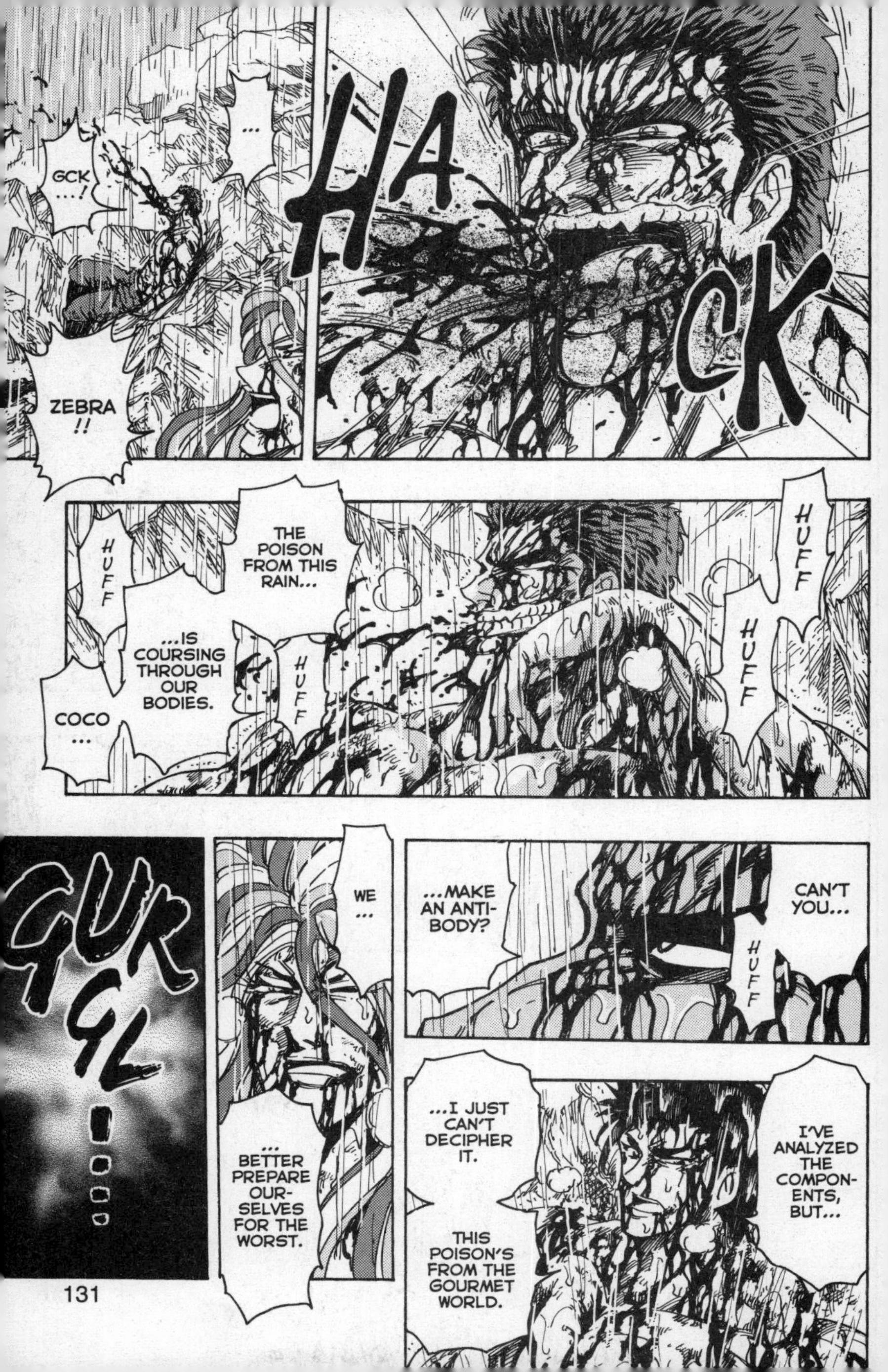
HACK
...
GCK...!
ZEBRA!!
HUFF
HUFF
THE POISON FROM THIS RAIN...
HUFF
...IS COURSING THROUGH OUR BODIES.
HUFF
COCO...
CAN'T YOU...
HUFF
...MAKE AN ANTI-BODY?
I'VE ANALYZED THE COMPON-ENTS, BUT...
...I JUST CAN'T DECIPHER IT.
THIS POISON'S FROM THE GOURMET WORLD.
WE...
...BETTER PREPARE OUR-SELVES FOR THE WORST.
GURGL.....

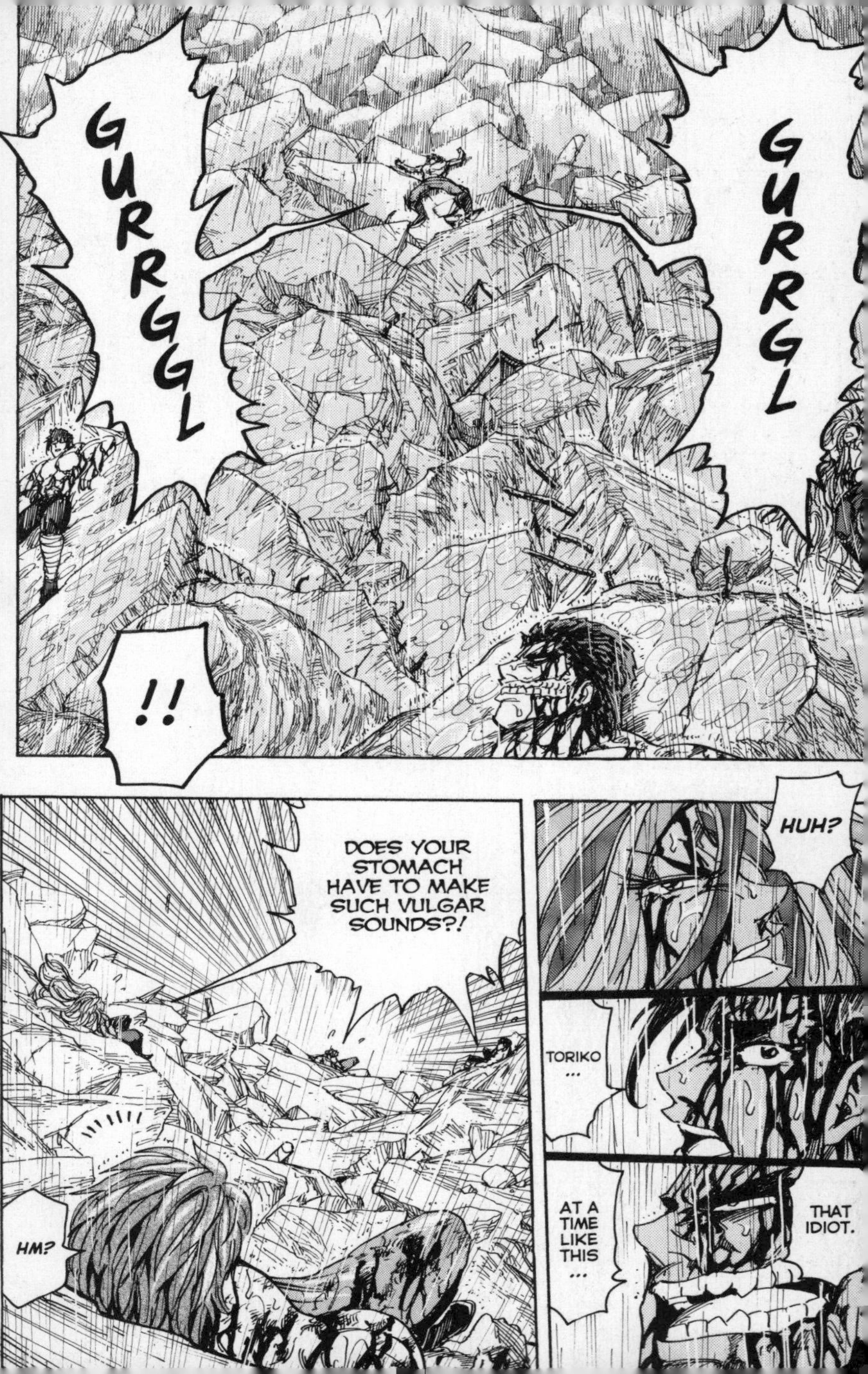
GURRGL
GURRGGL
!!
HUH?
TORIKO ...
THAT IDIOT.
AT A TIME LIKE THIS ...
DOES YOUR STOMACH HAVE TO MAKE SUCH VULGAR SOUNDS?!
HM?

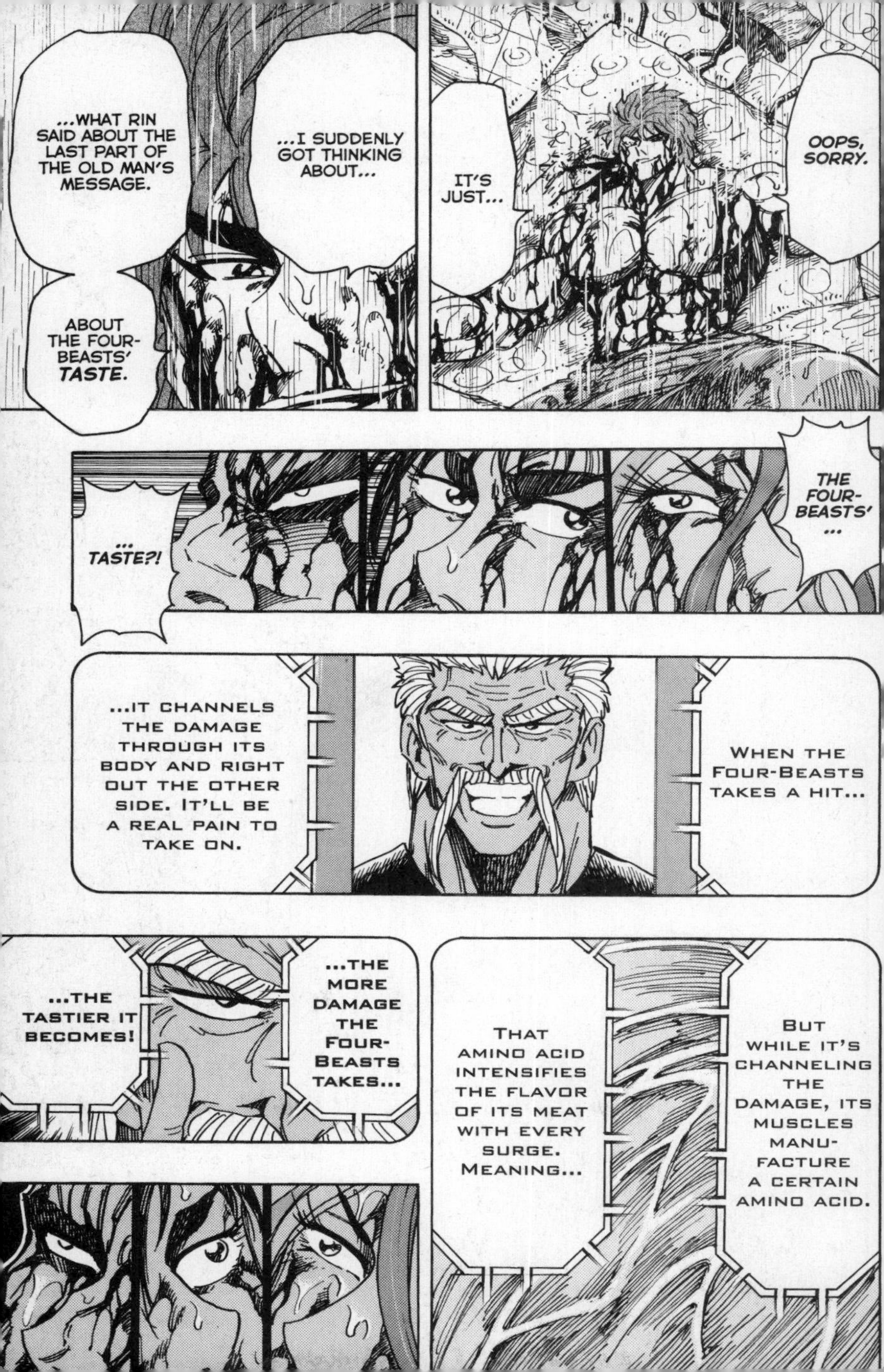
OOPS, SORRY.
IT'S JUST...
...I SUDDENLY GOT THINKING ABOUT...
...WHAT RIN SAID ABOUT THE LAST PART OF THE OLD MAN'S MESSAGE.
ABOUT THE FOUR-BEASTS' TASTE.
THE FOUR-BEASTS' ...
... TASTE?!
WHEN THE FOUR-BEASTS TAKES A HIT...
...IT CHANNELS THE DAMAGE THROUGH ITS BODY AND RIGHT OUT THE OTHER SIDE. IT'LL BE A REAL PAIN TO TAKE ON.
BUT WHILE IT'S CHANNELING THE DAMAGE, ITS MUSCLES MANU-FACTURE A CERTAIN AMINO ACID.
THAT AMINO ACID INTENSIFIES THE FLAVOR OF ITS MEAT WITH EVERY SURGE. MEANING...
...THE MORE DAMAGE THE FOUR-BEASTS TAKES...
...THE TASTIER IT BECOMES!

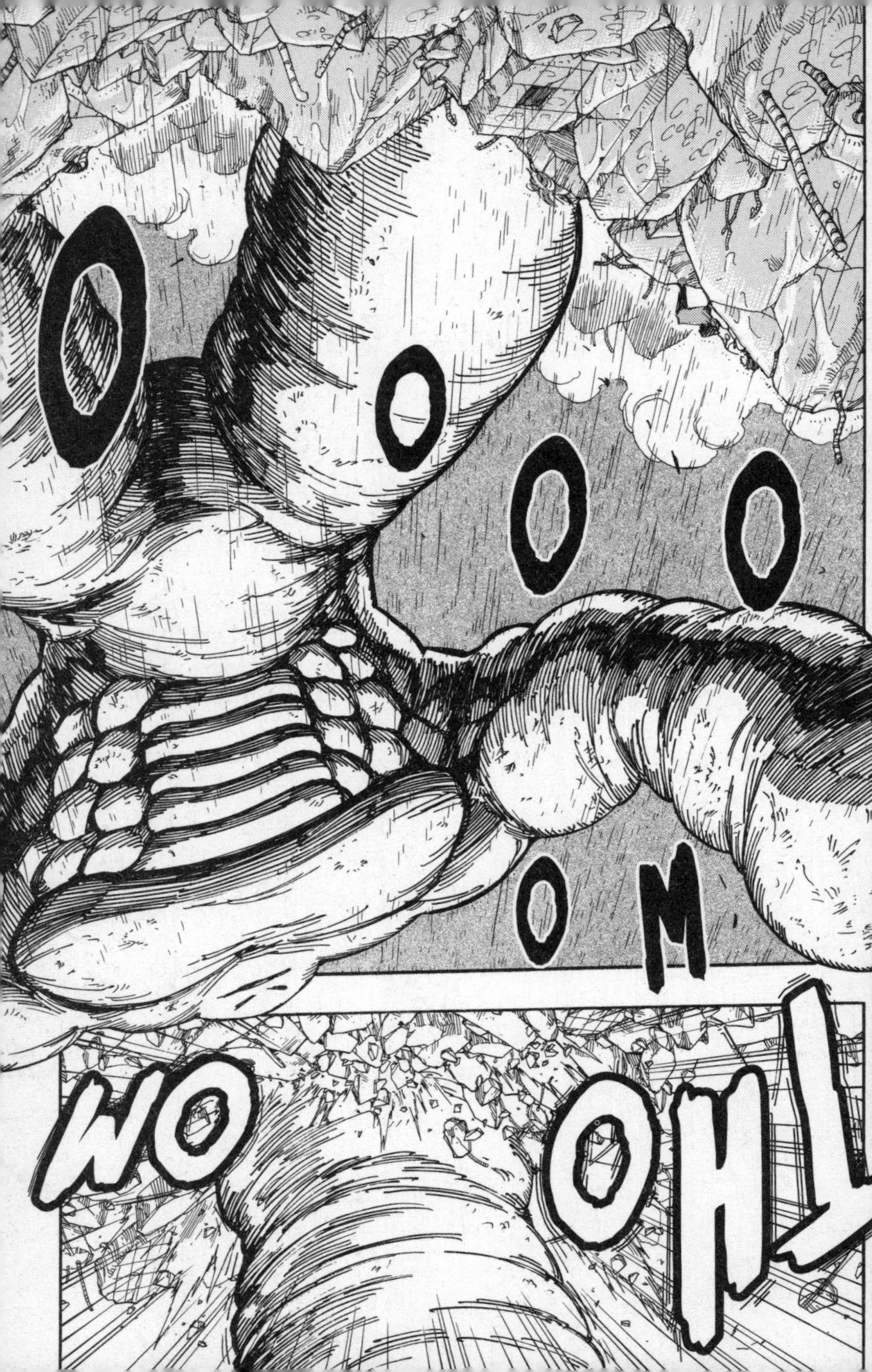
OOOOOOM
WO
OH!

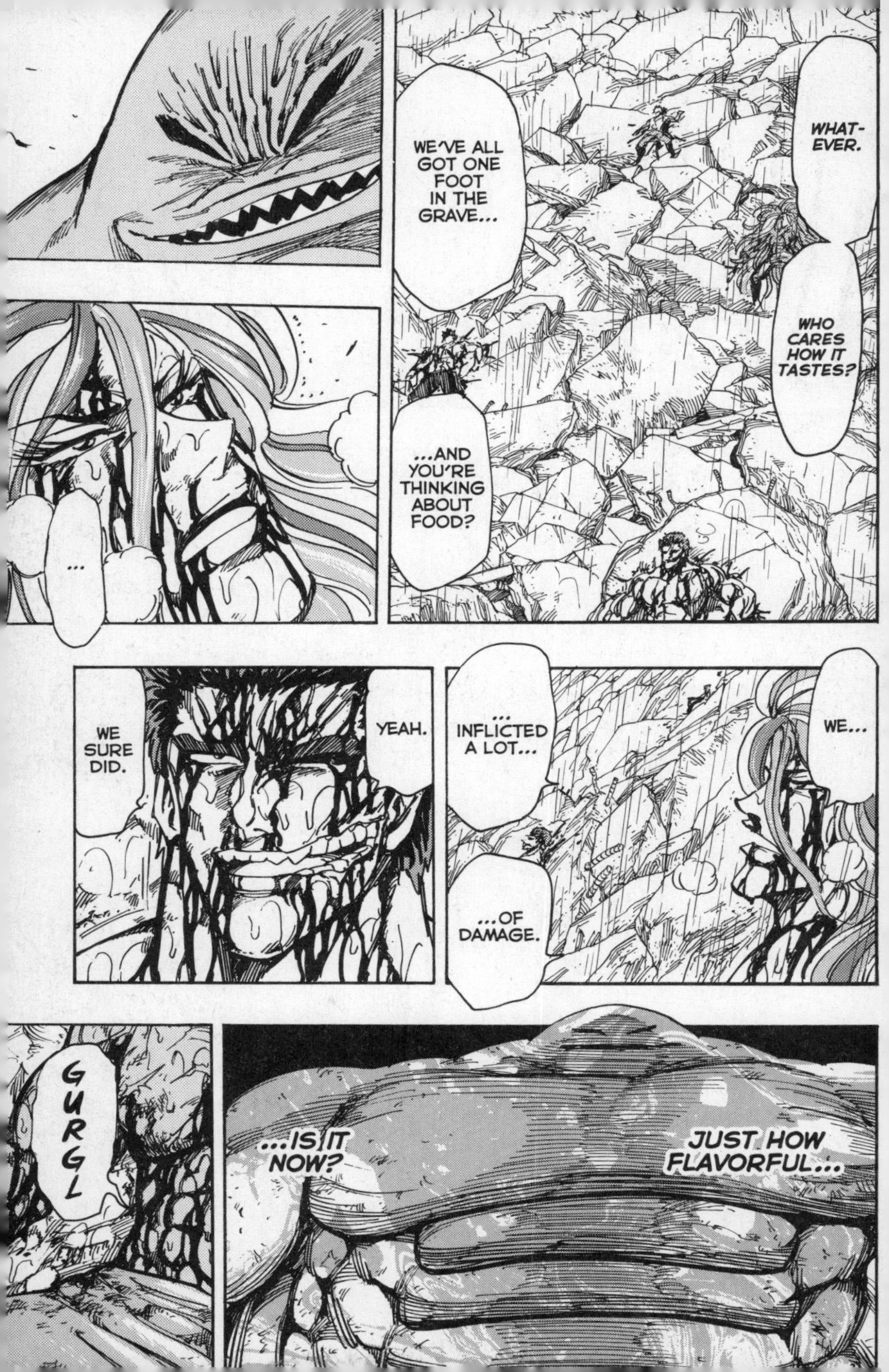
WHAT-EVER.
WHO CARES HOW IT TASTES?
WE'VE ALL GOT ONE FOOT IN THE GRAVE...
...AND YOU'RE THINKING ABOUT FOOD?
...
WE...
...INFLICTED A LOT...
...OF DAMAGE.
YEAH.
WE SURE DID.
JUST HOW FLAVORFUL...
...IS IT NOW?
GURGL

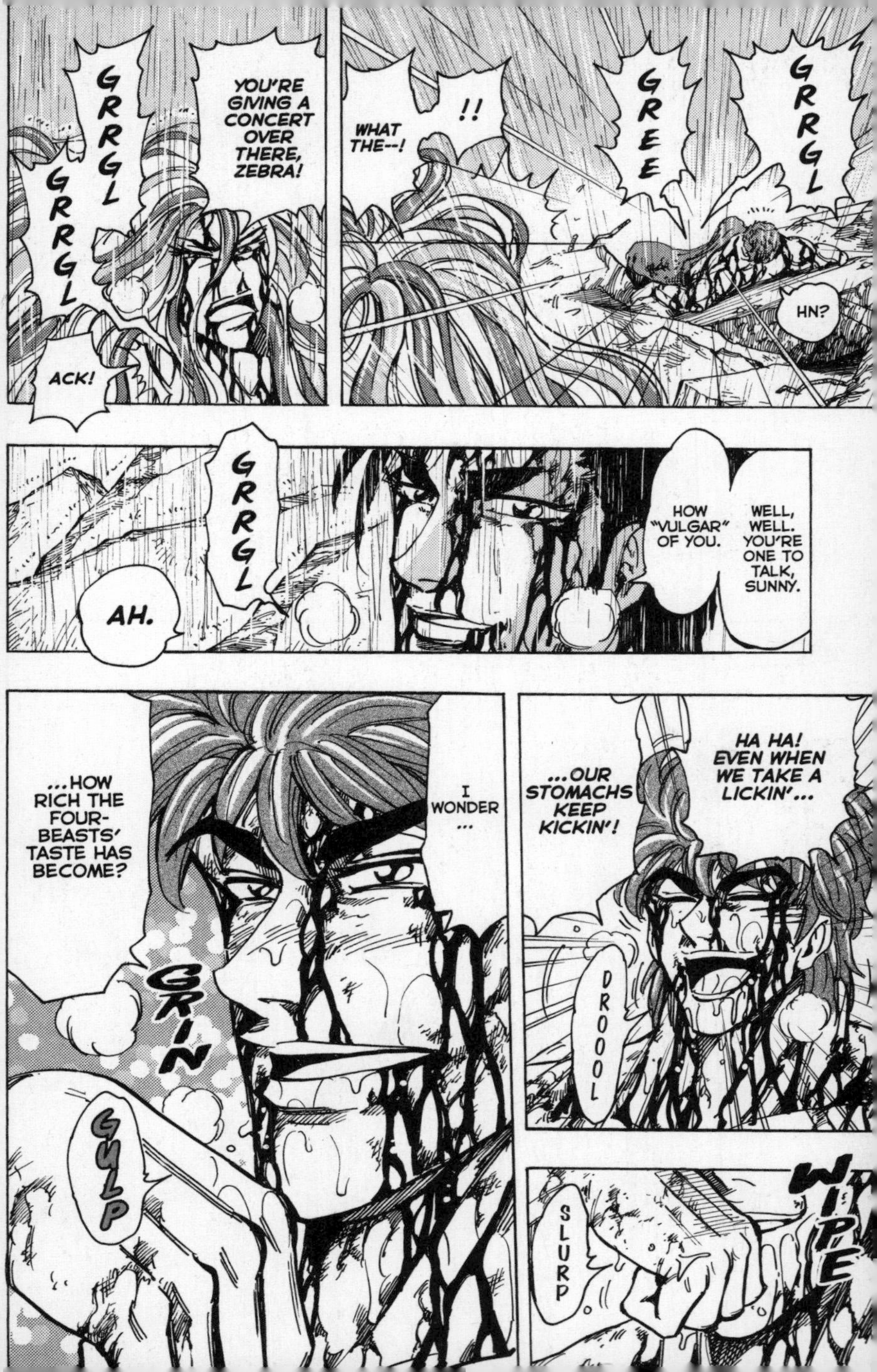
GRRGL
GREE
HN?
!!
WHAT THE--!
YOU'RE GIVING A CONCERT OVER THERE, ZEBRA!
GRRGL
GRRGL
ACK!
WELL, WELL. YOU'RE ONE TO TALK, SUNNY.
HOW "VULGAR" OF YOU.
GRRGL
AH.
HA HA! EVEN WHEN WE TAKE A LICKIN'...
...OUR STOMACHS KEEP KICKIN'!
DROOOL
WIPE
SLURP
I WONDER ...
...HOW RICH THE FOUR-BEASTS' TASTE HAS BECOME?
GRIN
GULP

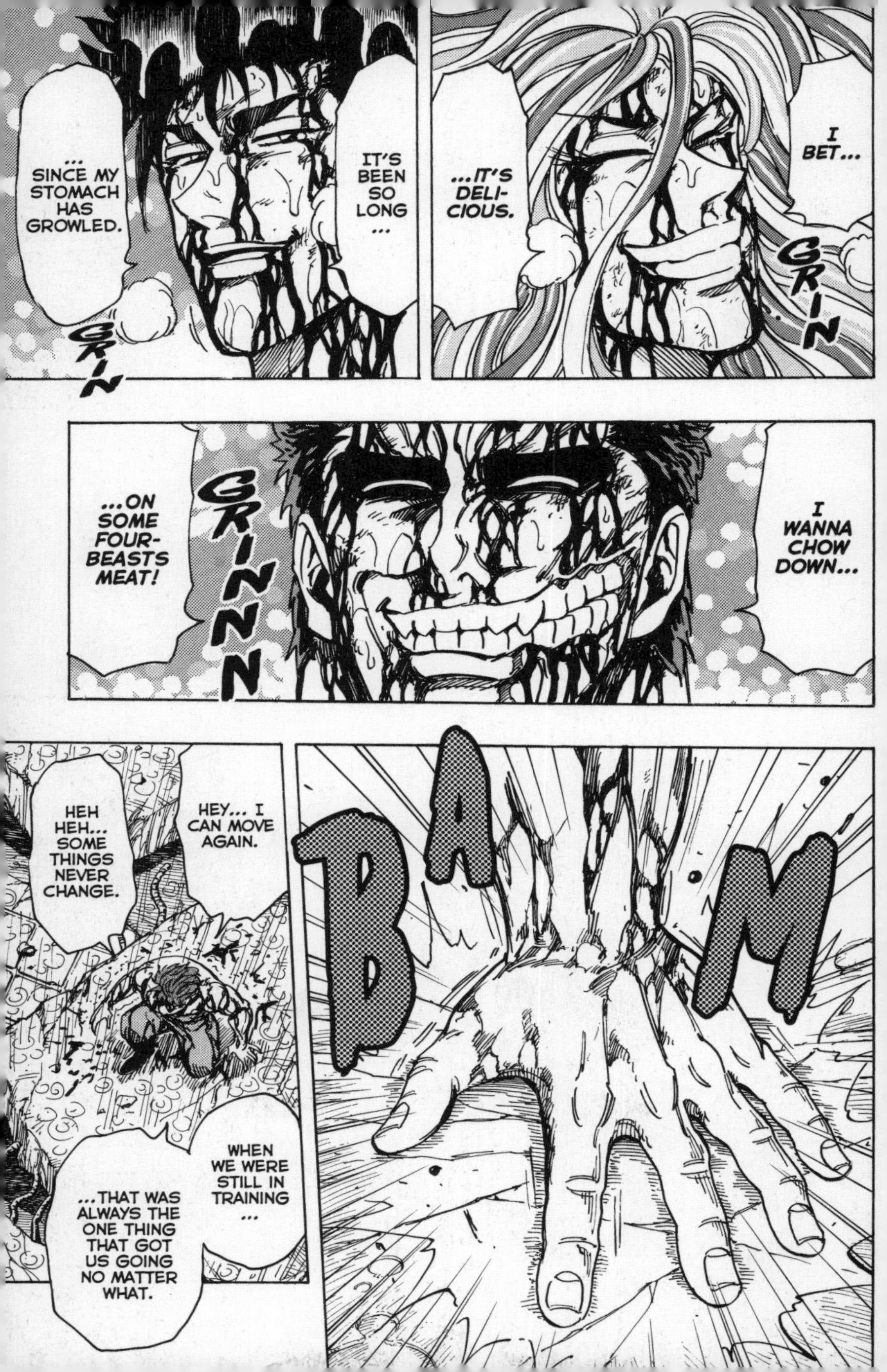
I BET...
GRIN
...IT'S DELI-CIOUS.
IT'S BEEN SO LONG ...
... SINCE MY STOMACH HAS GROWLED.
GRIN
I WANNA CHOW DOWN...
GRINNN
...ON SOME FOUR-BEASTS MEAT!
BAM
HEY... I CAN MOVE AGAIN.
HEH HEH... SOME THINGS NEVER CHANGE.
WHEN WE WERE STILL IN TRAINING ...
...THAT WAS ALWAYS THE ONE THING THAT GOT US GOING NO MATTER WHAT.

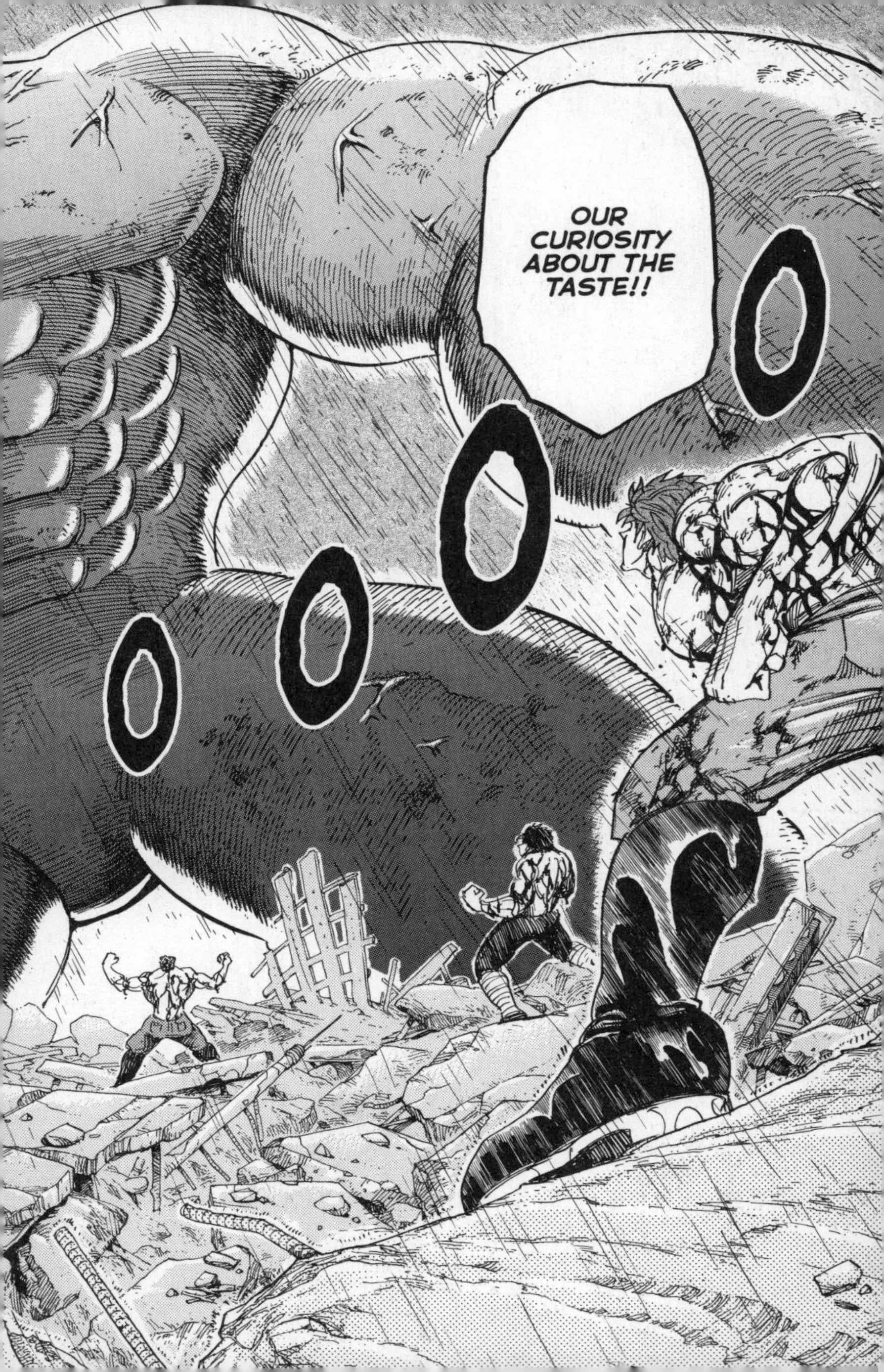
OUR CURIOSITY ABOUT THE TASTE!!

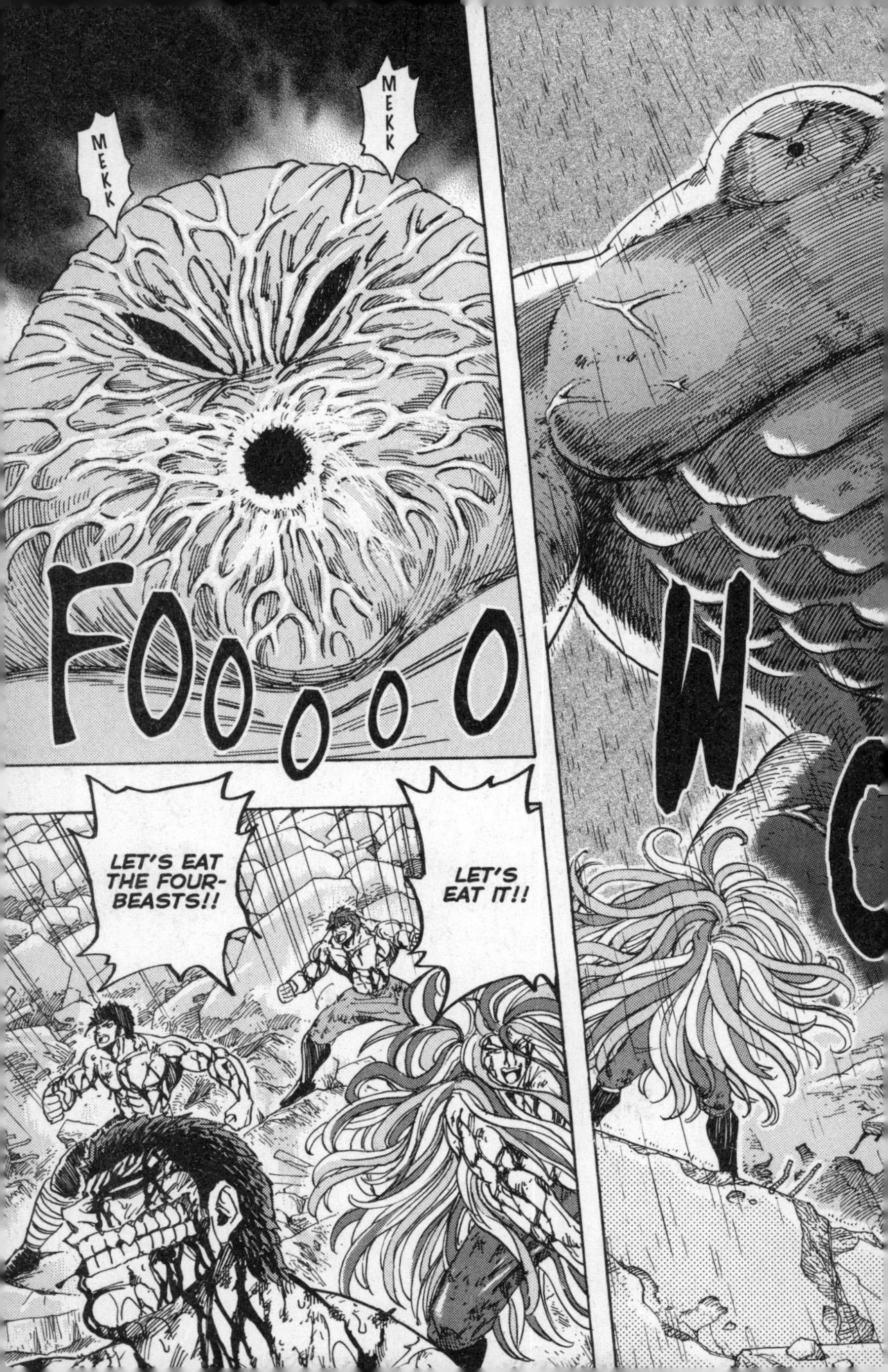
WO
MEKK
MEKK
FOOOOO
LET'S EAT IT!!
LET'S EAT THE FOUR-BEASTS!!

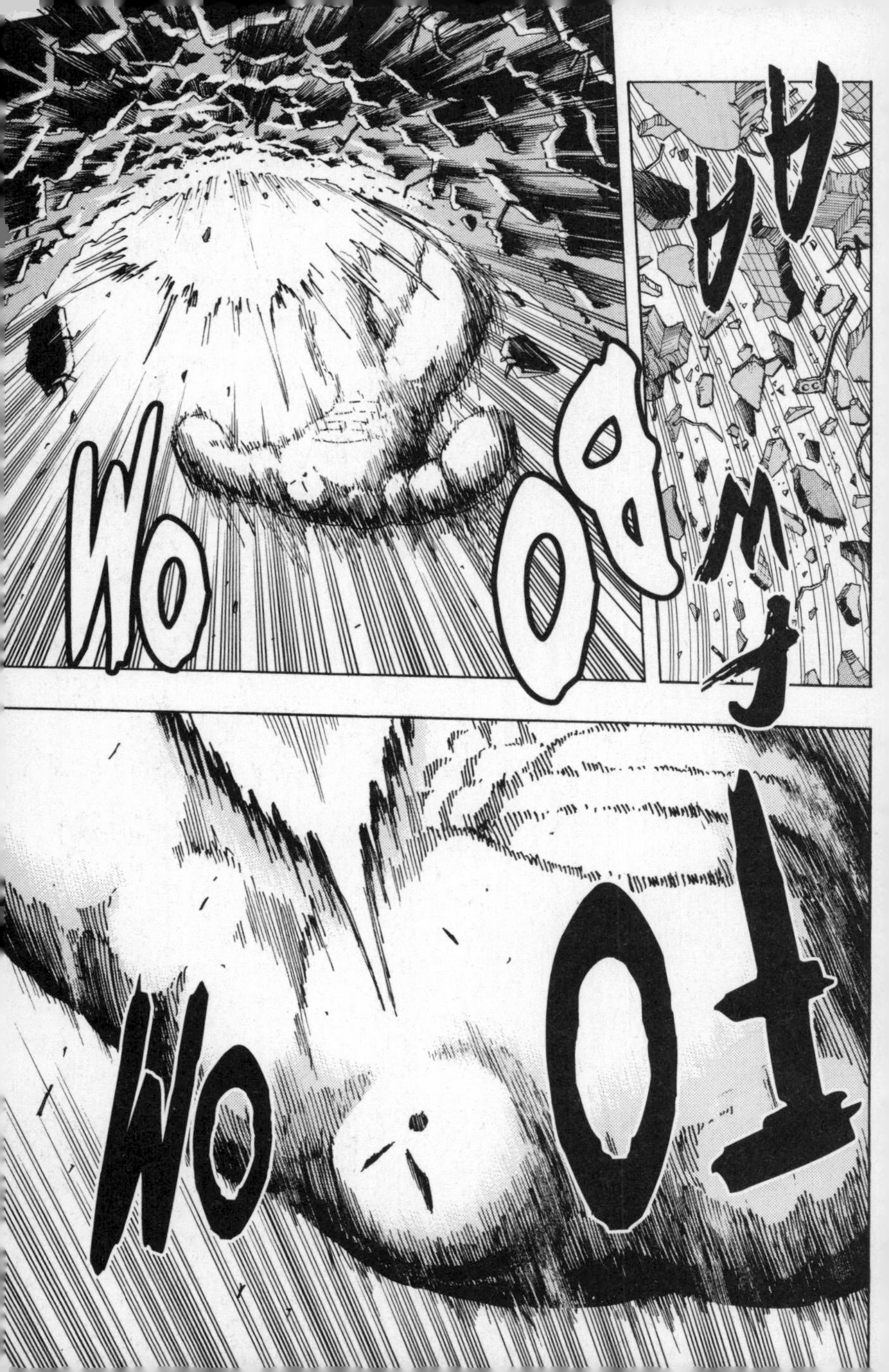
WO
O
WO
O

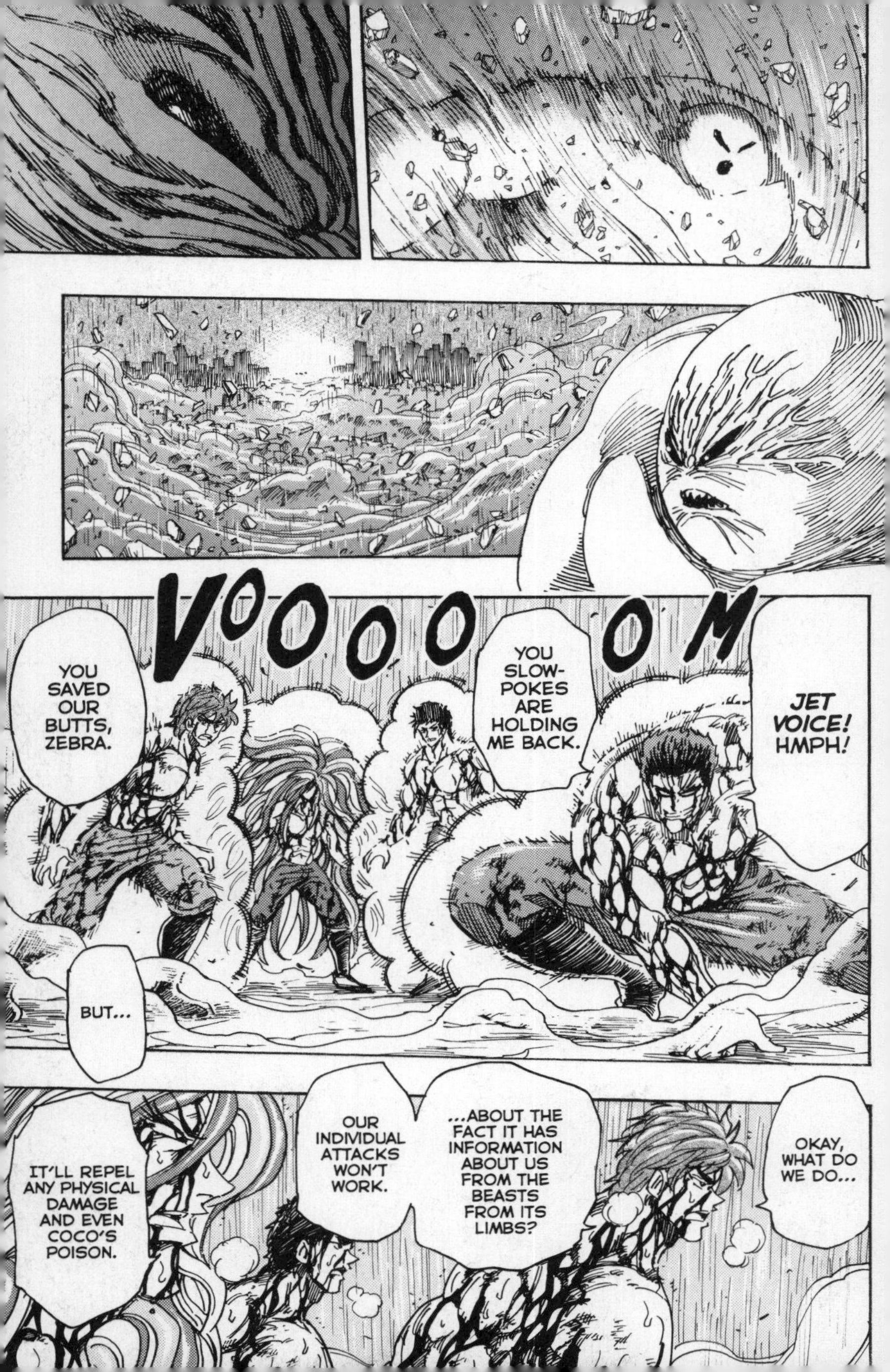
VOOOOOM
JET VOICE! HMPH!
YOU SLOW-POKES ARE HOLDING ME BACK.
YOU SAVED OUR BUTTS, ZEBRA.
BUT...
OKAY, WHAT DO WE DO...
...ABOUT THE FACT IT HAS INFORMATION ABOUT US FROM THE BEASTS FROM ITS LIMBS?
OUR INDIVIDUAL ATTACKS WON'T WORK.
IT'LL REPEL ANY PHYSICAL DAMAGE AND EVEN COCO'S POISON.

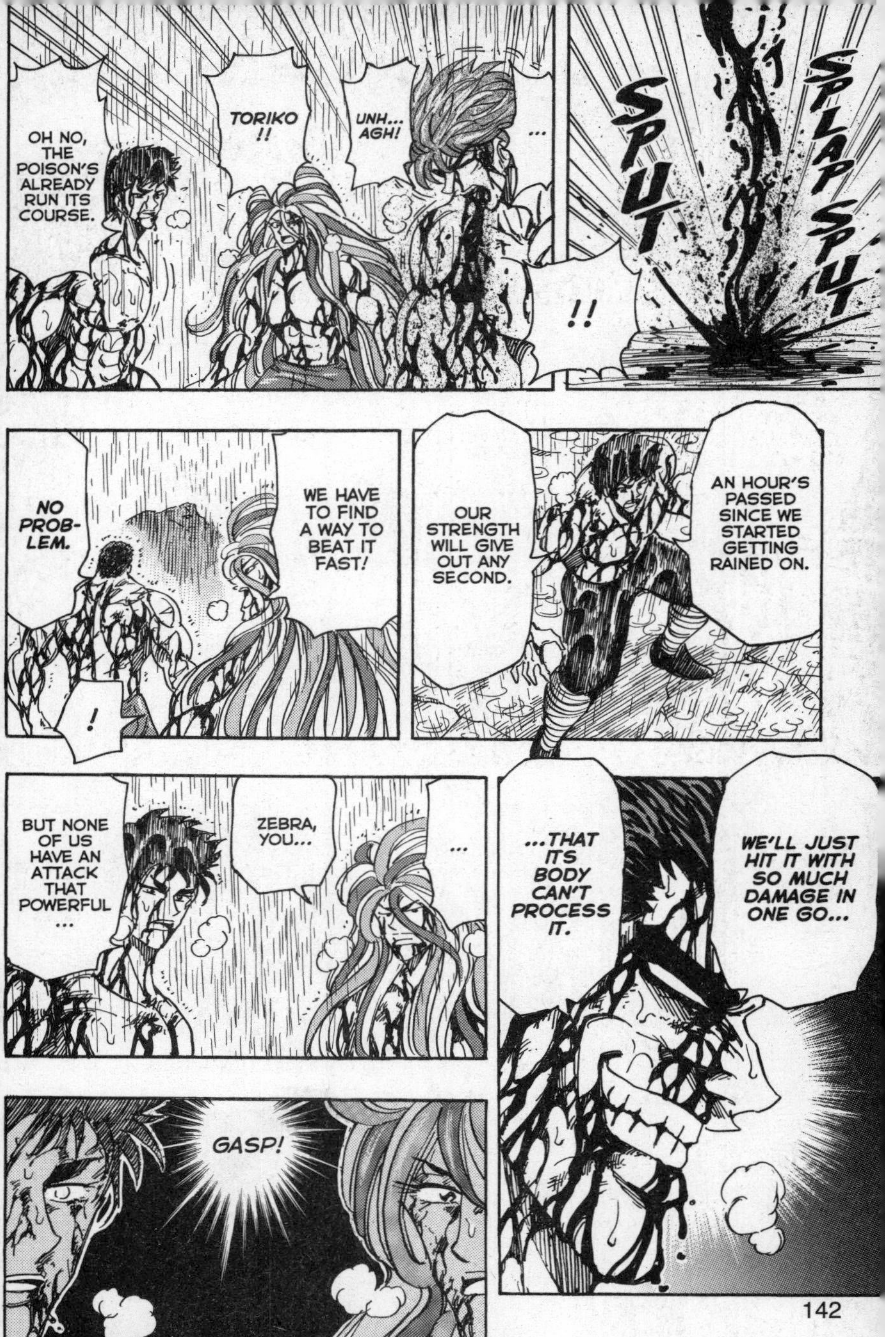

SPLAP SPUT
SPUT
!!
...
UNH... AGH!
TORIKO !!
OH NO, THE POISON'S ALREADY RUN ITS COURSE.
AN HOUR'S PASSED SINCE WE STARTED GETTING RAINED ON.
OUR STRENGTH WILL GIVE OUT ANY SECOND.
WE HAVE TO FIND A WAY TO BEAT IT FAST!
NO PROB-LEM.
!
WE'LL JUST HIT IT WITH SO MUCH DAMAGE IN ONE GO...
...THAT ITS BODY CAN'T PROCESS IT.
...
ZEBRA, YOU...
BUT NONE OF US HAVE AN ATTACK THAT POWERFUL ...
GASP!

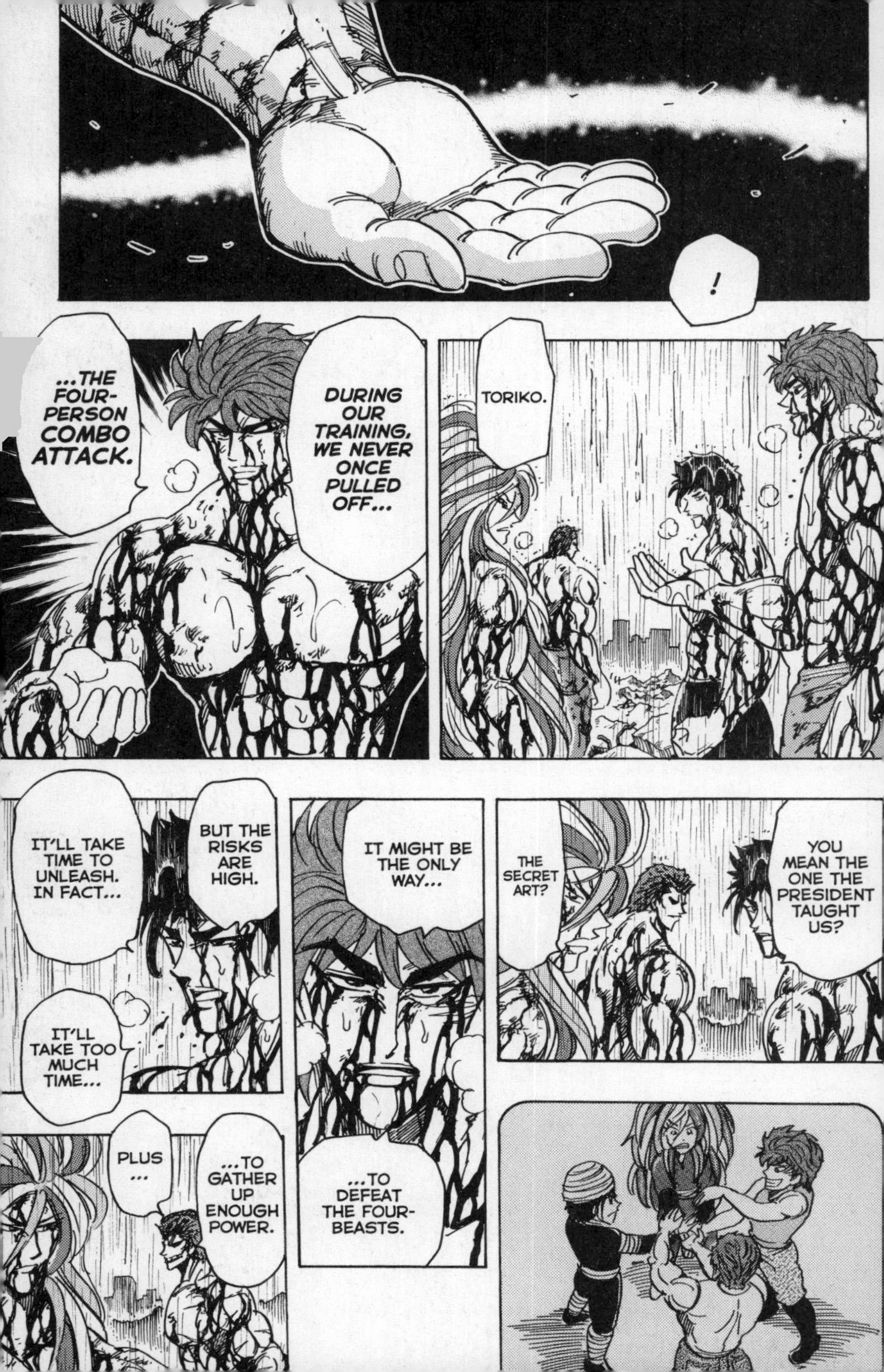
!
TORIKO.
DURING OUR TRAINING, WE NEVER ONCE PULLED OFF...
...THE FOUR-PERSON COMBO ATTACK.
YOU MEAN THE ONE THE PRESIDENT TAUGHT US?
THE SECRET ART?
IT MIGHT BE THE ONLY WAY...
...TO DEFEAT THE FOUR-BEASTS.
BUT THE RISKS ARE HIGH.
IT'LL TAKE TIME TO UNLEASH. IN FACT...
IT'LL TAKE TOO MUCH TIME...
PLUS...
...TO GATHER UP ENOUGH POWER.

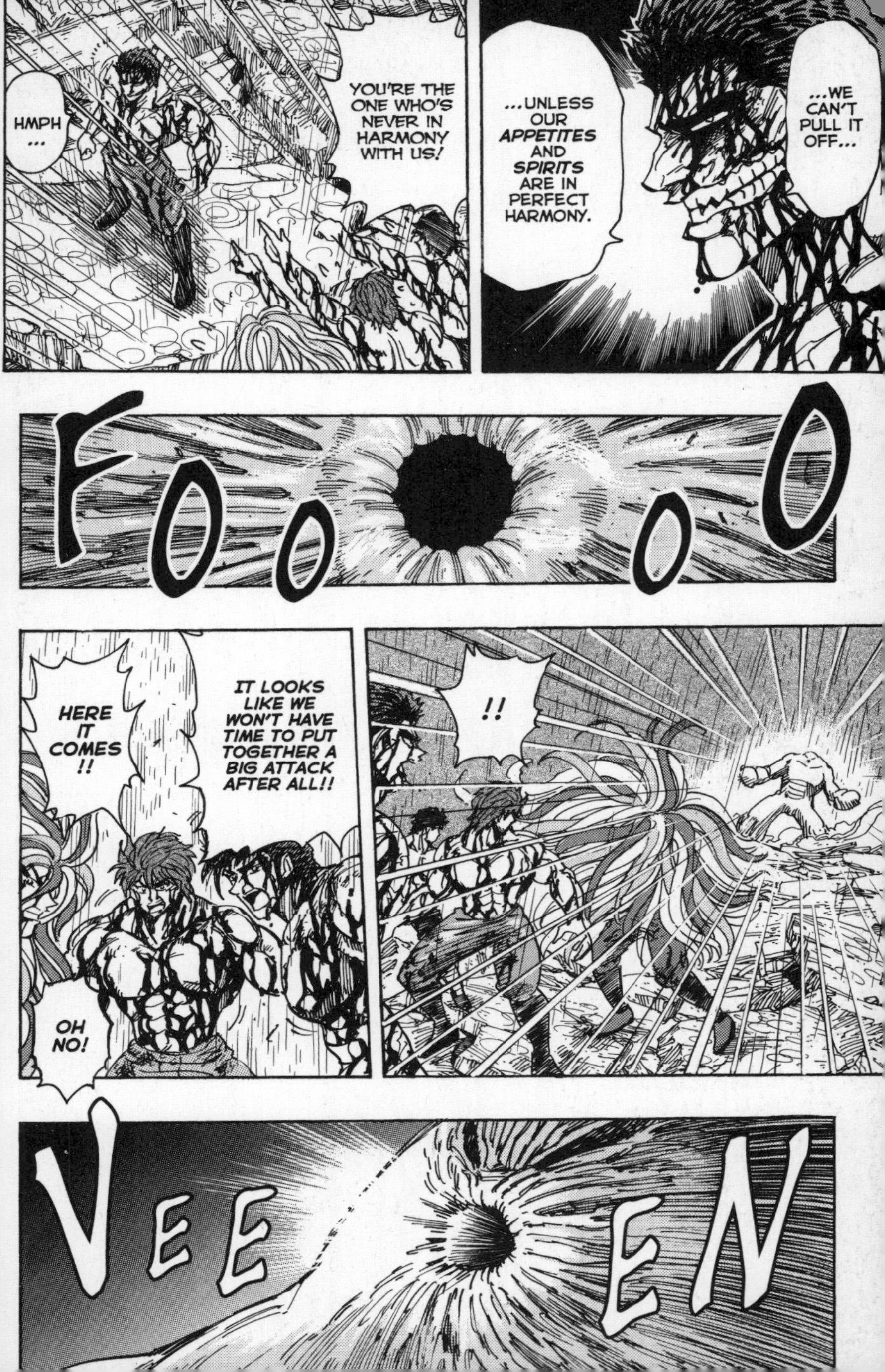
...WE CAN'T PULL IT OFF...
...UNLESS OUR APPETITES AND SPIRITS ARE IN PERFECT HARMONY.
YOU'RE THE ONE WHO'S NEVER IN HARMONY WITH US!
HMPH ...
FOOOOO
!!
IT LOOKS LIKE WE WON'T HAVE TIME TO PUT TOGETHER A BIG ATTACK AFTER ALL!!
HERE IT COMES !!
OH NO!
VEEEN

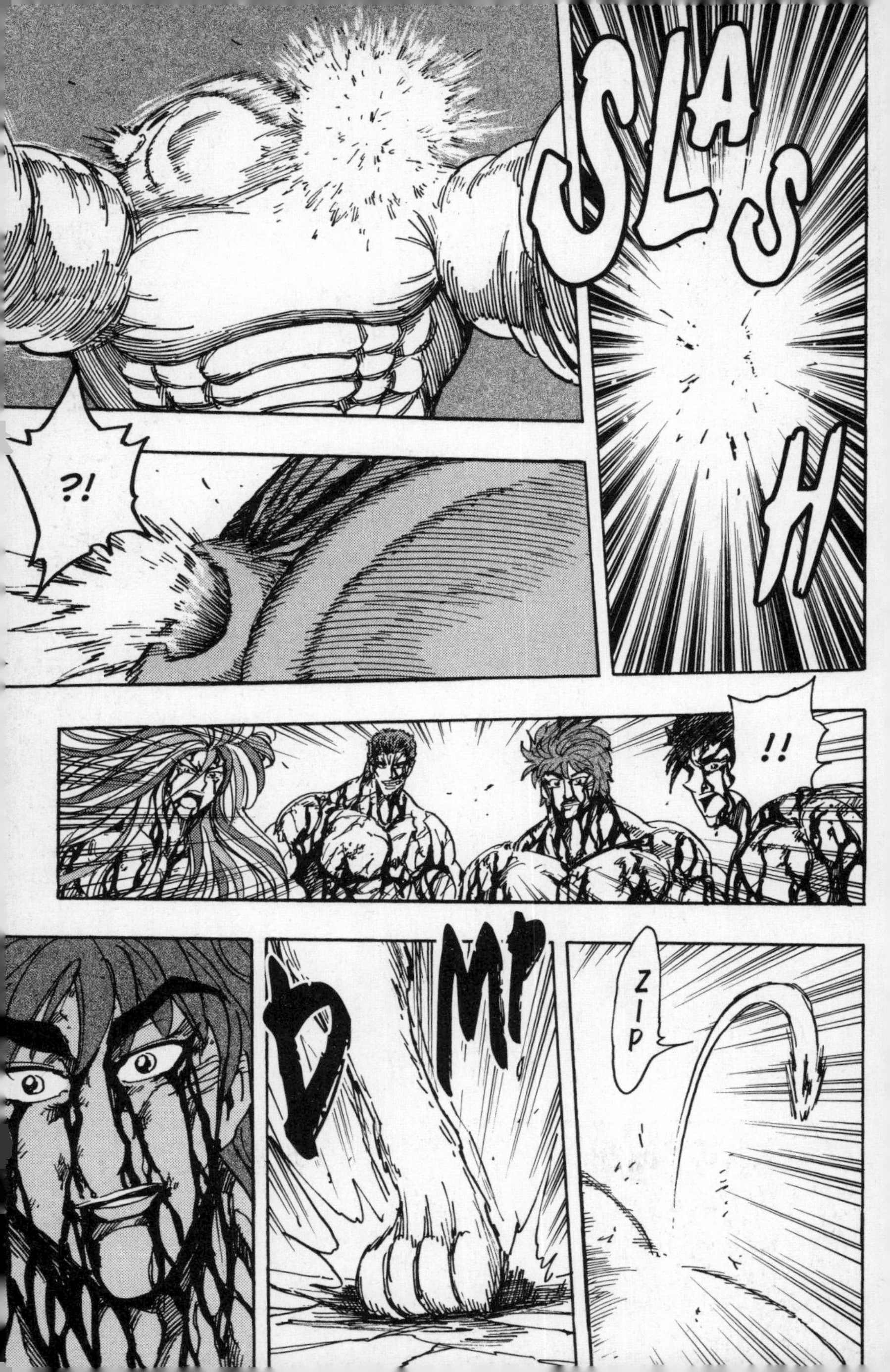
SLASH
?!
!!
ZIP
DMP

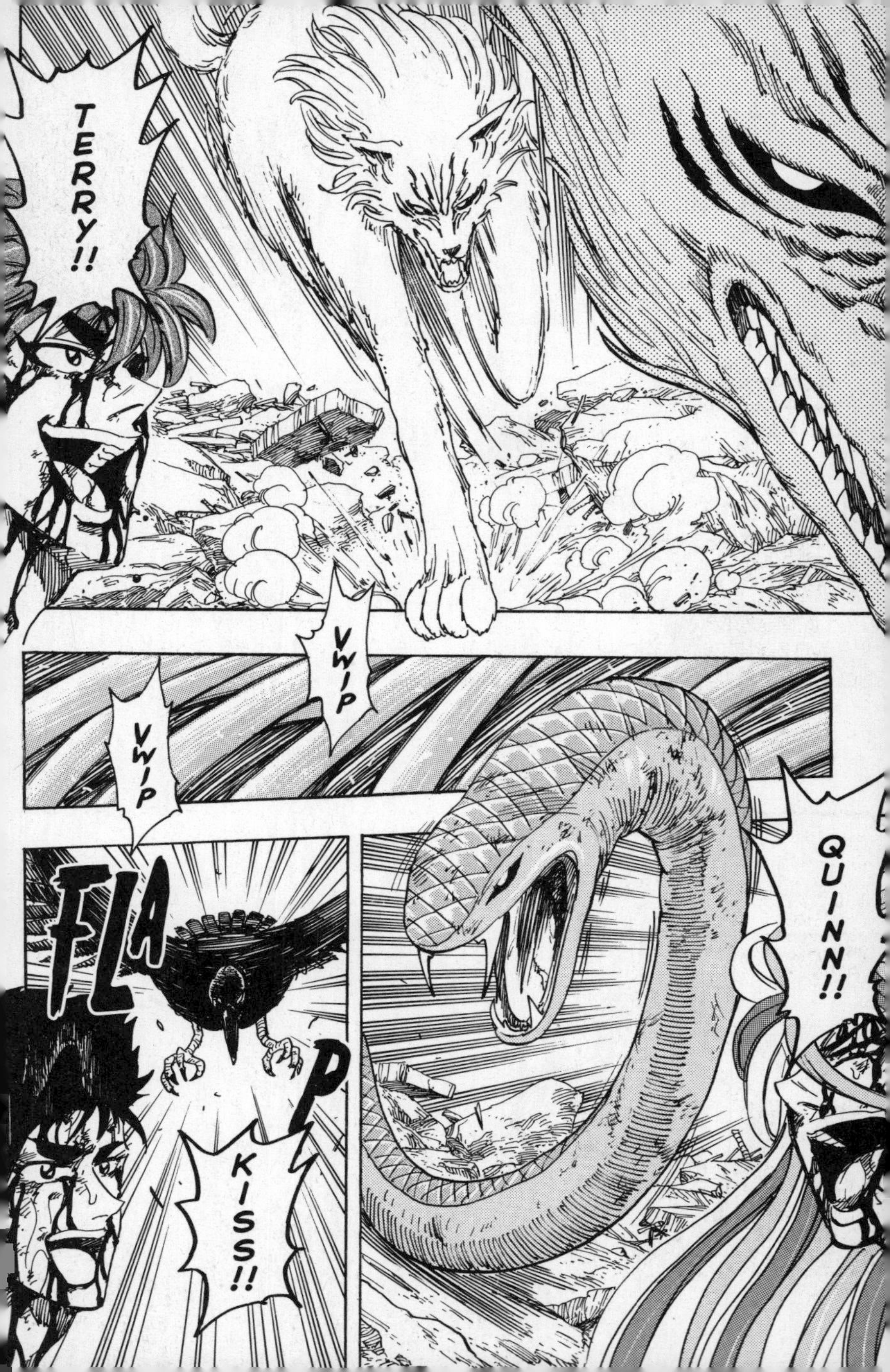
TERRY!!
VWIP
VWIP
QUINN!!
FLAP
KISS!!

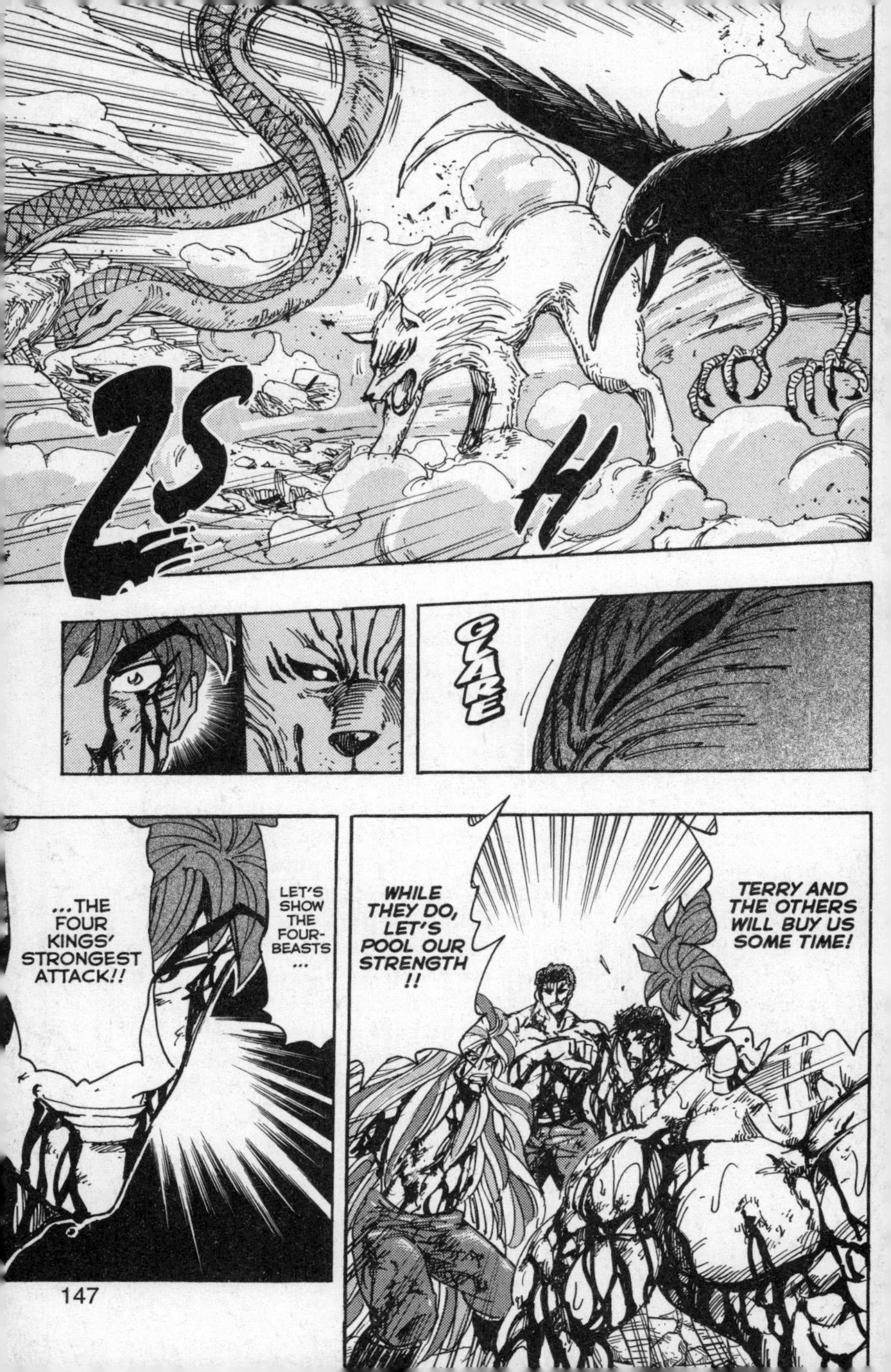
ZS
H
GLARE
TERRY AND THE OTHERS WILL BUY US SOME TIME!
WHILE THEY DO, LET'S POOL OUR STRENGTH !!
LET'S SHOW THE FOUR-BEASTS ...
...THE FOUR KINGS' STRONGEST ATTACK!!

SHIMABU SPEAKS

Hello, everybody! I'm the creator of *Toriko*, Shimabukuro! I think this is the first time I've ever written about *Toriko* here. I'm so nervous (Yet I write while totally sprawled out on my bed...) Anyway, I thought I'd take this time to explain a little bit about the "Reject Pages Corner" featured at the back of this book. To be honest, they're just there to fill space because I didn't have time to do the usual Gourmet Checklists! Yep! That's all! I hope you enjoy!!

The thing you should know is that when *Toriko* first began its serialization in the magazine, I would do proper storyboards for each and every pencil page. And I don't know why this is, but lately I just can't sketch storyboards to save my life (*heh*)! I even go so far as to do up the storyboards without any sketches to speak of. Yep. Though I really shouldn't be shrugging it off like that (*gulp!*). What I'm trying to say is that when you've been drawing manga for as long as I have, you have these weeks where nothing's coming to you. At all. I swear, my head feels empty as a hollow shell. The switch in my brain is in a complete "off" position. (I actually wish a switch like that existed!) Still, whether or not I can come up with anything, my deadlines just keep creeping up on me! And believe me, their approach feels so menacing... If they were just slowly but surely plodding along, that'd be one thing, but it feels like they're charging at me screaming "Waaaah!!" Oh, those deadlines... It reminds me of being a kid and sleeping in late while my mom ran the vacuum by my bed. (Why you gotta be like that, deadlines?)

Continued on page 168

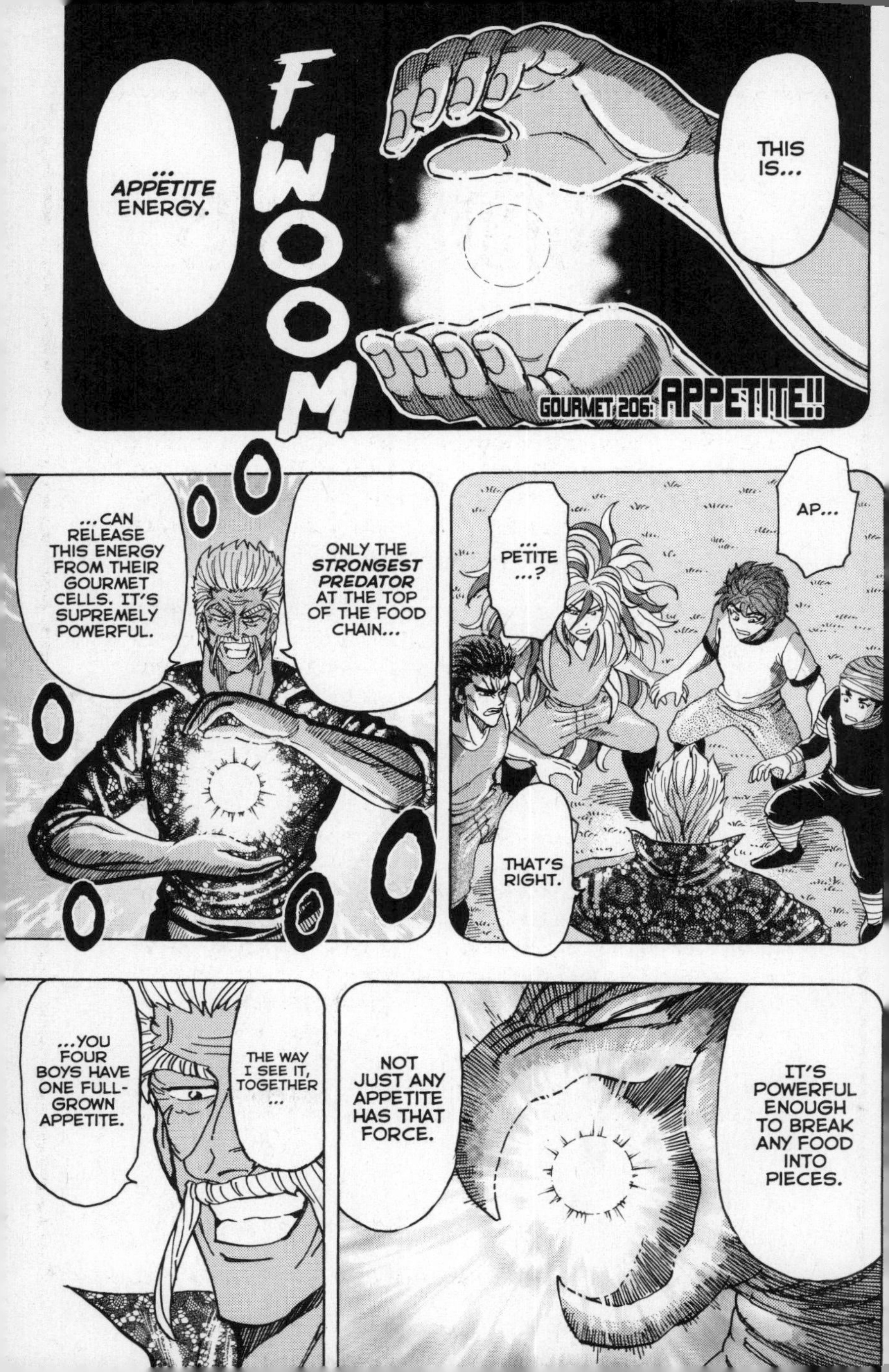
THIS IS...
GOURMET 206: APPETITE!!
FWOOM
...APPETITE ENERGY.
AP...
...PETITE...?
THAT'S RIGHT.
ONLY THE STRONGEST PREDATOR AT THE TOP OF THE FOOD CHAIN...
...CAN RELEASE THIS ENERGY FROM THEIR GOURMET CELLS. IT'S SUPREMELY POWERFUL.
IT'S POWERFUL ENOUGH TO BREAK ANY FOOD INTO PIECES.
NOT JUST ANY APPETITE HAS THAT FORCE.
THE WAY I SEE IT, TOGETHER...
...YOU FOUR BOYS HAVE ONE FULL-GROWN APPETITE.

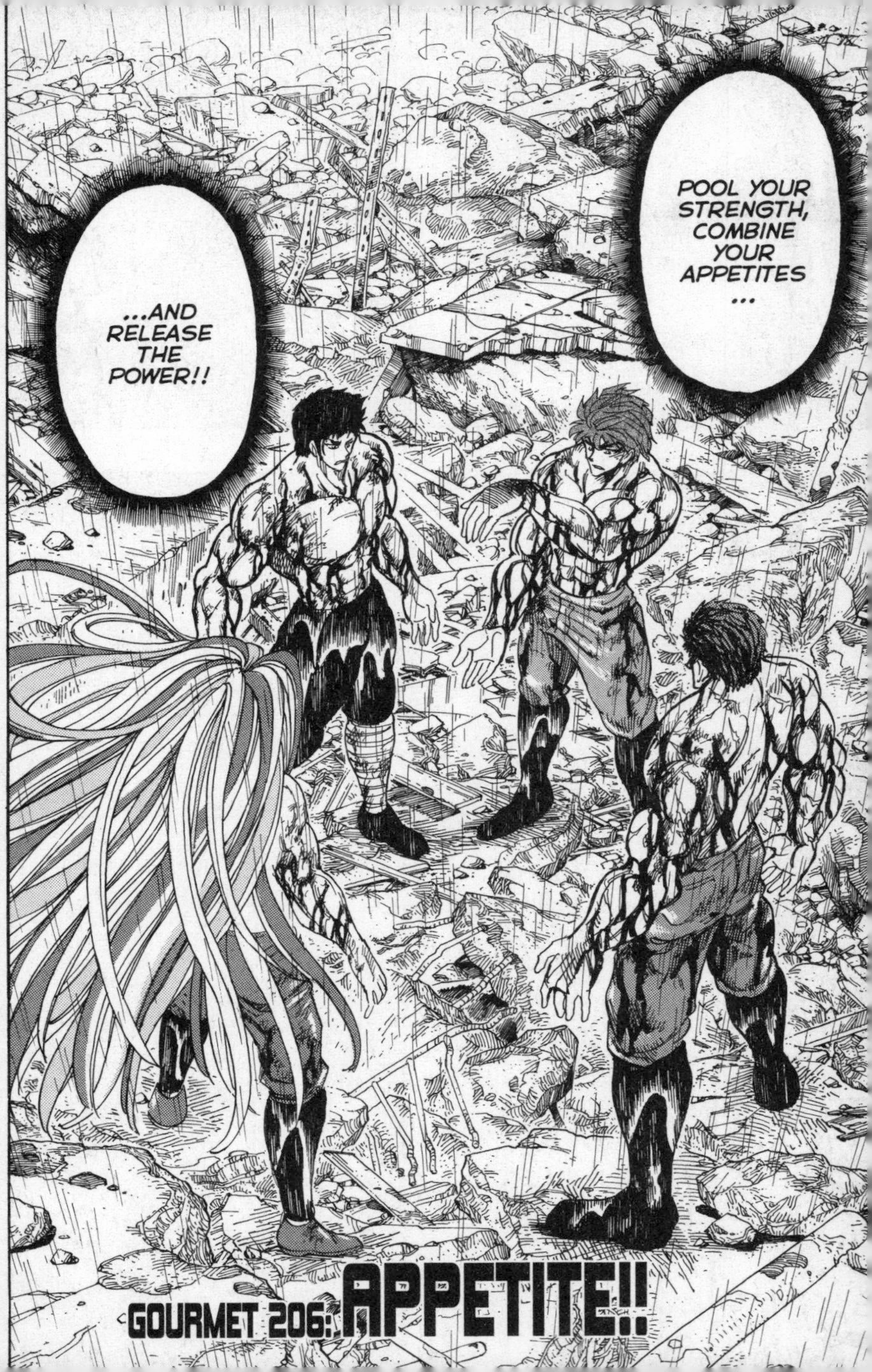
POOL YOUR STRENGTH, COMBINE YOUR APPETITES ...
...AND RELEASE THE POWER!!
GOURMET 206: APPETITE!!

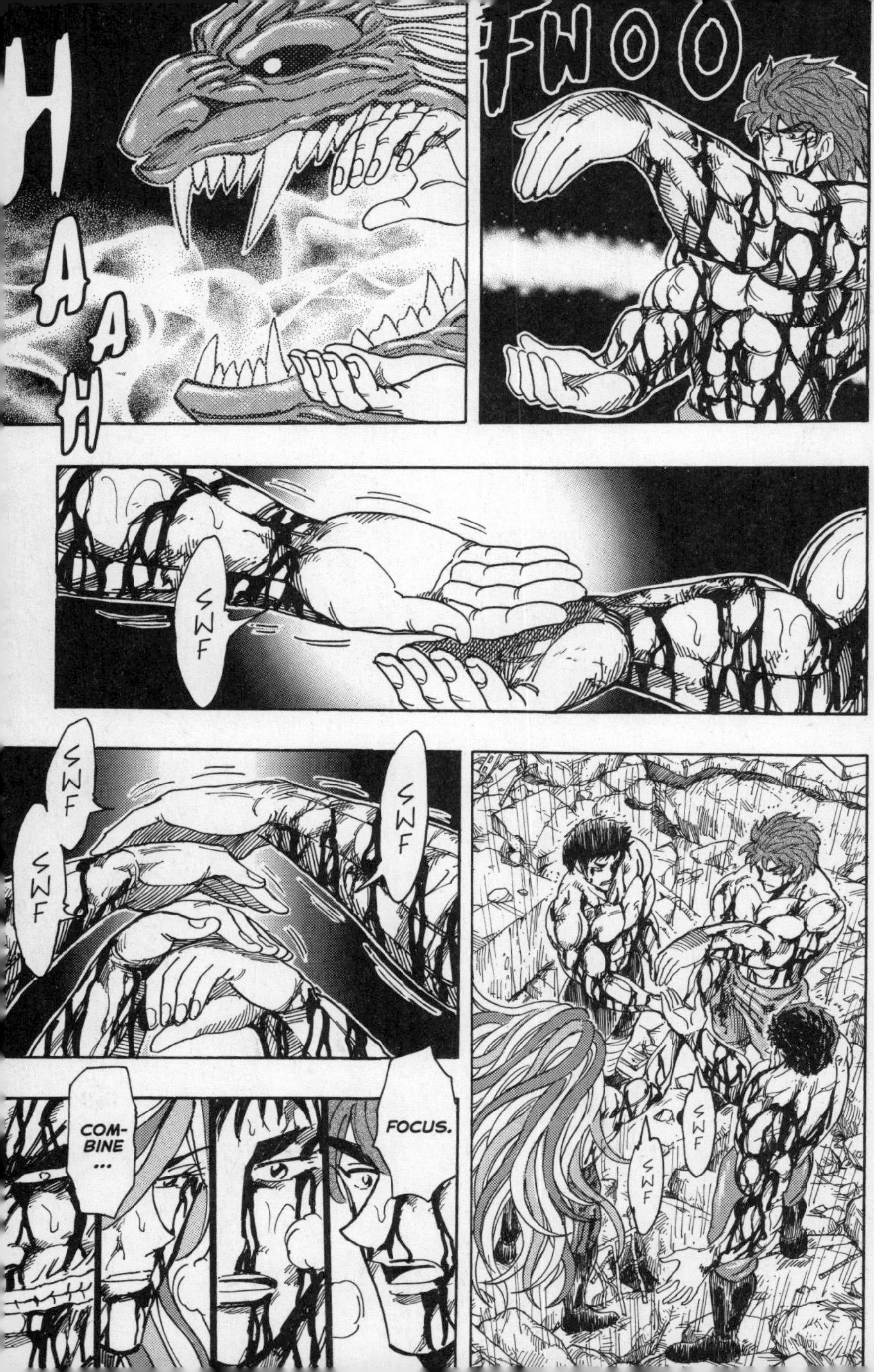
FWOOO
HAAH
SWF
SWF
SWF
SWF
SWF
SWF
FOCUS.
COMBINE...

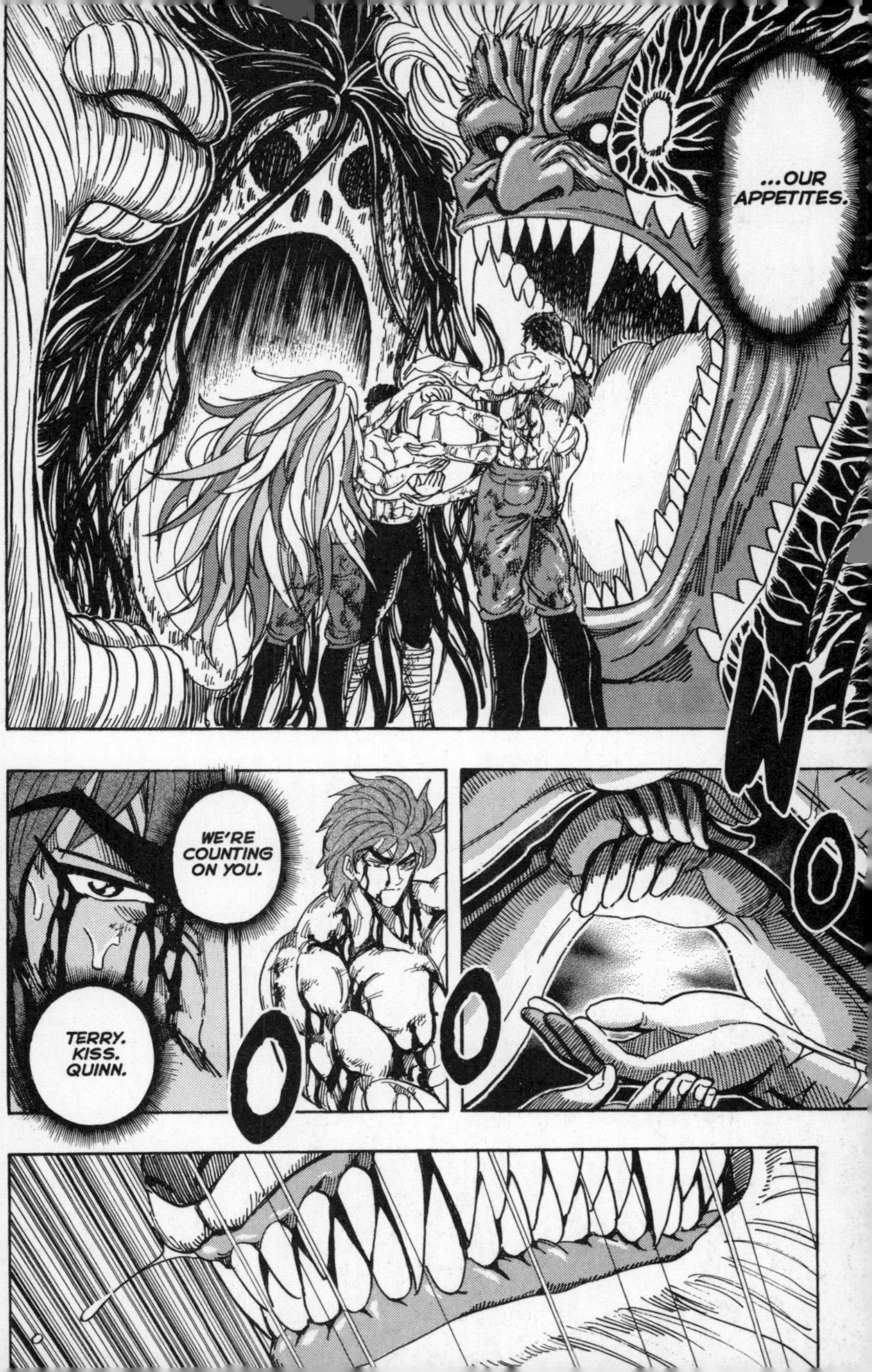
...OUR APPETITES.
WOOO
WE'RE COUNTING ON YOU.
TERRY. KISS. QUINN.

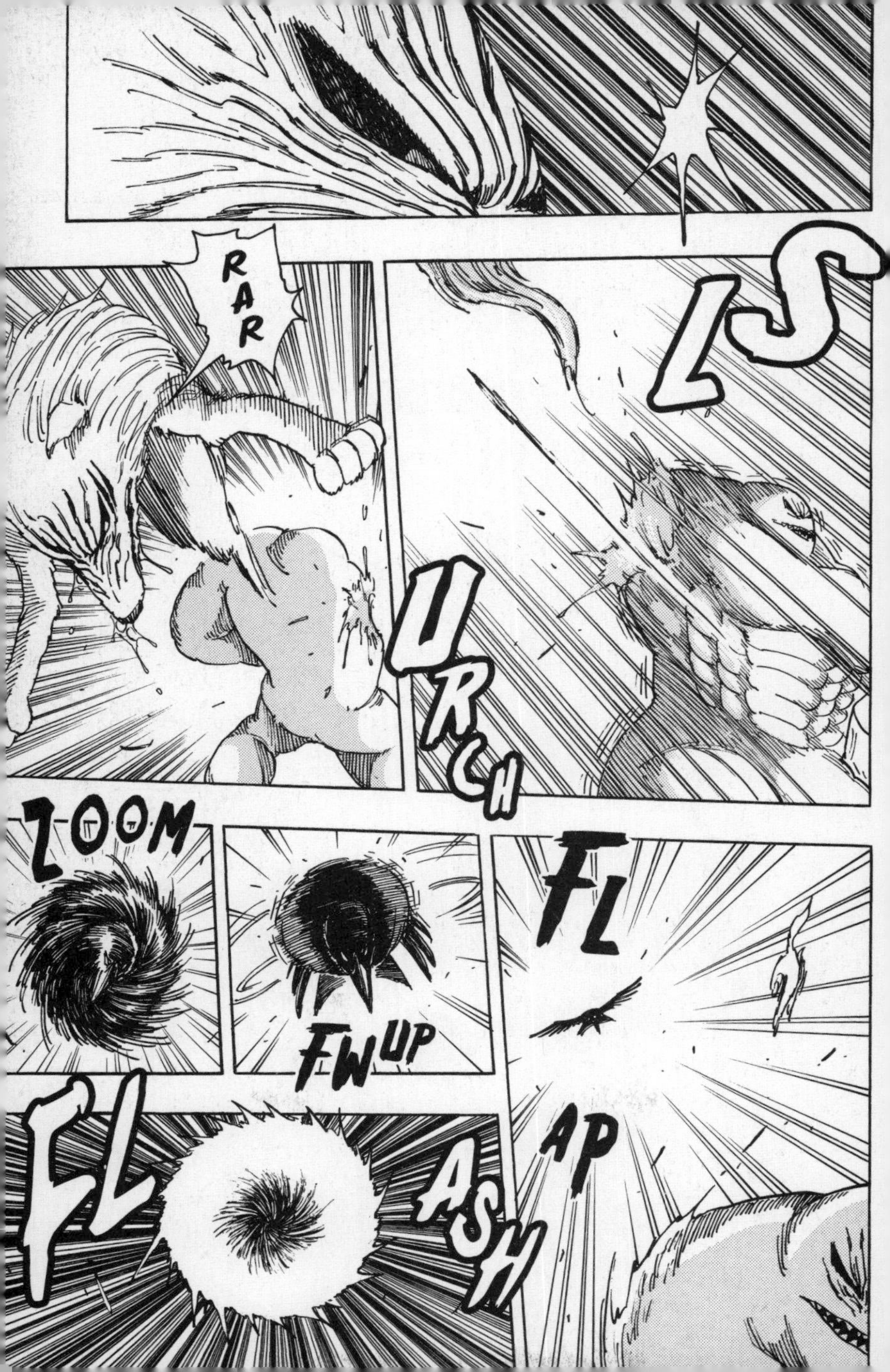

LS
URCH
RAR
FL
AP
FWUP
ZOOM
FL
ASH

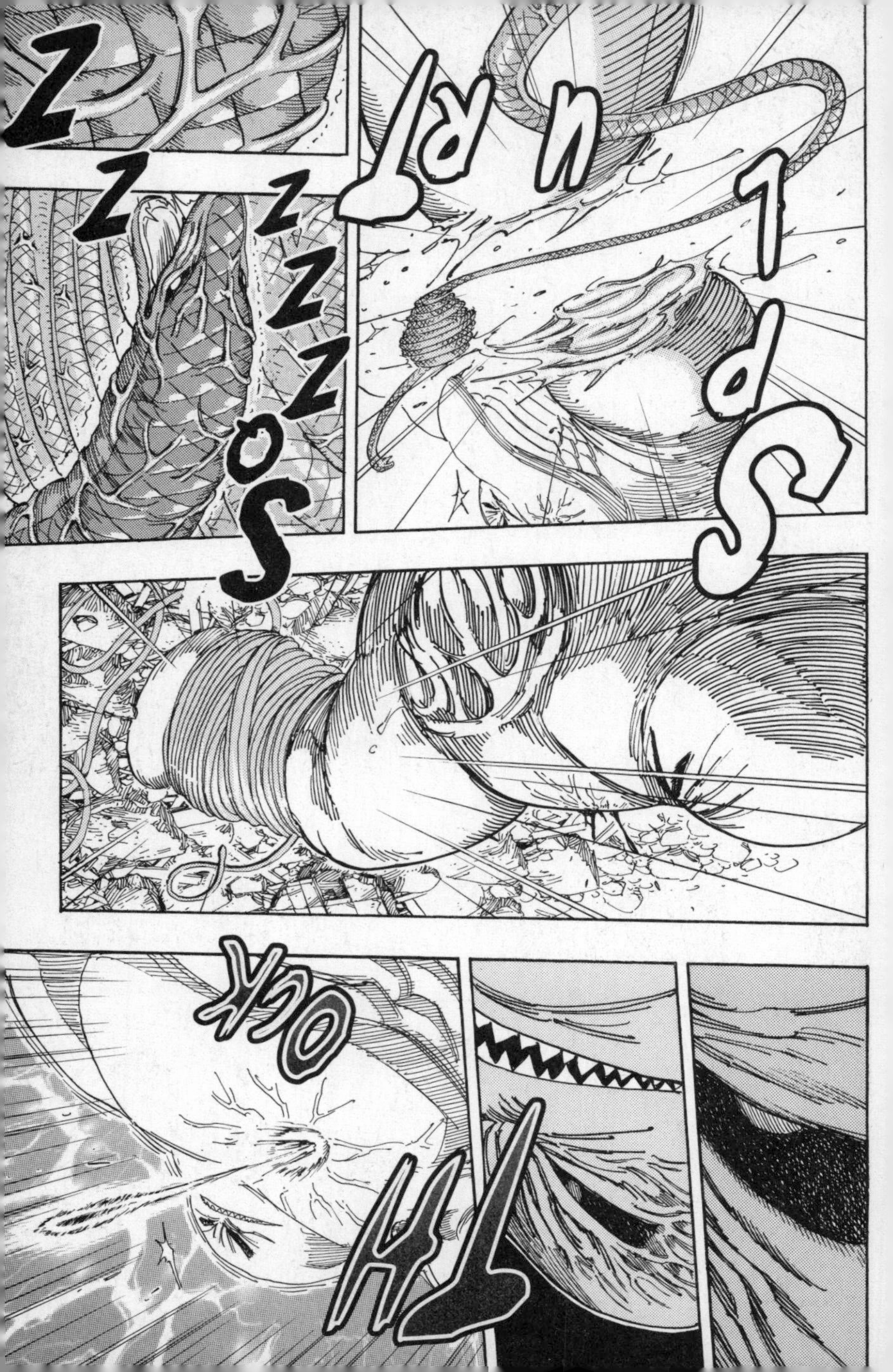

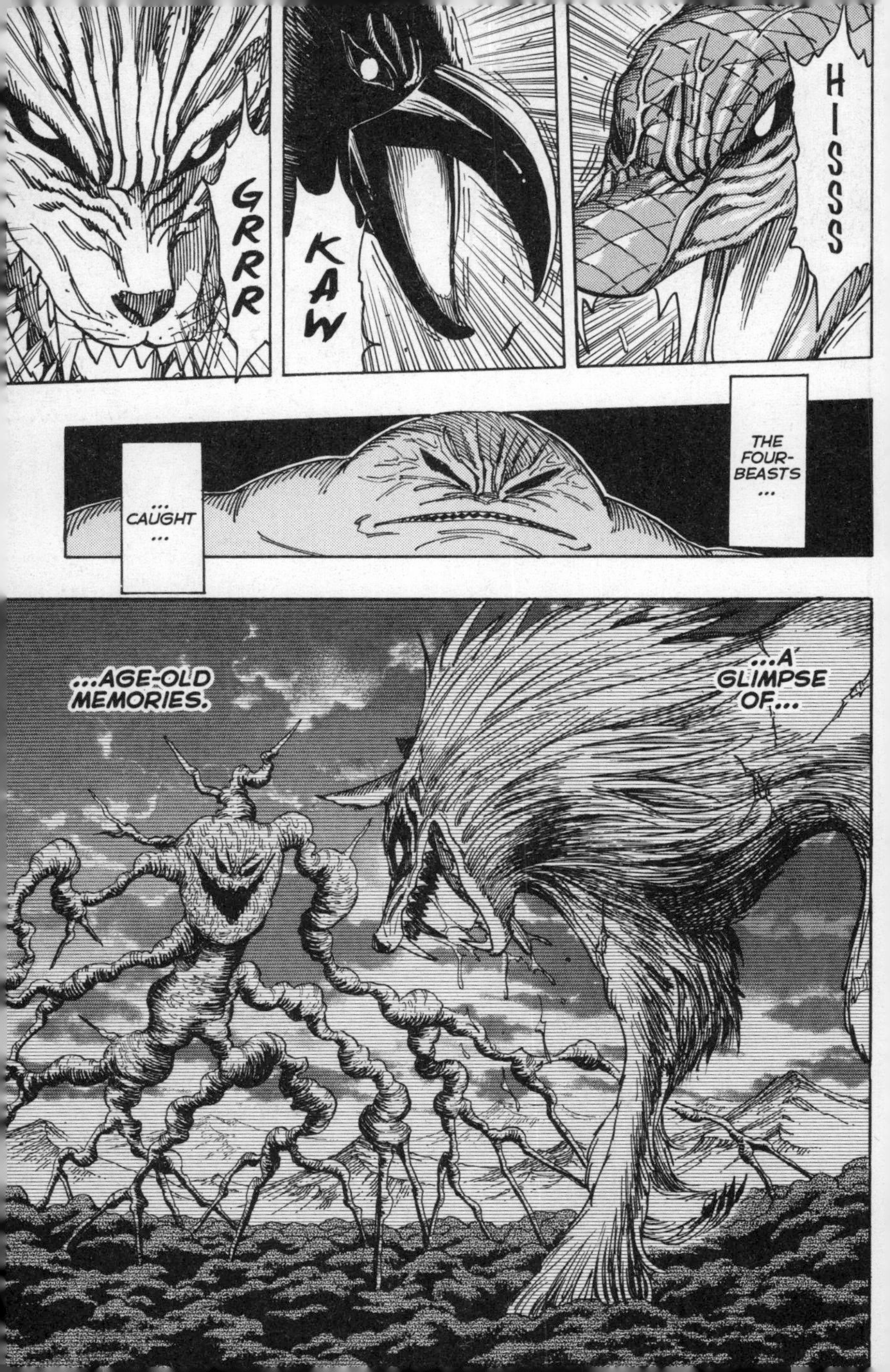
HISSS
KAW
GRRR
THE FOUR-BEASTS ...
... CAUGHT ...
...A GLIMPSE OF...
...AGE-OLD MEMORIES.

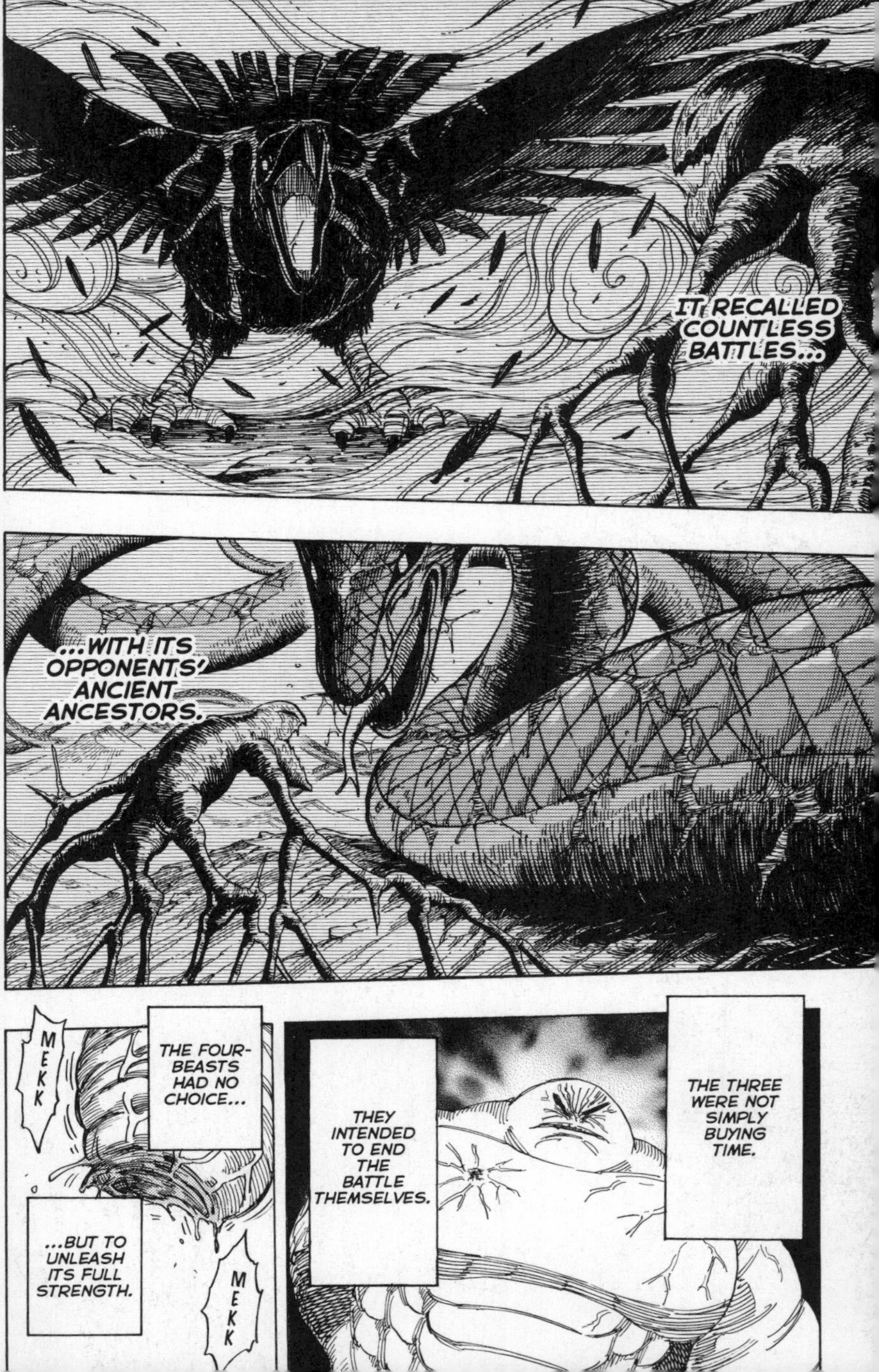
IT RECALLED COUNTLESS BATTLES...
...WITH ITS OPPONENTS' ANCIENT ANCESTORS.
THE THREE WERE NOT SIMPLY BUYING TIME.
THEY INTENDED TO END THE BATTLE THEMSELVES.
THE FOUR-BEASTS HAD NO CHOICE...
MEKK
...BUT TO UNLEASH ITS FULL STRENGTH.
MEKK

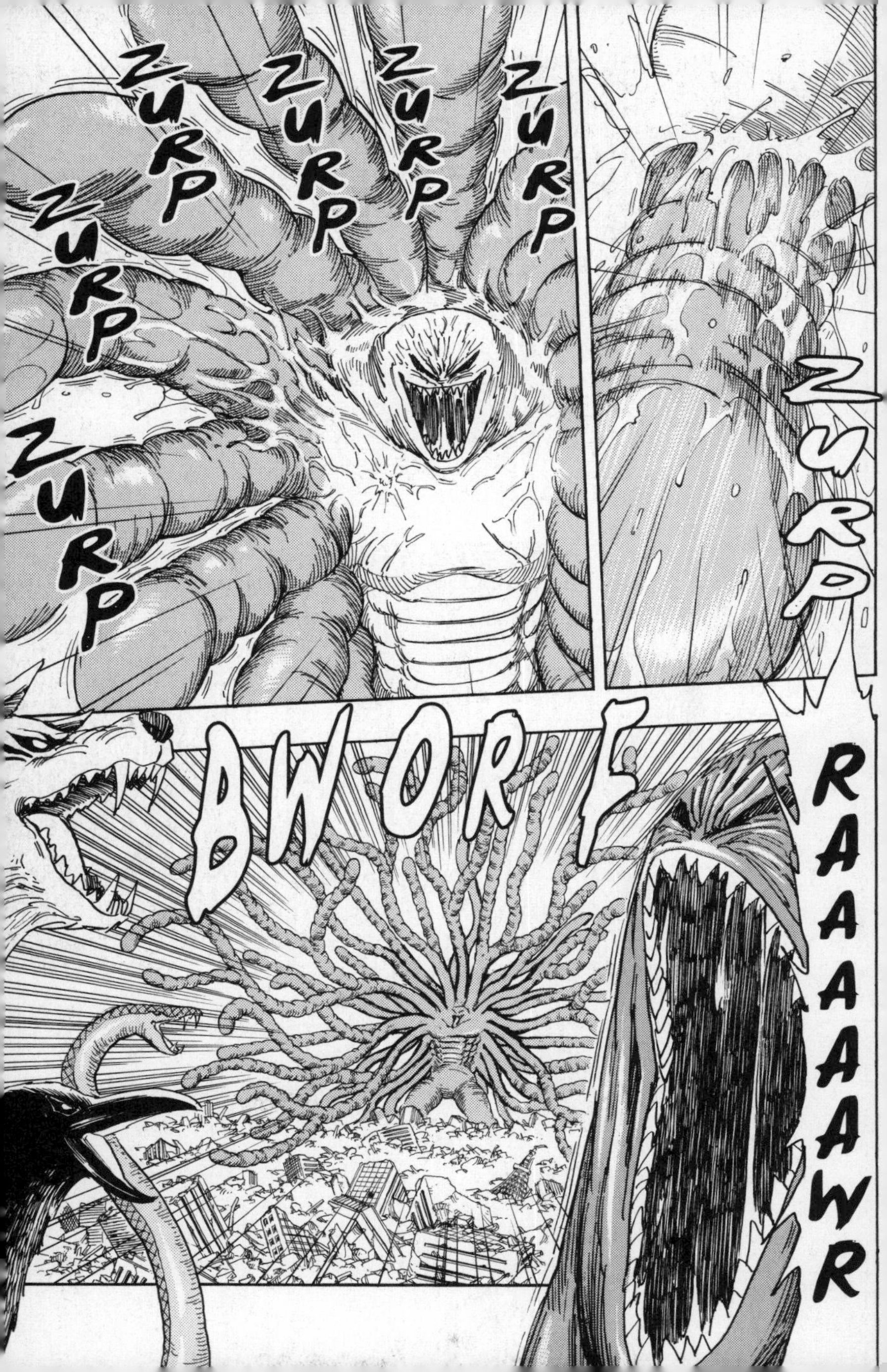
ZURP
ZURP
ZURP
ZURP
ZURP
ZURP
BWORF
RAAAAAWR

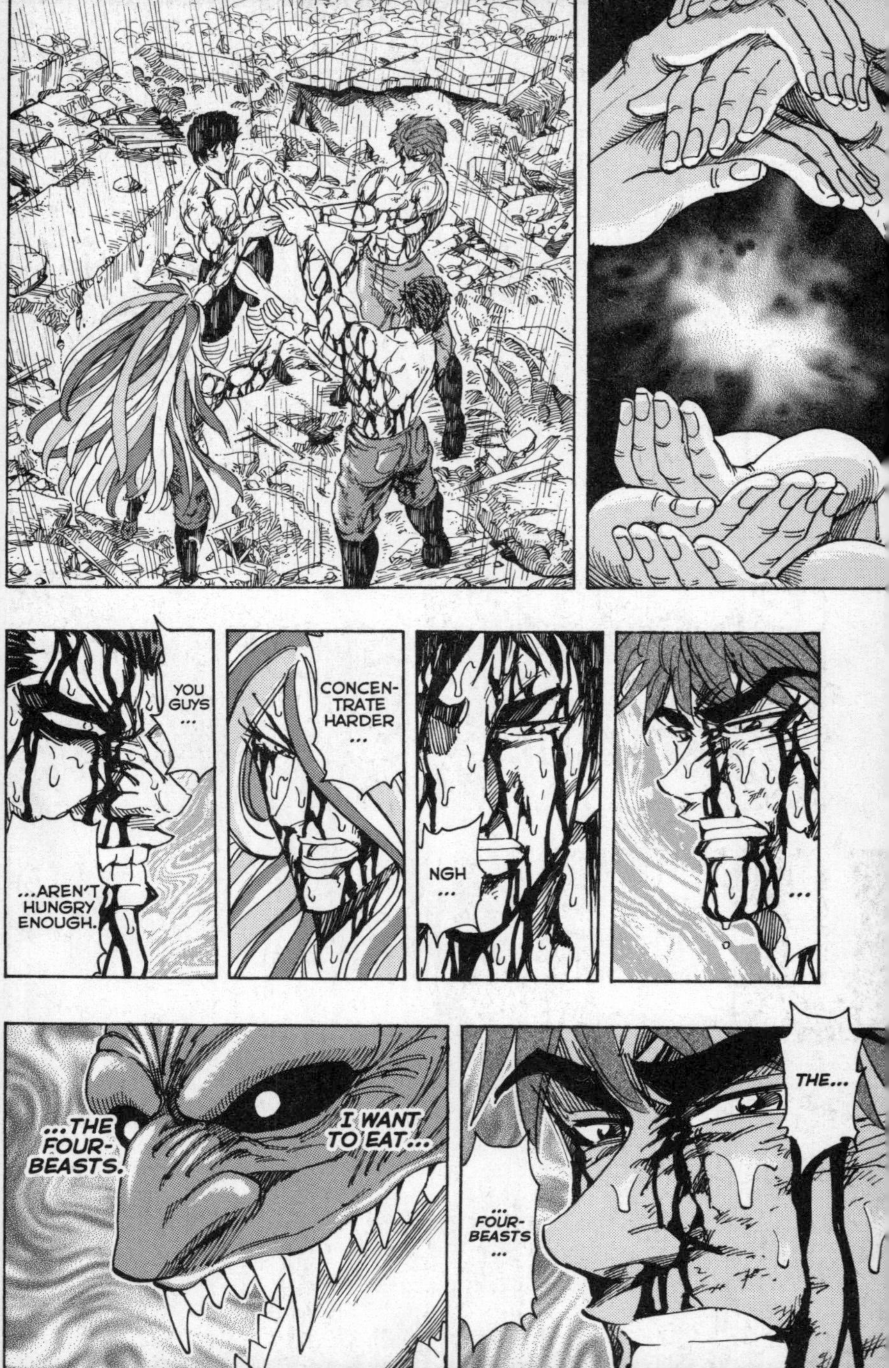
...
NGH ...
CONCEN-TRATE HARDER ...
YOU GUYS ...
...AREN'T HUNGRY ENOUGH.
THE...
... FOUR-BEASTS ...
I WANT TO EAT...
...THE FOUR-BEASTS.

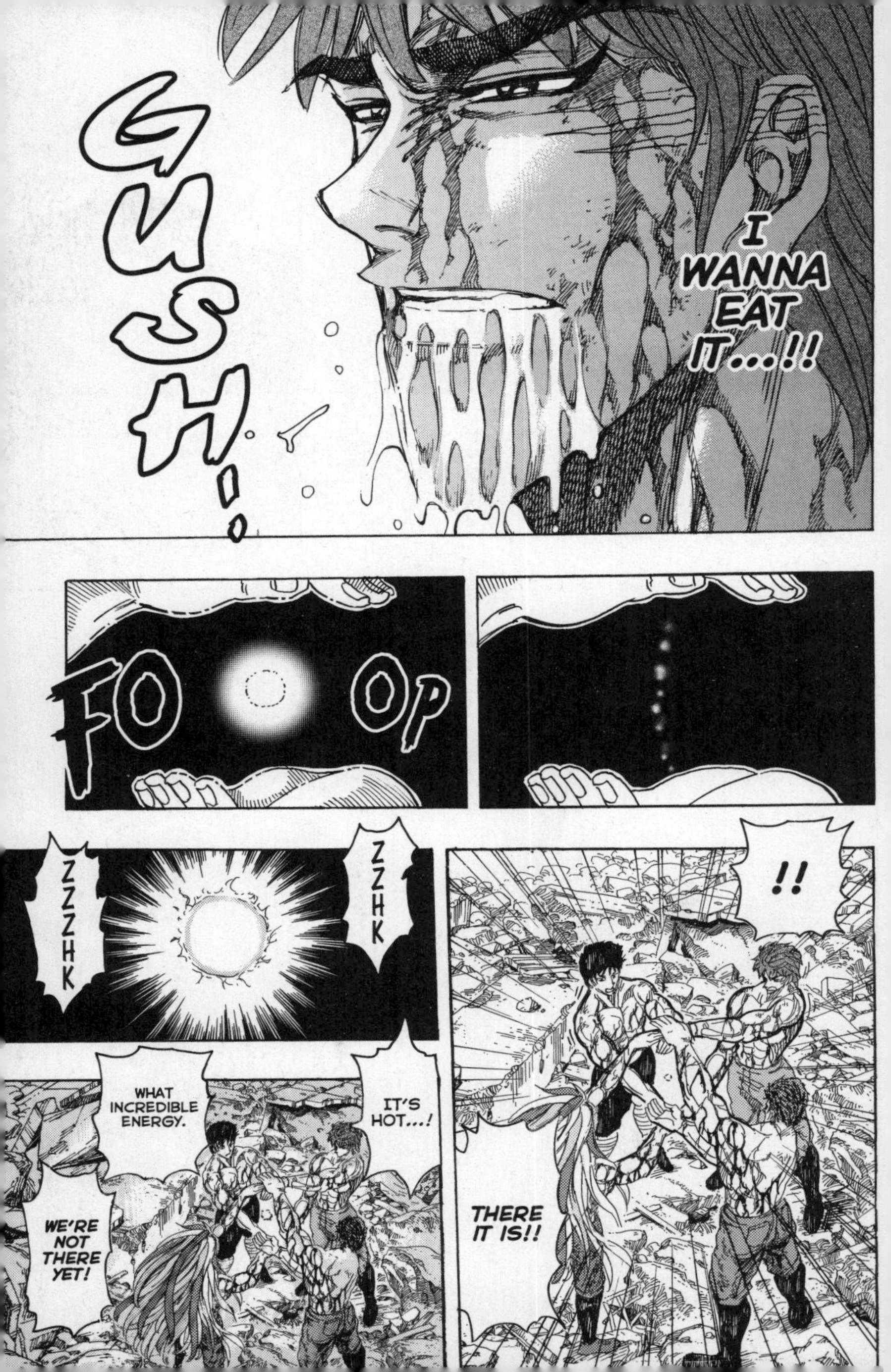
I WANNA EAT IT...!!
GUSH!
FOOOP
!!
THERE IT IS!!
ZZHK
ZZZHK
IT'S HOT...!
WHAT INCREDIBLE ENERGY.
WE'RE NOT THERE YET!

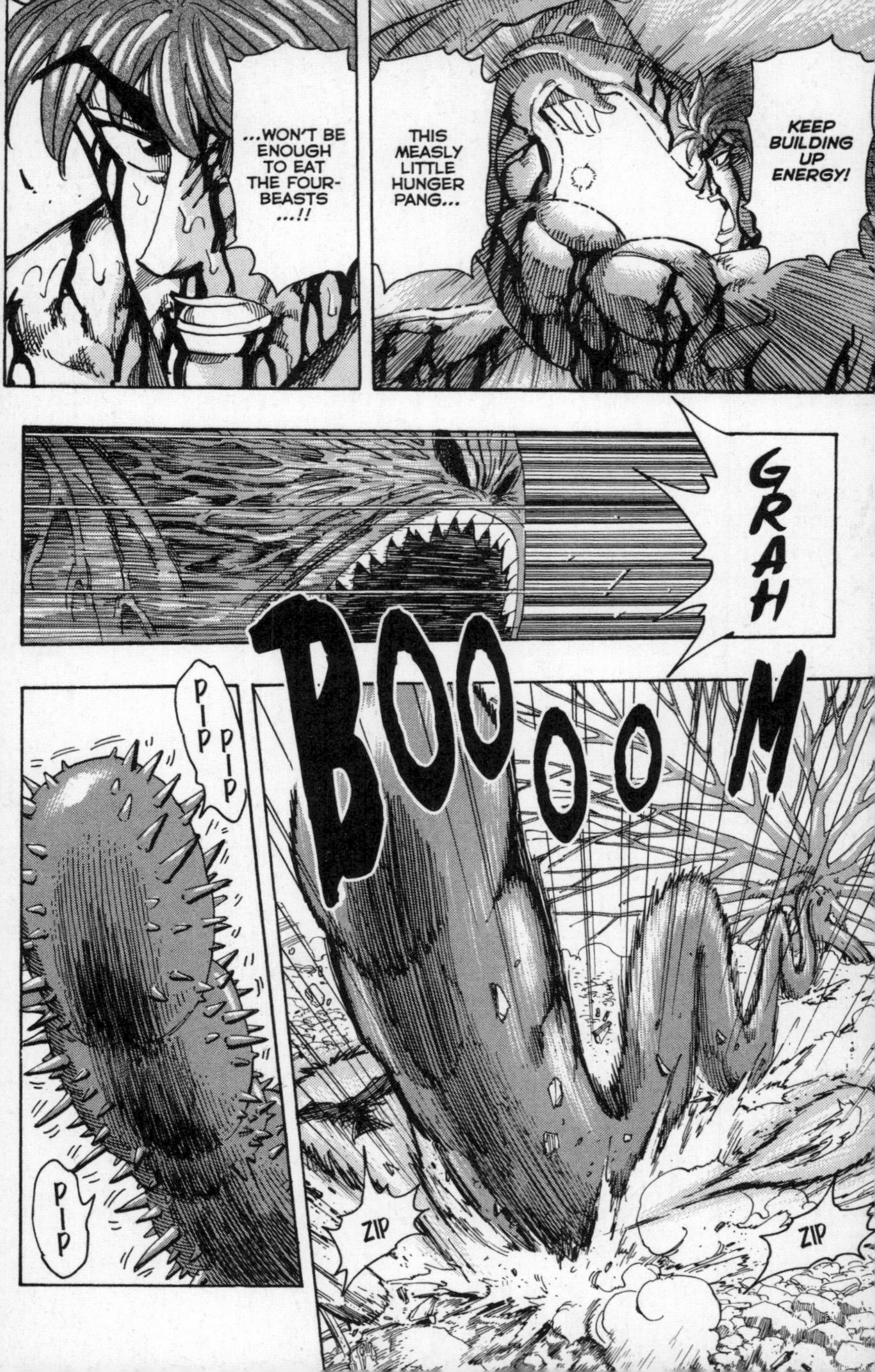
KEEP BUILDING UP ENERGY!
THIS MEASLY LITTLE HUNGER PANG...
...WON'T BE ENOUGH TO EAT THE FOUR-BEASTS ...!!
GRAH
BOOOOM
ZIP
ZIP
PIP PIP
PIP

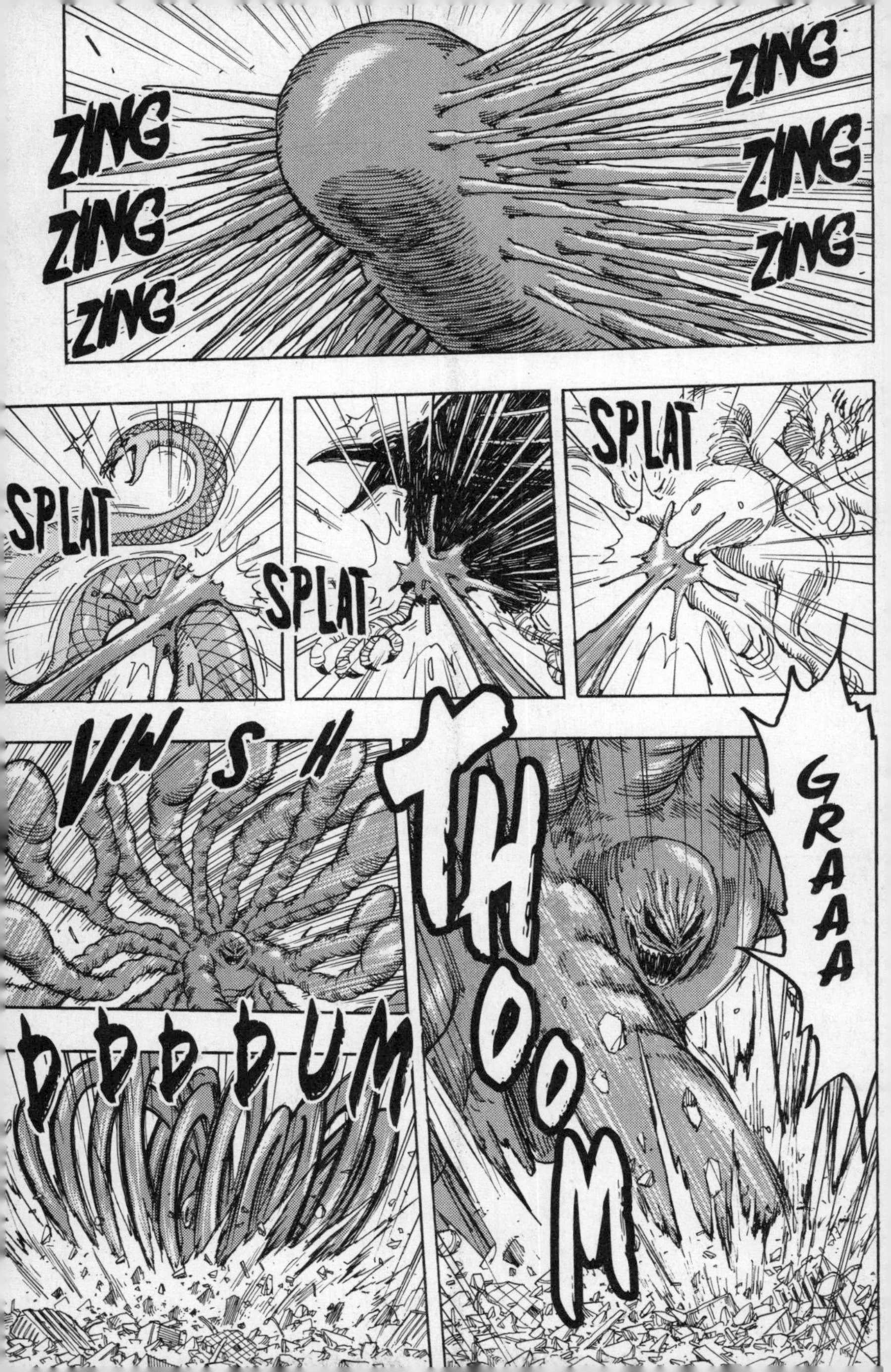
ZING
ZING
ZING
ZING
ZING
ZING
SPLAT
SPLAT
SPLAT
GRAAA
THOOOM
VWSH
DDDDUM

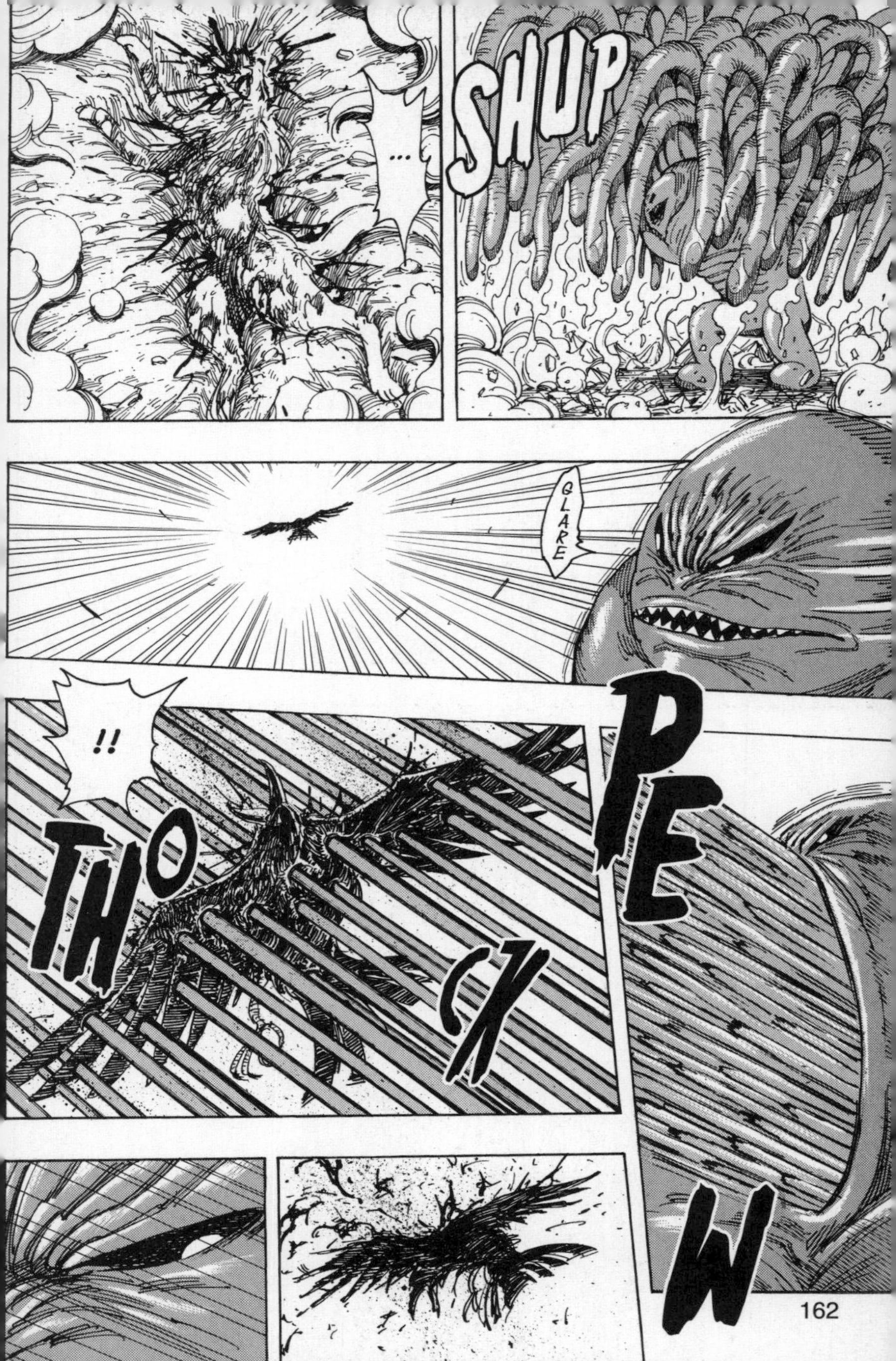
SHUP
...
GLARE
PEW
!!
THOCK

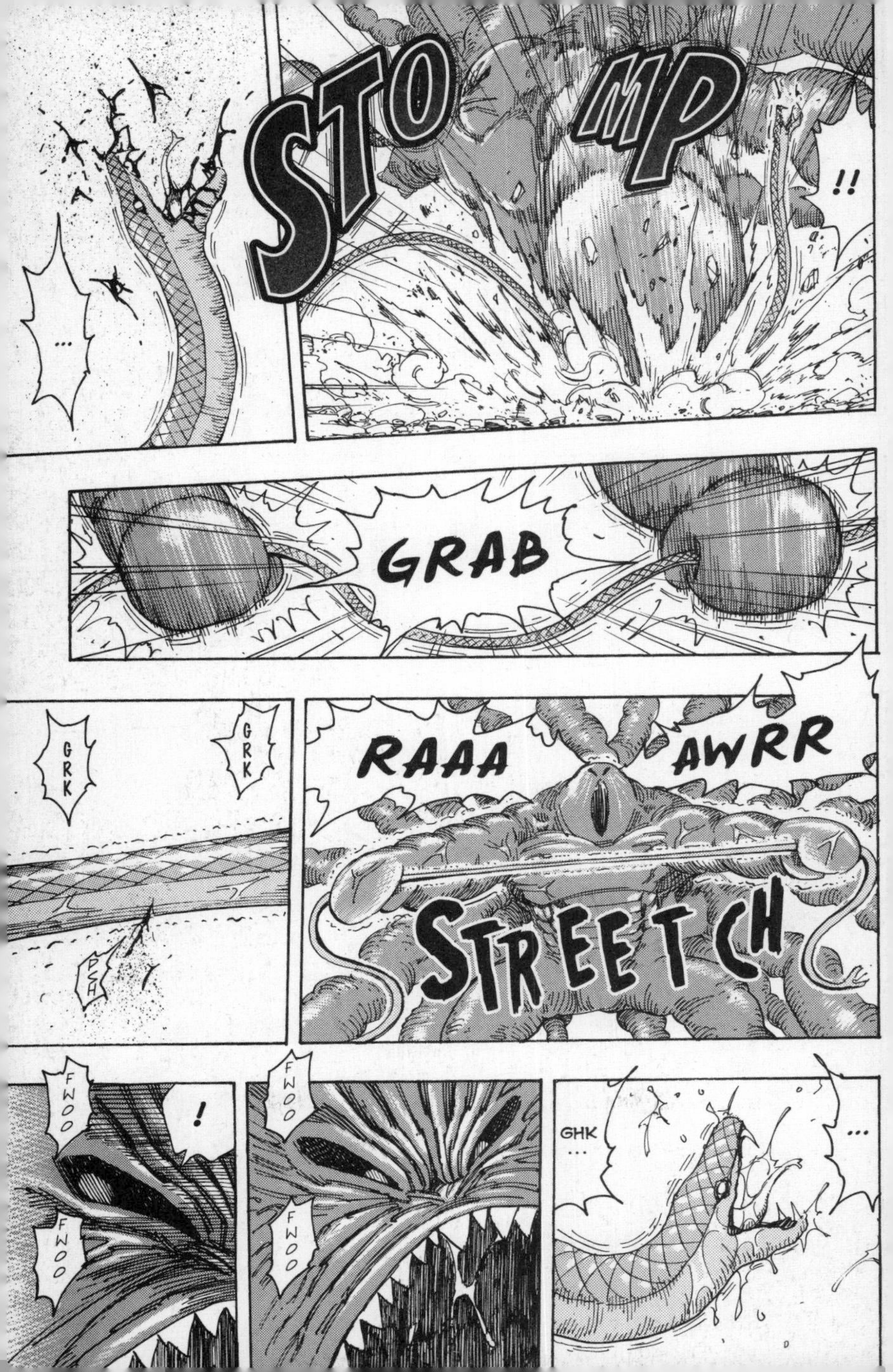
STOMP
!!
...
GRAB
RAAA
AWRR
STREETCH
GRK
GRK
PSH
...
GHK...
FWOO
FWOO
!
FWOO
FWOO

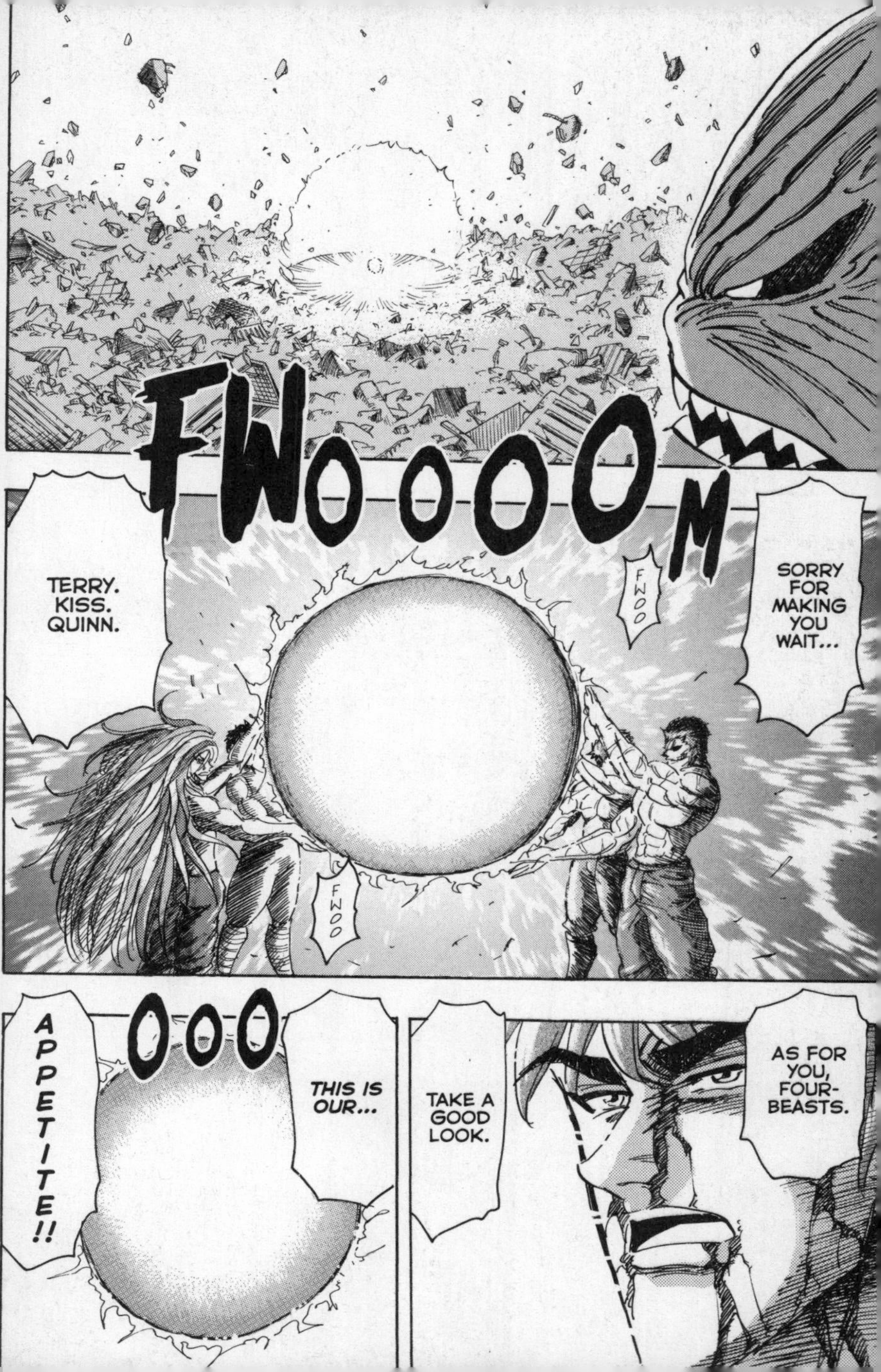
FWOOOOM
SORRY FOR MAKING YOU WAIT...
FWOO
TERRY. KISS. QUINN.
FWOO
AS FOR YOU, FOUR-BEASTS.
TAKE A GOOD LOOK.
THIS IS OUR...
OOO
APPETITE!!

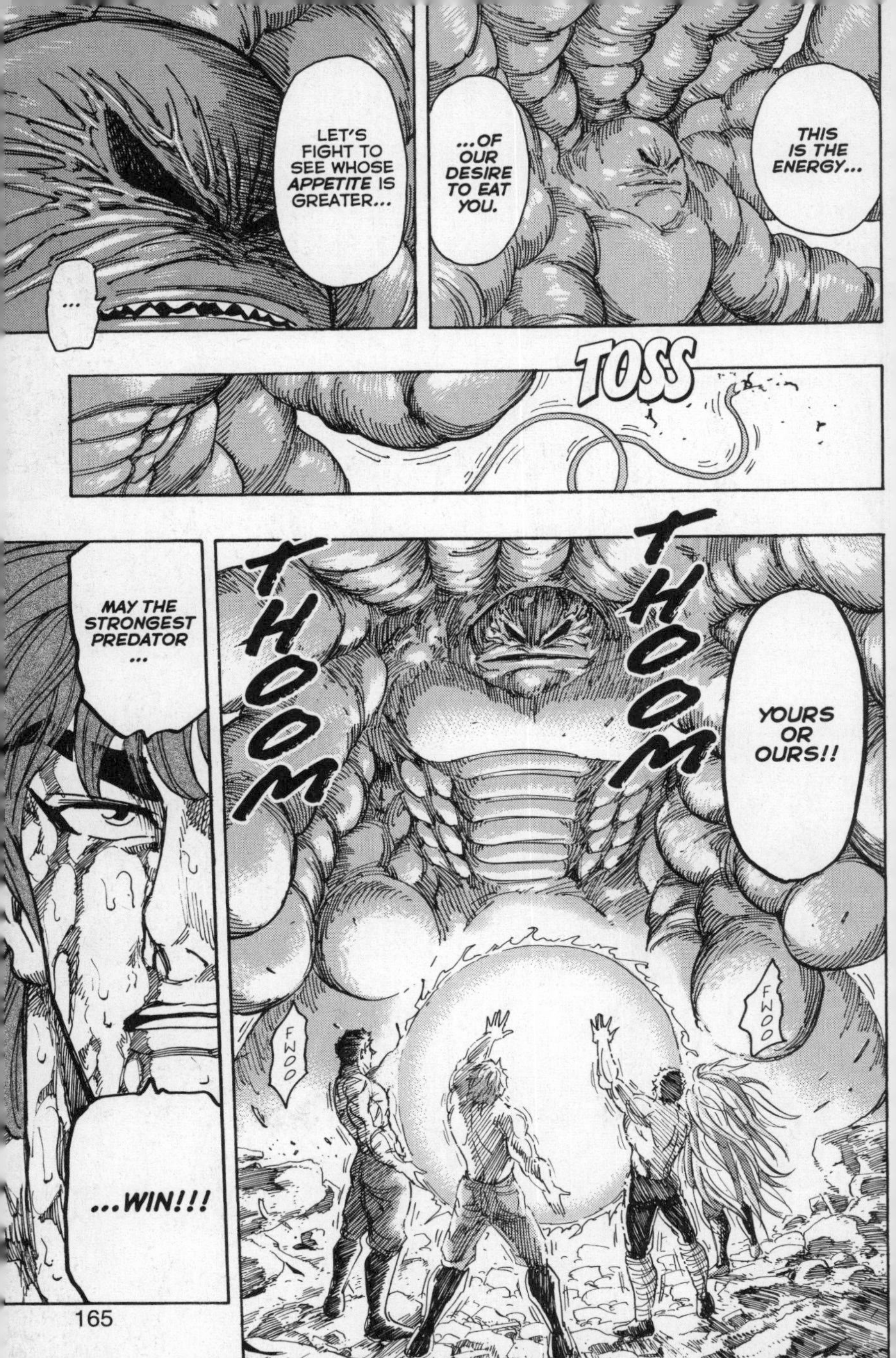
THIS IS THE ENERGY...
...OF OUR DESIRE TO EAT YOU.
LET'S FIGHT TO SEE WHOSE *APPETITE* IS GREATER...
...
TOSS
YOURS OR OURS!!
THOOM
THOOM
FWOO
FWOO
MAY THE STRONGEST PREDATOR ...
...WIN!!!

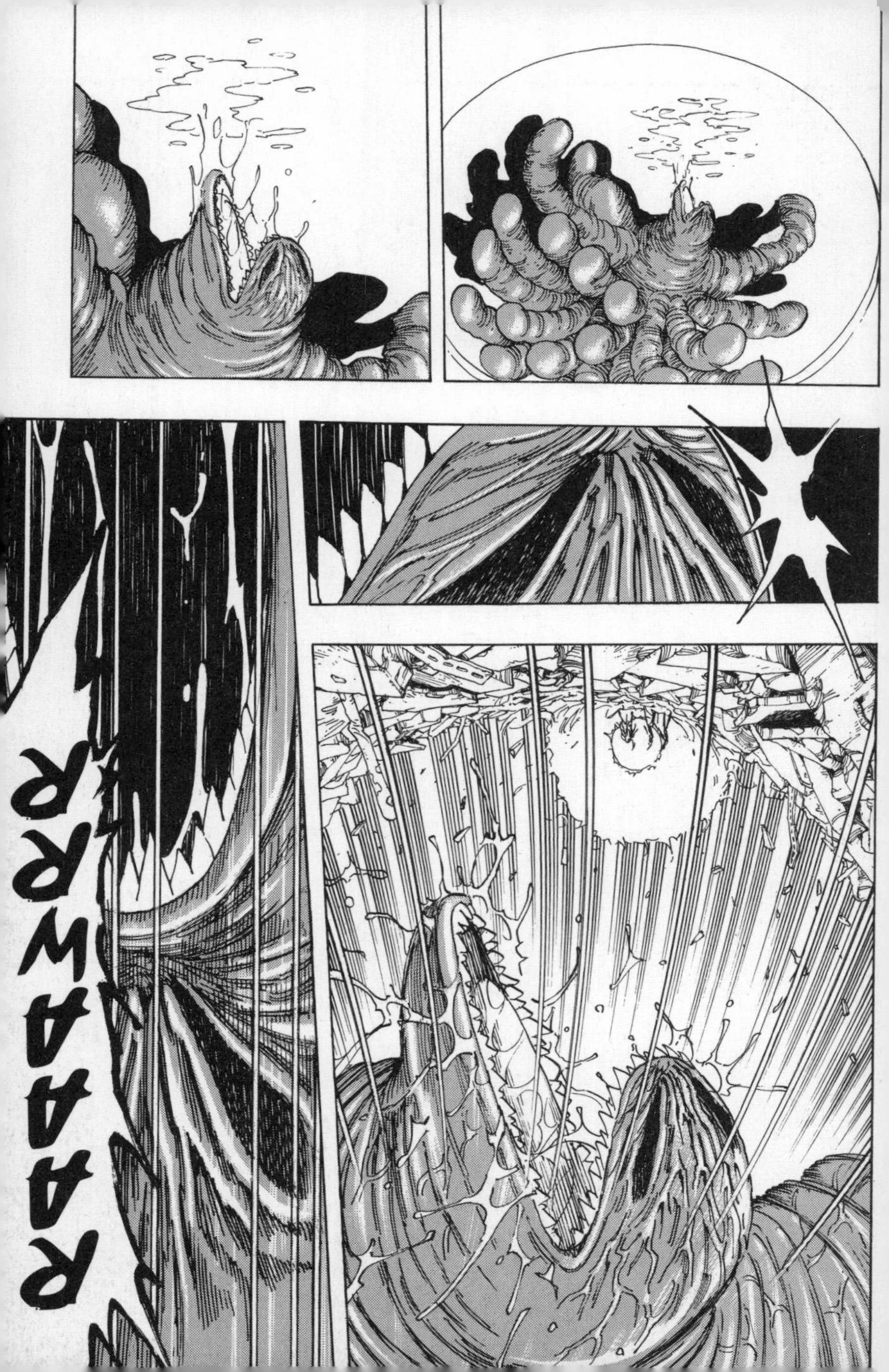
RAAAAWRR

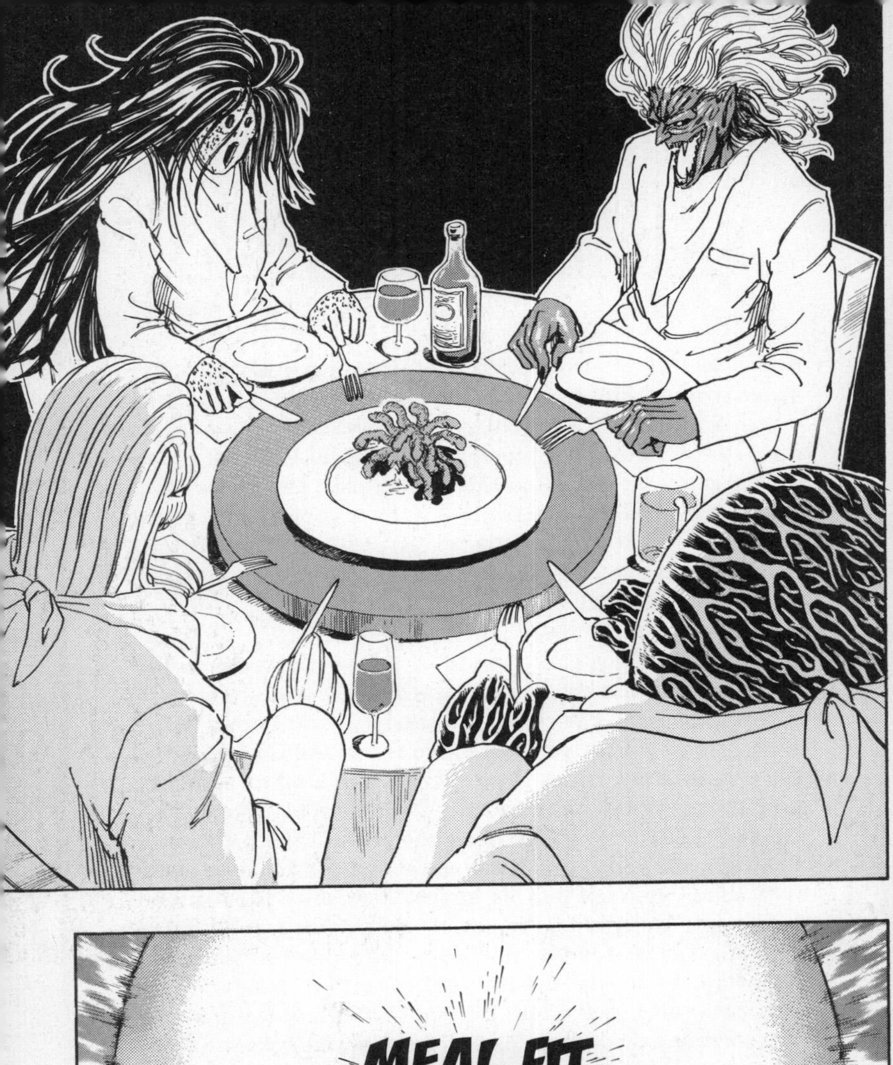

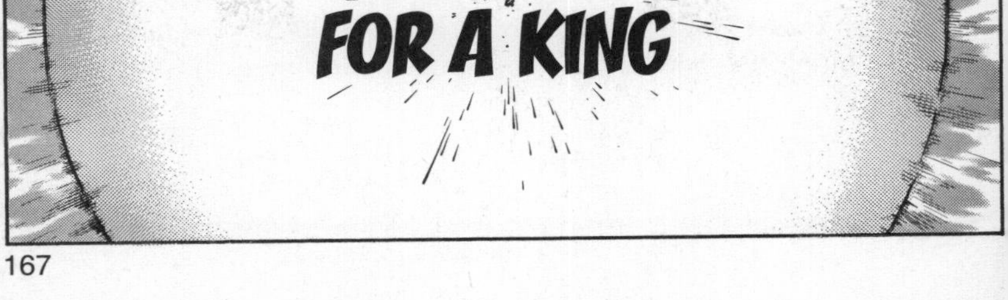
MEAL FIT
FOR A KING

SHIMABU SPEAKS

And worst of all, even with those grating deadlines fast approaching, I still can't come up with anything! Deadlines march on! Eventually, I have to put something, anything, on the paper because that blank piece of paper is what's going on the cover of the magazine! And then!! Get this!! What happens is I ad-lib all the content right onto the pencil page! That's right! That's the only way I can pull it off! Right?! So... there you have it. (Have what...? Sheesh, I gotta work harder on my storyboards!)

But I've got to say, this method of skipping directly to the pencil stage is a double-edged sword because when I want to make corrections I have to scrap a page that's practically to the inking stage. It nearly brings me to tears, and it's happened more than a few times. So I'm taking this opportunity to give those pitiful pencil pages their due by showcasing them as Reject Pages. I can hear my editor saying, "If you'd just done storyboards like you were supposed to, you could have saved yourself all this agony!" But since they served to fill some blank bonus pages, I'll consider it a good thing. (Though it's not good at all!!) If I get the chance, I'll feature more Reject Pages in the future! But so that I don't end up with pathetic pencil pages like that anymore, I'm going to try harder to sketch storyboards! I'm serious now, Mr. Editor! (*Rawr!!*) And with that, I look forward to seeing you next time I get my little Shimabu Speaks page! Until then, take care, everybody! This is Shimabukuro, who always fills the tank in his humidifier so full it ends up spilling, signing off! See you!!

END

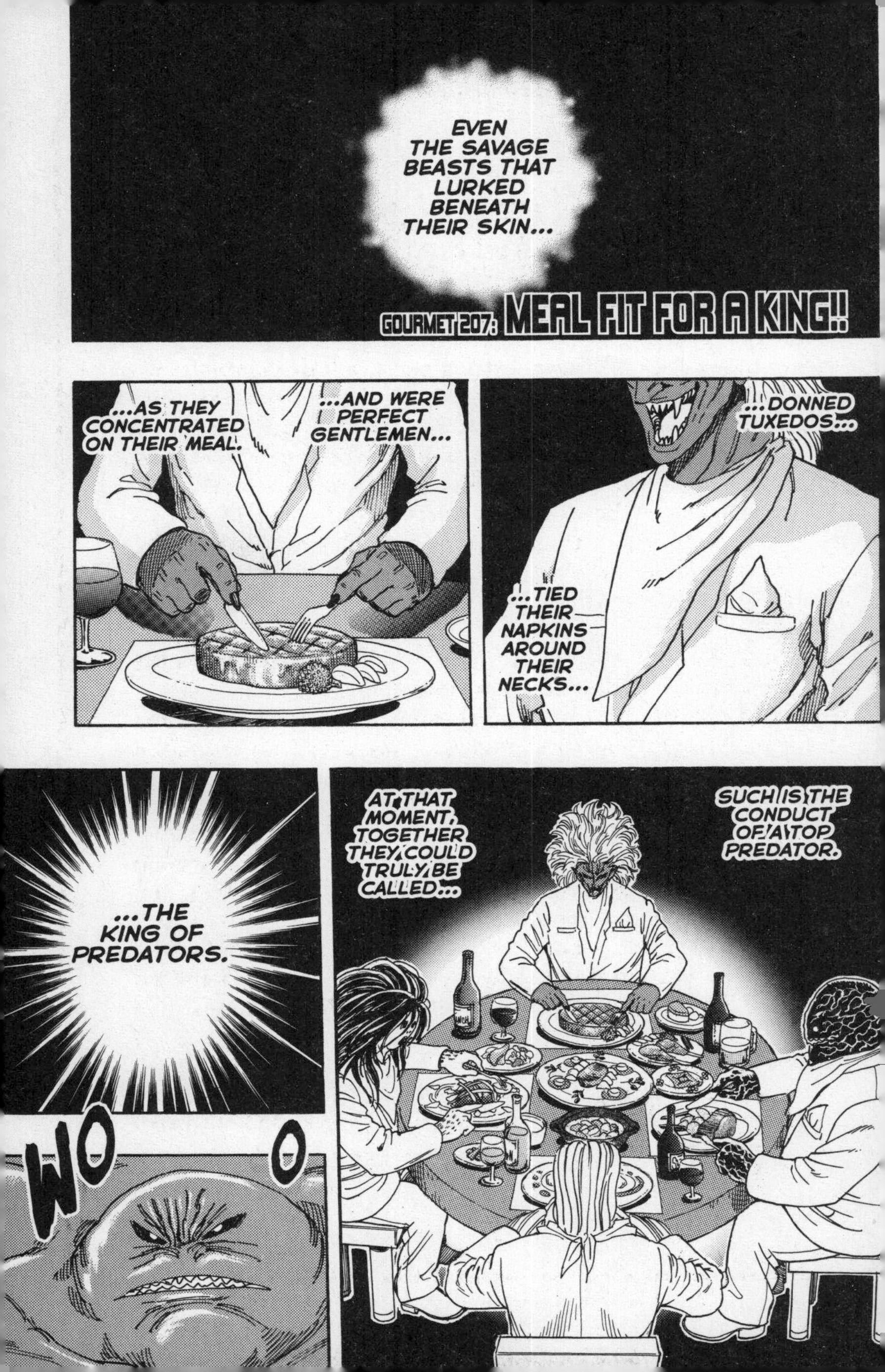
EVEN THE SAVAGE BEASTS THAT LURKED BENEATH THEIR SKIN...
GOURMET 207: MEAL FIT FOR A KING!!
...DONNED TUXEDOS...
...TIED THEIR NAPKINS AROUND THEIR NECKS...
...AND WERE PERFECT GENTLEMEN...
...AS THEY CONCENTRATED ON THEIR MEAL.
SUCH IS THE CONDUCT OF A TOP PREDATOR.
AT THAT MOMENT, TOGETHER THEY COULD TRULY BE CALLED...
...THE KING OF PREDATORS.
WO O

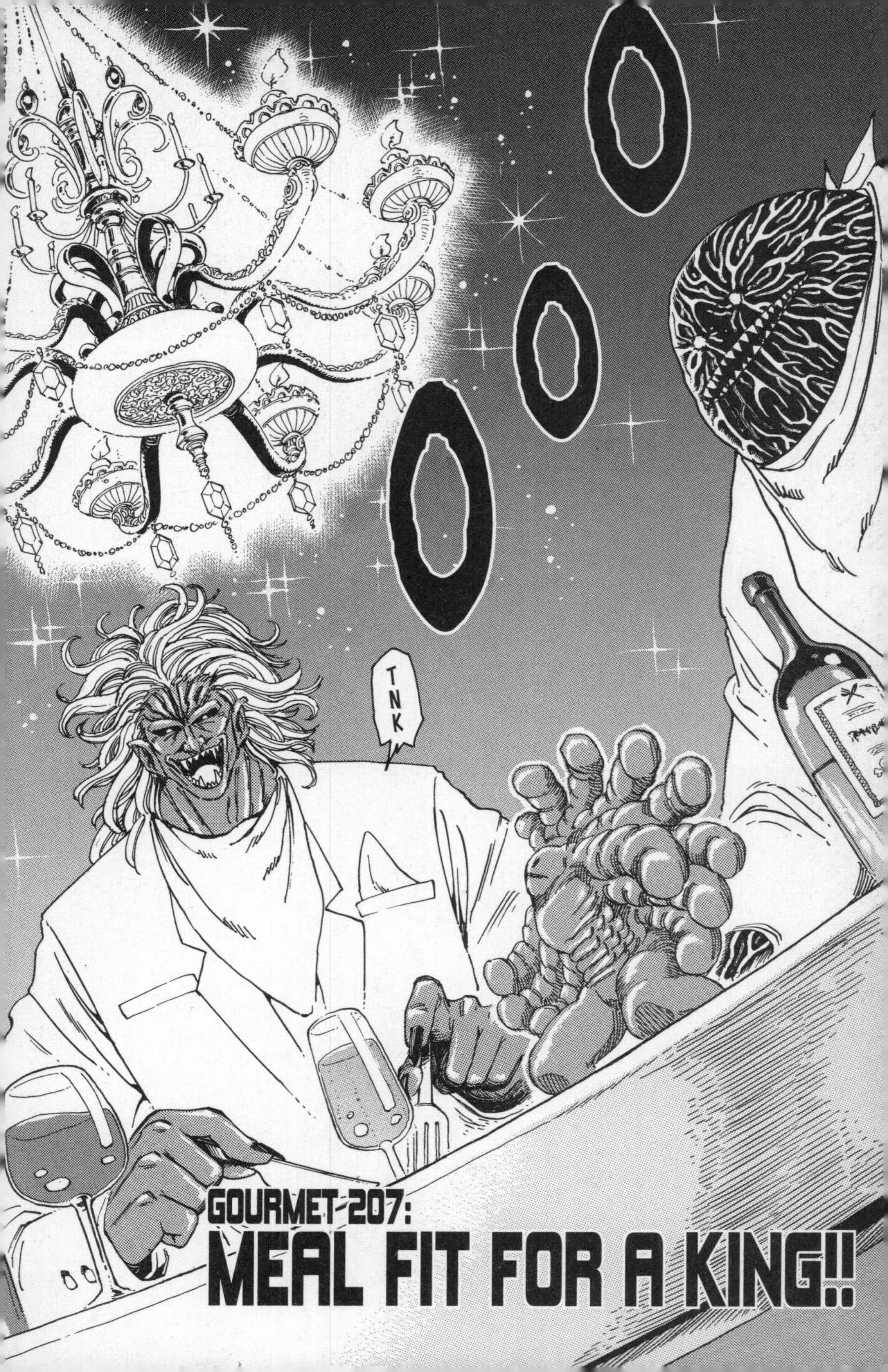
TNK
GOURMET 207:
MEAL FIT FOR A KING!!

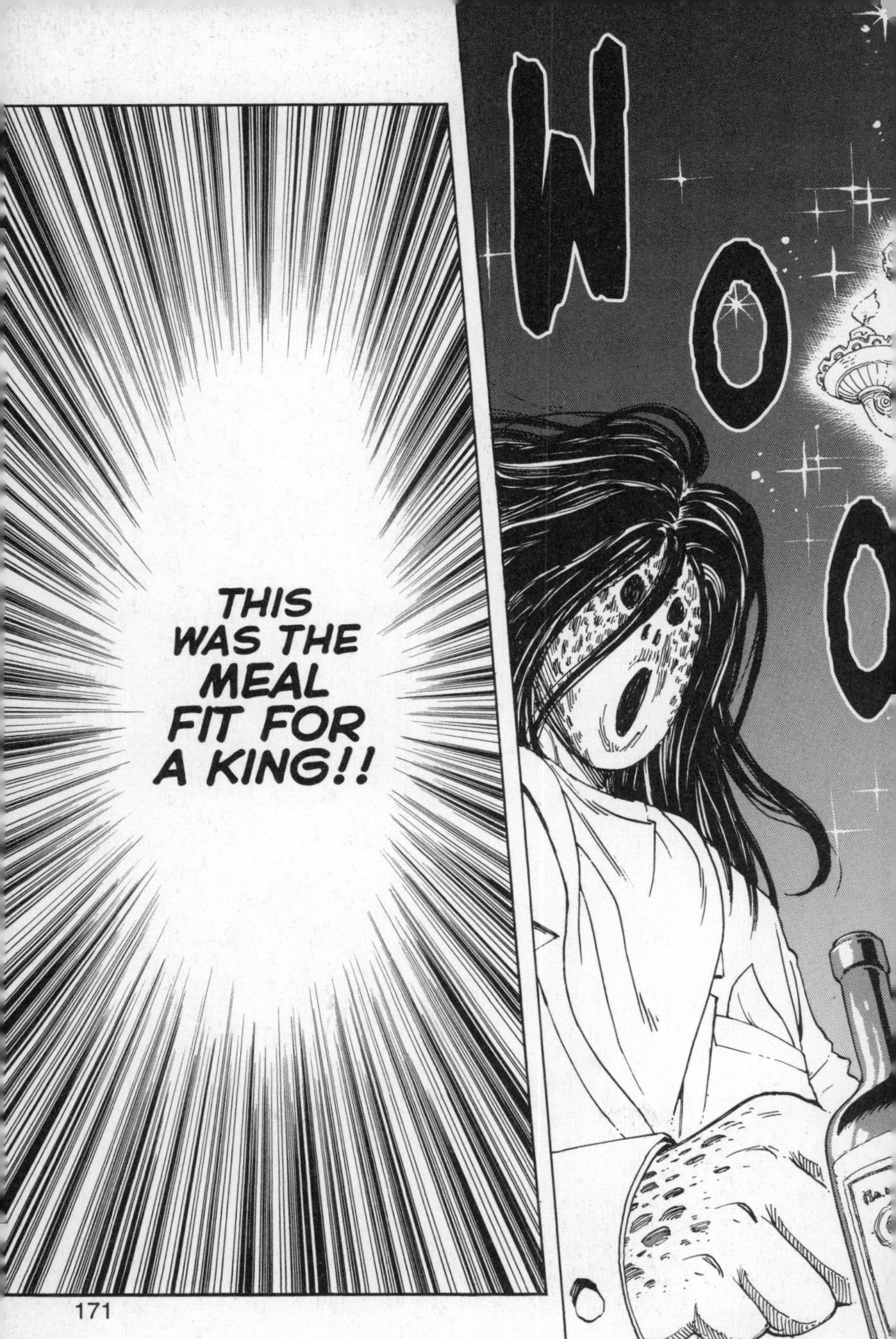
WOOO
THIS WAS THE MEAL FIT FOR A KING!!

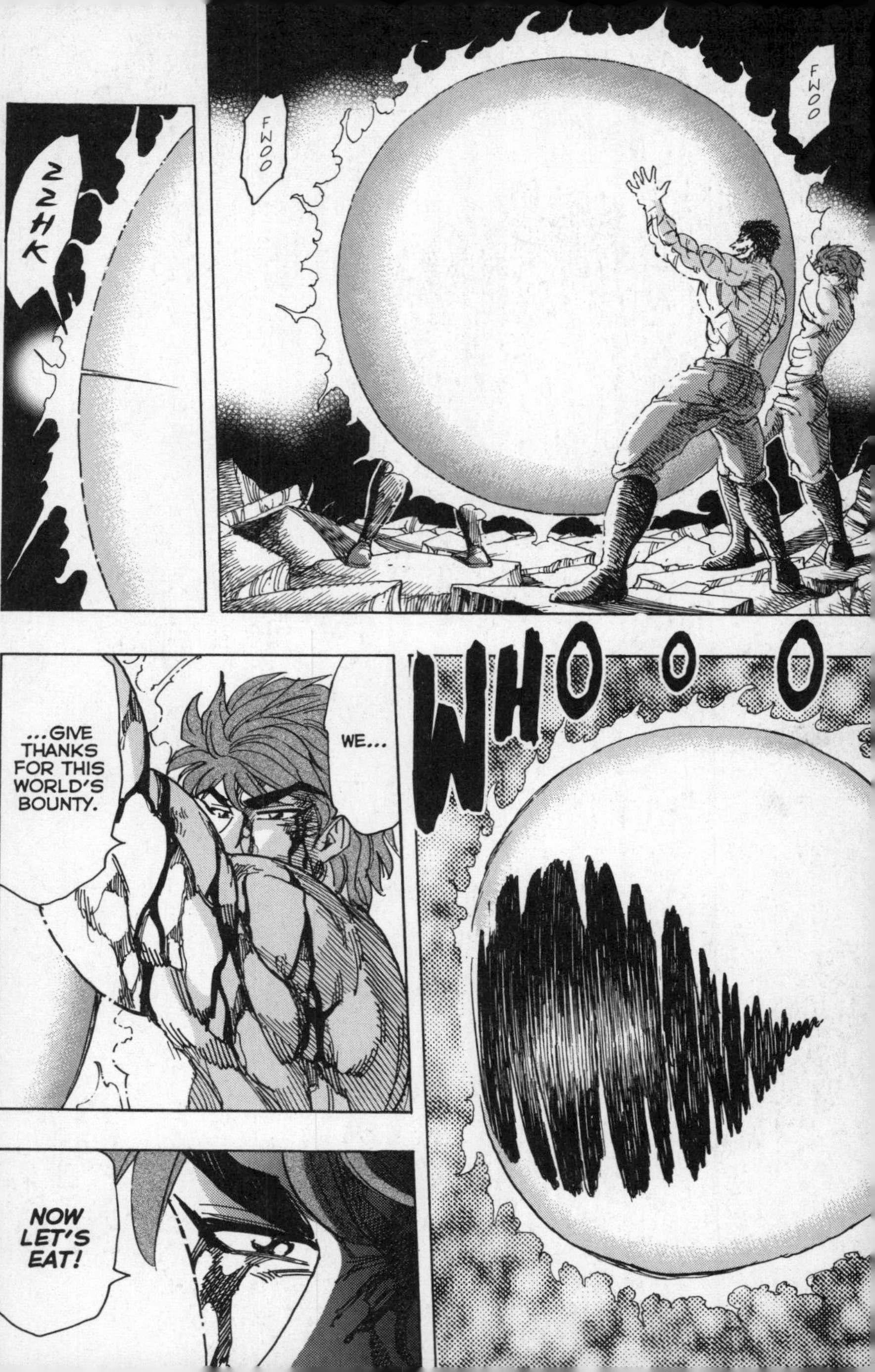
FWOO
FWOO
ZZHK
WHOOOO
WE...
...GIVE THANKS FOR THIS WORLD'S BOUNTY.
NOW LET'S EAT!

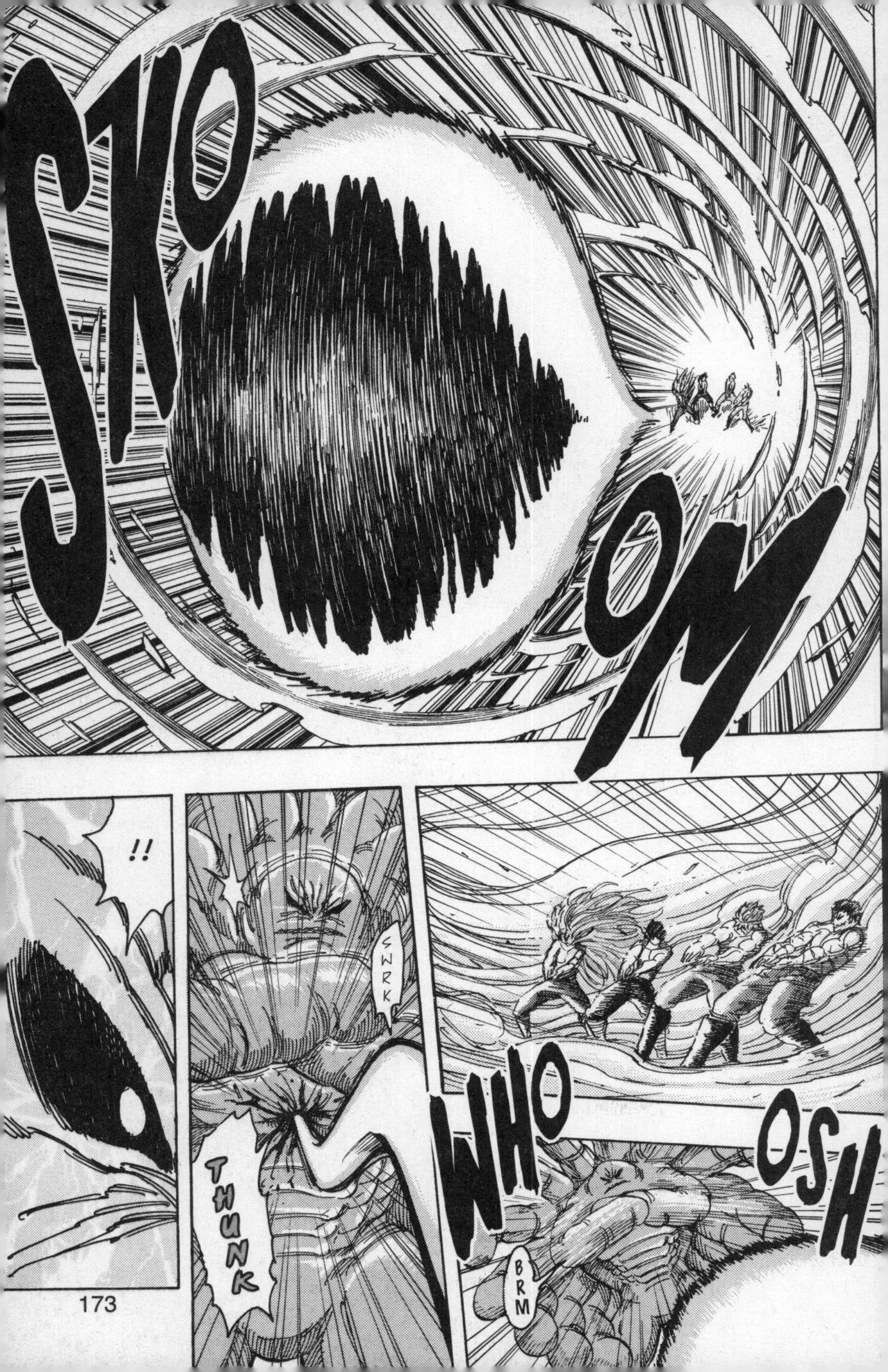
SKOOM
WHOOSH
BRM
SWRK
THUNK
!!

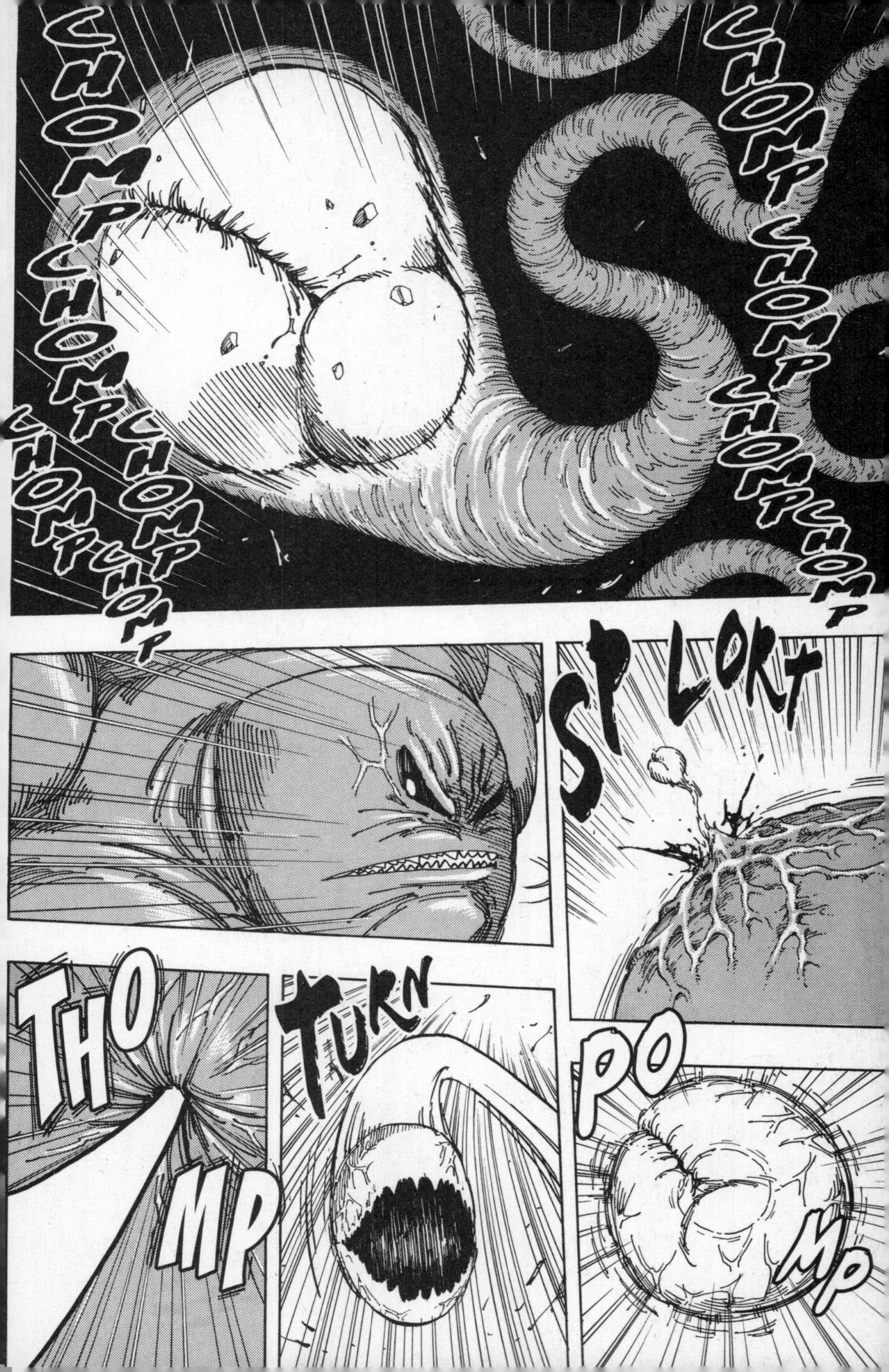
CHOMP CHOMP CHOMP CHOMP
CHOMP CHOMP CHOMP CHOMP
SPLORT
POMP
TURN
THOMP

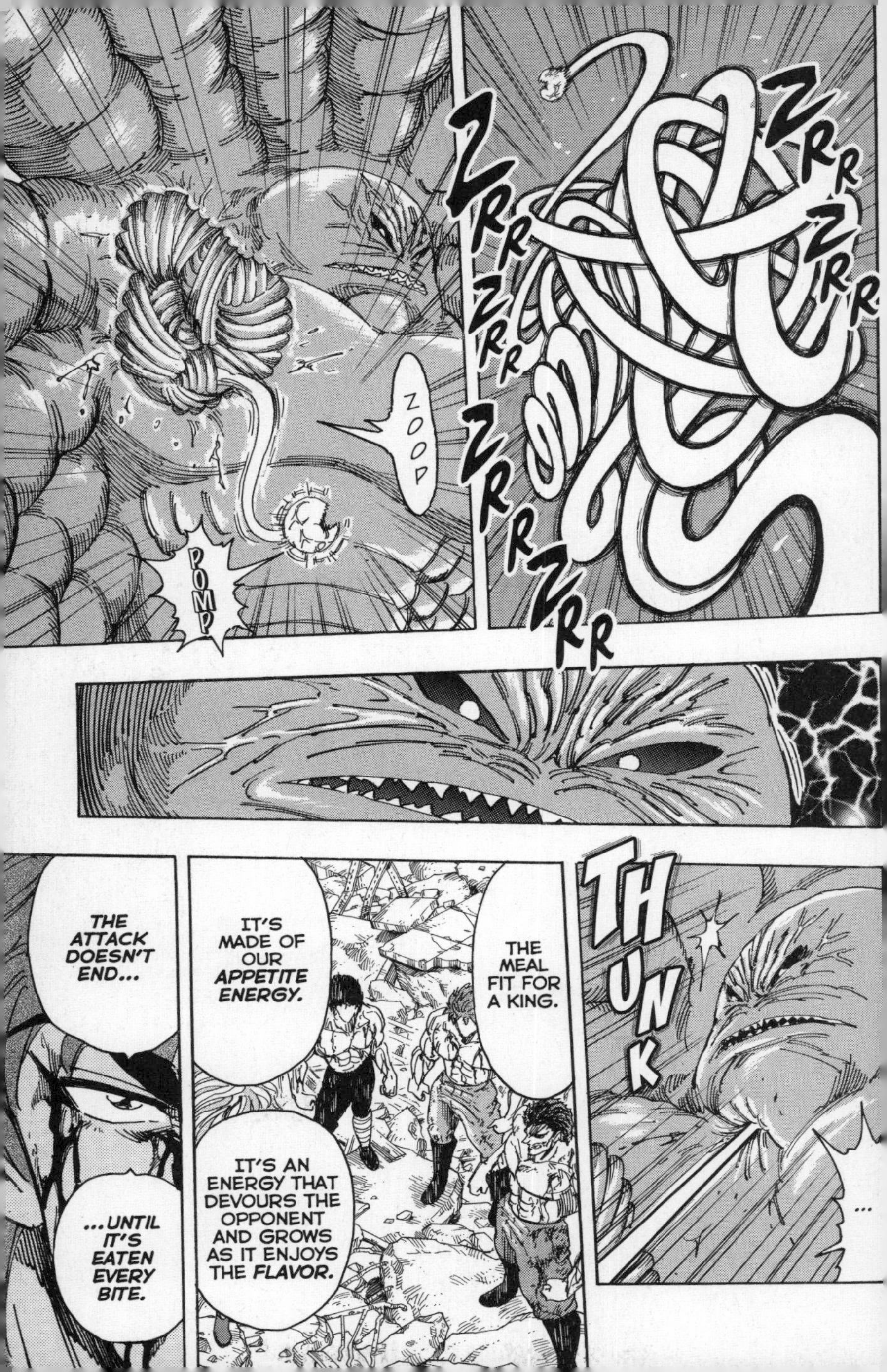
ZRRRZRRR
ZRRZRRRZRRR
ZRRZRRR
ZOOP
POMP
THUNK
...
THE MEAL FIT FOR A KING.
IT'S MADE OF OUR APPETITE ENERGY.
IT'S AN ENERGY THAT DEVOURS THE OPPONENT AND GROWS AS IT ENJOYS THE FLAVOR.
THE ATTACK DOESN'T END...
...UNTIL IT'S EATEN EVERY BITE.

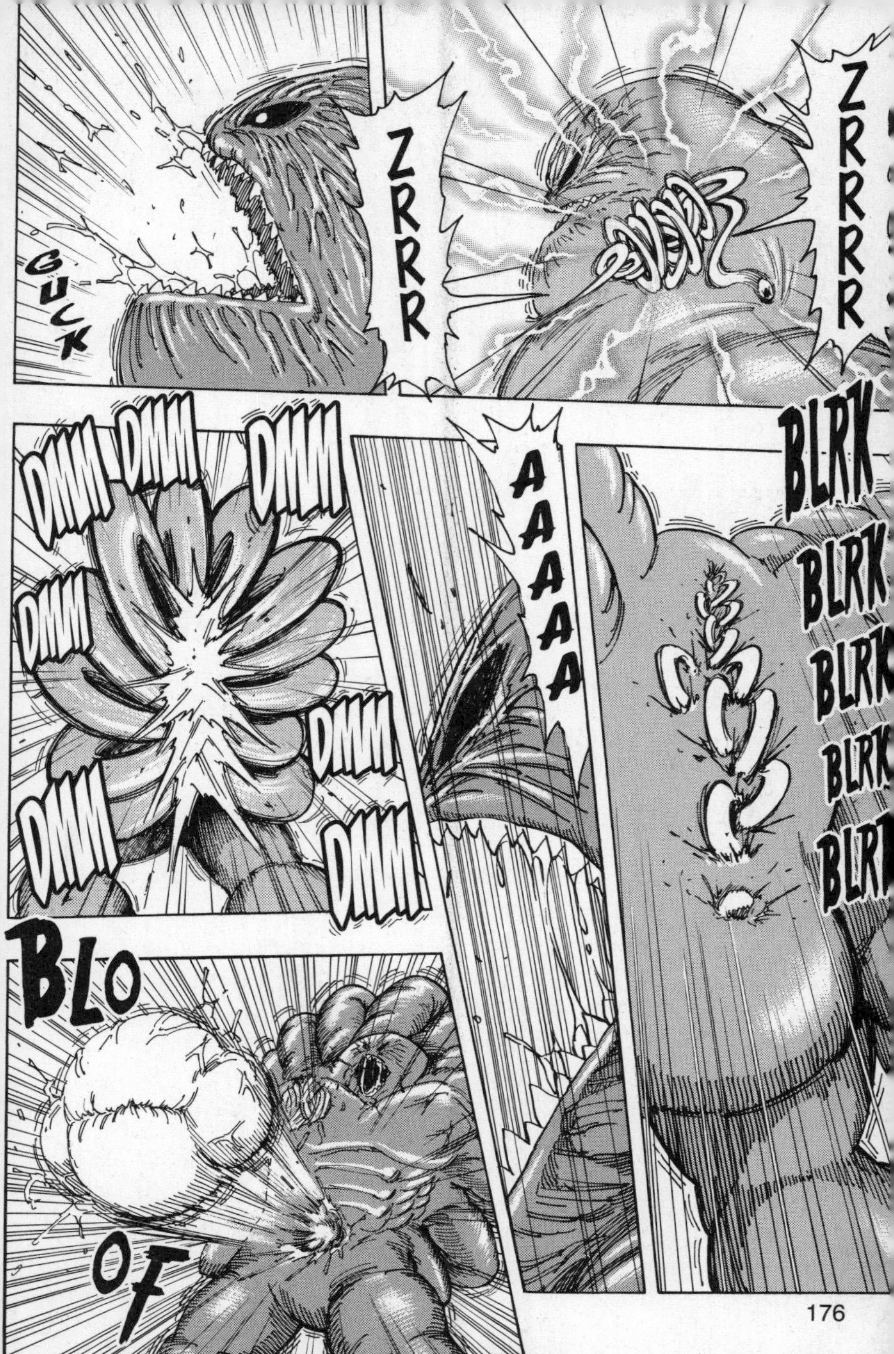
ZRRRRR
ZRRR
GUCK
BLRK
BLRK
AAAAAA
DMM DMM DMM
DMM
DMM
DMM
DMM
BLO
OF

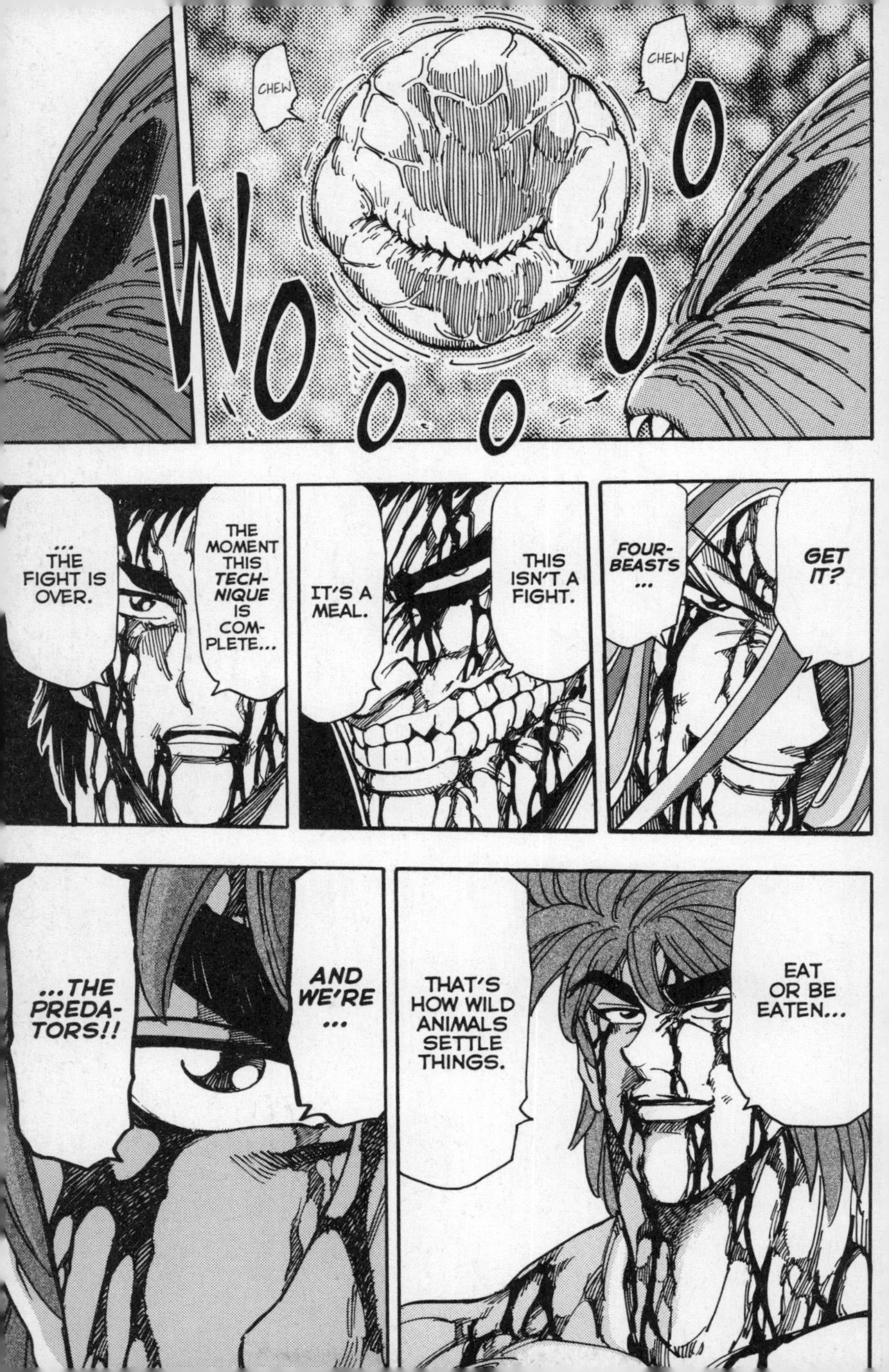
CHEW
CHEW
WOOOOOO
GET IT?
FOUR-BEASTS ...
THIS ISN'T A FIGHT.
IT'S A MEAL.
THE MOMENT THIS TECHNIQUE IS COMPLETE...
... THE FIGHT IS OVER.
EAT OR BE EATEN...
THAT'S HOW WILD ANIMALS SETTLE THINGS.
AND WE'RE ...
...THE PREDATORS!!

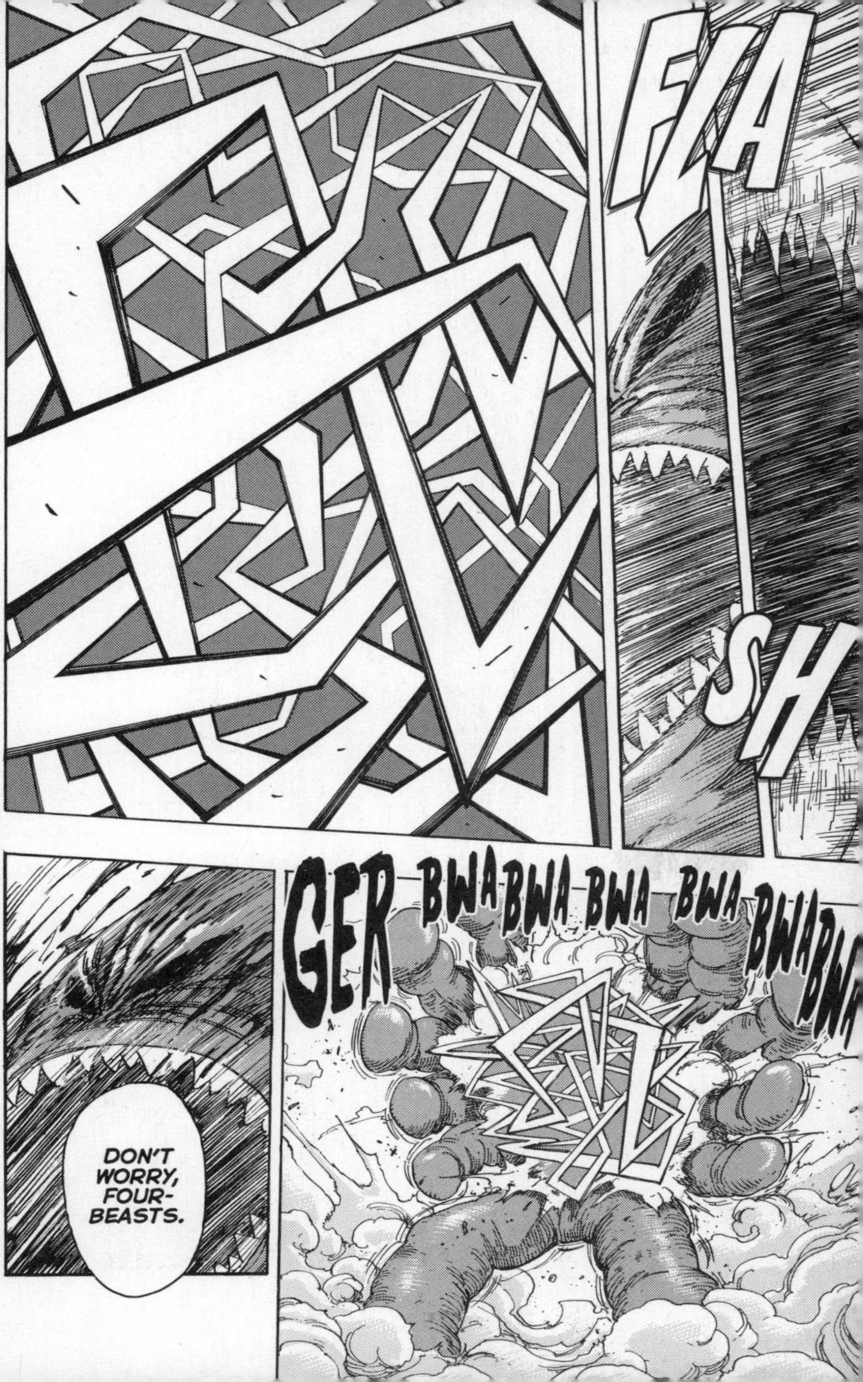
FLA
SH
GER BWA BWA BWA BWA BWABWA
DON'T WORRY, FOUR-BEASTS.

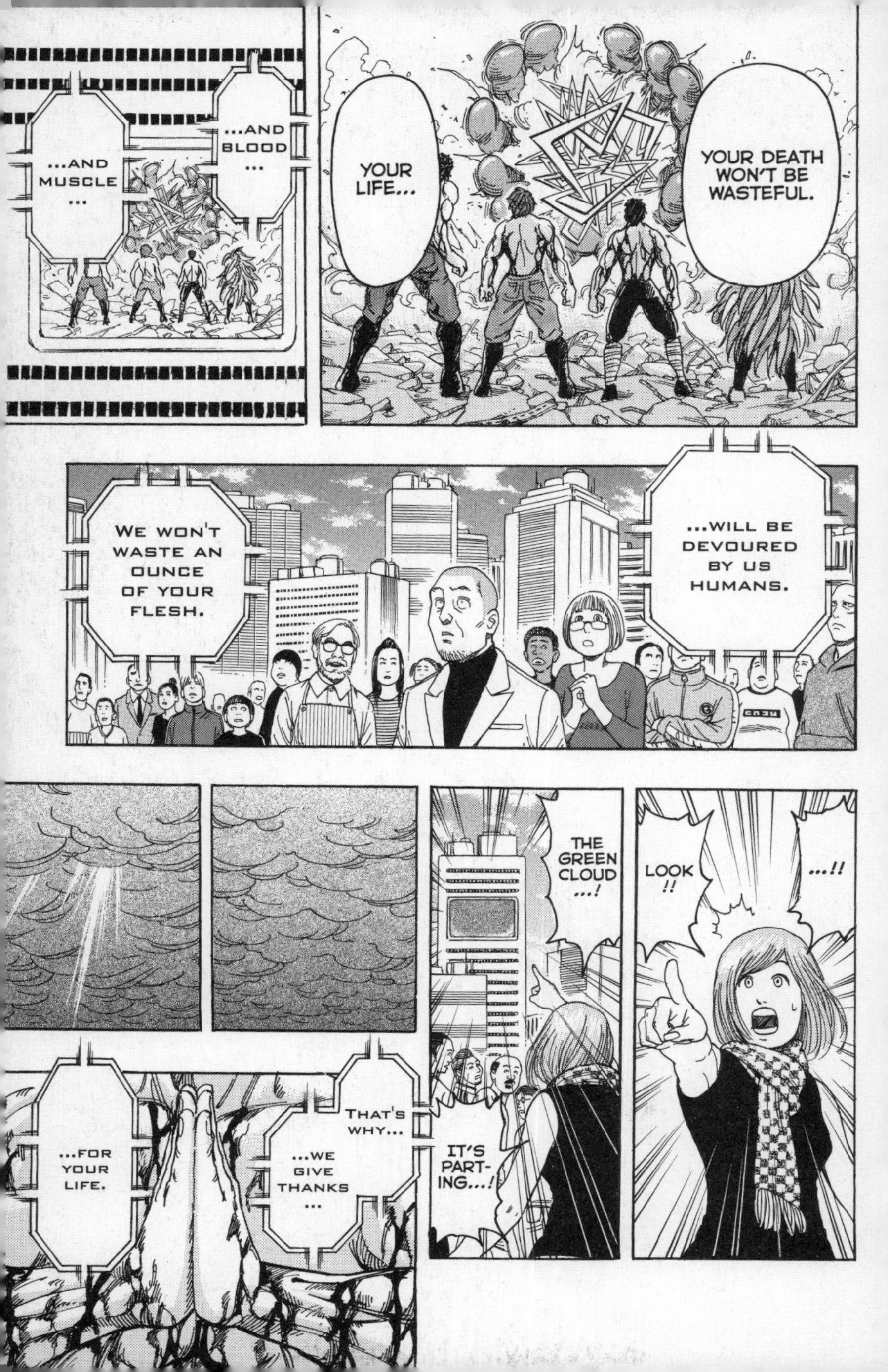
YOUR DEATH WON'T BE WASTEFUL.
YOUR LIFE...
...AND BLOOD ...
...AND MUSCLE ...
...WILL BE DEVOURED BY US HUMANS.
WE WON'T WASTE AN OUNCE OF YOUR FLESH.
LOOK !!
...!!
THE GREEN CLOUD ...!
IT'S PART-ING...!
THAT'S WHY...
...WE GIVE THANKS ...
...FOR YOUR LIFE.

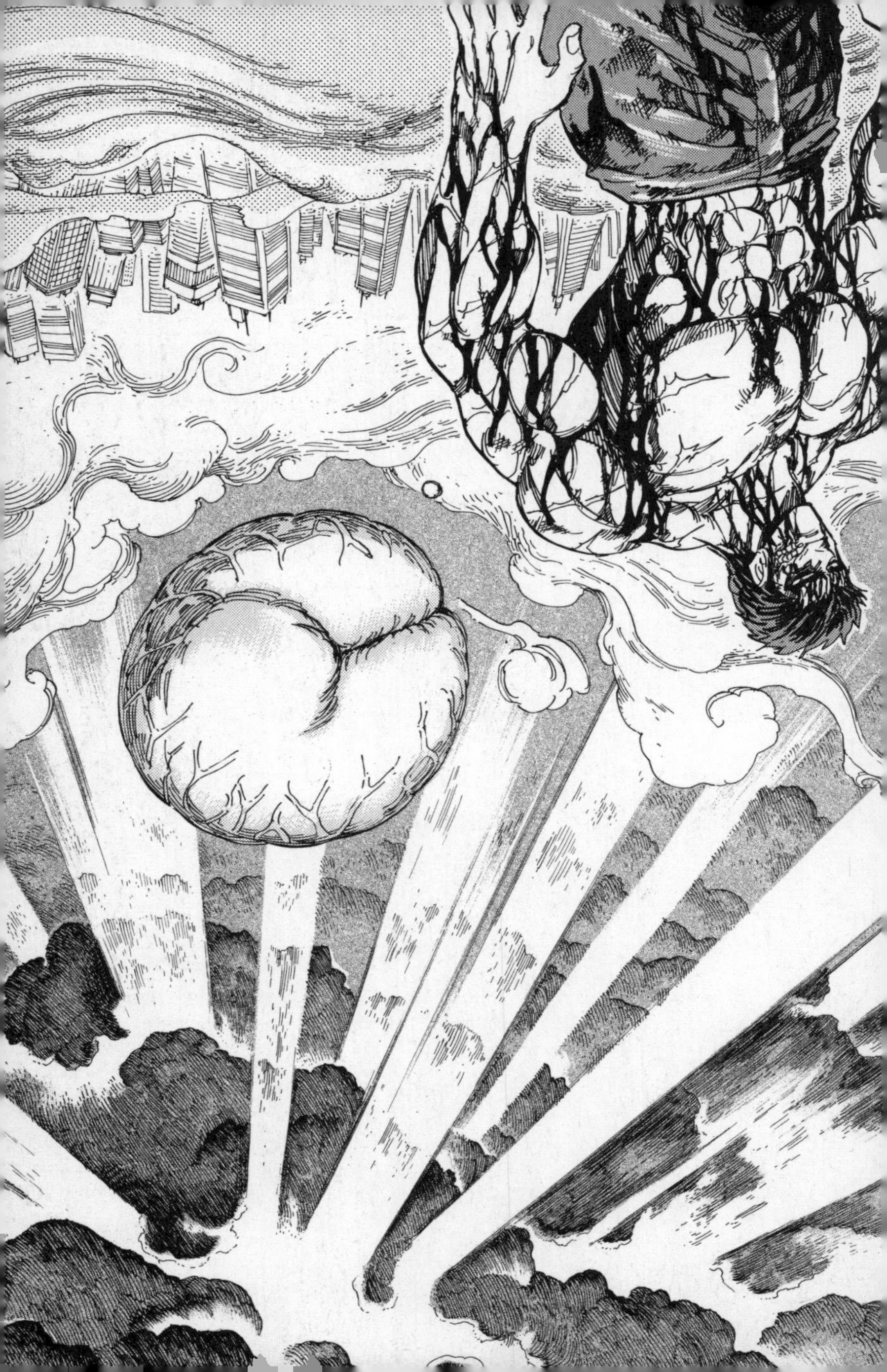

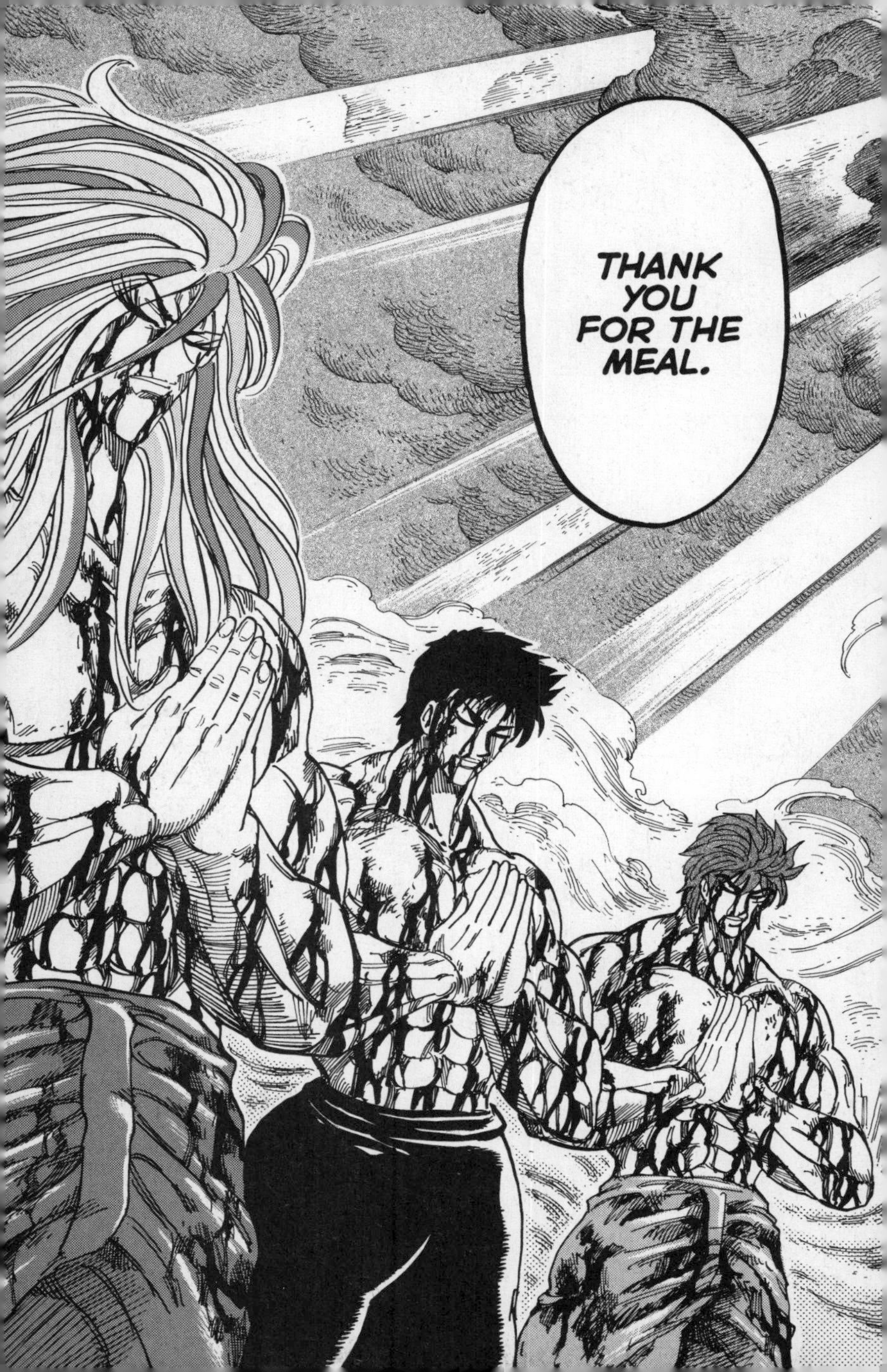
THANK YOU FOR THE MEAL.

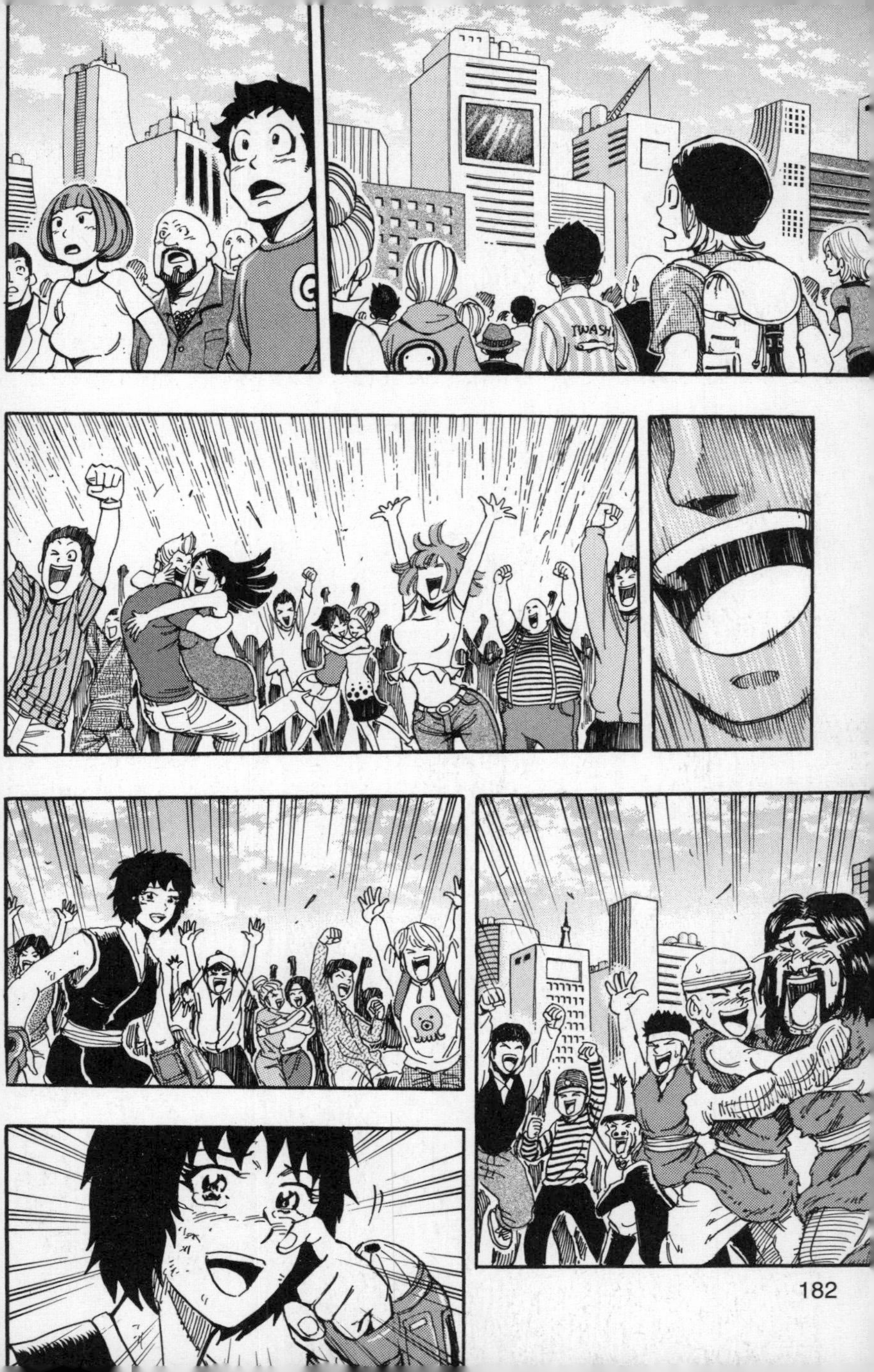
IWASHI

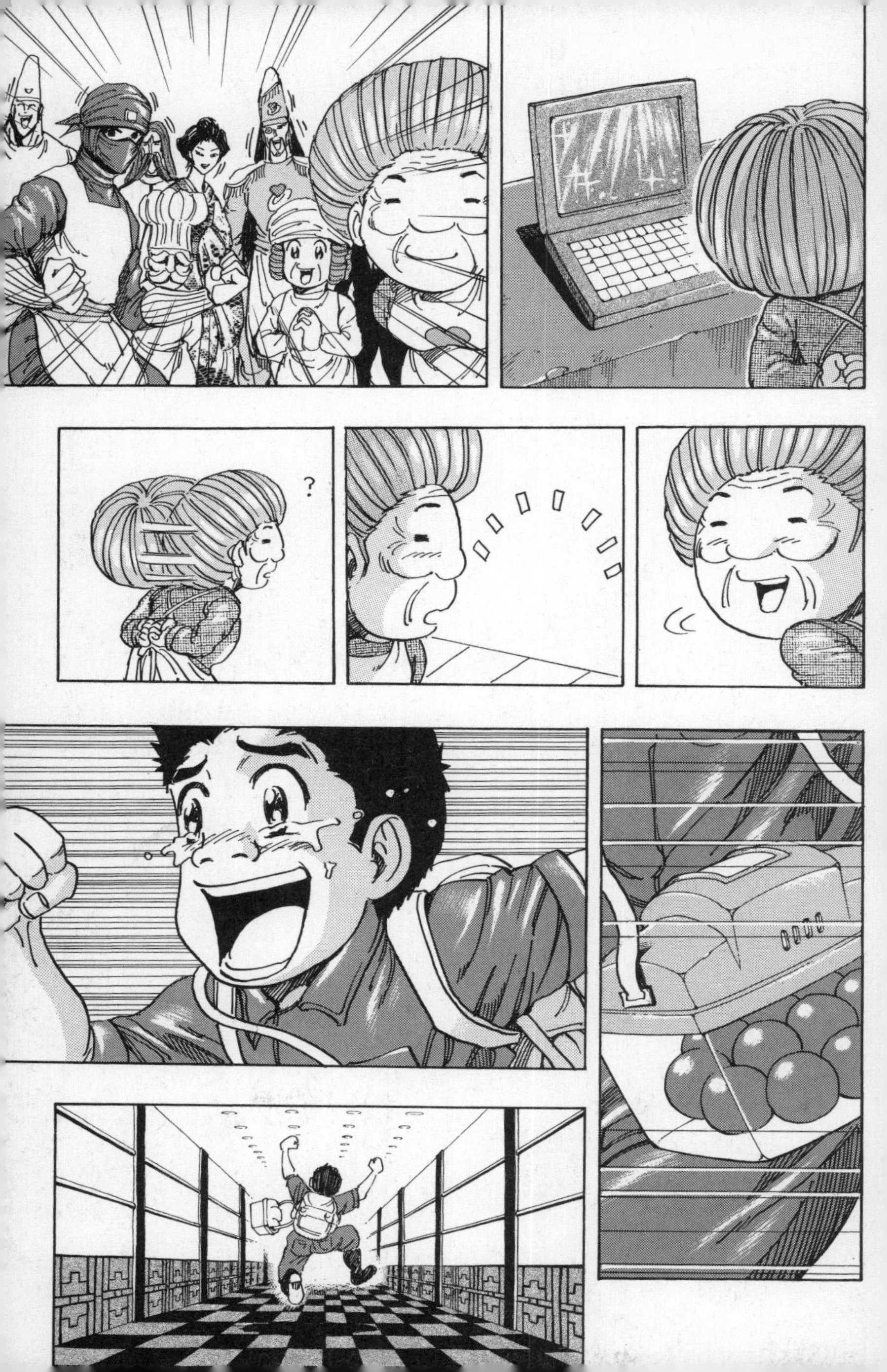
?

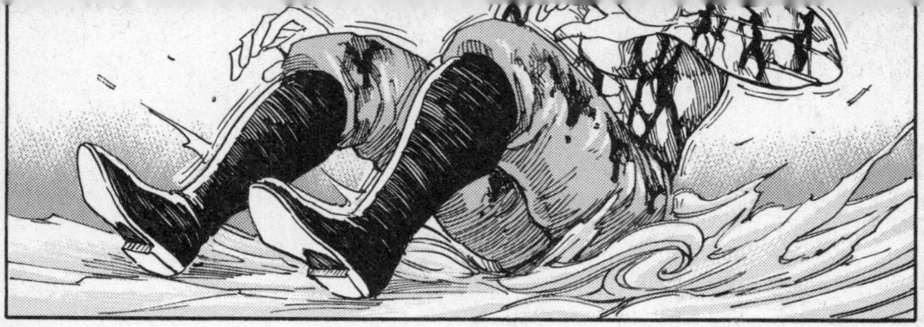
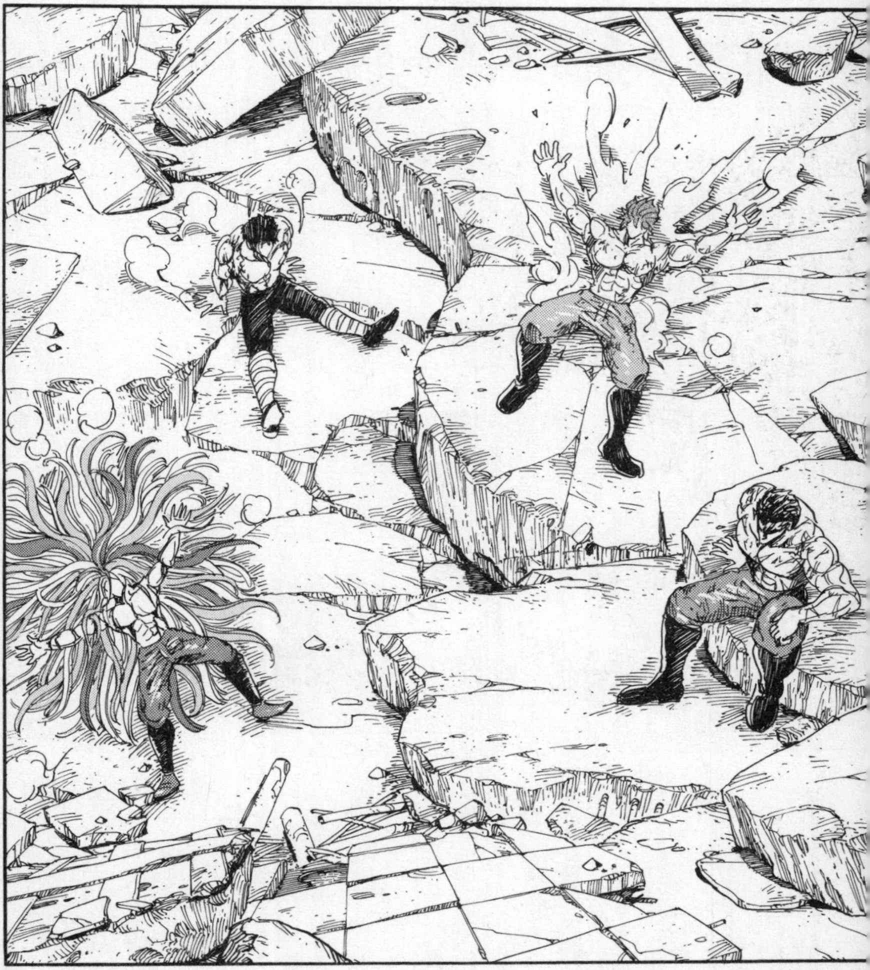

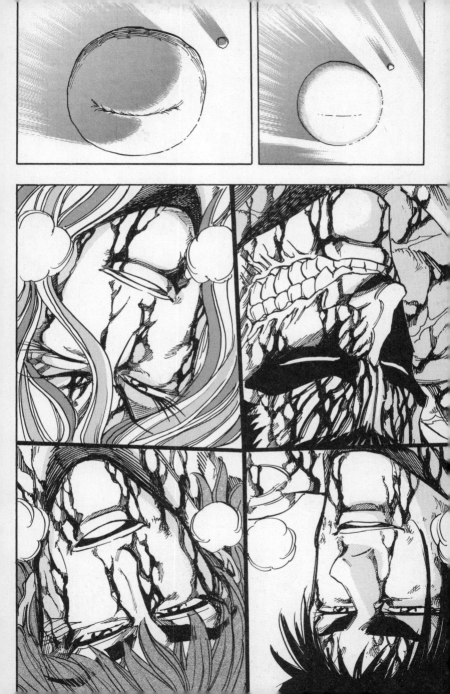

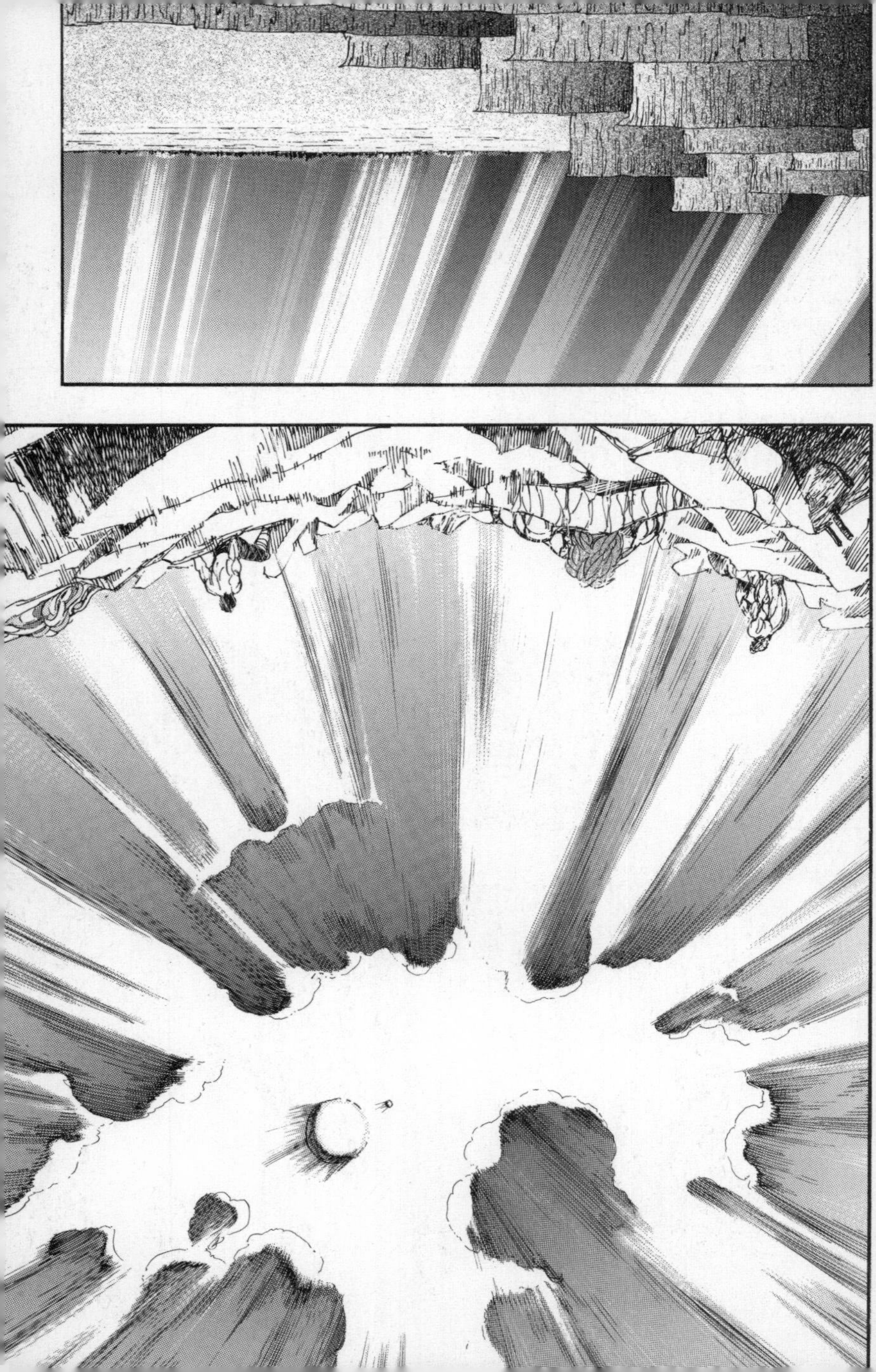

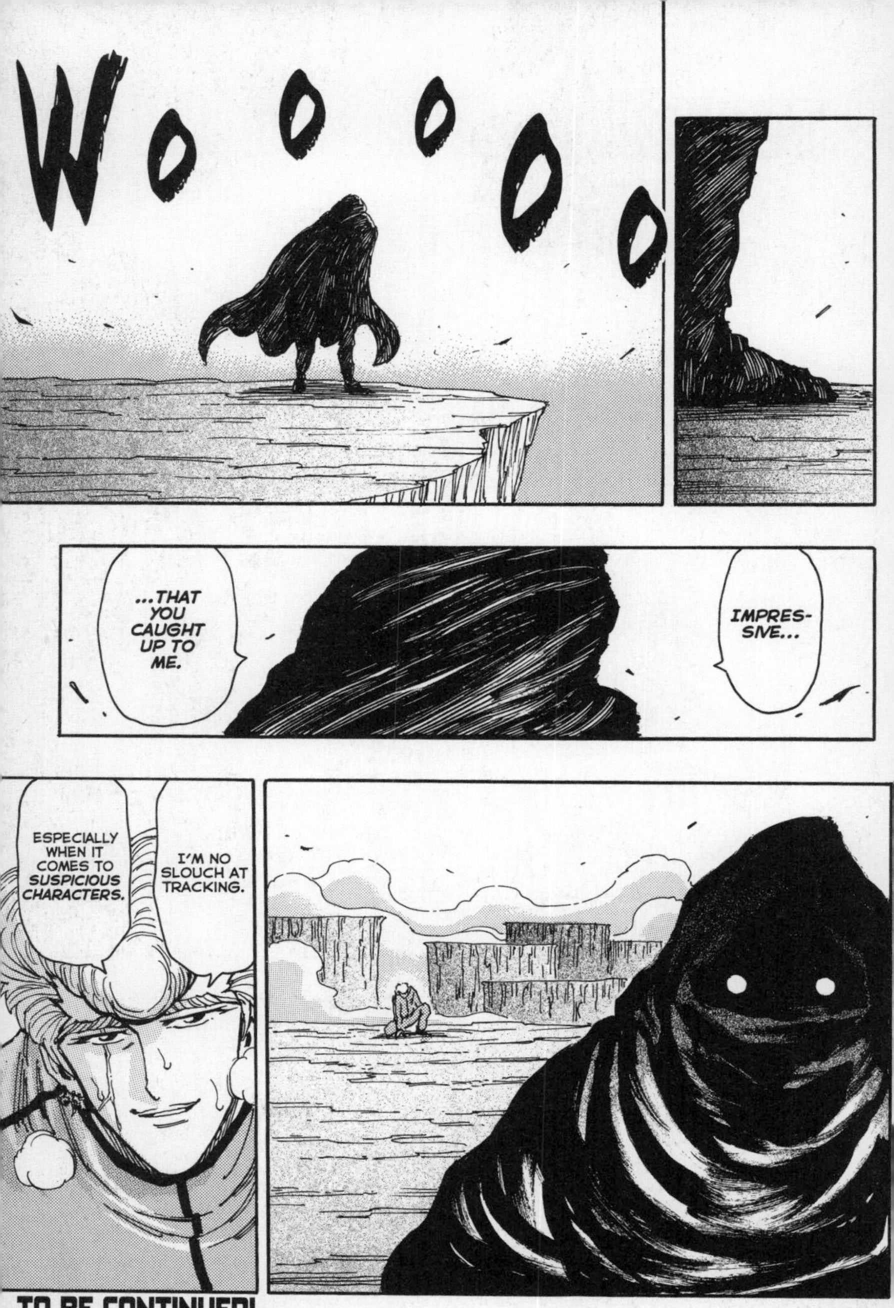
WOOOOO
IMPRES-SIVE...
...THAT YOU CAUGHT UP TO ME.
I'M NO SLOUCH AT TRACKING.
ESPECIALLY WHEN IT COMES TO SUSPICIOUS CHARACTERS.

TO BE CONTINUED!

TORIKO REJECT PAGES CORNER!!

(GOURMET 121)

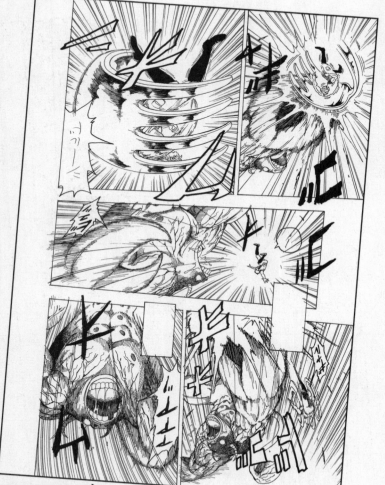

★ In this chapter, I drew Toriko and the Scorpion Demon Bull fighting, but halfway through I had to scrap it! I realized there wasn't time in the story for them to fight, so I had to redo it, even though I'd drawn so many pages of them in heated battle!! Uuugh!!

TORIKO REJECT PAGES CORNER!!

(GOURMET 126)

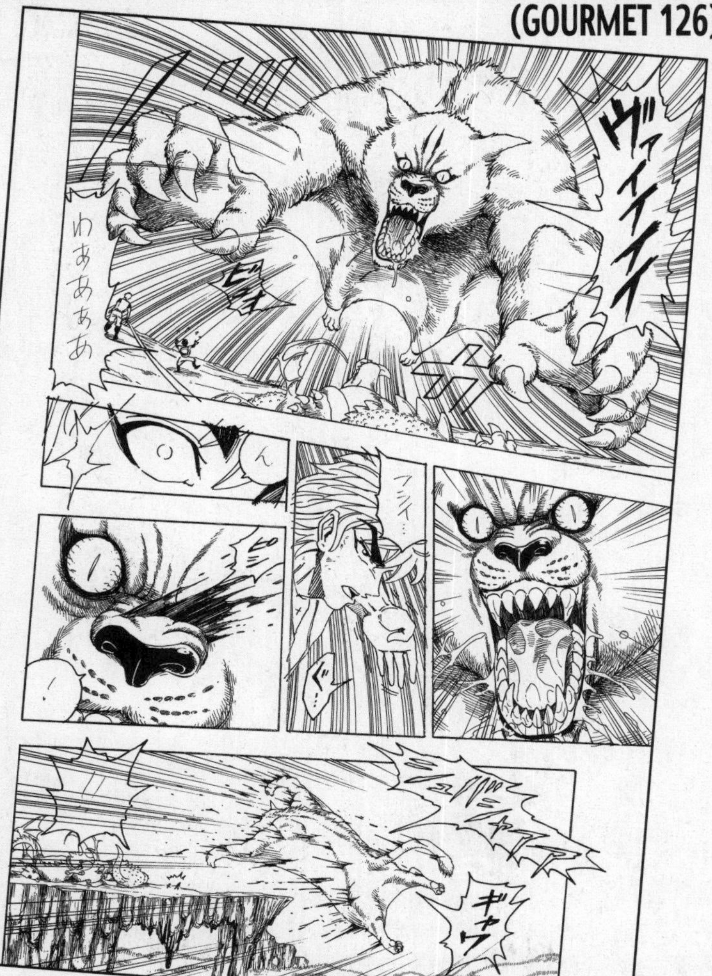
ヴァイイイイ
わあああああ
ギャワ

★ This was in the chapter where Toriko and Komatsu went to Honey Prison to meet Zebra. I'd penciled these pages of ferocious beasts attacking them, but once again realized there wasn't time for that and reluctantly sent them to the trash bin. This was a creature that a reader had thought up, so I felt bad that it didn't get to make an appearance!!

COMING NEXT VOLUME

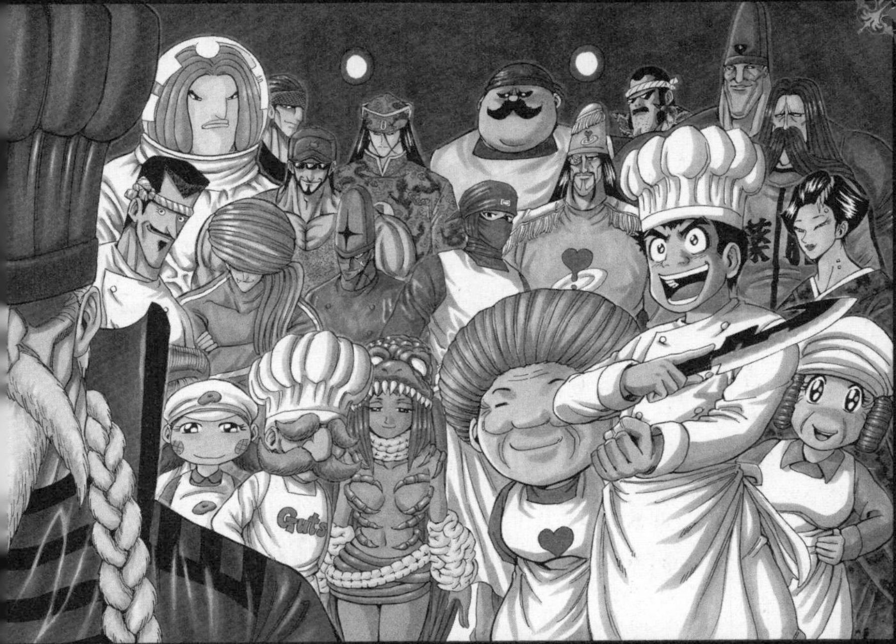
Guts

COOKING FESTIVAL KICKOFF

After playing a crucial role cooking up lifesaving mochi during the battle against the Four-Beasts, Komatsu rises to #88 in the World Chef Ranking. As a result, he gets to compete in the upcoming Cooking Festival against the world's top chefs. Whet your appetite for a more dazzling display of cooking by more crazy chefs than you can shake a ladle at!

AVAILABLE OCTOBER 2014!

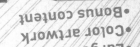

You're Reading in the Wrong Direction!!

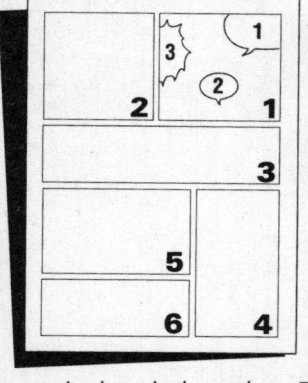

Whoops! Guess what? You're starting at the wrong end of the comic!

...It's true! In keeping with the original Japanese format, **Toriko** is meant to be read from right to left, starting in the upper-right corner.

Unlike English, which is read from left to right, Japanese is read from right to left, meaning that action, sound effects and word-balloon order are completely reversed... something which can make readers unfamiliar with Japanese feel pretty backwards themselves. For this reason, manga or Japanese comics published in the U.S. in English have sometimes been published "flopped" – that is, printed in exact reverse order, as though seen from the other side of a mirror.

By flopping pages, U.S. publishers can avoid confusing readers, but the compromise is not without its downside. For one thing, a character in a flopped manga series who once wore in the original Japanese version a T-shirt emblazoned with "M A Y" (as in "the merry month of") now wears one which reads "Y A M"! Additionally, many manga creators in Japan are themselves unhappy with the process, as some feel the mirror-imaging of their art skews their original intentions.

We are proud to bring you Mitsutoshi Shimabukuro's **Toriko** in the original unflopped format. For now, though, turn to the other side of the book and let the adventure begin...!

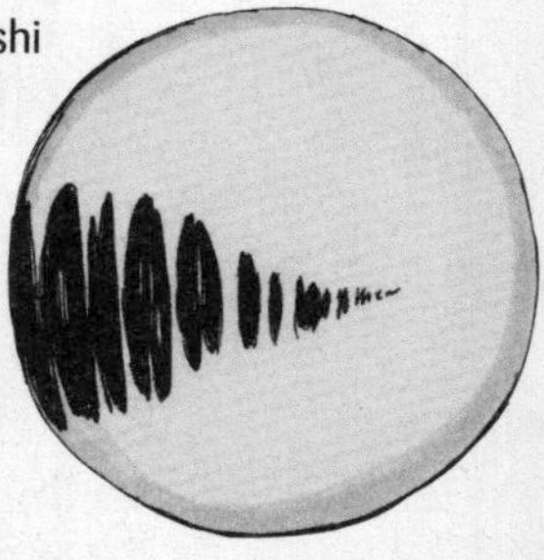

—Editor